SOMERSET CRICKETERS
1882 – 1914

SOMERSET CRICKETERS 1882 – 1914

STEPHEN HILL

With Additional Research by Barry Phillips

Foreword by Vic Marks

HALSGROVE

First published in Great Britain in 2016

Copyright © Stephen Hill 2016

British Library Cataloguing-in-Publication Data
A CIP record for this title is available from the British Library

ISBN 978 0 85704 291 0

HALSGROVE
Halsgrove House,
Ryelands Industrial Estate,
Bagley Road, Wellington, Somerset TA21 9PZ
Tel: 01823 653777   Fax: 01823 216796
email: sales@halsgrove.com

Part of the Halsgrove group of companies
Information on all Halsgrove titles is available at: www.halsgrove.com

Printed and bound in China by Everbest Printing Investment Ltd

Dedication

Gilbert Burrington (13.06.1879 – 21.11.1916) played three times for
Somerset with no great distinction. He lies buried in an unknown place,
having given of his best for his county and country. In a case of mistaken identity
he slipped from the archives, a war hero erased from cricketing history.
This book is dedicated to Gilbert and all the others who, like him, deserve
to be restored to their rightful place in the record books.

Somerset CCC autographs collected in 1902: S. M. J. Woods, A. E. Newton, D. L. Evans, P. Randall Johnson, Vernon T. Hill, O. M. Samson, C. E. Dunlop, A. E. Lewis, E. Robson, B. Cranfield, Geo Gill, F. T. Welman and Fred M. Lee

Contents

Acknowledgements

Eagle-eyed readers will spot that a number of dates, places, events and even first names differ from those previously held to be true. Where possible, I have relied on original press reports and documents rather than accepting 'folklore' or anecdote. Sources include birth, death and marriage certificates, wills, military papers, census forms, school and university records and correspondence. In an undertaking of this sort, where I have attempted to record as many hitherto unreported facts as possible, there is a strong possibility that I, too, have made mistakes. I apologise for any errors, oversights or sins of omission. I was disappointed not to have sourced an image of every player and I know the Somerset Cricket Museum would welcome copies of photographs of those who have eluded me. Where I have mentioned relatively unknown villages, I have only added the county if they are outside Somerset. In addition, at the risk of upsetting the purists, I have adopted certain conventions such as generally referring to rugby football as *rugby* and association football as *football*.

I am enormously grateful to those who have helped me. Barry Phillips has been a tower of strength with his unflagging support. I could not have completed the project without him. Richard Miller patiently showed me where and how to find much of the information I needed. Many others have provided facts, photographs or autographs. I will no doubt have missed some of them from the list, but I should like to acknowledge the following people who helped me in my quest. Those kind people are (in the order in which I encountered them): David Wood, Barry Clifton, Maureen Yardley, Susanne Price, Hazel Hudson, Geoffrey Bisson, Magnus Bowles of Sports Pages, Peter Wynne-Thomas, Andrew Leach, Richard Walford, David Lambden, Colin Johnston, David Bridges, John Brown, Steve Sheen, Sally Milsom, Phil Hill, Elizabeth Connelly, Helen Bridge, Julie Mather, Brian Mayled, Mandy Roe, Brian Hunt, Les Barden, Mike Tarr, Tim Davidson, Gloria Howells, Lesley Ross, John Hamer, Roger Gibbons, Phil Britt, Pat Hase, Brian Austin, Fr John Sharp, Kathryn McKee, Ian Quickfall, Gary Bode, Andy Clayton, Gay Sturt, James Bradby, Janet Owen, Christopher Dawkins, Ron Marrow, Christopher Saunders, Robin Brooke-Smith, Stephen Chalke, John Hill, Alice Noyes, Sydney Linyama, Libby Warren, Elaine Roydes, Simon Bennett, Duncan Davies, David Smith, Neil Gamble, Maggi Stowers, Chris McCormack, Simon Appleton, Julia Hudson, Janet Kennish, Henley Smith, John Lyddon, John Garbutt, Gervald Frykman, Alan Ramsay, Rob Campbell, Jane Lilly, Rab Barnard, Karen Clayton,

Alison Spence, Elizabeth Stratton, David Butterfield, Penny Baker, Crispian Beattie, Judith Curthoys, Robin Darwell-Smith, Michael Down, Steve Jennings, David Frith, Peter Hardy, Richard Hassell, Clare Hopkins, Michaele Jeavons, David Jeffery, Marg Thorne, Mary Jane Kirby, Tim Knight, Pat Lindegard, Ed Miller, Deirdre Parker, Michael Pitt-Payne, Josh Hill, Rachel Gardner, Patrick Thomas, Sharon Hendry, Eleanor Ward, Sue McCracken, Tony Powell, Barbara Stewart, Fr Andrew Hughes, Boyd Metzler, Clare Russell, Ian Leonard, Keith Walmsley, David Macklin, Liz Carter, Eileen Rowley, Claire Whickman, Dr C. S. Knighton (Clifton College Archive) and Guy Curry, who provided a wealth of wonderful images at the eleventh hour. My thanks, also, to everyone at Halsgrove. Finally, a big thank you to my wife, Kate, for her patience and support.

I also thank the following for permission to reproduce images: the families of many of Somerset's former players, Somerset Cricket Museum, Somerset Heritage Centre, British Museum, British Newspaper Archive, St John's College, Cambridge, The National Portrait Gallery, www.sportspages.com, British Medical Journal, Roger Mann, Barry Phillips, The Alfred Gillett Trust (C & J Clark Ltd), Durham County Council Archive, Sidmouth Museum, Cornwall Record Office, Bristol Record Office, the local history groups and the many schools and Oxbridge colleges whose archivists are included in the names above, Christchurch City Library in New Zealand, Oxford History Centre and the various club sides and county cricket librarians who have offered access to their collections. With the kind permission of Somerset Cricket Museum, I have also taken some images from Eddie Lawrence's *Players, Photographs & Statistics*. In the case of the following images, whilst I have no reason to doubt their provenance, I have been unable to find proof of their accuracy: Baily, Hotham, Selwyn-Payne, Swayne.

Somerset XI in 1890. The players shown are:
STANDING: J. A. Gibbs, E. W. Ebdon, A. E. Clapp
MIDDLE: J. E. Trask, G. B. Nichols, H. T. Hewett, C. J. Robinson, E. J. Tyler
FRONT: L.C. H. Palairet, J. B. Challen, V. T. Hill
Seated on the ground on the left is Henry Murray-Anderdon, who was instrumental in the county's
successful drive for inclusion in the County Championship.

Foreword by Vic Marks

Stephen Hill set himself a daunting task and we are the beneficiaries. He has tracked down every man who has played first-class cricket for Somerset – beginning, here, with those who appeared before the First World War – thereby assembling a fascinating catalogue, which contains some brilliant cricketers, some ordinary ones and countless remarkable characters. Not many of them raised a trophy but, as Stephen points out, Somerset teams were often building up a wonderful store of anecdotes while other counties were filling their trophy cabinets.

Somerset cannot boast more fine cricketers than any other county, but they may be able to claim a disproportionate number of larger than life personalities. Some of them, like 'Sammy' Woods, who is featured in these pages, or Bill Andrews, Bill Alley and Ian Botham, may be all too familiar, but many others have been rescued from oblivion by Stephen in pen portraits drawn with real warmth and affection.

I have a peculiar interest in the Rev. Stirling Cookesley Voules, who was appointed Somerset's first captain after the meeting at Sidmouth in 1875 when the club was founded. It tickles me that Cookesley Voules was born at the rectory 100 yards from my own birthplace in Middle Chinnock, in the south of the county. As a boy in the 1960s I scored a few runs in the backyard of that rectory against the vicar's two sons and, occasionally, his daughter.

Prepare to be surprised and enchanted at every turn of the page, not just by the biographies. You will also find fresh images of Somerset cricketers doggedly unearthed by the author as well as hundreds of autographs of players, which will, no doubt, excite the graphologists out there (which makes me unusually self-conscious as I sign off).

VIC MARKS

Somerset XI who played Worcestershire at New Road in August 1911.
STANDING: J. Bridges, H. Chidgey, F. P. Hardy, L. C. Braund, E. Robson, A. Young
SEATED: B. L. Bisgood, E. S. M. Poyntz, J. Daniell, O. M. Samson, F. D. H. Joy

Introduction

A brief canter through the history of cricket in Somerset offers some insight into how – through a combination of happenstance and persistence – the county came to be awarded first-class status. Somerset's first recorded county game took place at Devizes in 1798 when Eleven Gentlemen of Bath and the County of Somerset lost to Eleven Gentlemen of Wiltshire. Having decided that there was insufficient home-grown talent, Somerset called in five outsiders for the return match. They won and Wiltshire were incensed to find that they had been duped. The county then bumbled along, unsure if it was ready for any serious cricket. The Lansdown club in Bath led the way, formed in 1825 and employing a professional named John Sparkes. He was a hard hitter who played exclusively off the back foot and bowled slow, ineffective under-arm deliveries without a run up, as was then customary.

By the 1830s club sides had started springing up across the county, often failing to take root. Somerton, for example, formed a club but folded. Many of their players reappeared in a newly-created Langport team. Attractive fixtures were beginning to draw the crowds, although it was not always possible to get a team of eleven together.

Before the advent of the Penny Post or the telephone, players and the public were informed of any late changes by notices placed in the press. Witness to this is an announcement in the local paper of July 1839, placed by Eales White, the Honorary Secretary of Taunton Cricket Club, informing his members that Langport were unable to raise eleven men for their return fixture and that 'the Taunton club will make a match on their own ground at Orchard on that day. Wickets pitched at 12 o'clock.'

The *Somerset County Gazette* of 1867 reports the first 'meeting' played by Milverton CC in a field named Ladder Close, kindly donated by E. Fowler Esq, noting that 'great interest was shown in the manly game'. Indeed, it perhaps took courage to bat on a wicket that was little more than a recently-mown meadow with little or nothing in the way of protection. Unbeknown to the reporter, this was in fact at least the second attempt to form a club in the village. In the same year, local rivals Wiveliscombe CC were reformed. According to the same newspaper this was likely 'to revive a sport which was well kept up until the rifle corps absorbed the players'.

A re-established Somerton side were having something of a bumpy ride. The club's groundsman, Elias Hull, had been sacked without payment for doing his job badly and had taken the club captain, George Basham, to court. Elias put his case with 'great

In his memoirs, Rev. Ainslie freely admits that his ministerial duties involved little or no effort and that he filled his days with fishing, cricket and, perhaps more unexpectedly, building a locomotive he named 'Phoenix'. He also found time to complete such written works as his Smoking Fires, Their Cause and Cure, *published in 1869. He had previously founded, as he put it, 'a Taunton Cricket Club which played in the Vivary Park, but the men were not all very desirable and on the whole I never enjoyed cricket less. And when I had, after I had left Taunton for more than a year, to subscribe to pay off the debts of the club caused by champagne luncheons to the ladies, I did not much care for the T.C.C.' Disillusioned with Taunton, he started playing cricket at Tiverton and thereafter founded a club at Corfe, inviting a number of men who would form the nucleus of the newly-established county side.*

fervour', describing the team as 'a mean, shabby lot, who were not going to humbug him'. Having lost his case, he held out his hat and asked the judge for a contribution to his expenses, given that 'these cricketing fellows do go around the parish begging money to keep up theirselves and I ought to be helped the same way'. He was 'ignominiously expelled by the officer of the court'.

While the club at Taunton foundered, the folks at Yatton would in time style themselves as East Somerset and gain the support of Tankerville Chamberlayne, a sometime MP and enthusiastic club cricketer. Chamberlayne would be aggrieved when Yatton was not deemed worthy of being a county cricketing venue by the self-appointed Somerset hierarchy.

An attempt was made to reignite the county game with a 'Yeovil and County Cricket Club' in 1865 but the project lacked popular support. The seed had been sown on stony ground. Some of the names, particularly that of the Rev. Alexander Colvin Ainslie, would surface again ten years later. Ainslie was well-connected and was for a while Archdeacon of Taunton, prone to granting friends and family preferred appointments and happy to offer members of his circle the chance to engage in county cricket matches. Following a match between Gentlemen of Devon and Gentlemen of Somerset at Sidmouth in August 1875, the Rev. Ainslie chaired a meeting at which it was resolved that a Somerset County Cricket Club would be formed and that they would endeavour to organise matches against neighbouring counties on an annual basis, together with fixtures against highly-regarded opposition such as Incogniti.

Ainslie and the ad-hoc committee appointed Edward Western (who played for the Gentlemen of Somerset) as county secretary. Western's origins are a source of some mystery but he was at the time a teacher at Fullands School, Taunton. More of him, later.

Rev. Stirling Cookesley Voules was invited to become

the first captain. Described by *Wisden* as 'a free-hitting batsman, a good fast bowler and a capital field', S. C. Voules was born in 1842 in Middle Chinnock where his father was the rector. He attended Marlborough College and Lincoln College, Oxford, and was in the winning Oxford team in the Varsity match in four successive years. Aided by a mixture of Oxbridge-educated clerics and schoolmasters, wealthy amateurs and a limited number of professionals, Voules and others played their part in generating increased interest and knocking on the door of first-class status. According to the *Taunton Courier*, Ernest John Plantagenet Cassan 'bore the brunt of the attack' in the county's formative years, despite 'approaching the veteran stage'. An Oxford blue who played for Lansdown CC, he took his own life on Christmas Eve 1904, the death certificate noting 'suicide by shooting himself in the head during a fit of temporary insanity'.

A key moment in Somerset's development was the signing of the lease in 1881 of 7.5 acres of land in Taunton, beside the River Tone, from John Arundell Winter, a cricket enthusiast who played for the club. Winter was a landowner who needed ready cash and was prepared to offer the field to a collection of Taunton sporting clubs for £50 a year. After constructing a grandstand and a pavilion at a cost of £800, Somerset were admitted to the top table in 1882, though with some misgivings on the part of the cricketing hierarchy.

As subsequent events would show, they had neither the resources nor the infrastructure to justify their elevation. Somerset's first brief flirtation with first-class status was an unmitigated disaster. Fifty-nine different men played for the county over twenty-five games. Only a handful of those players were good enough cricketers to have graced any county team. Throughout the period from 1882 until 1885, there was disagreement among the periodicals and annual publications as to whether or not Somerset should be accorded first-class status. *Wisden* was

Somerset's first captain, S. C. Voules. After teaching for a number of years, including a spell as principal of Sydney College in Bath, he went into the ministry, first as the rector of Ashley on the border of Shropshire and Staffordshire and then as the rector of Heysham in Lancashire. In Fifty Years of Sport at Oxford, Cambridge and the Great Public Schools, *Lord Desborough quotes Voules at length, detailing his opinions on a number of matters, particularly the improvements in pitches during Voules's playing career. Voules notes that the wicket at Lords was prone to unpredictable bounce in the days before 'mowing machines' and heavy rollers became the norm. He also links pitch improvements with the lifting of the ban on round arm bowling.*

more generous than *Cricket: A Weekly Record*. *Lillywhite's* was ambivalent. The view of *Wisden* has prevailed.

Time and again, Somerset were comprehensively beaten, chalking up their only four successes against fellow whipping boys, Hampshire. By 1885, the powers that be had lost patience with both counties and rescinded their first-class status. Many expected a long, hard path back to the top flight. They had not counted on the inspirational leadership of Herbie Hewett or the organisational skills of Henry Edward Murray-Anderdon who replaced the county's first secretary, Edward Western.

Despite Henry's best efforts, Somerset had to content themselves with fixtures against other second-tier counties. Gloucestershire deigned to play their neighbours in 1887 but that proved a one-off and – predictably – Gloucestershire won by an innings. In other fixtures, Somerset's professional slow left-arm bowler, Teddy Tyler, was regularly among the wickets. Sam Woods of Cambridge University chipped in with some wonderful displays of pace bowling. Bill Roe hit some big scores and Herbie Hewett regularly tore into the opposition bowling. In one innings, against Wiltshire, he plundered eleven sixes in making 79. A team was coming together.

Then in 1890, Somerset enjoyed a remarkable run of success under the capable, unflinching leadership of Herbie Hewett. They won ten of their eleven games and tied the other. A high point was Hewett's brutal and exhilarating 203 not out in a total of 338 for 7 declared against Staffordshire. Among Somerset's victims was a Middlesex side who were one of the eight first-class county teams. The Somerset team and committee were invited to a celebratory banquet at the Castle Hotel in Taunton, a sumptuous menu reflecting the gratitude of the mayor for the fact that his town had been put on the cricketing map. Herbie Hewett subsequently presented Somerset's case for becoming a first-class county to the County Cricket Council. With him was Thomas Spencer,

Somerset XI who played Gloucestershire at Cheltenham in August 1887.
BACK: T. Knight (Scorer), G. B. Nichols, H. T. Hewett, H. F. Fox, H. E. Murray-Anderdon, Unknown
CENTRE: A. J. Fothergill, J. B. Challen, W. N. Roe, E. Sainsbury (standing), S. C. Newton,
S. M. J. Woods FRONT: E. W. Bastard

a local schoolmaster who by then shared secretarial duties with Henry Murray-Ander-don. In an unexpected turn of events, Somerset were granted their wish and the council dissolved itself, leaving the first-class counties to organise their own fixtures.

Who were the men who would play their parts – some pivotal, a great many marginal – in Somerset's cricketing odyssey? We begin with the eleven who appeared in the county's opening first-class fixture in 1882 and take each player in strict chronological order based on their debut appearance and their position on the scorecard. In this way, a clearer picture emerges of the melting pot of men from various strata of society and we are offered a much greater understanding of the changing backdrop to Somerset's many disasters and occasional triumphs. We might even understand with greater clarity why the Championship title continued to prove so elusive after well over a hundred years of trying.

Somerset were blessed with some fine amateurs as they re-established their first-class status. Clockwise from top left: L. C. H. Palairet, J. B. Challen, S. M. J. Woods, A. E. Newton and H. T. Hewett

1882

"These figures complete the statistics of the nine leading counties. Hampshire and Somerset have been omitted from this list as hardly entitled to positions of what is known as first-class cricket."

Cricket: A Weekly Record

In summarising the season, *Cricket: A Weekly Record* was not alone in believing Somerset to be unworthy of first-class status. Things began badly and this set the tone for much of what followed. At Old Trafford, Lancashire scored 237 in their first innings, having enjoyed the conditions before the rain came down in torrents, leaving the original wicket under water. Unwisely, captain Tristram Welman agreed to play out the match on a hastily-prepared wicket, with the unfortunate result that Somerset were twice skittled out for a combined total of 80 in two and a quarter hours. Humiliating defeats followed at the hands of Gloucestershire and Hampshire. S. C. Newton steadied the ship against MCC with his batting but could not prevent a narrow defeat and then Newton and Bob Ramsay combined to engineer the defeat of Hampshire. This would prove Somerset's only success. The season then tailed off, culminating with another trouncing at the hands of Lancashire. It had been a depressing season for the county.

1

William Herbert Fowler

8 June 1882 v. Lancashire, Old Trafford

W Herbert Fowler

Herbert Fowler was a great bear of a man, standing at nearly 6 ft 4 in. *Lillywhite's* describes him in 1882 as 'a giant hitter' and a 'very fast and dangerous bowler'. The *Observer* later noted that 'the advent of Fowler gave the game [in Somerset] a start'.

Herbert was born into a wealthy Quaker family in Tottenham on 28 May 1856. His father, William, an MP and a barrister, soon moved the family to Moor Hall, claimed to be the finest house in Harlow. Herbert was educated at Rottingdean and then at Grove House, a leading Quaker school based at the time in Tottenham. Two of his brothers – Gerald and Howard – went up to Oxford University where they gained reputations as fine cricketers and rugby players. Herbert opted to travel the world for three years after leaving school. In 1878 and at the age of twenty-two, he became a partner in Fox & Co, an independent bank based in Wellington, Somerset. He was clearly ill-equipped for such a challenge. An enthusiastic breeder of Guernsey cattle and an award-winning grower of chrysanthemums, he managed his financial affairs poorly and was on the point of bankruptcy in the late 1890s, having to sell his beloved Guernsey herd in 1898 for £1,000.

In 1890 he was married to Ethel Mary Brand, daughter of the chairman of the National Telephone Company. This would prove a fortuitous match when Herbert's fortunes began to fade in later years. In 1893, a daughter – their only child, Mabel Phyllis Joan – was born in Taunton. Mabel was seemingly offered little in the way of paternal affection and was rarely living with her parents, who were happy to lead separate lives. Herbert spent much of his time travelling and Ethel stayed with her sister and brother-in-law. Airbrushed for whatever reason from the family, Mabel died a spinster in Hampstead in 1946.

At the time of his marriage, Herbert was a director of the Castle Hotel, one of a number of directorships during his life that would result from connections rather than any track record of success. He was also active in local politics and was twice elected mayor of Taunton. Turning his attention to golf, he quickly mastered the game that he had tried for the first time in 1879. He soon became a scratch golfer and by 1900 was good enough to come 26th at the British Open. He would also represent England against Scotland between 1903 and 1905.

After teetering close to bankruptcy, he staged a recovery, helped by the intervention

Herbert Fowler was one of the better batsmen among the Somerset ranks, capable on his day of launching the ball regularly out of the ground. Although he was often among the county's top scorers, there was a certain inevitability that the excitement would not last. He averaged 18.20 in fifteen first-class appearances. He also took 22 first-class wickets at 22.54 apiece. He made his last appearance in 1888, with one report stating that his retirement from the game resulted from his having suffered sunstroke.

of his wife's brother-in-law, Sir Cosmo Bonsor, an influential MP and a director of the Bank of England. Sir Cosmo had purchased a large tract of land on Walton Heath and commissioned Herbert to design a golf course, subsequently inviting him to manage the course, which he did for forty years. Herbert had finally found his niche and would prove a hugely successful course designer, with commissions in various parts of the UK and also in America.

He died in Chelsea on 13 April 1941 at the age of eighty-four, still overseeing the Walton Heath golf course, although he had for a long while suffered from ill health.

2
Edward Sainsbury
8 June 1882 v. Lancashire, Old Trafford

Edward Sainsbury

Lillywhite's describes Ted Sainsbury as a 'first class bat against any bowling, combining the greatest patience with hard hitting'. He was one of the few Somerset amateurs of the time who understood how to construct and pace an innings. He was also a lob bowler, described delightfully to modern ears as 'a slow underhand bowler'. At club level, he was perfectly capable of registering double centuries. Although he scored four centuries for Somerset, only one was first-class. Despite being a consistently good performer for the county from 1877 until 1888, his first-class average over twenty-five fixtures was a modest 16.76. His underarm bowling brought him 25 wickets at 25.76 apiece. He also offered useful service as Somerset's captain in a number of games.

Ted was born in Bath on 5 July 1851 into a family of keen cricketers associated with the Lansdown club. He was educated at Sherborne School. He had played for the First XI in 1866 at the age of fifteen but he left before his sixteenth birthday in order to enter the business world. He continued to play cricket regularly and one week in August 1876 had him registering scores of 201 not out for Corsham and 116 not out for Lansdown. These sorts of performances must have been what led *Cricket: A Weekly Record* to state in their front page review of him that 'his is generally a difficult wicket to get', adding that 'though he can hit out on occasions, steady play is his forte and … he watches the ball carefully'.

Ted Sainsbury built up his business and wealth as steadily as one of his more successful innings. He had begun his career by training as a bookkeeper, taking lodgings in Banstead. Within ten years he was managing the Briton Ferry Chemical Company. Later he would set up a new limited company, the Avon Manure Company, based in Bristol, with an initial share issue in 1893, valuing the company at £65,000. Later, he was also running an oil cake manufacturing business. He was married in 1883 to Mary Stevens (née Chamen), with whom he would have two sons and two daughters. Although he settled eventually back in the Bristol and Bath area, his business interests had taken Ted and his young family at various times to Watford and then to Swansea. He severed his relationship with Somerset cricket when he was based in Swansea in 1889 and by the time he returned to county cricket in 1891, he had been persuaded by his good friend W. G. Grace to join Gloucestershire. He was forty years of age, though, and past his best as a batsman.

Ted retired to Weston-super-Mare, by then a widower, and died in the town at the age seventy-nine on 28 October 1930. His grandson, John Popham Sainsbury, would play twice for Somerset in 1951, also representing the county at rugby.

Ted Sainsbury – the first Somerset batsman to register a first-class century, 'his is a difficult wicket to get'

3
Harry George Tate
8 June 1882 v. Lancashire, Old Trafford

Harry George Tate.

Harry George Tate was born on 18 July 1862 in East Knoyle, Wiltshire. His parents, Bennett and Sarah (née Brockway) had been married ten months earlier. By the end of the year, Bennett, a railway guard, had died of a heart attack at the age of twenty-six, leaving mother and child to survive alone. Obliged to leave school at the earliest opportunity in order to earn his keep, Harry became a 'lad clerk' on the railways in Taunton on 4 June 1877 and just short of his sixteenth birthday, with an annual wage of £20. He took lodgings in the nearby village of Trull, staying with Eliza Nichols, who hailed from the village of his birth. Presumably this was the time when he met his future wife, Eliza (née Southwood), the daughter of a tallow chandler. If so, theirs was a protracted courtship, possibly as a result of George's work that would take him away from Somerset.

This promising teenager was very soon accumulating runs for Taunton and was offered the chance to prove his worth in a trial game at the end of May 1882. He made 46 while opening the batting for the Colts against the county side and was more or less immediately given his chance in the game against Lancashire at Old Trafford. This proved a damp squib. Somerset's captain on the day, Tristram Welman, had put his faith in the nineteen-year-old by deploying him as the number three batsman. George suffered the indignity of what was at the time referred to as a pair of spectacles – nowadays shortened to a pair. He was not alone in failing. Six Somerset batsmen were dismissed for a duck in each innings. It would have been a source of regret that George never had the opportunity to prove his worth for the county. He was obliged to leave Taunton in June 1882, a matter of days after his debut. His work with the railway took him to Reading, where he was immediately drafted into the local cricket team and proceeded to top the batting averages in his debut season. His temporary transfer became a permanent move in February 1883.

Thereafter, he played regularly for Caversham Cricket Club in Reading. In one report of May 1893, where he scored over half his team's runs, he is described at the age of thirty as 'the veteran H. G. Tate', perhaps reflecting the fact that he had represented the club tirelessly for ten seasons. He remained a mainstay of Caversham CC until the end of the nineteenth century. He had been married to Eliza in 1891 and they moved to Birkenhead in 1907, where they brought up their two sons and a daugh-

23

The County Ground in its original more pastoral setting that would have greeted Somerset's pioneering first-class cricketers

ter. Also staying in their home was Eliza's father, by now a widower. They remained in Birkenhead until George's retirement.

George and Eliza spent their final years in Bishop's Hull, near Taunton. He died there at the age of eight-six on 9 March 1949. His had been a long life, in marked contrast to his father's. A gifted cricketer, perhaps he was disappointed that he never had the opportunity to atone for the ignominy of his pair on an unplayable track in his only first-class game.

4
Frederick Tristram Welman
8 June 1882 v. Lancashire, Old Trafford.

A wicket-keeper of some renown, Tristram Welman had first played for Gentlemen of Somerset v. Gentlemen of Devon in1876. He and his siblings were brought up as Roman Catholics and this would have a profound influence on him. He was born at Norton Manor near Taunton on 19 February 1849 and sent to St Mary's College, Oscott, in Birmingham, a Roman Catholic institution, many of whose pupils opted for the priesthood. Coming from a hugely wealthy family, Tristram had the means to adopt a peripatetic lifestyle that involved a cocktail of cricket, partying and devotion, but not, it would appear, a career. He volunteered as an idealistic young man for the Pontifical Zouave, an infantry force created in 1860 to defend the Papal States, although he probably never actually saw action.

Tristram was a popular socialite, a frequent guest of others who rarely stayed long in one place. But he was also attentive to his duties as a Catholic with at least two pilgrimages to Rome, one in March 1869 and another in May 1877, where he was among those 'occupying the most prominent positions around the Pope's throne' and 'had the honour of kissing the hand of his Holiness'. Pope Pius IX would in fact reward him with the medal *Bene Mereti*, possibly in gratitude for financial support. In 1883, Tristram married Mary Moore (née Ray), the daughter of a successful merchant from Melbourne, Victoria. The *Bath Chronicle* announced that the 1884 Gentlemen of England team to face the Australians included 'Mrs F. T. Welman (Somerset)': it is arguably a disappointment that this was merely a misprint rather than a snook cocked at the tourists. The birth of a first child is recorded in 1886 in Torquay but Tristram's wife was not destined to live a long life. The couple spent time lodging at seaside locations and this may possibly have been linked to her health. She died on 6 December 1902. Tristram would live for another twenty-nine years, many of them spent playing the game he loved.

His last appearance for Somerset was in 1901 when the *Taunton Courier* informs us that 'age had robbed him of his former brilliance'. His had been a long cricketing career, stretching from a first-class debut for the MCC in 1874, followed by appearances for Middlesex and Somerset. He was not an outstanding batsman, averaging 13.22 for Somerset over nineteen games, but contemporaneous reports praise his keeping. They also reveal the hazards of playing the game at the time. In1901 'F. T. Welman the veteran Somerset stumper had to retire from the position when operating for

Tristram Welman, who captained Somerset in their opening first-class fixture. He played his first game for them in 1876 (aged twenty-seven) and his last game in 1901 (aged fifty-two). An image taken in Rome (bottom) shows him in the uniform of the Pontifical Zouave.

the MCC … a ball from A. J. Miller re-opening a wound on the finger received when keeping wicket against the South Africans in June.' Then in 1904, the *Bath Chronicle* reports a broken arm.

Never remarried, he died at the age of eighty-two on 30 December 1931 in South Ascot, Berkshire.

5

Arnold James Fothergill
8 June 1882 v. Lancashire, Old Trafford

a. J. Fothergill

Arnold Fothergill holds a special place in Somerset's history, being the first player from the county team to represent England, though his status is more a matter of interest than a recognition of greatness. The son of an engine fitter, he was born on 26 August 1854 in Newcastle-on-Tyne. A fast-medium left-arm bowler and sufficiently competent a batsman to be regarded as an all-rounder, he cut his teeth as a teenager playing for two seasons for Benwell High Cross in 1870 and 1871. He was also selected by Northumberland CC and would represent them from 1870 until 1879. He was rewarded with his first professional engagement in 1879 by the Manchester Clifford club based at Old Trafford. In the same year, he was married to Isabella (née Hymners), with whom he would have ten children. Although he had no familial connections with Somerset, he was almost certainly recommended to the county by a teammate at Manchester Clifford, Somerset amateur William Massey. Lacking a pool of professionals, owing to the absence of the competitive club matches enjoyed in the North, Somerset registered the hard-working pro. He was given lodgings in Taunton in 1880 and was drafted into the side before he had officially qualified by residence. There was controversy in 1881 when the visiting Kent team refused to play at Bath unless he was removed from the team sheet. There are reports of a heated exchange. A nineteen-year-old trainee civil engineer named Francis Sacheverell Coke, lodging in nearby Pulteney Street, was drafted into the team but Kent need not have worried as they cruised to a comfortable victory.

Arnold Fothergill set the trend for Somerset's hardworking and over-bowled pros and, between 1880 and 1890, would take 157 (including 57 first-class) wickets for the county. For the last eight of those years, he also served on the MCC and Lord's ground staff. His extensive use in the nets is offered as a reason for his accurate bowling. At 5 ft 9 in, and weighing 11 st 7 lb in his prime, he relied on strength and a good line and length. On the basis of his performances as a member of the ground staff, he joined Major Warton's Tour of South Africa in 1888/9, where he played in two matches that were subsequently granted test match status.

Apart from this one tour, he spent his winters working as a clerk, either in Taunton or in Newcastle, where he was employed by a ship-building company. He lodged at various times with fellow Somerset cricketers William Massey and George Nichols. His wife, Isabella, bore the brunt of the child-rearing duties. Having been released by Somerset in 1890, Arnold spent five weeks as the pro at Oswestry, but his efforts had not been forgotten. He was awarded the 1892 fixture against Middlesex at Taunton as a benefit match (in which he did not feature): a gesture of thanks to a loyal servant of the county in the dark days as a second-tier county. By 1894 he had taken up the position of coach at Repton School, where he would remain for many years. He then retired to Sunderland, where he died at the age of seventy-seven on 1 August 1932.

*Arnold Fothergill
Somerset's first England
international*

6
Herbert Francis Fox
8 June 1882 v. Lancashire, Old Trafford

Herbert Fox is described by *Lillywhite's* as a stylish batsman and he was certainly capable of some significant innings at a Minor Counties level. Regrettably, his contribution was modest on the first-class stage. He was born on 1 August 1858 in Brislington, where his father, a qualified medic, owned the lunatic asylum at Brislington House. Herbert attended Clifton College and University College, Oxford, where he shone more brightly as an academic than he did as a sportsman. After graduating in 1881 he became a school-master at Bath College until 1889, when he left to become first a fellow and then a tutor at Brasenose College, Oxford. In 1892 he was married to Rachel Mary (née Garrett) who was sixteen years his junior. They would have two children together.

Herbert wrote books on the Classics. His *Westminster Versions: Renderings into Greek and Latin Verse* (published in 1906), reprinted from a regular column in the *Westminster*

Herbert Fox, whose major triumphs were as an academic rather than as a cricketer

Gazette, found a wider audience than some of his more esoteric publications. Whether by dint of inheritance or scholarship, he had acquired sufficient wealth by 1900 to commission a family home to be built in Headington, Oxfordshire. It offered a convenient location while he was tutoring at Brasenose College. He lived in 'Mendip House', as he called it, until 1908, the name indicating his continued attachment to the place of his birth, though the family were in fact frequent visitors to Suffolk and in time he moved there.

Herbert Fox had first turned out for Gentlemen of Somerset for their fixture against Gentlemen of Devon in August 1877. Thereafter, he had played intermittently over the years, taking part in nine first-class matches during Somerset's initial spell as a first-class county. His tenth first-class game – the 1891 encounter with Gloucestershire at Taunton – was his one and only Championship appearance. In the course of his fragmented cricketing career, he had averaged only 7.82. Although an occasional bowler, he was never risked in first-class games. Between 1902 and 1908 he appeared in Minor Counties cricket, firstly for Oxfordshire and then on a number of occasions for Suffolk, his last appearance coming shortly after his fiftieth birthday. In an environment less challenging than the Championship, he notched up a century and a 99.

He died at the age of sixty-seven on 20 January 1926 in King's College Hospital, London.

7
Frederick John Potbury
8 June 1882 v. Lancashire, Old Trafford

F. J. Potbury

Major Frederick John Potbury was a member of a well-known Sidmouth family whose name is still attached to a retailing business and auction house which he and a younger brother, Herbert, set up in the East Devon town.

Their father, John, was a coal, timber and slate merchant. One of twins, Frederick was born on 7 November 1862 in Ottery St Mary, a few miles north of Sidmouth. While his twin brother, William Henry, left for South Africa to seek his fortune as a gold prospector – and died in Rhodesia (now Zimbabwe) in 1939 – Frederick remained in the West Country for most of his life. After training initially as a draper's assistant on Taunton High Street (in all likelihood in the Hatcher's Department Store) he decided to start his own business. This coincided with his marriage in 1890 to Isabella Maria (née Tighe), who hailed from Exeter and with whom he would have two children. After a brief period as a house furnisher in Putney, he returned to Devon, setting up in furniture retailing with younger brother, Herbert, before also becoming an auctioneer and estate agent. Frederick was active in the Sidmouth sporting scene and was regarded as an accomplished club cricketer and rugby player. His home ground at Sidmouth, overlooked by the Belmont Hotel, is the location of the match between Gentlemen of Devon and Gentlemen of Somerset in 1875 which sparked the formation of Somerset CCC. On one occasion the ground was used for a rugby match. Sidmouth played host to Newton Abbot, though perhaps on the insistence of an apoplectic groundsman, the experiment was never repeated. F. J. Potbury had been a member of the home XV.

As well as playing cricket for Sidmouth, he also played on occasions for Taunton, whilst also representing both Devon and Somerset. Regrettably, his first-class career with Somerset was ill-starred. In his only game for the county he registered a pair and did not bowl.

As a young man he became the local commander of the Sidmouth Company of Volunteers and is described as 'a remarkably good shot'. At the outbreak of the First World War he volunteered promptly, rising to the rank of major. His wife, Isabella, died in 1921 but within a year Frederick was remarried to Catherine (née White), who would also predecease him, in 1937.

He was 'a staunch churchman' and for many years warden of the parish church. He also remained active in business and was regarded as an influential figure in local politics, leading the efforts to rebuild the town's defences after severe storm damage, in order to protect the important holiday trade. He also successfully challenged what were regarded as iniquitous inconsistencies in the rating valuations.

Frederick Potbury died in Sidmouth on 4 April 1943 at the age of eighty.

F. J. Potbury: a pillar of the Sidmouth community

8
Henry Fox
8 June 1882 v. Lancashire, Old Trafford

Henry Fox

Harry Fox was possessed of an irrepressible spirit of adventure

Few men have had both a rugby stand and a cricket pavilion erected in their memory and even fewer have had a mountain named after them – in this case Mount Fox in the Dawson range in Canada. But Harry Fox was no ordinary man. The son of Dilworth Crewdson Fox and a member of the family who ran the world-renowned woollen manufacturing company, he was born and raised in Tonedale (now Tone Dale) House, Wellington. His date of birth was 30 September 1856. Educated at Sherborne, he was destined to become a partner in the family business.

In truth, Harry was a decent but not a great cricketer. Deployed as a middle-order batsman by Somerset, his one moment in the sun came in a non-first-class match against Kent in 1881, when he scored 42. In three first-class games for the county, he began with a pair against Lancashire and would average only 2.50 in three matches. He offered greater service to the team with his financial support and his role as a vice president, a position he held until his death. He performed more successfully at rugby, being instrumental in setting up both the Wellington rugby club in 1874 and the county side in 1877. In 1874 he had called a meeting of a number of able-bodied Wellingtonians in his house, where he explained the rules of rugby to them with the aid of a blackboard and chalk. He became treasurer, coach and captain of the club, as well as its founder. One account describes him as 'a fine three-quarter and tremendously speedy, so much so that when he received the ball and started running, the rest of the team have been known to actually stand still and clap, so useless was it to try and back him up.' He was also the benefactor, captain and leading light of the Somerset rugby team until obliged to cease playing as a result of a knee injury. Thereafter, he became a referee (or umpire as it was then known) in club and county matches.

His spirit of adventure remained undaunted by injury and in the mid-1880s he took up mountaineering with great enthusiasm. After having conquered the most challenging peaks in Europe, including the Eiger and the Matterhorn, he set out with two colleagues – W. F. Donkin and C. Dent – to become the first men to scale Koshtan-Tau in the

Caucasus mountains. Dent was soon obliged to give up the attempt but Fox and Donkin pressed on with their Swiss guides. They were never seen again and although subsequent search parties found their base camp supplies and, higher up, their bivouac, none of the bodies was ever recovered. It is assumed that they were victims of an avalanche. His death at the age of thirty-one is given as 'on or since 30th August 1888, at some place unknown'. Harry had never been married. A stand was built at the ground of the Wellington rugby club he had formed and a pavilion at the local cricket ground where he had been an enthusiastic participant. Tributes flowed to a popular and generous-hearted man. A glowing obituary in the *Bristol Mercury* states that 'the bright, eager face and the cheery ring of his voice were warmly welcomed in the cricket or [rugby] football field, whether he appeared as player, umpire or keen onlooker'.

A brilliant organiser and a fearless adventurer, Harry had pushed himself to his limits until, ultimately, he fell short, both on the first-class cricket field and, more tragically, in the Caucasus mountains.

9
William Trask
8 June 1882 v. Lancashire, Old Trafford

William Trask

The Trask family made their fortune from the mellow hamstone in South Somerset. Charles Trask had started up a business combining the mining and carving of stone with a highly-regarded workshop in Norton-sub-Hamdon. His sons joined the business but not before William, born in the village on 15 July 1859, had been educated in Crewkerne and then at Sherborne School, in Dorset. For a while William assisted in the business but his younger brother would take over the day-to-day management. In 1891 William was married to Margaret Stancomb (née Le Gros) in a lavish

William Trask – prolific at club level

society wedding in Frome. He was appointed chairman of the Ham Hill and Doulting Stone Quarries, though he lived for much of the time in London and Eastbourne, eventually settling in Frome, just down the road from the Doulting quarry.

What of his efforts at cricket? A prolific accumulator of runs for Lansdown CC, he is described as a steady batsman who was hard to remove once he had established himself at the crease. He played forty-seven times for Somerset, but at the first-class

William Trask

level, his batting rarely rose above mediocrity and he only bowled occasionally. William also found time to pursue his other great love – golf – and the *Bath Chronicle* of 9 May 1936 reports that at the age of seventy-seven he had achieved his seventh (and presumably final) hole-in-one.

By the time of his death on 24 June 1949 just short of his ninetieth birthday, William Trask had been back in Somerset and living in Frome for nine years. A life of relative ease had perhaps contributed to his longevity.

10
Henry George Hamlet Hall
8 June 1882 v. Lancashire, Old Trafford

Henry George Hall

Hamlet Hall – 'an inveterate stonewaller'

He signed himself as 'Henry George' but he was normally referred to in cricketing circles as 'Hamlet'. The son of a customs officer, George Harris Hall, and his wife, Jane, Hamlet was born in Bedminster on 24 December 1857. Brought up in Bedminster, he and his younger brother, Ernie, became schoolmasters in the area. Hamlet taught at Dr Bell's National School, an elementary school run by the Bristol Education Committee. Later, in retirement, he would become one of the men responsible for setting up the school's Old Boys' Association, established in 1924.

He and his brother played for Bedminster CC and on two occasions, Hamlet played in first-class fixtures for Somerset. In four innings he was dismissed three times and managed a grand total of 2 runs. His bowling was marginally more successful, with 1 wicket at a cost of 57 runs.

He was married in 1884 to Millicent Jane (née Pope). They had two daughters. There are press reports of his having penned what are described as 'amusing ditties' which he performed locally. If he was an entertainer when standing on a stage, the same could hardly be said when he took to the crease. Hamlet was capable of carrying his bat on occasions but not of batting with any adventure or abandon. In a game for the Gloucestershire XI v. Colts (who numbered Somerset player Tom Gregg among their ranks), the reporter informs us that 'Hamlet Hall … held his position while his companions did the hitting'. In another reference, he is described as 'one of the steadiest bats we have had in Bristol, who would stay in for hours and never vary his tactics'. Rev. George Wood, a player who appeared in later years for Somerset, notes in a letter: 'I remember well those happy days when I played cricket … fairly regularly for Bedminster from 1893 to 1898. Your mention of Hamlet Hall – an inveterate stonewaller – reminds me how hard we tried to teach him that a cricket bat was an offensive and not only a defensive weapon.' Perhaps the Somerset supporters were grateful that Hamlet's cameos for the county proved unusually brief affairs.

For the twenty-five years leading up to his death he was a widely-known and well-regarded umpire in club cricket in the Bristol area. He stated publicly that poor and partial umpiring had caused frictions between teams in his playing days and that he had resolved to remedy this during his own time as an umpire. He believed that it had led to much greater trust and more socialising between the competing club sides.

He died at the Southmead Institution in Bristol on 13 February 1934 at the age of seventy-six. There was genuine sadness attached to a tribute to him in the *Western Daily Press*. 'A. G. P.' writes about hearing that Hamlet 'whose name was as well known as any in the game, locally, 40 years ago', was seriously ill. The reporter approached the hospital to offer help only to find that Hamlet was dead. He writes that 'times have been hard with our old friend for some years past; this fact was only made known … a few days ago, otherwise something might have been done. It seems to me that the Bristol Cricket Association might well consider the possibility of a fund from which small grants could be made to old cricketers in times of great need.' Too little and too late for Hamlet.

At the opening of the new Bedminster pavilion in 1921, Hamlet Hall stands to the far right in his umpire's coat. Somerset cricketer Ernest Murdock is in the foreground on the left, next to Hamlet's fellow umpire. At the back, centre, stands Somerset cricketer A. E. C. (Bert) North.

11
Henry Scott
8 June 1882 v. Lancashire, Old Trafford

Harry Scott

Harry Scott – who worked in the framework knitting industry from the age of eight until the age of seventy-five

Known as Harry, he hailed from Nottinghamshire, a rich source of professional cricketers in the 1870s and 1880s. At 5 ft 11.5 in and with an athletic frame, Harry Scott is described in *MCC Scores & Biographies* as 'no batsman but a useful slow bowler with an off break'.

Born in Sutton-in-Ashfield on 28 October 1851, he was one of fifteen children of Samuel and Mary Scott, who were stocking framework knitters. The majority of their offspring would either follow a similar path or become miners. Harry began his working life at the tender age of eight, employed as a winder before becoming a hand framework knitter when he reached thirteen. Once into his twenties he combined summer work as a professional cricketer and coach with winter work as a framework knitter. His first professional appointment was with Northallerton in 1873, when he was twenty-two. One-year appointments followed at Preston and Oxford. In the winter of 1875 he was married to Jane (née Knowles), who would pre-decease him by twenty-nine years and with whom he would have seven children, three of whom reached adulthood. The following year he began to spend his summers plying his trade in the West Country in Taunton, Ilfracombe, Weston-super-Mare and finally, in 1882, Clifton College, where he was employed as the coach. After having qualified for Somerset by residence, he made useful contributions prior to the county's elevation to first-class status, including a hat-trick against Sussex at Hove. In 1879, at Clifton, he claimed the prized wicket of W. G. Grace for 113, although Grace gained ample revenge by twice bowling Harry for a duck. By 1882, his career with Somerset was petering out. He made two first-class appearances, averaging 4.00 with the bat and taking 2 wickets at 49.50 each. After returning to Nottinghamshire, he played in a trial match but was never selected to play for the county of his birth. From 1891 he settled for the life of a framework knitter, back in his native Sutton-in-Ashfield, working for the firm of Dove & Clarke until 1926, by which time his eyesight was failing him.

Blind for the final fourteen years of his life, Harry died in Sutton-in-Ashfield on

11 November 1941 at the age of ninety, still living in the house he had purchased back in 1891 with his earnings as a pro – 28 Langford Street. None of his three children was ever married. Frank, Eliza Ann and Ethel continued to live in the family home long after their father's death.

12
Dudley David Pontifex
13 July 1882 v. Gloucestershire, Gloucester

Dudley David Pontifex

Dudley Pontifex was born on 12 February 1855 in Weston, near Bath. His family had accrued their wealth over two generations through manufacturing, specialising in the production of chemicals and metals. After attending Sydney College in Bath, described as 'a prominent independent school' and based in the building where the Holburne Museum of Art is now housed, he went on to Trinity College, Cambridge. After graduating he pursued a career in law, having been accepted into the Inner Temple. He was called to the bar in 1885.

D. D. Pontifex – an excellent all-round sportsman and a brilliant billiards player

Although he played in the 1876 trial match, he failed to make it into the Cambridge University XI. He was, however, awarded a blue as a billiards player, also winning the cue as the top billiards player at the university in three successive years from 1876 until 1878. An all-round sportsman, he also played tournament tennis with some success, but it was at billiards that he truly shone. He is described as one of the leading amateurs of his day. Breaks in excess of 300 were commonplace and he also wrote on the subject, with published articles and contributions to the authoratative book entitled *Billiards*, by Major Broadfoot, published in 1896.

When turning his attention to cricket, Dudley Pontifex was a batsman who kept wicket on occasions. He first appeared for Gentlemen of Somerset in 1877, although his debut in first-class county cricket was for Surrey. He played for them on nine occasions in 1881, his best performance being against Nottinghamshire at The Oval, when he opened the batting and scored 89. In 1882 he offered his services to the county of his birth as they struggled to justify their first-class status. He played for them in one match, against Gloucestershire, where he resided at the time. His subsequent commitments as a barrister living in Dulwich made it impossible for him to play more regularly, but he would also represent MCC in a number of first-class fixtures.

He was married in 1879 to Clementina Mary Jane (née Salmon), with whom he had three children. Ten years after his marriage, the *South Wales Echo* reports a stand of 159 by Dudley Pontifex and Hamilton Ross for Lansdown CC. It adds that this was supposedly the largest stand by two men both wearing spectacles, beating the previous record of 130, of which Pontifex was also a part. He took up golf at the age of forty-five and, demonstrating his natural flair as a sportsman, succeeded in becoming a scratch golfer.

Dudley Pontifex died on 27 September 1934 at the age of seventy-nine, still living in Dulwich and having suffered for many years from the crippling and painful effects of severe arthritis. His obituary in *The Times* informs us that 'he combined great skill at games with a charming, modest and generous appreciation of others'.

13
William Massey
13 July 1882 v. Gloucestershire, Gloucester

William Massey

William Massey was born on 11 April 1850 in Manchester (and not 1846 as stated in *MCC Scores & Biographies*). His father, also William, married to Elizabeth, was a successful businessman who worked in the hosiery trade and became a respected figure in the area.

On leaving school, William and his younger brother Herbert became print salesmen. Taunton-based historian H. J. Channon, writing in the 1940s, describes Massey as 'a giant in stature and a boxer' and whilst evidence of his career as a pugilist is elusive, the description rings true, given that at athletic meets, William starred both as a sprinter and at 'putting the weight'. The same could be said of his brother who on one occasion won the 'throwing the cricket ball' competition with an impressive distance of 116 yards. Both brothers also played rugby for Free Wanderers and cricket for St Helens, although William seemed happy to play cricket wherever the opportunity arose, with appearances for a variety of teams, including Manchester Clifford and Stand. Whereas Herbert remained in Manchester, ultimately setting up a successful company in Burnage that manufactured velveteen, William bought an ailing silk manufacturing company in Ottery St Mary, Devon. He became a partner of John Collin Newbery in the firm of J. C. Newbery & Co. in 1874. He made an immediate impression on the social and sporting scene in East Devon, demonstrating his speed and strength at the 1874 athletics meet, playing cricket for Ottery, Sidmouth and indeed, by 1875, for Gentlemen of Devon for whom he played against Gentlemen of Somerset at Sidmouth. By 1876 he was playing regularly for Exeter Rugby Club as a full-back and was captain of the newly-formed Devon rugby team. He starred in a rare victory when Somerset amassed a number of tries at a time when the only points to be gained were one for each conversion. Somerset missed every kick. In the dying seconds, Devon landed a breakaway try which Massey converted from near the touchline. Devon had won 1-0. In *The Story of Devon Rigby Football Union*, F. A. Davey incorrectly states that Massey's usual team was Newton College, but it is certainly true that he was happy to play for any team for miles around. He also clearly retained his links with Manchester – perhaps owing to connections with the Manchester rag trade – and continued to make occasional appearances for Free Wanderers RFC and Manchester Clifford CC. In 1880, his silk manufacturing business was bankrupted and he began to engage his passion for rugby and cricket in Somerset. He captained the Somerset rugby team in 1879 and also appeared for Weston-super-Mare and St George's Hospital (Easton-in-Gordano). He also played for Fullands and Somerset at cricket, making 120 for the county against Sussex at Bath in 1880. The 1881 census sees William as a guest of Somerset CCC Secretary Edward Western in Weston-super-Mare. By then he had begun to refer to himself as William M. Massey but this was an affectation as he continued to appear as plain William Massey on legal documents.

William's father died in 1882, leaving a sizeable estate of over £4,000 to his offspring. For a while, William Jnr continued to enjoy his cricket, appearing in his only first-class game for Somerset in 1882 (scoring 0 and 4) and once for Lancashire in 1883 (with scores of 5 and 1). But in November 1885, he arrived in New York to begin a new life as an agent, presumably importing fabrics. He cannot be accused of allowing his business interests to stand in the way of his cricket. In 1886 he played for Staten Island, including in a match against a touring England XI, as an

The Somerset and Lancashire cricketer is often referred to as 'William Morton Massey', but this may have resulted from an assumption that he was the man of that name who played for Toronto and Quebec in the 1890s. The confusion is understandable as William, who liked to style himself 'W. M. Massey' had by then emigrated to the United States. It is, however, incorrect. William Morton Massey (pictured above) was born in Canada in 1867, the son of William Morton Massey Snr, a partner in the exclusive New York perfume retailer and druggist, Caswell Massey & Co, who have long been purveyors of fine goods to the great and the good, from George Washington to John F. Kennedy.

attempt was made to improve the infrastructure of competitive cricket in the USA. There were grand plans to create a league organised by the Order of the Sons of St George, a society of ex-pats with 200 lodges and 17,000 members.

By 1887, William was based in Orange County, Florida. Peter Roebuck recounts the tale of William Massey's having scored 1,998 runs in a season and hastily arranging a further match in order to accumulate a further two runs, only to suffer a pair. If the tale is true, then it applies to the 1887 season, when William made scores of 264 not out, 177 not out and 101 not out in a matter of days. This was also the year in which he married Elizabeth McLain Saunders, a widow who had recently moved to the area from Canada with her two children. At the age of thirty-seven, William had found love and set down roots. His breathless round of cricket matches became a thing of the past. In 1891, he built a 'packing house' on land which Elizabeth handed over to him for a nominal fee.

He never took out American citizenship so that when he died suddenly, at the age of forty-nine, on 17 April 1899 while visiting New York, probate was settled by his brother Herbert, still based in Burnage, Manchester. William left his estate to his 'beloved wife' Elizabeth.

14
Robert Christian Ramsay
13 July 1882 v. Gloucestershire, Gloucester

R. C. Ramsay.

Bob Ramsay appeared all too briefly on the Somerset cricketing scene. A well-built young man, 5 ft 6 in tall and 12 stone, he is described in *MCC Scores & Biographies* as 'a useful batsman and an effective slow bowler with a variety of pace and a curly leg-break'. The latter fact had led to his moniker of 'Twisting Tommy'.

His father had emigrated in 1839 to Queensland where he was a successful sheep farmer and a politician. Robert Snr and his wife, Susan, had fourteen children, only nine of whom reached adulthood. The family were on an extended holiday in England when Bob was born in Cheltenham on 20 December 1861. When Robert Snr retired to England, Bob and his brother, Marmaduke Francis (known as Frank), were sent first to Elstree Preparatory School and then to Harrow, where they excelled at sports. In 1879 the pair took seventeen Eton wickets in the annual fixture at Lord's. Bob was a pace bowler at that time but when he left Harrow he reinvented himself as a leg spinner, finding he could turn the ball a considerable distance whilst keeping the bounce low. On going up to Trinity Hall, Cambridge, he continued to play cricket, earning his blue in 1882, although he opted not to complete his degree. His parents were then residing in Dinder House, Wells, and so Somerset claimed him as one of their own.

He played four first-class matches for the county, averaging 20.71 with the bat, including a highest score of 71. He also took nine wickets at 32.11 apiece, never quite capturing the form he showed for Cambridge University, for whom he secured victory against the touring Australian XI in May 1882, claiming twelve wickets in the match.

Despite his modest record for Somerset, they would have rued the loss of a potential match-winner when Bob returned to Australia. He joined his brother, Frank, and together they learned the trade of sheep farming at the livestock station at Eton Vale, near Toowoomba. In time all five Ramsay brothers would form a business partnership. Bob was determined that the company should expand through the early adoption of technology in order to maximise efficiency. He was an astute businessman with excellent man-management skills and noted for his judicious movement of stock during

Known as 'Twisting Tommy', Bob Ramsay went on to enjoy a hugely successful business career

drought and his flair for establishing underground aquifers. A grandson, Alan Ramsay, modestly adds that Bob possibly enjoyed an element of 'uncommon good luck'.

In 1907, Bob was married to Olive Zillah (née Voss) in Queensland and they would have seven children together. During the First World War, he was a member of the Queensland Recruiting Committee. Described by one opponent as 'a blood and fire conscriptionist', he resigned after the 1916 referendum, where the proposal to introduce conscription was rejected. In 1920 he returned to England, living at the Howletts estate in Bekesbourne, Kent, where his father had been a tenant for many years and which Bob had purchased a decade earlier with two of his brothers. A man of unbounded energy, he took up flying at the age of sixty-nine, gaining his pilot's A Certificate five months later. When the Bekesbourne Flying Club found itself in financial difficulties, he purchased the aerodrome and aeroplanes so that the club could remain a going concern. Already reputedly the oldest pilot in the country, he would undoubtedly have continued flying but for the ban on private flights resulting from the Second World War.

Bob Ramsay remained at Bekesbourne until his death at the age of ninety-five on 25 June 1957.

15
Charles Francis Long Sweet
13 July 1882 v. Gloucestershire, Gloucester

C. F. L. Sweet.

Rev. Charles Sweet – described by his tutor as 'rather idle', he was more successful as a footballer than as a cricketer

Lillywhite's describes Rev. Sweet as 'a fine field', their default description for someone who never rose above the average with bat or ball but showed enthusiasm or athleticism as a fielder. Born in Bath on 29 November 1860, he was the eldest son of a clergyman. Educated at Winchester College, he went on to gain a BA in Modern History at Keble College, Oxford, though according to the reports still held in the college's archive, he was 'rather idle'. One tutor concluded in Sweet's final year that 'he has not done much this term … I don't think he ever will do much'. Having already appeared as a schoolboy for Somerset in two non-first-class fixtures, he played in a Varsity trial match but failed to make it into the Oxford University side. He was, however, captain of the Keble College side in 1882. An active sportsman, he also played rugby for his college and captained them for two years at association football. This last was clearly the sport at which he excelled, given that he played for the University XI and was awarded a footballing blue. As for cricket, he played five first-class games for Somerset and in nine innings totalled 67 runs, his average of 16.75 having been bolstered by the fact that he was not out in over half his visits to the crease. His love of the game remained undiminished and he would represent Dorset and Wiltshire as his work took him to those counties.

In 1885 Charles Sweet was appointed a curate at Paignton. Then in 1887 he was married to Edith Maud, eldest daughter of Lt Colonel Walrond. Their three children all adopted the name Walrond Sweet. This was also the year in which Charles became curate of Bere Regis and Winterborne Kingston, in Wiltshire. In 1892 he was appointed Assistant Inspector of Church Schools in the deanery but he only had to wait one more year for his elevation to the role of vicar of Milton Lilbourne, also in Wiltshire. He remained there until he became vicar of Stourpaine, Dorset, in 1902. He was briefly Rural Dean of Blandford until being offered the living as Rector of Symondsbury where he would remain from 1914 until his retirement owing to ill health in September 1930. During his time there, he was instrumental in reviving the Symondsbury Cricket Club and was for many years their president. He also oversaw the restoration of the parish church. Tragedy struck in 1919 when his son, Rev. G. C. Walrond Sweet (at the time chaplain to the Army on the Rhine), drowned while on honeymoon.

Charles Sweet died in Teignmouth on 24 January 1932 at the age of seventy-one.

16
Richard Ernest Hill
13 July 1882 v. Gloucestershire, Gloucester

R.E.Hill

He was born on 12 August 1861 in Timsbury, where his father, Rev. Richard Hill, was the rector. Richard Snr had benefitted from a sizeable inheritance. Richard Jnr's paternal grandfather, John Hill, had been a successful merchant based in St Petersburg and had also brought fifty acres of land when the city of Canterbury was being established in New Zealand. He succumbed to gout and gangrene in 1861, suggesting that he might not have been the most abstemious of men. Russian enterprise's loss was Rev. Richard Hill's gain when the estate of the late merchant fell into his lap.

On leaving school Richard Jnr embarked on a military career, becoming a lieutenant in the 2nd Royal Cheshire Militia in 1881. He was married in 1883 to Isabel Fielding (née Holt), with whom he would have two sons. He saw service in Dublin with the Manchester Regiment before returning to England with the rank of major. In 1904, by then a Lieutenant Colonel on active service in Pretoria, he was transferred to the Army Service Corps and in 1907 he was added to the reserve of officers as a brevet colonel. He would be recalled to service in 1914 as Assistant Director of Supplies and Transport, Northern Command.

Richard Hill was educated at Marlborough College where he played for the First XI in 1879 alongside fellow Somerset cricketer, J. B. Challen. A left-arm pace bowler and lower-order right-handed batsman, he played his club cricket for Lansdown. Having already appeared for Somerset as a twenty-year-old in 1881, he made his only first-class appearance in 1882. It was a game in which Somerset were roundly thrashed. W. G. Grace offered no favours, taking ten wickets, while Woof put in a dogged performance to claim a further nine. Hill made 0 and 7 not out and took 1 for 21. Others among Somerset's five debutants had fared worse.

His younger son, Roy Fitzgerald, became a farmer in South Africa. His elder son, Richard Blundell, volunteered for the war effort in May 1918. Sadly, he lost his life five months later in Flanders. In retirement, Richard Hill resided with Isabel in Weston-super-Mare, though he died at Westminster on 25 December 1924 at the age of sixty-three.

17
Francis John Hill
24 July 1882 v. Hampshire, Southampton

Frank J Hill

Frank Hill in the 1880 Marlborough College XI. He subsequently played for Lansdown CC alongside older brother Richard. Although both all-rounders at club level, Frank was primarily a batsman. In his only match for the county of his birth, he made scores of 29 and 2. He also played rugby as a three-quarter for Bath and Somerset.

The brother of fellow Somerset cricketer Richard, Frank Hill was born in Timsbury on 1 October 1862. His mother had given birth to three sons and four daughters when she died in 1871. Frank was approximately nine years old at the time.

Educated at Marlborough College and Exeter College, Oxford University, where he opted not to complete his degree, Frank emigrated to Canada in 1883 in order to begin a new life as a rancher. Initially he settled in the Territories of McCleod, Alberta. But he soon purchased 500 acres of land in the Qu'Appelle district of Saskatchewan and built a homestead that still stands. Frank was not occupied entirely with farming. In 1885 he served with Boulton's Scouts during the crushing of the North-West Rebellion, led by Louis Riel, who was hung for his pains. This was followed by a spell serving in the 16th Light Horse. In 1887 he was married to Augusta Cosgrave, known as Daisy, with whom he would have seven daughters and a son. Theirs was a double ceremony at which Daisy's sister was also married. From 1920 Frank lived in the town of Whitewood. In 1922, having presumably handed over the management of the farm to his son, Richard, he made an extended visit to his family in Timsbury before returning later in the year to Canada. Frank and Daisy moved to Saskatoon in 1926. Frank died on 11 September 1939 at the age of seventy-six in Saskatoon. He lies buried in the Woodlawn Cemetery. Daisy died in Edmonton in 1957.

18
Francis William Terry
24 July 1882 v. Hampshire, Southampton

F. W. Terry.

Francis Terry emigrated to Canada in 1891. He would become a local hero in Canadian cricketing circles, captaining the national team on a number of occasions, becoming the leading scorer of centuries in club cricket and, with his score of 111 against the USA in 1893, establishing a highest total by any Canadian batsman in an international match – a record that would stand for 70 years. As the leading light in Canadian cricket, he was asked by J. E. Hall and R. O. McCulloch to write the foreword to *Sixty Years of Canadian Cricket*, published in 1895. In it he reveals his love for 'a game … that combines mind, eye, and muscle in one, together with fresh air, summer weather, the smell of mown grass, the fragrance of flowers'.

Born in Wells on 26 October 1860, Francis was the son of George Terry, a local GP. Whereas his older brother chose to pursue a medical profession and became a surgeon, Francis entered the ministry. Educated at St Edward's School, Oxford, he went on to Merton College. Although he played in a Varsity trial match he failed to make the Oxford University XI, owing to some stiff competition. He did, however, play on a number of occasions for Somerset and for representative sides between 1881 and 1890. With a low centre of gravity, a strong physique and an excellent eye, he was a hugely versatile cricketer, at times a brilliant batsman, a medium-pace bowler and a fine wicket-keeper. *Lillywhite's* describes him as 'a first class wicket-keep [sic]' and 'a plucky and determined bat'. In ten first-class matches for Somerset he averaged 32.47 scoring one century and three half-centuries as well as taking thirteen catches and completing two stumpings.

He left the county in 1886 to take up the curacy at Horsham for six years before emigrating to London, Ontario, to take up an appointment at the recently-built Chapel of Hope in the grounds of the London Asylum for the insane. Francis Terry played his cricket for London Asylum and Canada, proving a prolific run-maker and well-

Francis Terry – a brilliant wicketkeeper and batsman who briefly lit up Somerset cricket

regarded wicket-keeper. He returned to England for a brief period from 1900 when he assisted Rev. Tremenheere as a curate at Madron, near Penzance. He lit up the Madron cricketing scene, reviving the village's fortunes in 1900 with his 'brilliant' and 'powerful' batting complimented repeatedly in the local press. It was announced ahead of the following season that he would no longer be able to play for Madron, being 'hampered by serious illness'. Returning to Canada, he took up a post in the outskirts of Toronto at the Mimico Asylum, whom he represented at cricket between 1902 and 1908. He continued his pastoral work for the mentally ill in MimicoAsylum and died in the Ontario Hospital of Senility in Toronto. The date stated on his death certificate is 6 October 1936 (a day later than some sources record). He was never married.

19
Francis Reed
24 July 1882 v. Hampshire, Southampton

Francis Reed.

Frank Reed was born on 24 October 1850 in Ottery St Mary, Devon. His story is a cocktail of genteel privilege and the depths of despair. His father was a schoolmaster and a member of the Royal College of Preceptors who ran a small school on Broad Street in Ottery St Mary. William Reed's wife, Ellen (née Farrant) had given birth to a daughter and two sons, William Jnr and Frank, but died of tuberculosis four months after Frank's birth.

Ellen's unmarried sister, Emma, moved in to help with the care of her niece and two young nephews. Then, in 1854, she was married to William and would give birth to a number of daughters and a son, Herbert Farrant Reed. Frank's half-brother would also represent Somerset at cricket.

Frank went up to Exeter College, Oxford, where he played for the college but failed to make the University XI. On graduating, he became a chaplain and teacher at Fullands School, Taunton, of which his father was the proprietor and principal. Fullands, with its superb wicket, would for a while be the epicentre of the Somerset cricket scene.

These were perhaps among Rev. Frank Reed's happiest years. He appeared regularly for Somerset, first representing Gentlemen of Somerset in 1871 as a twenty-year-old and playing his last game for the county in 1884. 5 ft 10 in tall and with a slim frame, he was primarily a right-arm medium-pace bowler, tidy rather than penetrating, but was also good enough as a batsman to score an unbeaten first-class fifty. In ten first-class matches, all of which came in the latter part of his playing career, he averaged 11.64 and took 12 wickets at 31.66 each.

He also played rugby for Somerset in 1879.

By the time William Reed Snr died in 1881, the eldest son, William Jnr, had taken over as headmaster-proprietor of Fullands School, with Frank acting as vice principal, classics teacher and chaplain and Herbert Farrant Reed also a member of staff. Frank also supplemented his income by working as a curate at nearby Bickenall. Perhaps he needed to do so because the school was still heavily mortgaged and the brothers were struggling to keep the enterprise afloat, putting it up for sale in 1886.

In 1885, he was married to Margaret (née Trenchard), who came from a wealthy, well-connected family, and he also took up an appointment as headmaster of Donington Grammar School, Lincolnshire, chosen from 117 applicants for the post. Frank would have anticipated a rosy future as a provider for his family, particularly when his son, Cecil, was born in Donington. However, he did not stay there long. In 1887, he was offered the headmastership of Lady Lumley's Grammar School in Thornton-le-Dale, Yorkshire, with the additional role of warden of Lady Lumley's Hospital. Something went horribly wrong because by 1889 he had been replaced and was living in Middlesbrough, advertising his services as a tutor and in the administering of sacraments. In advertisements placed in the local press he refers to his time as headmaster at Donington but makes no mention of his time at Thornton-le-Dale. Not for the last time, he swept a part of his life under the carpet.

His daughter, Elinor, was born that same year, but hereafter things went downhill. The 1891 census shows Frank visiting his friend and fellow teacher and cricketer, Edward Western, who was by then a headmaster at Langport. He and his family began to lead separate lives, with Margaret eventually managing a large boarding house in Bournemouth. She described herself somewhat prematurely as a widow, either because she had no idea of her husband's whereabouts or she wished to distance herself from him. (Interestingly, his son, Cecil, would change his surname to Reede, pointing to the latter explanation.)

William Reed, who was the proprietor and headmaster of Fullands School in Taunton and father of Somerset cricketers, Frank and Herbert Farrant Reed. The school's 'much-admired' cricket pitch was home to the Somerset side in the early years. After William's death in 1881, William Reed Jnr would take over the running of the school but, crippled by too ambitious a loan, the project foundered. Frank and Herbert Farrant Reed would both end their lives in a state of destitution.

Exeter College, 1873, when Francis Reed was in his final year

Frank's physical decline can be charted from his regular admissions to the Whitechapel Infirmary and the Stepney Workhouse in the East End of London, beginning in 1901 and ending in 1912. An early visit to the infirmary has him described as a 'commercial clerk', though this may have been a fabrication. Reliant on charity, Frank was admitted for ailments such as swollen or ulcerated legs. These admissions lasted for a few days in the first instances but the duration grew over the years. His final spell in the Stepney Workhouse, suffering from bronchitis, was in the spring of 1910 and lasted four months. Further admissions to the Whitechapel Infirmary followed and this is where he would live out his final days. For a number of years, he had denied the existence of a wife and children, describing himself as either a single man or a widower and giving his next-of-kin as his brother, William, whose whereabouts were known to Frank.

For over a decade, Frank Reed had endured a depressing existence, lodging in doss houses such as Wildermuth House, which took in up to 900 men. Conditions were wretched: such places were filthy and flea-ridden. Petty crime and prostitution were rife and fear would have stalked the streets, given that this had not long since been the hunting ground of Jack the Ripper. A charitable explanation for his presence might be that he was seeking redemption by working among the poor and dispossessed, but the nature of his illnesses and regular admissions to charitable institutions suggest otherwise. Francis Reed died on the 30 April 1912 at the Whitechapel Infirmary. Margaret, almost certainly oblivious to his demise, never remarried and lived in Bournemouth with her spinster daughter until her death in 1950.

20

Herbert Farrant Reed

24 July 1882 v. Hampshire, Southampton

Herbert. Farrant Reed.

Herbert Farrant Reed's life story is not dissimilar to his stepbrother Frank's sorry tale of decline. He was born on 10 September 1865 in Wilton, Taunton. Some sources state that he was registered as 'Albert', but they are incorrect, as the parish records testify. Taught by his father, William, the proprietor of Fullands School, Herbert benefitted both from an excellent education and good sporting facilities. In 1879, at the age of thirteen, he was already in the Fullands XI and by 1881, aged fifteen, he was selected for Somerset, whom he would continue to represent until 1886. In eight first-class matches for the county he averaged 11.50 and took 2 wickets at 30.50 each. As with the trajectory of his life, the averages are remarkably close to his brother's. He also played rugby for Taunton and then for Somerset against Devon in January 1886.

He was offered a place in 1883 at Queens' College, Cambridge, as an 'admitted pensioner', a scholarship offered to talented or well-connected undergraduates who were unable to pay their way. He appears to have squandered the opportunity. In his second term he was caught drunk and disorderly by the proctor and a curt note on his examination results records: 'Classics abominable; mathematics bad'. By 1884 a despairing tutor recorded: 'I can make nothing of this man: fit for the poll [non-honours degree] scarcely'. He delayed taking his finals with 'bad eyes' in 1885 and a 'bad foot' in 1886, though in his favour he was captain of the College XI in 1886. During the vacations he continued to appear for Fullands. Writing in the *Taunton Courier* in 1943, H. J. Channon refers to an old scorebook confirming that Herbert scored 133 for Fullands against The Wesleyan College in 1885.

After a 'very bad failure' in Theology, he managed to scrape a third class degree in History in 1890. He took up a post as an assistant schoolmaster at Temple House School, Sandhurst. He almost certainly remained a teacher at the school for some years, given that he was visiting his step-sister, Edith, in nearby Newbury at the time of the 1901 census and his occupation is given as 'schoolmaster'.

Over the next decade tragedy befell him, just as it had befallen his brother, Frank. By 1906, he had been admitted to the British Home for Incurables in Streatham, Surrey. This was a charitable hospital for middle-class professionals who had hit on hard times. Although sufficiently in command of his faculties to sign his will and appoint his older step-brother William as executor, Reed was suffering from locomotive ataxia, where he was unable to control his movements. The affliction, caused by a degeneration of the spinal cord, is almost invariably brought about by syphilis. To add to his woes, this led to nephritis, or acute kidney failure. We can only guess the chain of events but we can surmise that the heart attack that killed Herbert Farrant Reed at the hospital on 9 March 1911 at the age of forty-five would have been a merciful release from his suffering. One wonders whether or not his half-brother, Frank, lurching between the workhouse and the infirmary, was aware that Herbert, a handful of miles away, was in an even more wretched state than he was.

Never married, he left his estate of £97 to his only full sister, Rose, and her husband.

21
Charles Edgar Winter
24 July 1882 v. Hampshire, Southampton

Charles Winter - the subject of a later myth that he had played for Somerset as a twelve-year-old

A familiar Somersetshire tale. An exhilarating young cricketer fails to build on his early promise. Charles was not, as is commonly supposed, the son of a tanner from Bermondsey, mysteriously called up by Somerset as a twelve-year-old. That is a myth promulgated in more recent times. He was in fact the son of Henry Winter, a baker at the time of Charles's birth in Wellington on 9 October 1865, but later an agent for an auction house. Whilst not quite the astonishing child prodigy of some accounts, Charles Winter was nevertheless a promising young cricketer. A right-arm fast bowler who was no mug with the bat, he made his first-class debut when he was approaching his seventeenth birthday. Somerset lost heavily but the young bowler acquitted himself well. His best first-class performances came during Somerset's first brush with first-class status and his powers had waned by the time he appeared in his first Championship game in 1892, by then aged twenty-six. His final appearance for the county was in 1895. Charles was also a fine rugby player, representing Somerset on eleven occasions. A full-back, he was first selected early in 1882. His last appearance for the county at rugby was in the 1893/4 season.

Beyond the world of sport, Charles Winter became a pupil teacher (or classroom assistant) in Wellington, often a first step on the employment ladder for bright young men, but he took up a position in the woollen industry as a clerk at Fox Brothers, who were the major employers in Wellington. Harry Fox was almost certainly his sponsor. Married to Edith Ellen (née Hebditch) in 1894, Charles moved to London, where he raised his family, acting as an agent for the company before setting himself up as a manufacturer of woollen goods in Hornsey. Between 1921 and 1925 his son, Charles Arthur Winter, would also represent Somerset. In 1939 and seventy-three at the time, Charles Snr was married for a second time. His bride, Bridget (née Swowden), was forty years his junior.

He died in London on 3 April 1954, at the age of eighty-eight, leaving Bridget the princely sum of £23,000, confirming that he had made a success of his business venture.

22
Cleveland Edmund Greenway
4 August 1882 v. MCC, Lord's

Born in Buenos Aires on 29 October 1864, Lt Colonel Greenway was a right-handed batsman who played in two first-class games – one for Somerset and one for MCC – and averaged only 7.75 with the bat. Between 1900 and 1902 he played for Northumberland on thirteen occasions, scoring three half-centuries but never going on to amass a big score. He was also a member of George Vernon's touring party to Ceylon and India in 1889/90, keeping wicket and registering a top score of 130 not out. According to *Cricket: A Weekly Record* he was an attacking batsman – 'a leather mover'. The magazine reports a friendly game played at Wellington

C E Greenway appearing for Northumberland in 1900

where he was caught and bowled by Sam Woods but had 'got so well of and under the ball that he spanked it up among the birds and made two runs and was off for the third' before the ball finally nestled in Sam Woods's hands.

Cleveland's father, John, was a merchant, originally from Guernsey, who had become one of the early British settlers in Buenos Aires and remained there for the rest of the life. John was in his early fifties when Cleveland was born and his wife, Martha Elizabeth Anne, was in her early thirties. Buenos Aires was no place to bring up a child at the time. Because it was more or less impossible to leave the crowded city by land, epidemics were frequent. A cholera outbreak at the time of Cleveland's birth was followed by an outbreak of yellow fever in 1871. By this latter date, Cleveland had already been despatched to England. It is possible that he never saw his father again as John died in Buenos Aires in 1877.

Cleveland was educated at Cheltenham College and then at the Competitive College, Bath, before being offered his commission as a lieutenant in 1883. The following year he was transferred from the 3rd Battalion of the Bedfordshire Regiment to the King's (Liverpool) Regiment. He was promoted to the rank of captain in 1890.

He was married in 1894 to Maud Mary (née Sykes). They would have one child, a son, who would also pursue a military career. Cleveland retired from regular army service in 1902, his last appointment having been as adjutant of the 1st Volunteer Battalion of the Northumberland Fusiliers. For eleven years he oversaw the training of volunteers, rising to the rank of honorary colonel.

In 1913 he had time to lead a cricketing tour, taking the prestigious Incogniti team to North America. He was recalled to service for the First World War and appointed a draft conducting officer in July 1915, taking a group of reinforcements to France. In December 1916 he took command of the regimental depot of the East Surrey Regiment at Kingston-upon-Thames.

He died on 17 June 1934 at the age of sixty-nine in West Wickham, Kent.

23
Stephen Cox Newton
4 August 1882 v. MCC, Lord's

Stephen Cox Newton

Born in Nailsea on 21 April 1853, Stephen Newton was the son of Robert Newton, a carpenter and timber merchant. Stephen's mother, Elizabeth Catherine, died while giving birth to a daughter at the age of thirty-nine, when her son was only six. Unable to cope with the demands of business and the upbringing of eight children, Robert despatched Stephen and three of his sisters to an aunt of theirs in St Helier. Here they were raised in what must have been a vibrant household with two cousins and two second cousins also residing there.

Educated at Victoria College, Jersey, Stephen was captain of the First XI for three years in succession and the college's star batsman. He graduated from Corpus Christi, Cambridge, in 1876, the year in which he was awarded his blue. He played for Somerset in nine seasons, the first being in 1876. His last appearance came in 1890, the season before Somerset's entry into the County Championship. During their first brush with first-class status, he was captain of the side from 1882 until 1884, although being based in London he was only available during the summer vacations. *Lillywhite's* describes him as a 'brilliant field, especially at cover point, with a very quick return' and *MCC Scores & Biographies* notes that he was 'a fine and free hitter'. Bill Roe stated in his notes on teammates that he never saw a man more inclined to use his pads. It was certainly the case that he offered useful support to Ted Sainsbury and that the two of them often formed the backbone of Somerset's innings in those lean years. Where others had reputations as big hitters, Newton and Sainsbury understood how to build an innings. Newton made useful contributions without ever hitting the heights. In sixteen first-class matches for Somerset he averaged 24.56, including five 50s and he took 2 wickets at a cost of 80.50 apiece. He also played in first-class matches for MCC and Middlesex.

S. C. Newton at Cambridge University

S. C. Newton – captain of Somerset from 1882 until 1884

On graduating from Cambridge he became a schoolmaster, teaching classics in the venerable Highgate School, founded in 1565. The school magazine entries reveal that he threw himself into school life, for example acting in the masters' play and coaching the pupils at cricket. He remained there from 1876 until 1884.

In 1883 he was married to Sophia Catherine (née Bell), who hailed from Belfast and was five years his senior. Her father was a leading businessman in the province.

From 1888, Stephen was the proprietor and headmaster of Loudon House School (a small school taking in approximately six boarders), which he ran from his own home in 1 Loudon Road, St John's Wood. He remained there at least until 1912, when one of his pupils is recorded as having won a scholarship to Uppingham.

Catherine died in 1906 and though the couple had no children they had perhaps managed to recapture at Loudon House School the vibrant family atmosphere of Stephen's own upbringing. Never remarried, he retired to Yoxford in Suffolk. He died at the age of sixty-three on 16 August 1916 following an operation at the Fonereau Nursing Home in Ipswich.

24
Frederick William Hotham
4 August 1882 v. MCC, Lord's

F.W. Hotham

Rev. Hotham, who played football for Wanderers FC

Frederick Hotham was born in Bath on 17 January 1844. His father, John, was an officer in the Royal Navy who had married Sarah (née Hawsley) in the city. Francis was educated first at Rossall School and then at Eton College. He then graduated from Queen's College, Oxford, in 1868. On leaving university he became a schoolmaster at Elstree. On a number of occasions he played as a batsman for Hertfordshire, though there is little indication that his was a distinguished cricketing career. He also played for a while in the late 1870s for Wanderers FC. For a decade they were a dominant force, winning the F.A. Cup on five occasions in the first seven years of the competition. Drawn from the large pool of former public schoolboys, the team plunged into sudden decline when the schools began to field their own teams of old boys. Frederick Hotham did not appear in any of the FA Cup finals but played when the team was already in decline. Ironically, it was his old school, Eton, who triggered the collapse by defeating Wanderers FC in the first round of the 1878-9 competition.

After receiving his MA in 1878, he became the curate of Radlett, Herts, for four years and then from 1883 until 1888 held a similar position in Brome, Suffolk.

We are informed in *MCC Scores & Biographies* that he was 5 ft 10.5 in tall and that he was a 'useful batsman and a good fielder at point'. The description is perhaps generous in the context of county cricket. He represented Somerset against MCC at Lord's in 1882 and then in the following year played for MCC against Somerset at the same ground. He totalled 18 runs in his four innings.

From 1888 until the time of his death he was rector of Cricket Malherbie and in addition (from 1890) Knowle St Giles, near Ilminster, also acting as chaplain of the Chard Union Workhouse. Frederick Hotham is described in an obituary in the *Western Times* as being 'of a retiring disposition, probably accounted for by his delicate state of health'. For many years he had suffered from a heart complaint.

He died at the age of sixty-four on 23 June 1908. The circumstances of his death are outlined in local newspaper reports. The son of the local schoolmistress had been sent with a message for the Rev. Hotham but raised the alarm when there was no response. On entering the rectory via a bedroom window, a neighbour found Rev Hotham dead in his bed as a result of a heart attack. Never married, he had left his effects to his sister, Rosetta Ann Carew.

25
Lyonel D'Arcy Hildyard
4 August 1882 v. MCC, Lord's

L. D. Hildyard

Born in Bury, Lancashire, on 5 February 1861, Lyonel was the third son of Charles Frederick Hildyard, the headmaster of Bury Grammar School. Educated at Birmingham Grammar School (now King Edward's School), he left to become an assistant schoolmaster in Devon at St Andrew's College, Chardstock. An accomplished musician, he performed on the harp and was a member of the school orchestra, playing the viola. He also performed as the college organist. Between 1878 and 1882 he represented St Andrew's College at rugby as a three-quarter and at cricket as an all-rounder who generally opened the batting. One highpoint was an unbeaten century for the college against Ilfracombe on a tour of North Devon in 1879. Somerset noted his prowess. In 1880 and at the age of nineteen, he appeared in a non-first-class fixture versus Sussex. Selected as a batsman who also bowled, he is credited with a stumping in Sussex's second innings, suggesting that he took the gloves towards the end of the game. He would play seven first-class games for Somerset with an average of 21.10. His top score of 59 not out came in his first game, in a tenth-wicket partnership of 83 with his captain, the doughty S. C. Newton. A press report from 1883 praises

Lyonel Hildyard – 'a most brilliant field'

his 'capital, steady innings' against Gloucestershire, suggesting that Hildyard's approach was less cavalier than many an amateur. He only bowled three (four-ball) overs for Somerset and failed to take a wicket. He was apparently an excellent fielder both in the covers and in the slips. *Lillywhite's* describes him as 'a most brilliant field and covers any amount of ground; a very steady bat'.

On leaving his teaching post at St Andrew's College he went up to Magdalen College, Oxford, in order to train as a clergyman. He would represent the university in each of his four years there, from 1884 until 1887. *Wisden* informs us that 'Hildyard was fortunate to get his blue [in a strong 1884 side], for he only came into the side at the last minute'. By this time, he had switched his allegiance from Somerset to Lancashire, the county of his birth. Lyonel Hildyard was no fool. He would play seventeen first-class games for Oxford University and eight for Lancashire. As with his Somerset career, his success was modest. A further (non-first-class) appearance for Glamorgan in 1891 resulted from his close friendship with the Glamorgan captain, Hildyard's fellow Oxford blue J. H. Brain, whom he had played alongside at the university.

For fourteen years after graduating, Lyonel was a minor canon at Windsor. He was married in 1895 to a distant cousin, Annie Florence Thoroton (née Hildyard), who had been born in Malta in 1872 and with whom he would have a son and daughter. In 1908 he became rector of St Peter's Church, Rowley, near Hull. His family had long been patrons of the living there, with his paternal and maternal (Thoroton) ancestors having been rectors for a period of more than two centuries. Rev. Lyonel Hildyard would remain the rector of Rowley for twenty-seven years until his death on 22 April 1931 at the age of seventy. The following year, an oak portal to the vestry was dedicated to his memory.

26
William Nichols Roe
8 August 1882 v. Hampshire, Taunton

At 5 ft 9 in, already weighing nearly 12 stone when seventeen and having filled out further by the time of his debut as a twenty-one-year-old, Bill Roe was a well-built batsman, described by *Lillywhite's* as 'plucky and sterling'. In sixty-six first-class games for Somerset between 1882 and 1899 he completed four first-class centuries and six half-centuries, averaging 22.46. He was also an occasional bowler who chipped in with 21 wickets.

Bill was a teacher and something of a bombast, always ready to call on his canon of anecdotes, invariably about his own exploits. John Poynton was a teammate in the Championship era and hinted that Roe might have liked the sound of his own voice when writing that his colleague was 'not easy to know, as is so often the case with schoolmasters'. We should remind ourselves that he was speaking of the teaching profession within the private sector in the Victorian era.

Although born in Closworth, Somerset, on 21 March 1861, Bill was educated at the Clergy Orphan School, Canterbury, and then went up to Magdalene College, Cambridge. One of his oft-repeated tales, related by Peter Roebuck, was of how while still a schoolboy cricketer Bill 'played against Chatham lunatic asylum and was chased from the field by an inmate who took exception to losing his middle stump'. His early promise came to something approaching fruition when he

Bill Roe – a commanding presence and a tireless raconteur

scored 415 not out for Emmanuel Long Vacation Club against the Caius Vacation XI. As he liked to remind people, his innings had lasted five hours in sweltering heat and it is said that he kept his precise score in his head whenever he batted, so that on this particular occasion he upbraided the scorer for having robbed him of one run. Quite why he was playing for Emmanuel is not entirely clear.

Married in 1892 to the confusingly named Zoe Susanna Charlotte Jennings Crew Crew, Bill taught at Elstree School (a feeder school for Eton and Harrow) between 1883 and 1900. He left in order to set up a new preparatory school at Stanmore Park near Harrow with former England cricketer Rev. Vernon Royle. The pair seemed to regard cricketing prowess as a criterion for appointing staff. Among their employees, though only briefly, was future Somerset captain John Daniell. Bill Roe died in a nursing home in Marylebone on 11 October 1937 at the age of seventy-six. His son (also named William Nichols Roe) played for Buckinghamshire and edited a book entitled *Public Schools Cricket*.

27
Edward Western
8 August 1882 v. Hampshire, Taunton

Edward Western

In *MCC Scores & Biographies*, Edward Western is described as 'a good average batsman and field'. Nothing more. We are also informed that he was 5 ft 9 in tall and 10 st 7 lb in his prime. Where there is uncertainty is in relation to his birthplace. The date is clear: 12 May 1845. The place is a blank. A glance across the census entries over the years reinforces this confusion, with the birthplace variously given as Brislington or Poulton, near Marlborough. Later attributions of Taunton or Paulton in Somerset are entirely wide of the mark. We are further hindered by the fact that his birth appears never to have been registered.

At a young age Edward was placed in the care of two elderly spinster sisters – Jane Amelia and Mary Edols, living on Church Hill, Brislington – who took in abandoned children and orphans, offering them a home and an education in their school. If Edward was abandoned at birth, it is perhaps worth noting that a servant girl, Mary Western, was at that time working for an accountant, Henry Howell, and his two young children, five miles down the road on St Michael's Hill, Bristol. Whatever the true story of Edward's parentage, it is clear that someone took the trouble to fund his private education.

Having left the care of the Edols sisters, Edward Western became a pupil at Fullands School and, perhaps in the absence of other information, he is described as hailing from Brislington. A very able pupil, he stayed on at the school, teaching maths. While at Fullands he became immersed in the county cricketing scene. Having played his part for Gentlemen of Somerset against Gentlemen of Devon in 1875 with scores of 28 and 4 not out, he was asked by Rev. Ainslie to become the secretary of the newly-formed team and charged with negotiating fixtures against established counties in the hope that Somerset's stock would rise. Judging by the fact that the county team was accorded first-class status in 1882, we can deem his efforts a success. Less so his playing career. In two first-class matches for Somerset he mustered 6 runs at 3.00. He also played one first-class fixture against Somerset when MCC were presumably a man short and he stepped into the breach. He resigned as secretary after Somerset lost their first-class status. The reins were handed to Henry Murray-Anderdon, who had the time and money to oversee an upturn in Somerset's fortunes.

By then Edward was working as a private tutor in Weston-super-Mare and was also a lieutenant in the 1st Devonshire Volunteers. In the 1881 census he lists fellow cricketer William Massey as a visitor. Two years later Edward Western was appointed head-master of Langport Grammar School and he would remain in the role from 1883 until 1892. After leaving Langport, Edward taught for a while in Ilfracombe (where he met his future wife) before setting up a private school in Alcombe, Minehead. It is described as having taken a small number of boarders and had a large upper room with a stage, near the Britannia Inn. He was joined in the enterprise by Mabilla (née Chanter), whom he was married to in 1898. The school operated from 1897 until 1901. Edward was fifty-six by then and Mabilla also of mature years, so that there was never a question of their having any children. The couple remained in Minehead and Edward was still listed as a schoolmaster in 1911.

He died in the town on 16 October 1919 at the age of seventy-four.

28
Walter William Giffard Tate
11 August 1882 v. MCC, Taunton

No relation to fellow Somerset player H. G. Tate, he was referred to in adult life as William Giffard Tate. Although Walter is given as his first name on his birth certificate, he was already known as William at a young age. His father, Rev. Francis Tate, was a brilliant but feckless man who gained a first at Baliol and married Emma Giffard, daughter of the late Sir Ambrose and Lady Giffard. Rev. Francis Tate was appointed as the vicar of Axminster in Devon but in 1862 he was declared a bankrupt with debts in excess of £16,000 and a yearly income from the incumbency of Axminster of only £1,200. The vicarage of Axminster was sequestered but Francis was later restored to his position. Perhaps he had been bailed out by his wife's family. The reprieve was relatively shortlived. Francis died in 1867. His widow had already borne the death of her father at the age

William Giffard Tate - at the time of his appointment as Secretary of the National Roads Association of Adelaide

of two and was now left with eight children, although one of them would soon be making his own way in the world. Francis Alban Arthur Giffard Tate would rise to the rank of admiral.

Among the children mourning the loss of their father was three-year-old William, born in Axminster on 27 August 1863. He was educated at the Clergy Orphan School in Canterbury. Here, in a match for the school versus the Upper Sixth XI, the sixteen-year-old William pitted his wits against a nineteen-year-old Bill Roe, who would become an important figure in Somerset's cricket in the 1880s. Bill Roe claimed nine wickets in the match, clean bowling William twice. Something of a merciless accumulator of runs against inferior club opponents, Roe then went on to plunder 223 runs from the youngsters.

In Somerset's 1882 home fixture against MCC, William scored 0 and 19 and took 0 for 27 in ten overs. It was his only appearance for the county.

His mother, Emma, opted to make a fresh start in Australia along with some of her offspring but, sadly, she died there in May 1885. In 1892 William joined the Colonial Sugar Refining Company, employed at various times as a salesman and accountant. He was based for much of his time in Adelaide although there are reports of his involvement in amateur dramatics in Sydney, perhaps at a time when he was a salesman there.

He was married to Amy Grace (née Charsley) in 1894 and they had three children, a daughter, Emeline Grace, followed by two boys, both of whom would predecease their father. Francis signed up for the war as an eighteen-year-old-boy in 1916, still only 5 ft 2 in and 7 st 10 lb. Wounded in 1918, he was dead by 1920. Arthur later served as a lieutenant commander in the Australian Royal Navy, but he died in 1941 and is buried in Gaza. William and Amy continued to live in Adelaide and judging by press reports were regarded as pillars of society there. Certainly the visit of William's brother – Rear Admiral Alban Giffard Tate – caused a stir.

Having left the business of sugar refining, William turned his attention to the repair and construction of highways, first as the secretary to the National Roads Association of Adelaide and then in 1916, perhaps 'gamekeeper turned poacher', as company secretary to the newly-formed South Australia Roads Construction Co. Ltd.

William's wife, Amy, died in 1928 and after returning to England for an extended fifteen-month stay, William moved to New South Wales where he resided at 'The Cairo', an exclusive hotel in MacLeay St, Sydney. At the time of his death at the age of eighty-three on 29 December 1946 he was residing in Randwick, Sydney. He had enjoyed a more productive and fulfilled life that that of his father – a man who had squandered his gifts and of whom William would perhaps have had no memories.

29
William Whicher Cookson
11 August 1882 v. MCC, Taunton

William Whicher Cookson
Captain Royal Artillery

William Cookson was born in India on 29 August 1862. His place of birth is variously given as Mussoorie and Meerut, but his mother, Laura (née Whicher), whose opinion should presumably be regarded as relevant, stated that her son was born in Naini Tal (now Nainital), a hill station where the conditions would have been more conducive to childbearing than in nearby Delhi. William's father, Major General George Remington Cookson, served in the Bengal Infantry. After retiring, the major general moved to Easterland House in Sampford Arundel near Wellington, thus establishing his son's links with Somerset. Young William was educated firstly at a preparatory school in Kingston-upon-Thames and then was sent in 1877 to his father's old school, Clifton College. He was awarded a place as a gentleman cadet at the Royal Academy in Woolwich in1880 and received his Royal Artillery commission in October 1881. He had already played cricket for the Royal Artillery in 1882 when, perhaps on a visit to his family in August of that year, he was invited to play for Somerset in the match against MCC at Taunton. In his one innings he scored 8 runs. This remained his only appearance for the county.

William Whicher Cookson during his time at Clifton College

His entire army career was spent in the North West Frontier. In 1887 he was married in Meerut, India, to Adelaide Frances Elizabeth Chicheley (née Plowden), known as Fanny. The couple had four children, one of whom died in infancy. Laura was born in Kohat in 1888 whilst William was stationed at L Battery Peshawar, now in Pakistan. A second daughter, Alice, died aged two months in 1891, the year in which William was promoted to captain. Their twins – Margaret Remington and George Plowden – were born in Bombay in 1892.

William rose steadily through the ranks, gaining promotion to major in 1900. His official retirement from the Army was in 1908 but he and his family were already in England by this time and living with his widowed mother in Clifton. The family were making preparations for the marriage of William and Fanny's eldest daughter, Laura, who was married in Clifton. Fanny and her two daughters returned to India but William was unable to follow as he suffered a stroke and was confined to a wheelchair by 1909. His son, George, remained in Clifton following the well-trodden Cookson path of Clifton College and military service.

William was unable to attend his younger daughter Margaret's wedding at Karachi in 1911 and was still marooned in Clifton when Fanny died in India in 1913. William continued to live with his mother and his three unmarried sisters, cared for by a hospital-trained nurse. In 1915, following the marriage of one of the sisters, they moved to The Brook, Winscombe.

William Cookson died there on 23 December 1922 at the age of sixty.

30
Alfred Henry Evans
14 August 1882 v. Lancashire, Taunton

Alfred Henry Evans.

By the time of his first-class debut for Somerset, A. H. Evans was already an established figure within the sporting world and had indeed played for the county on a number of occasions prior to their elevation to first-class status. His appearances between 1882 and 1885 were limited to the summer vacation, given his commitments as a schoolmaster. He would also play for Hampshire in 1885. One report on his career notes that he 'assisted Somerset and Hampshire'. The wording is commonplace. Amateurs 'appeared for' or 'represented' or were 'selected to play for' the leading counties. The lesser counties regarded it as an honour when an excellent cricketer deigned to help them out.

Alfred Evans was born in Madras on 14 June 1858. His father, Dr William Evans, was at the time Inspector General of the hospitals in Madras but the family moved to Bath while Alfred was still an infant. He was sent to Rossall School where he played for the First XI as a sixteen-year-old. From 1875 until 1877 he attended Clifton College, captaining the cricket team in his final year. While at Oriel College, Oxford, he gained his blue in the four years between 1878 and 1881, captaining the team in his final year. On the basis of his performances he was invited to play for Gentlemen v. Players at Lord's. He also gained rugby blues in 1877 and 1878 and was appointed captain in 1879, although he resigned the post at Christmas. At just under 5 ft 10 in and weighing a little over 11 stone, he relied on superb athleticism rather than brute strength. Selected as a forward for the England rugby team scheduled to play Ireland in 1879, he failed to win his cap when the match was cancelled owing to fog.

On graduating from Oxford he was offered the job of assistant master at Winchester College. He taught there for six years from 1882 until 1888 and was described as 'the moving spirit in cricket at the college'. Alfred Evans was at times a devastating fast bowler and it was Somerset's misfortune that he was unable to appear for them more regularly during their first-class years. He played six first-class games for them, achieving his best bowling return in his debut match against Lancashire with 6 for 75. Despite his heroics, Somerset lost by nine wickets. Although he took over 200 first-class wickets, more than a half of these were for Oxford University and perhaps a high point of his career was taking 9 for 59 for an England XI in 1880. *Lillywhite's* describes him as 'a first class bowler; wonderful field at short slip, and most effective anywhere'. His career was not without controversy, though. During their triumphant 1878 tour, the Australians registered their objections over his suspect action.

In 1888 he was married to Isabel Aimee Houssemayne (née Du Boulay), a vicar's daughter. They would have seven children. Two sons – Alfred John and Ralph – would play first-class cricket. The former, known as John, was awarded an England cap. 1888 was also the year in which Alfred was appointed headmaster of Horris Hill Preparatory School in Newton, Newbury. He would remain there until 1920.

By the time of his death at the age of seventy-five, he was living in Shawford, Winchester. He died on 26 March 1934, having collapsed whilst playing a round of golf at Saunton, in Devon. A supremely talented sportsman, he could have done much to boost Somerset's fortunes had he been more readily available.

A. H. Evans – a sometimes devastating fast bowler whose pace was perhaps derived from a suspect action

1883

"The record of the shire is far from satisfactory ...
The scoring has been fairly good, but ... the less
said about the bowling the better."

Bath Chronicle

The opening fixture against MCC at Lord's ended in a draw, after Somerset's opponents had been forced to follow on. In the following game, Somerset were routed by a rampant Surrey. Thereafter, defeat followed defeat with predictable regularity, although a bright spot was a century by Ted Sainsbury - the first to be scored by a Somerset player in a first-class fixture - which failed to prevent Gloucetershire from winning with ease at Taunton. And then, in the final game of the season, Rev. F. W. Terry led Somerset to victory against Hampshire with a wonderful innings of 121. It was perhaps typical of Somerset's ill luck that Terry had been unavailable for the bulk of another woeful season.

31
Hamilton Ross
30 July 1883 v. MCC, Lord's

Yours Sincerely
Hamilton Ross

Known as 'Hammy', Hamilton Ross was born on 26 August 1849 in Gouyave, Grenada, in the Windward Isles. His connection with Somerset began when he was educated at the Hermitage School in Portland Place, Bath. He is particularly noteworthy for being possibly the first man of Afro-Caribbean descent to play first-class cricket. His father, Henry James Ross, was a barrister who had practised in and around London and is described by Grenada's Lieutenant-Governor in February 1841 as 'a native, a West Indian'. Henry Ross's wife, Mary Philippa (née Bradburne), was born in Cumberland, England. Henry had purchased the Plaisance Estate, a coffee plantation near the town of Gouyave, in

Hamilton Ross – an Afro-Caribbean pioneer

1835. He became a leading member of the House of Assembly and the Legislative Council of Grenada before later becoming the Chief Justice of St Kitts and Nevis.

Having played one match for Middlesex in 1878, Hamilton represented Somerset from 1878 until 1891. A prolific batsman in club cricket and for MCC, he was unable to make the step up and his first-class average was decidedly mediocre. Described by *Lillywhite's* as 'a hard-hitting batsman, rather too eager to score', he was also an occasional wicket-keeper. He made one Championship appearance for Somerset in 1891, in the twilight of his cricketing career. Coming in at number ten he suffered the indignity of a pair, becoming the county's first player to record no runs and no wickets in his entire Championship career. He had endured the same fate in his initial first-class game for Gentlemen v. Players in 1874, seventeen years earlier.

Trained as a barrister, Hamilton practised in Bath and London. A popular figure in Bath, he orchestrated a number of well-attended charitable functions, though his work became increasingly centred on London. He was never married and led a peripatetic life, lodging in Bath or staying with his mother in Montague Square when visiting London and then residing with her in Hove once she had retired. After her death in 1901, he purchased a house in Worthing where he was based for the remainder of his life. His retirement from the bar in 1911 coincided with the death of his brother, Charles, who had been based in Grenada. Thereafter, Hamilton visited Grenada and other West Indian islands each winter, suggesting that the family still had extensive business interests there. While at home in Worthing, he was submitting newspaper articles and working on his reminiscences, for which he failed to find a publisher. Perhaps in another age his status as a pioneering Afro-Carribean cricketer would have elicited a more positive response from the publishing industry. He was on his annual trip to the West Indies when he died in Grenada on 29 March 1938 at the age of eighty-eight.

32
Albert Lavington Porter
30 July 1883 v. MCC, Lord's

*Rev. A. L. Porter – a
'muscular Christian'*

The *Graphic* of June 1889 reports in jocular tones that 'there are some muscular Christians down at Fareham. Playing against South Hants last week the local club ran up 426 to which the Rev. A. L. Porter contributed 185, and the Rev. A. C. Hayes 114.' Albert Porter's efforts on behalf of Somerset some six years earlier had been less impressive. In two first-class matches for the county he averaged 4.00 with the bat and took no wickets at a cost of 20 runs. He would later play one game for Hampshire.

He was the son of Robert Porter, a prosperous Australian export merchant, and his young wife, Sarah. Her father, James Blanch, had been transported to Australia for stealing and remained there after his seven-year sentence, becoming the continent's leading manufacturer of mathematical and navigational instruments and its first meteorologist. The couple came over to England after their marriage and Albert was born in Croydon on 20 January 1864. He was educated first in an elementary boarding school in Kingston-upon-Thames and then at Marlborough College before going on to Trinity College, Cambridge. He graduated with a BA in 1886, having been more successful as a rower than a cricketer. By this time his parents had moved the family to Westfield House near Bath and it was whilst at Cambridge that Albert made his two first-class appearances for Somerset. He worked briefly in Guildford before being appointed to his first curacy at Fareham in 1888. He remained there until 1898. In 1894 he was married to Constance Deverill (née Richardson), who hailed from Sydney. They would have one child, Francis, who predeceased them. Interestingly, Albert's nephew, Robert Bamford, founded the firm that became Aston Martin. They were clearly a bright family. In 1899 Rev. Porter was appointed the vicar of Braishfield, Romney, Hampshire. Here, as reported in the *Graphic*, he continued to indulge his passion for cricket and in 1904 was president for a year of the Hampshire Hogs club. He remained vicar of Braishfield until 1917, combining this with duties at Eldon between 1901 and 1907.

He lived for many years at Hartland House in Woolacombe, Devon, where he stood in and officiated at church services during two terms of sequestration and took a keen interest in local affairs, becoming treasurer of the Nursing Association. He died on 14 December 1937 at the age of seventy-one at his final home of 'Westfield' in Tiverton, named perhaps after Westfield House in Bath.

33
Thomas Gregg
30 July 1883 v. MCC, Lord's

Thomas Gregg

Tom Gregg was born in Wilford, Nottinghamshire, on 18 April 1859. His mother was a laundress and his father, also named Thomas, was an agricultural labourer and later a miner. By the age of twenty he had opted for a career as a professional cricketer but although a trialist he failed to make it into the Notts team. One of a large number of professional cricketers emerging from Nottinghamshire at the time, he was 6ft tall, weighed 13 stone and had a superb physique. He is described in *MCC Scores & Biographies* as a 'hard and powerful hitter and a fast bowler'. On moving south he was employed as a pro at Newent in Gloucestershire and subsequently at Oxford. From 1891 until 1893 he coached at Clifton College, where a number of fine young cricketers came under his wing. He played only once for Somerset, being used primarily as a batsman by his captain, Tristram Welman, although he took 2 for 34 when brought on to bowl in the second innings as MCC hung on for a draw. W. G. Grace saw something in Gregg and grasped immediately that his skills

Tom Gregg, who played for Somerset and Gloucestershire and died at the age of only thirty-six

lay primarily in fast bowling. With a better eye for a player's strengths and a willingness to poach talent from across the county border, he encouraged Tom to join the Gloucestershire side as an opening bowler. Tom played 33 games for Gloucestershire between 1884 and 1889 and represented the South v. North, led by his mentor, Grace. His 55 first-class wickets came at an average of 28.00.

Tom was married in 1883 to Frances Alice (née Ford) with whom he had two daughters and a son. His life ended tragically early. At the age of thirty-four, for reasons that are unknown, his body underwent a general paralysis and he was committed to the Gloucestershire County Lunatic Asylum in Wotton Vill, a hamlet since swallowed up by the city of Gloucester. He died there at the age of only thirty-six on 20 March 1896, his death certificate describing him as 'Formerly a Professional Cricketer of Bedminster, Bristol'.

A benefit match for Tom's widow, Frances, originally scheduled for August, was twice postponed owing to inclement weather. It finally took place – albeit still in unsuitable conditions – in October 1896, raising the sum of £30. By 1901 Frances had become a shopkeeper in Frenchay, Bristol.

Writing in the *Bristol Evening Post* in 1939, the reporter 'Blue Feather', who had seen Tom Gregg in action, informs us that he 'had all the requisites of a fast bowler. Tall, well proportioned, and lissom, he never made good because he lacked that first essential – length. His end was very sad.'

34
Joe Ambler
30 July 1883 v. MCC, Lord's

Joe Ambler

Asked to name the greatest batsman to have represented Rishton, most of the fans of the Lancashire League club based not far from Blackburn would probably cite Somerset legend Viv Richards, who played for them in 1987. Asked the same question by the *Lancashire Evening Post* in 1901, Billy Hulme, at the time one of the mainstays of the club, replied that it was Joe Ambler. Frustratingly, the records that might support this claim are scant, an unnamed and overly-zealous groundsman having decided to rid the club of its archive in order to tidy the place up. It is, however, reported that in the 1886 season, employed as an all-rounder, Joe averaged 37.80 with the bat and proved a major wicket-taker.

Born in the Lepton district of Huddersfield on 12 February 1860, Joe was one of two brothers who played as cricketing pros. Their father, Jeremiah (or Jerry), worked as a skilled handloom weaver. Sarah Anne Ambler had already turned forty when Joe came along and Jeremiah was in his mid-forties. Older brother John was already a teenager by then. It is safe to assume that John's relative success as a cricketing pro would have influenced his younger brother in his decision to follow suit but Joe was undoubtedly a talented player. He represented the Twenty-Two of Wakefield against an All England XI at the age of fourteen. In that match he opened the bowling, took three wickets and was the only member of his team to reach double figures with the bat. Perhaps the youngster was given some encouragement by the opposition but he must nevertheless have been regarded as a fine prospect. He established his reputation with the Lascelles Hall cricket club, founded in 1825 and regarded in the late nineteenth century as something of a breeding ground for young pros.

A right-handed batsman and fast-medium right-arm bowler, Joe would play both for Somerset and his home county of Yorkshire. Whilst qualifying for Somerset he played as a professional for Yatton, who also included Somerset regular Albert Clapp among their number. Joe also made occasional appearances for Taunton and Bedminster. In 1883, the *Bristol Mercury* informs us that 'Ambler batted and bowled in excellent style'. He was a versatile cricketer whose fielding is praised in the local press and who was capable of standing in as a wicket-keeper (as was the case in Somerset's fixture with Surrey in 1883). He played for Somerset on four occasions between late July and mid-August in 1883. His batting average of 18.42 was boosted by a score of 76 in his first match against the MCC at Lord's and by what the *Western Daily Press* described as a 'vigorous innings of 35, consisting of 6 fours' in the match in which he kept wicket, sharing the gloves with Tristram Welman. That game, where he also turned his arm for four overs, would prove his swansong.

Leaving the county and returning north, he would play for Rishton and East Lancashire, and on four occasions in June 1886 for Yorkshire. Married in 1890 to Mary (née Jessop), he was employed as a power loom weaver while residing in the village of Lascelles Hall near Huddersfield, supplementing his summer wages as a pro.

Joe Ambler died of pneumonia in Lascelles Hall at the age of only thirty-eight on 10 February 1899. His widow, Mary, worked as a woollen weaver in order to provide for their young children, Arnold and Sarah Ann. Any historian attempting to source an image of Joe Ambler will be hampered not only by the efforts of the

Rishton groundsman who consigned his club's archive to oblivion but also by the arsonist who burned down the pavilion at Lascelles Hall, destroying a treasury of old photographs.

35
Edward William Bastard
30 July 1883 v. MCC, Lord's

Edward Bastard – 'the mainstay of the Somerset bowling when the county was in the second class'

Edward Bastard was born on 28 February 1862 in Wilton, Taunton (not Wilton in Wiltshire as sometimes stated). His father, Henry Horlock Bastard, was a 'clergyman without care of souls' based in affluent Haines Hill in the Wilton parish. Whilst to be ministered to by a Bastard without care of souls might sound unnerving, the term in fact refers to a clergyman without a parish. Anna and Henry Bastard's three sons – John, James and Edward – would choose different paths in life. John followed his father into the ministry and James became a teacher at Banstead Hill School, Surrey, while Edward was only briefly gainfully employed and embarked on a slow descent into depression, induced by alcoholism.

A brilliant scholar and talented cricketer, Edward was educated along with his brothers at Sherborne and then went up to Baliol College, Oxford, where he gained a blue. In an obituary, he is described as the 'mainstay of the Somerset bowling when the county was in the second class' (i.e. the period between 1886 and 1890) and that 'he was also a useful bat'. The obituary failed to mention that he had in fact taken 57 first-class wickets for Somerset at 20.77 runs apiece with his slow left-arm deliveries. He had also enjoyed three 5-wicket hauls and a best bowling analysis of 8 for 59 against Hampshire at Southampton in August 1885. Having performed well for Oxford University and for Dorset, there was little doubt that Somerset would call on his services. Perhaps he might have served them for longer had it not been for his chronic alcoholism. By the late 1880s his position as the slow left-armer was threatened by the rise of the young

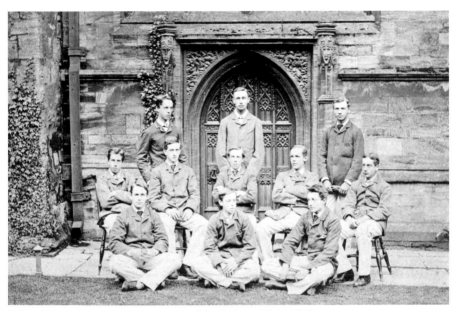

Edward Bastard, seated centre, as captain of the Sherborne XI in 1881

pro Teddy Tyler. It is perhaps no coincidence that once Herbie Hewett – a no-nonsense disciplinarian referred to as 'The Colonel' – had established himself as captain, Edward Bastard's services were dispensed with. Thereafter Edward sank into a spiral of decline. Never married and rarely in employment, he was an assistant schoolmaster for a while but generally referred to himself as a gentleman of independent means. He remained a member of Somerset CCC and, having resided for a while in Babbington, Torquay, he returned to Taunton He lodged for a period not far from his parents' home in the residence of a painter, William Millet Turner, who was perhaps more tolerant of his drinking and his eccentricities than Edward's parents would have been. His death – a short while after his brother, John, had been offered the living at St George's in Wilton – was attributed to an 'accidental fall'. However, it became clear from the description of his lifestyle at the subsequent inquest that he spent much of his time in bed, either in a drunken stupor or, in more lucid moments, reading. From the details elicited from his landlord and landlady, it is apparent that he was in the grip of delirium tremens.

His death occurred on 2 April 1901 at the age of thirty-nine. A sad and wretched end for a man who had shown great promise but whom alcohol had destroyed.

36
James John Alexander Parfitt
9 August 1883 v. Gloucestershire, Clifton

James John Parfitt KC.

His Honour Judge James Parfitt

James Parfitt was born on 23 December 1857 in Slwch Villa in the town of Brecon. The son of a lawyer who hailed from Bruton, he attended Prior Park Roman Catholic School near Bath. He went up to the University of London and gained his BA in 1884. He taught for three years at Cardinal Newman's School in Edgbaston and would remain a committed Roman Catholic throughout his life.

In a change of career, he was called to the bar by the Middle Temple in 1887. In 1900 he was married to Elizabeth Mary (née Reynolds), with whom he would have one child, a son who died shortly after his first birthday in the winter of 1903. He was appointed junior counsel to the Post Office on the Midland Circuit and then counsel to the Birmingham Assay Office, taking silk in 1908. He was also invited to become a governor of the University of Birmingham.

From 1916 until 1918 he was the Recorder for Northampton, overseeing the work of the magistrates. For the following three years he acted as judge of the county courts for Leeds and Wakefield, then Sussex and finally Clerkenwell. He became a popular figure famed for his ready wit and pithy aphorisms that were often quoted in the press. He had no time for prolixity and could be withering in his treatment of the verbose or pompous. A favoured observation was 'now you are wandering around the Wrekin', referencing the place of his birth. At the same time, he was noted for his humanity. His allusions to cricket during court cases were frequent. His favoured expression of condemnation was to describe something as 'not cricket' and when summing up one court case he opined: 'Verdict for the defendant. Plaintiff is out, bowled middle stump and in any case, he'd have been stumped.'

His debut in first-class cricket could hardly have begun better. *Wisden* recounts that on 11 August 1881, playing for Surrey against Yorkshire, Parfitt 'bowled from the pavilion end and with the first ball he delivered Ulyett was bowled, amid much applause'. *Lillywhite's* describes him in 1882 as 'a fast bowler' and 'a very hard hitter' but adds that 'he has not had much practice this season'. James Parfitt was an extraordinarily tall man. He would unfurl himself to his full height to dramatic effect in the courtroom and his height was no doubt an asset when he was bowling. He represented Surrey a total of eight times in 1881 and 1882. Then over the 1883 and 1885 seasons he played six times for Somerset, for whom he averaged 11.1 with the bat and took 13 wickets at 35.00 apiece. His appearances were all in August or September, during his university or school summer breaks. He also turned out for Warwickshire in 1886.

His Honour Judge James Parfitt died in Wimbledon on 15 May 1926 at the age of sixty-eight.

37
George Godfrey Lillington
9 August 1883 v. Gloucestershire, Clifton

George Lillington was born in Bedminster on 31 October 1843. He was the eldest child of George Snr, a 'tobacco spinner' who made and sold cigars and snuff in an age before the industrial manufacture of cigarettes had arrived. W. D. & H. O. Wills, for example, would introduce their first cigarette brand, the *Bristol*, in 1871.

Thirty-nine years old at the time of his first-class debut, George Jnr completed three stumpings but made little or no impact with the bat. He in fact managed an average of 1.00 in the course of two first-class games for the county. He had been a stalwart of Bedminster CC for many years. Although a tail-ender at county level, he had his moments in club cricket. Indeed, he is reported as coming second in the batting averages for the club in 1870 with an average of 34.60, being awarded a bat for his efforts. As well as being a keen wicket-keeper and batsman for Bedminster CC, George Lillington was a member of the Redcliff Rowing Club and was for a while their treasurer.

He was married in 1872 to Ann (née Sweet). The couple would have no children. George spent his working life in the employ of H. M. Customs, perhaps encouraged by a father who wished to ensure his tobacco business was not being undermined by smuggled goods. It seems that patience was required for a working man to progress through the ranks of the civil service. He was thirty-one years old when promoted from supernumerary at the Bristol docks to the dizzy heights of second class outdoor customs officer at Cardiff. It would be some years before he would finally enjoy the privileges of a more deskbound role.

George demonstrated great rectitude as he went about his work, unimpressed by status but treating all culprits in a similar manner. The same cannot be said of the judiciary. In one reported case, Alfred York Brown was acquitted when 6 lb of undeclared cigars were found hidden in his luggage in 1894. The judge was inclined to believe the word of a clergyman's son over that of a humble customs inspector such as George Lillington.

He resided throughout his adult life in Brislington and died there on 25 August 1914. He was seventy years old. His wife, Ann, lived until 1927, leaving her modest estate to her younger sister.

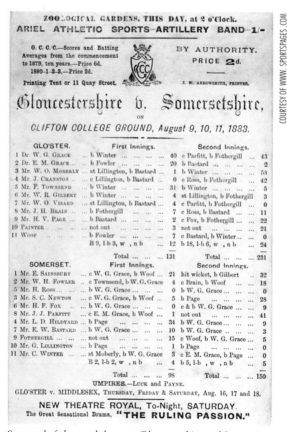

Scorecard of the match between Gloucestershire and Somerset on 9 August 1883: George Lillington completed three stumpings

1884

"The county eleven is now degenerating into one of those
nomadic teams who go about the country during the
university vacations amusing themselves by playing cricket."
Somerset County Gazette

"It is much to be regretted that an influential paper like
the County Gazette – ignoring the difficulties under
which the club labours – should so persistently decry
the efforts made to establish county cricket in Somerset.
Such disloyalty is unparalleled.
Yours faithfully, EDWD. WESTERN, Hon. Sec."

The were some different fixtures this time around with Kent having agreed to play
Somerset home and away, but the picture proved familiar with Somerset suffering
resounding defeats in all bar one game. The nadir was the innings defeat at the hands
of fellow strugglers Hampshire who had racked up 645 runs, with every Somerset
player bar wicket-keeper Rev. F. W. Terry turning their arm. There was some measure
of revenge when Hampshire were defeated by an innings in the return fixture at
Taunton, where Bill Roe scored a hard-hitting 132 runs.

38
William John Jewell
8 May 1884 v. Kent, Taunton

[signature: W. Jewell]

Known in cricketing circles as John Jewell, he was born in Newcastle-upon-Tyne after April 1855 but before 24 February 1856, when he was baptised in St Andrew's church of England in the city. There is a certain irony in the fact that the man who would become a senior probate officer should never have had his birth registered and would die intestate. Not a good example to others. His father, William, had joined the 85th Light Regiment in 1840 and would retire as a sergeant major twenty-one years later. William and Catherine lived a peripatetic and sometimes chaotic life typical for those in the military but it is frustrating for cricket historians that they should have registered the births of John's four siblings but not his. By 1861 the parents had taken the family to live in Exeter before their final move to Taunton. John became chief clerk to the probate registry in Taunton and would live in the town throughout his adult life, much of it in elegant Hammet Street. He played as an all-rounder for Taunton and also represented Somerset before their elevation to first-class status and then once in 1884. One of three debutants, he mustered ten runs in a slow-scoring game – a war of attrition in which he bowled twelve overs and conceded only 14 runs without taking a wicket. Kent's application paid off when they won by an innings.

John had been taken on as a supernumerary office boy at the Taunton probate registry in 1869. He had to wait a further five years before being granted a permanent role by Lord Hannen. He was married in Taunton in 1888 to Sarah Ann (née Evans). Two of their daughters – Norah Mary and Lilian – reached adulthood.

John rose through the ranks until he became chief clerk in 1890 and he also assisted the archdeaconry of Taunton for many years, becoming registrar. The Rev. A. C. Ainslie, for a while Archdeacon of Taunton and the guiding light of the formation of Somerset CCC, was among his champions and we are left with the impression of a diligent and efficient administrator.

A keen student of cricket, John Jewell wrote on occasions to the press. A letter printed in the *London Evening Standard* in 1891, reads:

SIR, - In a match between Bishop's Lydeard and Nether Stowey, in Somerset, played a few years since, the latter team were disposed of for two leg-byes, not a run being scored off the bat. The most remarkable part of the innings, however, was that the ball never once came in contact with the bat, the whole side being clean bowled. The gentleman who performed this extraordinary feat was the late Rev. C. P. Winter.

In his history of Somerset CCC, Peter Roebuck attributes the feat to Charles Winter's brother, John Arundell Winter, but Jewell is more likely to be correct. Whilst the account begs some questions – e.g. if the ball never touched the bat then did another bowler miss stumps and bat with every delivery? – the letter offers an insight into the woeful pitches village cricketers were expected to put up with on occasions.

After a short illness, John Jewell died, surrounded by his family at his home in Taunton on 3 March 1927. He was seventy-one and was about to enjoy a belated retirement. An obituary informs us that as well as having been a keen cricketer, he was 'formerly one of the most talented players' in the Taunton Bowling Club and an active member of the local Conservative Association.

39
Frederick Aitken Leeston-Smith
8 May 1884 v. Kent, Taunton

He was born in Paddington, London, on 10 May 1854. Initially named Frederick Aitken Smith, he assumed the name Leeston-Smith along with the rest of his family in 1880. His father, Frederick James Smith, was a man of leisure who described his occupation as 'esquire' and his mother was Mary Catherine Sydney (née Pennington). After the family had moved to Leeston House, Great Malvern, Frederick was initially sent for two years to Malvern College but transferred in 1869 to Christ College in Brecon. Why this was so is unclear, given that a brother continued to be educated at Malvern. It is of course possible that he committed some misdemeanour. On leaving school in 1871, he spent time in Scotland, appearing regularly for Carlton CC in Edinburgh and coming second in their

Frederick Leeston-Smith – a fearsome striker of the ball

batting averages in 1874. He then went up to Marischal College (part of Aberdeen University) to study medicine, although he seems to have concentrated more on cricket than on his studies, with appearances for Aberdeenshire. Judging by the press reports, he had by now established a reputation as a fearsome striker of the ball. He also played rugby for the college as a half-back and the goal kicker. He never graduated, leaving the college in 1878 after two years.

Returning to Weston-super-Mare, where his parents were now living, Frederick would appear to have settled for a hedonistic lifestyle. 5 ft 10.5 in tall and powerfully built, he could be a destructive batsman when on song. In *First-Class Cricketers from Christ College, Brecon*, D. T. and J. B. Smith note that 'he joined Weston-super-Mare CC in 1880 and over the next eleven seasons, for many of which he was captain, he made seven centuries'. He was also often among the wickets with his slow off-breaks. The *Western-super-Mare Gazette* reports one innings in an away game at St George's, Bristol, where 'one of the sixes was a splendid off-drive which, going over an adjoining house and garden and pitching into the road is well worthy of mention'. Dr E. M. Grace was once on the receiving end of Leeston-Smith's powerful hitting while captaining Thornbury. In a letter to the cricket historian, F. S. Ashley-Cooper, written in 1902, Grace states:

> F. A. Leeston-Smith and F. L. Cole came in together for Weston-super-Mare. It was then five balls to an over. Cole made 1 off the first ball, Leeston-Smith 6 off the second, 6 off the third, 6 off the fourth, 6 off the fifth, when the umpire said, "I'm afraid it is over, Doctor". I said, "Shut up! I am going to have another"; and off this one he was stumped. Weston-super-Mare had to follow their innings. The first ball I bowled to him he hit for 6, and the second for 6; but off the third he was stumped again.

Perhaps this brief cameo serves as a useful summary of his entire career. Having first appeared for Somerset in the second tier, he then played three first-class games between 1884 and 1885. He totalled 130 runs, many of them no doubt in boundaries, at an average of 21.66. He is described in one reference as 'a casual and indolent fielder'. In cricket as in life.

His death is wrongly reported in *Wisden* as having occurred in 1903. He had in fact died of 'Russian flu' at the age of only thirty-nine at Parkstone in Dorset on 27 January 1894.

40

John Arundell Winter
8 May 1884 v. Kent, Taunton

John Arundell Winter's census return for 1911 offers an insight into his character. Ensconced in Twickenham and living with his wife, a son and a servant, the retired major writes that since his eight children are 'scattered all over the world' it is 'quite impossible to say if alive or dead', suggesting either paternal indifference or a group of offspring with the good sense to steer well clear of their father. He then goes on to deface his census form with a long rant:

Many of the questions are of an <u>impudently inquisitive nature</u>, no statistics resulting from them can in any way benefit anyone; the idiots who devised or sanctioned this ridiculous waste of money ought to be made pay {sic} the entire cost of carrying it through; it would have been wiser to spend the amount alleviating … the overwhelming taxation of the present day.

Note that he advocates a reduction in the level of tax (including his own) rather than suggesting that the money be used to help the poor.

John and his brother, Harry, came from a farming family made good. Originally owners of a small farm in Ash Priors, their forebears gained much of their land when Taunton Priory was dissolved in the reign of Henry VIII. Thereafter, the Winters owned great swathes of land in Somerset, although their principle residences were at Ash Priors and nearby Watts House in Bishops Lydeard. These were not, however, manorial residences. The lords of the manor were the Lethbridges, with whom John and Harry's father, John Snr was in constant dispute, with at least fifteen lawsuits recorded. These ranged from arguments over diverting of streams to quarrying, trespass and even assault. In short, John Winter Snr was the proverbial 'neighbour from hell' and it is clear from whom John Arundell Winter had inherited his arrogance and irascibility.

Born at Priory House in Ash Priors on 28 July 1851, he was brought up there and also in neighbouring Bishops Lydeard and in Bampton, Devon. Educated for a while at Uffculme Grammar School in Devon, he attended the Royal Military College and was appointed a lieutenant in the 70th Foot Regiment in 1871. Two years later he inherited Watts House when his father died at sea on a White Star liner, the *SS Asiatic*.

In 1875 he was married to Rosa (née Norman), a banker's daughter from Staplegrove. As he would confirm when defacing a later census form, they had eight children.

At some point – perhaps in 1881 when the 70th Foot regiment was merged – he joined the West Somerset Regiment of Yeomen Cavalry, regarded as the preserve of the wealthy and well-connected. He rose to the rank of brevet major but appears to have seen no action. Meanwhile, not all was well in terms of Major Winter's finances. Perhaps he had engaged in some ill-advised business dealings. Alternatively, if his estate was all tied up in land, he may have required the cash to provide for the needs of a large family. He certainly seems often to have been in need of cash as evidenced by his readiness to lease what became Somerset's County Ground in the early 1880s. Worse still, he was obliged to sell his principle residence, Watts House, and other family possessions. Based at the time in Lewisham, he remained in Greater London for the rest of his life. It is perhaps telling that he had ceased referring to himself as a 'landowner' but now merely styled himself a 'retired major'.

By the time of the 1911 census he gives the impression of believing that the whole world is against him. He perhaps felt something similar on the occasion of his only first-class match for Somerset, when he came in as a tail-ender and scored a 4 and a duck. His cricketing career was as ill-starred as his management of the family finances. He had however made two major contributions to Somerset cricket. In 1885 he had been appointed honorary treasurer of the club and he had also leased the land for the County Ground. Somerset perhaps owes a greater debt to Henry VIII and his henchman, Thomas Cromwell, than is commonly acknowledged. Having dissolved Taunton Priory, they had sold to J. A. Winter's forebear both the priory lands and the buildings, including the barn that now houses the cricket museum.

John Arundell Winter died on 15 May 1914 in Hampton Wick at the age of sixty-two.

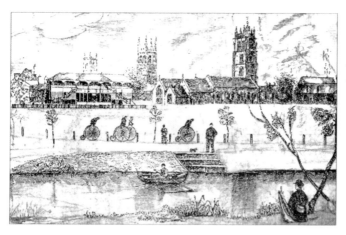

The County Ground, Taunton, sketched in 1882, a year after it had been leased by J. A. Winter

41
John Bonamy Challen
7 August 1884 v. Hampshire, Southampton

J. B. Challen.

A headmaster for many years, John Challen was referred to by his pupils as 'Venus'. He hated the moniker but it stuck as stubbornly irremovable as chewing gum on the underside of a schoolboy's desk. Born in Ruthin in Denbighshire on 23 March 1863 and educated at Marlborough College, he was a dapper, well-turned-out man. He was also a technically sound batsman and an athletic fielder. In 1875 and at the time a sports-obsessed teenager, he had been one of only 112 people (and very probably the youngest) to respond to Edward Western's appeal for contributions of half a guinea each to support the establishment of county cricket in Somerset. Presumably his was a generous pocket money allowance and there was little else to fritter it on in Ruthin. A graduate of Trinity College, Dublin, he was a good all-round sportsman who played football for Corinthians at a time when they were thought by many to be the leading English club (although as part of their constitution they eschewed competitive matches). He also played football for Wales. As for his cricketing skills, a beautiful timer of the ball capable of taking the fight to the bowlers, he was often obliged to adopt a more cautious approach when batting, while those around him failed to temper their attacking instincts. There is no better example of his cool head than the time in 1891 when he steered Somerset to victory against

J. B. Challen was often obliged to adopt a cautious approach as a batsman while other Somerset amateurs were inclined to chance their arms

Surrey with only two minutes left on the clock. This was in the days when shameless time-wasting tactics on the part of the bowling side were unthinkable.

In 1893 he was married to Amy (née Price) a rector's daughter from Willey, Warwickshire. At the time, he was headmaster of Crediton Grammar School. In 1895 he was appointed headmaster at the Devon County School in West Buckland. He played his last game for Somerset in 1899, having represented them in fifty-two first-class matches. He came away with a batting average of 19.71 including one century

*'Venus' Challen offered
his pupils a 'thoroughly
sound modern education'*

and he took 16 wickets at 35.75 apiece. In 1900 he founded the North Devon School, in Barnstaple. An advert from that time offers his pupils a 'thoroughly sound modern education'. In 1907 'Venus' departed, leaving the school in the hands of his son and promising that the ethos would remain unchanged. He had opted to reopen the Philberds School in Maidenhead. The school had originally been founded by his father-in-law, Rev. E. H. Price. Challen was a former pupil. In the event the North Devon School closed its doors in 1910 and Challen similarly moved on to Eastbourne for his final stint as a schoolmaster. Although he retained his links with North Devon and with Somerset cricket, he made Eastbourne his home, retiring eventually to a nursing home in the town. He died there on 5 June 1937 at the age of seventy-four.

42
Theodore Robinson
7 August 1884 v. Hampshire, Southampton

Theodore Robinson

Theo in 1883

Theo Robinson was a man more noteworthy for his wealth and generosity than for his prowess as a cricketer. A loyal servant of Somerset, he made ten first-class appearances over a ten year period from 1884 to 1894. Never a stellar performer, he averaged 8.44 with the bat, including one 50. Only used as an occasional bowler, he took 2 wickets at 43.00 apiece. When not playing for Somerset, he would often turn out for Glamorgan. With the Welsh county not yet accorded first-class status, there was no conflict in terms of registration.

He was born in Beaminster in Dorset on 16 Feb 1866. The family became hugely important employers in the Bristol area. Theo and his brother and fellow Somerset cricketer, Crescens, were sufficiently wealthy to pursue their sporting interests. In Theo's case this extended to archery, where he would represent Great Britain at the 1908 London Olympics. In time he would set up a seed crushing business and would take up residence with a sister, Isabel, and their team of servants. Throughout his life he remained concerned for the welfare of the inhabitants of his village of Backwell and neighbouring Flax Bourton, donating the land for the new Backwell playing fields in 1929 and funding the construction of tennis courts and a bowling green to encourage young and old alike to take up sport. Lord Bath joined Theo to lead the opening ceremony on 6 June 1929. Later donations of land were made in 1932 and 1945.

He died on 4 October 1959 at the age of ninety-three in West Town House, Backwell, where he had lived for much of his adult life with his sister, Isabel. Theirs had been a genteel existence. Neither of them was married, both of them content to spend their lives in one another's company and taking delight in nurturing the local community.

Theo in the Somerset XI, 1894

The Robinson family played annual fixtures against invited teams at Backwell. Photographed in 1883, a seventeen-year-old Theo is standing far left. Fellow Somerset cricketer, Cres, is seated in front of him, holding a bat. Their cousin Arthur (centre, standing, facing sideways with a studiedly 'man of destiny' look) played for Gloucestershire.

43

Horatio Ernest Hall

7 August 1884 v. Hampshire, Southampton

Horatio Ernest Hall

Born on 25 April 1861 in Bedminster, the son of a customs officer, he was registered as Horatio Ernest but used the name Ernest in adulthood, preferring to be referred to as E. H. Hall on scorecards, leading to the incorrect assumption in some sources that he was 'Egerton Hawkesley Hall'.

Ernie and his brother, Hamlet, played their club cricket for Bedminster and would both represent Somerset. He is described in a history of Bedminster CC (published in 1947) as 'one of the stalwarts of the First XI' and 'a capital batsman and a good medium pace bowler'. The *Western Daily Press*, reporting a match between Bedminster and East Somerset in September 1885, praises the 'excellent bowling of Ernest Hall, who dismissed eight of the opponents for 24 runs'. In other local press reports he is spoken of as a mainstay of the Bedminster club and capable of bowling a persistently good line and length, moving the ball off the seam and proving deadly in the right conditions. In his three first-class matches for Somerset he was less effective, taking 3 wickets at 48.33 each and averaging 8.60 with the bat.

He was married in 1899 to Beatrice Maud, younger sister of Ernest George Murdock, who also played cricket for Bedminster and Somerset and lodged for a while with the Hall family. Their daughter, Eileen Clare, was born early in 1902 in Bedminster but was christened in Stafford. Why this should have been so is not immediately apparent. He was employed as a schoolmaster in Bedminster by the Bristol Education Committee and the 1911 census lists him as a headmaster.

Ernie Hall died at the age of fifty-eight on 01 December 1919 in Caledonia Place, Clifton, leaving his estate to his brother-in-law, E. G. Murdock. An obituary in the *Western Daily Press* describes him as having been 'one of the best bowlers in the district.' It also adds that, as a 'medium-pace bowler with a nice action, he commanded a good length with a quick spin, and on a wicket which suited him was at times unplayable'. The tribute also informs us of some diffidence on Ernest's part, stating that 'there is no doubt that if he had had full confidence in his own ability he would have been in the front rank of bowlers'.

44
Frederic Marks
7 August 1884 v. Hampshire, Southampton

Frederick Marks

Born on 21 June 1868 in Clevedon, the year before the coastal town's famous pier was completed, he is 'Frederic' on official documents, he signed himself as 'Frederick' but he was known as 'Fred'. His father, William, was a baker and confectioner based in Clevedon. Fred made his first appearance as a club cricketer at the age of only twelve in a side captained by W. G. Grace. His only game for Somerset came in 1884. It was not a great success. He scored 2 runs, although he was only once dismissed and he took 0 for 3. He played on a number of occasions for Wiltshire, demonstrating versatility and being deployed at various times as a batsman, bowler and wicketkeeper. He would perhaps have been relieved to have been keeping wicket and not bowling on the occasion in 1888 when MCC racked up 735, with former Somerset captain Ted Sainsbury plundering 180 runs before he was finally caught behind by Marks.

Fred Marks – a well-known sportman and dispensing chemist in Clevedon, Somerset

Fred's brother, William Marks Jnr, took over the running of the family bakery and confectionery business while Fred worked as an apprentice in a chemist's shop in Clevedon. He lived for a while in Swindon, where he played cricket for the town and for Wiltshire. It was at this time that he was married to Mary Elizabeth (née Deacon) at the Baptist Tabernacle in Swindon. The couple remained committed Baptists and they would have two children, Frederic Hubert Benjamin (known as Ben) and Gladys Mary. After he had qualified as a dispensing chemist, Fred moved again, opening his first shop in Barnstaple. In 1903, he and his family moved to his birthplace of Clevedon when he had the opportunity to purchase the chemist's shop that had belonged to J. Henry Hart. He continued to find time for cricket and indeed, in *Fools on the Hill: an Appreciation of Clevedon cricket 1874-1974*, Piers McBride states that 'of all the cricketers to represent Clevedon down the years, few, if any, have rendered such wonderful service as that remarkable and gifted cricketer, Fred Marks'. He would score over 10,000 runs and take nearly 2,000 wickets for the club. In

a report of the wedding of his daughter Gladys Mary to Archibald Edward Macklin, Fred is described as 'as well known in the Bristol district as he is in local [Clevedon] cricketing and golfing circles'.

Mary Elizabeth died in 1912 and Fred was married for a second time in 1917 to Annie Edith (née Merrifield) who was nineteen years his junior. They had no children.

Fred Marks handed over his chemist shop to his son, who predeceased him, though his grandson also became a chemist. Fred had played cricket for Clevedon for thirty years. He would play for the town's golf club for forty years and was also accomplished at hockey and tennis.

He died in Clevedon on 6 May 1952 at the age of eighty-three, a celebrity in his beloved town.

45
John Ernest Trask
18 August 1884 v. Hampshire, Bath

A cousin of fellow Somerset cricketer William Trask, John Trask was born on 27 November 1861 in Brympton d'Evercy near Yeovil. His father, James, was a gentleman farmer who later retired to the grander location of Bayfield House in Bath. John was educated at Somerset College, Bath, and then went on to study medicine at Bristol Medical School after a brief flirtation with clerical work. For a while he became house surgeon of the Bath Royal United Hospital but then opted to join the military. After further training at the Royal Military Hospital he went to Poonah in India for four and a half years, captaining the Gymkhana Cricket XI in his leisure time.

In his youth he had turned out regularly for Lansdown in Bath and he played for Somerset on a total of three occasions in 1884 and 1885. Home on leave for less than three months in the summer of 1895, the returning hero managed to squeeze six Championship games for Somerset into his schedule. He came away with a first-class average for the county of 15.20.

Seconded to the Egyptian Army at the end of August 1895, he was struck down by cholera within a year, though not before 'at the battle of Firket he showed himself a very capable officer, behaving with the greatest bravery and coolness while tending the wounded under heavy fire' as *The Graphic* reports. The article goes on to tell us that on 25 July 1896, Captain-Surgeon Trask and Captain Fenwick arrived in the morning at Kosheh, Sudan, in the middle of a prolonged heatwave, weakened and exhausted by the grip of cholera, although generally in 'ordinary health on the Saturday morning, but dead by four in the afternoon'. Trask was only thirty-four years old. He was not married. In Arthur Conan-Doyle's book *The New Revelation*, the author would write a fanciful account of having communicated with the spirit of John Trask in Cairo, referring to the late captain-surgeon under the pseudonym of 'Dodd'.

Trask's image appears above the brief tribute to him in *The Graphic*. We can assume that he wore a cap rather than a fez when walking out for Somerset. If he demonstrated the same precision, care and attention to detail when wielding his surgeon's knife as he did when grooming his moustache, then his patients will have been in very safe hands and we can forgive him any sartorial faux pas.

John Trask in Somerset (top) and in Cairo (above).

His brother, Charles William Trask, a Bath schoolmaster, devoted time to instilling a sound batting technique in his pupils, who would include Somerset and England batsman Jack MacBryan.

46
George Tierney Mirehouse
18 August 1884 v. Hampshire, Bath

George T Mirehouse
24/10/13

George Mirehouse was born on 11 May 1863, along with a twin sister, Milly, in the village referred to either as St George's or Easton-in-Gordano. His father, Henry, was Somerset County Registrar and the rector of St George's. His grandfather, Rev. Thomas Henry Mirehouse (also a twin) had caused considerable upset when, as the local squire, he had ordered the fourteenth century church to be replaced by a structure that one contemporaneous report described as 'cold, staring, barn-like and bare, thinly sprinkled with worshippers'. On his death after fifty years as the rector in 1867, the monstrosity was taken down and replaced, with building works completed in 1872. Perhaps a young

G. T. Mirehouse, who took his own life in Australia

George witnessed the removal and replacement of his grandfather's ill-judged place of worship.

He attended Westminster School and Jesus College, Cambridge University, where he represented the university side primarily as a fast-medium opening right-arm bowler between 1884 and 1886. He played in a total of thirteen first-class matches for Cambridge University, Somerset and MCC, claiming a total of 22 wickets. In his four appearances for Somerset over the 1884 and 1885 seasons, he took 8 wickets at 24.00 apiece. Not a batsman by any stretch of the imagination, he averaged 3.50 for the county.

Although he eventually settled in Richmond Park Road, Clifton, he was a frequent overnight guest at clubs in London. He may for many years have enjoyed a carefree bachelor's existence but he clearly had an interest in economic matters, becoming an early member of the Bristol Bimetallic League – a group of people who argued for the use of a flexible gold and silver standard. He also wrote to the local papers expressing strong views on matters such as taxes on sugar. An active investor, he was managing a sugar refining business in Australia when he ended his own life at the age of fifty-nine while residing in Turramurra, New South Wales. At the time of his death on 5 March 1923, his main residences were given as Clifton and the New University Club, St James's St, London. His body was found in his bedroom on 6 March, 'hanging by a piece of sash-cord from the top rail of his bed'. It was noted at the inquest led by the city coroner in Sydney that 'Mirehouse had stated a few days previously that he was very worried over business matters'. A verdict of suicide was recorded. Having never been married, his estate was granted to his cousin (who was also his brother-in-law), Captain Egerton Bagot Byrd Levett-Scrivener, who owned Sibton Abbey, in Suffolk. Levett-Scrivener had been married to George's twin sister, Milly, after his first wife had met her end by falling from a horse.

47
Herbert Tremenheere Hewett
25 August 1884 v. Kent, Tunbridge Wells

Herbert Hewett

Born on 25 May 1864 in Norton Fitzwarren into a family of brewers and wine merchants, Herbie Hewett was educated at Harrow and Trinity College, Oxford, where he played in the University XI alongside fellow Somerset cricketer Lyonel Hildyard. Tall, burly and a left-handed batsman who 'smote the ball mercilessly', Hewett is a towering figure – perhaps the most important – in Somerset cricket's early history. He arrived on the scene as an Oxford undergraduate when the county was at a low ebb. He led from the front during their brief period in the wilderness and by 1891 he had wrenched them back to first-class status with his batting and his uncompromising captaincy. Although regarded by many as difficult, he was a born leader and had been offered the captaincy at the relatively young age of twenty-six. Trained as a barrister, he developed an idiosyncratic habit of utilising a toothpick while he pondered tactics. Once he was set on a course, he would often prove immoveable in his opinions. Herbie could be brooding as well as stubborn, not one to forgive easily.

Herbert Hewett – a superb captain and a brilliant batsman who 'smote the ball mercilessly'

If his performances in 1890 and 1891 established his reputation as a captain, then 1892 was a triumph for Hewett the batsman. He was a forceful and intimidating left-hander who bludgeoned opponents right from the start of an innings, not with agricultural slogs but with generally aggressive intent and powerful stroke play. In 1891 he was the only player to reach 1,000 runs in county games in a season where runs were hard to come by and rain was plentiful. The highpoint was his remarkable opening stand of 346 with Lionel Palairet, against Yorkshire. *Baily's Magazine of Sports and Pastimes* reported that 'the cricket season of 1892 … presented no feature more brilliant that the batting of Mr Herbert Tremenheere Hewett'. In 1893 Hewett and Somerset were consolidating their burgeoning reputations but this would be his last season with the county. Somerset's cricketing folklore has it that Hewett resigned as a result of a fiasco where play against the Australians was abandoned, only for the tourists to be tracked down later in the day in order to calm the baying multitudes who had come from afar to see them in action. A limited amount of play was possible on a stinker of a rain-affected wicket. Hewett unfairly shouldered the blame for the about-turn. Yes, he was in high dudgeon, but he did not resign. The club had already announced the previous April that he would be forsaking county cricket in favour of a career in law. He left on a high, having blasted a couple of quick-fire centuries to round off the season. He was considered a huge loss to the game.

COURTESY OF BARRY PHILLIPS

Herbie lived in London while he practiced as a barrister, unmarried and perhaps wisely so, given his inability to accept the idea of compromise in his relationships with others. He died in Hove on 4 March 1921 at the age of fifty-six, though he was buried at Norton Fitzwarren. Sadly, having reversed Somerset's decline, he had seen their fortunes plummet after his departure. Herbie Hewett's resignation would prove one in a series of disasters to befall the club. It could even be regarded the greatest misfortune in its long history. Had he remained in situ, he would never have countenanced the happy-go-lucky amateurism that once more engulfed the club.

48
Harry Edmund Winter
25 August 1884 v. Kent, Tunbridge Wells

Harry E. Winter

The younger brother of fellow Somerset cricketer, John Arundell Winter, Harry was born on 7 December 1857 at Coombe Head House in Bampton, Devon. The family moved to Watts House in Bishops Lydeard shortly after his birth, when Harry's father, John, inherited the estate. The house had been built in 1829 for Harry's grandfather, Charles Winter, and would remain in the Winter family's possession until 1902, when it was purchased by Lt Col Dennis Fortescue Boles, later an MP and baronet. The private cricket ground would be the scene of a number of country house fixtures featuring various Somerset players. In *46 Not Out*, R. C. Robertson-Glasgow recounts his first experience of such a game, where, unaware of the fact that he was supposed to address Sir Dennis with due deference, he caused hilarity by shouting 'Up a bit, Boles' to his host, who was standing by the sight-screen at fine leg in conversation with his butler, a wag named Burgess whose party piece was to feign tripping up when his master's back was turned.

Educated at Taunton College School (later renamed King's College), Harry was entering his teens when his father died. He made only one appearance for Somerset. Coming in at number 11, he hit 24 not out in a last wicket stand of 29, suggesting that he adopted a devil-may-care approach to batting. This is perhaps reinforced by the fact that he was stumped for a duck in the second innings. He also bowled one over at a cost of 9 runs. Harry trained to become a solicitor, practicing in London. Initially lodging in Westminster, he later lived in Fulham before moving first to Warwick Gardens and then to the rarefied atmosphere of Earl's Court Square, Kensington. He was married in 1885 to Jessie (née Hall), with his eldest brother Charles (at the time curate of St John's, Bridgwater) officiating. The couple would have two daughters –Winifred Mary and Frances Lesley.

In the latter part of his career, Harry left mainstream practice as a solicitor and became involved in 'exploiting industry and patents'. Perhaps surprisingly for a solicitor, he died without a will on 17 January 1921 in the village of Stone, near Dartford in Kent. He was sixty-three and still residing at the time in Earl's Court Square. His widow, Jessie, was left with the relatively modest sum of little more than £70. She continued to reside in Kensington with her unmarried daughters until her death in 1945.

49
Edward Stanley
28 August 1884 v. Lancashire, Old Trafford

Having completed the match against Kent at Tunbridge Wells, eight of the Somerset eleven had to make their way by rail to Manchester for their fixture against Lancashire, the following day. They were to be joined by John Challen. Bill Roe and Herbert Fowler, but Fowler was obliged to withdraw at the eleventh hour. Permission was sought to include Capt Edward Stanley a Somerset-born man who was based at the time in Manchester. Lancashire agreed, aware that Somerset would be thrashed, however many men they had fielded.

He came in at number 11 in both innings. In the first, he was struck on the second ball he faced and had to retire hurt. In the second, he made a duck, thus signing off a miserable season for his county.

Edward Stanley – a last-minute substitute who made only one appearance for Somerset

Born in Charlton Horethorne near North Cadbury on 29 June 1852 and the son of Rev. Edmond Stanley Stanley [sic], his family were lords of the manor of Charlton Horethorne. Edward did not stay long in the family home as his father's role in the ministry took them to first to Pembroke and then overseas as an army captain and chaplain in St Saviour in Jersey. Edward was educated at Victoria College, Jersey, where he played for the First XI from 1868 until 1870. At the age of sixteen he won the mile race by a considerable distance in an impressive time of 5 min 45 seconds, though his movements were later restricted when in 1872 he was out with friends and was accidentally shot in the back.

For a brief period before joining the army he was an assistant master at a school near Ledbury in Herefordshire but he soon embarked on a military career, his first appointment being in the 2nd West Indian Regiment. Married in 1877 to Mary Louisa (née Deane), who was known as 'Sunny' and with whom he would have six children, he and his family were rarely in one place for any length of time. His first child was born in Demerara, British Guiana (now Guyana) but by the time of the birth of a second child in 1880 he was based in Ipswich. In September of that year he was transferred to the 2nd Regiment of Foot and soon posted to Ireland. In 1884 he was stationed in Manchester where he undertook the examinations required to qualify as a major. His next appointment was with the North Staffordshire Regiment, with whom he sailed to the West Indies later that same year, but 1886 saw him living in Lichfield where he is recorded as playing an active role for Lichfield CC. After further brief spells at Devonport and Portsea he retired as a major in 1888, granted a gratuity but no pension. In 1890 he entered the Colonial service and he was appointed Inspector-General of the Houssa Force – the armed wing of the local constabulary – in Lagos, Nigeria in 1892.

He was only forty-three when he died of malaria on 7 April 1896 while stopping off at Accra in Ghana, having recently departed Lagos for England. His family resided at the time in Southsea, Hampshire, where some of his wife Sunny's relations lived. After being widowed, Sunny returned to her native Suffolk. The children would later state that they had little knowledge of their father, who had been obliged to be away from home for much of his working life. Most Somerset cricket supporters had little knowledge of him, either.

1885

"As usual, [Somerset] have had a disastrous season,
and of the six matches played have won but one,
the home contest with Hampshire."

Taunton Courier

Somerset were in some ways unlucky during their first brush with first-class status.
The weather played into their opponents' hands more often than not, but – above
all else – it was their inability ever to pull together a full strength side that was their
undoing. For four seasons they had scratched around to find eleven players. In one of
their final matches before their ignominious loss of first-class status – the away fixture
with Hampshire – they were able to conjure only nine men. And yet, perhaps typically
for Somerset, they confounded everyone by almost stealing victory in that particular
match. Almost, but not quite. It was a season in which a youthful Herbie Hewett had
established himself as the county's leading batsman and Edward Bastard had bowled
well, with 25 wickets at 15.80 apiece. Among the debutants, only O. G. Radcliffe
would make telling contributions in first-class cricket, though the vast majority of
them would come in future years, after he had been poached by Gloucestershire.

At the AGM in September, Edward Western tendered his resignation as secretary
and proposed Henry Murray-Anderdon as his successor. John Arundell Winter was
appointed as treasurer. A new committee was formed with formal representation from
eleven club sides. At the end-of-season celebrations, it was noted that 'all wished that
under the new management, Somerset would rank as one of the first cricketing counties
in England'. Their optimism was neither tempered by realism nor matched by their
ability.

50

Octavius Goldney Radcliffe
16 July 1885 v. Hampshire, Taunton

Yrs sincerely,
O. G. Radcliffe

O. G. Radcliffe was not alone in being persuaded by W. G. Grace to forsake Somerset and throw in his lot with Gloucestershire

On Monday 12 May 1890, Goldney Radcliffe would earn the distinction of having scored the first ever run recorded in the 'modern' era of the County Championship. Coming in at number three for Gloucestershire, and with his team already stumbling when E. M. Grace was dismissed for a duck, he took a single. Whether or not W. G. Grace, watching from the bowler's end, was irked at having had the honour plucked from his grasp is not recorded. In fairness, W. G. was an admirer of Radcliffe's, writing that 'until he was seventeen years of age, he played little or no cricket, but after that he cultivated the game with great perseverance, and is now one of the most punishing bats in England'.

Goldney Radcliffe was born on 20 October 1859 in the hamlet of Hilcott, in the parish of North Newnton, Wiltshire, where his father Rev. Alston Radcliffe was the rector. Although his parents had clearly opted to begin numbering their children when their eighth child, Octavius, appeared on the scene, he was always known as Goldney. Educated privately and having only taken up cricket in 1876, he mastered the art of batting but his technique was at times 'agricultural'. One description talks of 'a batsman with great freedom, he scored very fast when in the mood, hitting all round well without any regard to style'. He was also 'a serviceable off-break bowler'. He came to the fore playing for Yatton, whom he captained for two seasons in the early 1880s, topping the batting in 1884 with an impressive average of 122. W. G. Grace had already persuaded him to begin the process of qualification for Gloucestershire by arranging for lodgings in Thornbury and Peter Roebuck suggests that the Oxbridge crowd who ran Somerset CCC proved reluctant to welcome

Goldney on the basis that they considered him ill-educated and insufficiently refined. As supporting evidence, Roebuck quotes a report in the *Somerset County Gazette* condemning the 'quidnuncs who did not think [Radcliffe] good enough' and who were obliged in later years to eat humble pie when Goldney Radcliffe blasted a century against Somerset. It will not have helped that there were tensions between Yatton (sometimes referred to as East Somerset) and the leading lights, based at Taunton. If there was reluctance on Somerset's part, they would have overcome their doubts when he averaged 32.30 – including a century – in his five matches for the county in 1885. Goldney was already destined to play for Gloucestershire after having been tempted away by W. G. Grace, but the rescinding of Somerset's first-class status would have been the final straw. He would go on to play 119 times for Gloucestershire, notching up four further centuries. He was also invited by England captain Grace to join Lord Sheffield's tour of Australia in 1891-2 but made no test appearances.

After retiring from first-class cricket he was appointed captain of the newly-formed Wiltshire county team and was instrumental both as a player and administrator in establishing organised cricket in the county of his birth. He was described as 'the moving spirit of Wiltshire cricket'. He remained unmarried and settled for many years in Bell Farm House, Cherhill in Wiltshire, where he was looked after by his house-keepers. There are no records of his ever having engaged directly in any business. He died at his home on 13 April 1940 at the age of eighty-one.

51
Albert Edward Clapp
16 July 1885 v. Hampshire, Taunton

Albert Edwards Clapp

Born in Congresbury on 3 May 1867 and educated at Long Ashton School, Albert Clapp was drafted into the Somerset team as a promising, strongly-built eighteen-year-old middle-order batsman who could also turn his arm. His employers – Great Western Railway, who took him on as a clerk – were supportive, allowing him time off to play as an amateur until 1890. From then on, he offered his services on a professional basis both to Somerset and Shropshire. In the early days, he had made some telling contributions for club and county. W. G. Grace was sufficiently impressed to invite Albert to play for Bedminster, but the bulk of his club cricket was played for Yatton, for whom he also played rugby. Although he enjoyed some considerable success in non-first-class games (such as his 10 for 30 for Gentlemen of East Somerset v.

Gentlemen of South Hampshire in 1889), he failed to live up to his rich promise in first-class games. Over ten matches he averaged 10.85 with the bat and took no wickets.

Given his modest performances for Somerset, it is unsurprising that he only played first-class cricket for them on ten occasions. He notched up two half-centuries on a benign track against the touring South Africans in 1894, though this was not registered as a first-class fixture. Playing in the second tier for Shropshire against lesser opponents, he had much more success, scoring centuries and being utilised on occasions as a medium-pace bowler.

In 1893 he was married to Clara Louisa (née Gough), a farmer's daughter from Long Ashton. Census entries reveal that both were obliged to spend time apart while they cared for their ageing parents.

Somerset did not simply cast him adrift. Sam Woods led out a team in a benefit match for Albert in 1901. He was still residing in Yatton with his parents at the time and working as an insurance agent. He had originally joined the Great Western Railway as a clerk at the age of sixteen, earning the princely sum of £15 per annum, and later, by then living with his widowed mother, he would return to the fold as a railway accountant, suggesting that he had turned to insurance sales as a temporary measure to supplement his income while a professional cricketer.

He died in the Bristol General Hospital on 3 June 1936, aged sixty-nine, still living at the time in Yatton and working as a supplementary postman. A report in the *Western Daily Press*, written after his death, reads rather harshly:

Albert Clapp – a talented young all-rounder who never quite fulfilled his early promise. Pictured (front) with fellow Somerset cricketer, Monty Sturt (back)

> *What a disappointing cricketer he was. Full of promise as a recruit to the Somerset XI, he failed to come anywhere near expectations.*

Shropshire fans would have expressed a more generous view. At least he strove to reach the top and in doing so carved a useful career in the second tier.

52
Thomas Crump
16 July 1885 v. Hampshire, Taunton

Thomas Crump

Born in Cleobury Mortimer, Shropshire, on 12 March 1845, he was the son of Thomas Crump, a man of means who described his occupation as 'gentleman'. Thomas Jnr was educated at Lucton School, Herefordshire, before going up to Wadham College, Oxford, where he trained for the ministry and graduated with a BA in 1868. His first curacy was in Bitterley, Shropshire, and after three years he was appointed the vicar of Leintwardine in North Herefordshire, where he would remain until 1876. In 1876, he was married to Josephine Helen (née Colvin), a daughter of Colonel John Colvin of Leintwardine House. From 1876 until 1880, he was vicar of nearby Downton-on-the-Rock.

Rev. Thomas Crump, who made his debut at the age of forty

How did a man whose family was so ensconced on the Herefordshire-Shropshire border become vicar of Corfe in Somerset in 1880 and debut for Somerset at the age of forty? As is so often the case in the early days of Somerset county cricket, the answer lies with the man who pulled the cricketing strings: Rev. A. C. Ainslie, who rose through the church hierarchy to become Archdeacon of Taunton. Ainslie was a cousin of Thomas Crump's wife, Josephine, and writes in his memoirs of pleasant trips to visit Thomas's father-in-law at Leintwardine House:

> *I kept my hand in for fishing at Upottery, about nine miles from Corfe, where the Helyars had a nice reach of the Otter. But chiefly I fished at Leintwardine – a fortnight in the spring after Easter, for trout, and a fortnight in the autumn for grayling. I think I hardly missed a year for 20 years, and delightful visits they used to be to my dear old uncle John ...*

Nepotism was as rife in the Church of England as it was in Somerset cricket, so it comes as no surprise that Thomas should have been granted the living as rector of Corfe, where he would remain from 1880 until 1897. In addition, he would supplement his income by becoming the diocesan inspector of schools from 1890.

Although his contribution to Somerset's victory over Hampshire was minimal, with an innings of 8, he had turned in some decent performances at club level. The local paper talks of his 'remarkable innings of 120' for Fullands against Taunton in 1882. He also appeared on a number of occasions for the Somerset Club and Ground team who played approximately twenty games a season, seeking to increase gate receipts and offer useful practice for potential county players. In 1891, immediately prior to Somerset's first County Championship game, he was a member, at the age of fifty-five, of the team when the Somerset pro George Nichols blasted the Glastonbury attack for a quick-fire 311 not out. Thomas Crump's own contributions were never quite so telling.

From 1897 until 1907 he was the vicar of East Pennard. Despite having three daughters and two sons, Rev. Crump was able to enjoy considerable leisure time. Cricket gave way to golf when he became a keen member of the Burnham and Berrow Golf Club. He was also a member of the Somerset CCC committee. He died on 18 January 1907 in East Pennard at the age of sixty-one. An obituary informs us that he had suffered for a long while from 'an internal complaint which he bore with the greatest fortitude'.

53
Edward Caldecot Marsh
3 August 1885 v. Gloucestershire, Moreton-in-Marsh

Edward Caldecot Marsh could boast a distinguished lineage. A notice of his death, presumably placed by his mother, describes him as the 'beloved only son of the late Colonel Newnham Marsh, Indian Army, and of Mrs. Newnham Marsh of Grosvenor Villas, Bath … and grandson of the late Captain Edward Marsh, Lord of the Manors of Snave and Ivychurch, Romney Marsh, County Kent and of Nethersole House, Bath.' Edward's grieving mother had failed to add that her own father had been the Lord of the Manor of Holton, Lincolnshire, and that she had spent her formative years in Holton Hall. In addition, the grand lady had dismissed the background of Edward's wife, Fanny, as an irrelevance.

Edward was born in Belgaum, India, on 7 May 1865. Brought up in the city of Bath, he was educated at Malvern College, where he played in the First XI. He appeared for Somerset as a twenty-year-old and would play for the county in two first-class fixtures during his summer vacations, mustering an average of only 4.50 as Somerset were overwhelmed, as they so often were – in these instances by Gloucestershire and Surrey. He also played locally for Yatton and Weston-super-Mare and on occasions for Devon.

He graduated from Merton College, Oxford, in 1887. By 1892 he had taken up a position as a schoolmaster at Kendal Grammar School. He played for a successful

Kendal CC side between 1892 and 1894, opening the batting and enjoying a hugely successful season in 1893 as the leading batsman in the North Lancashire and District League with an average of 64.83. He would return in the early 1900s to take part in the club's late summer tours.

E. C. Marsh – his lineage was impressive but his county career less so

He was married in 1896 to Fanny Maria (née Leeming), daughter of a late surgeon. Fanny lived with her brother, a GP, in Kendal. Edward was by this time a schoolmaster at Pocklington Grammar School, east of York. In 1899, a year after the birth of their only child, he became proprietor and headmaster of Burstow Preparatory School in Horley, Surrey. He would remain there for twenty-seven years. His son, Neville, was killed in action on the Western Front at the age of nineteen. Neville had volunteered as a seventeen-year-old and after serving with the King's Own Scottish Borderers in Gallipoli was posted to the Western Front, where he died of his wounds in 1917.

On tour with Kendal CC (20 August 1903, Carlisle), fresh from having scored a century against Northumberland in the preceding match

Edward died, suddenly and unexpectedly at the age of sixty-one on 27 November 1926 while visiting Kendal with his wife, Fanny. At the time of his death he was still involving himself in sport as a vice president of Burstow FC. His death had a profound impact on the community as his school was forced to close with immediate effect. Edward Marsh was given a fine send-off by the residents of Burstow with a peal of muffled bells, a service in which his old friend from his Merton days, the Archdeacon of Bedford, read the collect, the boys from his school sang and the church was packed to overflowing. A more glorious exit than had been the case in his four first-class innings for Somerset.

54
Charles Henry Hulls
3 August 1885 v. Gloucestershire, Moreton-in-Marsh

Charles. Henry Hulls.

Born on 18 March 1861 in Luton, Charles was the son of Charles Henry Hulls Snr and his wife, Eliza. C. H. Hulls Snr had established himself as a schoolmaster in the

The coach of the 1885 King's School Rugby XV, almost certainly a twenty-four-year-old Charles Hulls

Home Counties before venturing west in 1871 to become the proprietor of the Corsham School, buying the enterprise from Mr Cloutte, who reassured parents that his successor was 'a gentleman from London of great experience in tuition'. The school was a success and indeed a Girls' School was opened in 1883, while the Boys' School was moved at the same time to Rudloe, Box, near Bath.

Charles Jnr had meanwhile been sent to Blairlodge, a school in Falkirk with a fine reputation both academic and sporting. He played for the school XI – well, but not outstandingly so, and he proved a finer musician than he was a cricketer. One report tells us that Charles Hulls the schoolboy 'played a pretty and careful innings of 30'. The school would in fact close in the early 1900s following a series of misfortunes including the death of the headmaster and an outbreak of 'an infectious disease' (possibly measles) two years later. Charles had long since left the school and by 1882 had been appointed music teacher at King's School, Warwick. Here he engaged his passions for music (organising and performing in school concerts) and cricket (first appearing for Warwickshire as a twenty-one-year-old). Warwickshire were not at the time a first-class county.

Charles Hulls Snr appeared in club cricket, primarily for Corsham and on occasions for the venerable Lansdown club in Bath and would have taken some pride in the fact that his son was asked to make the short trip from Warwick to Moreton-in-Marsh in August 1885 to represent Somerset against Gloucestershire. It was a match in which Somerset were roundly thrashed by an innings and 268 runs. Charles Hulls made 0 and 8 and was one of eight bowlers, returning figures of 0 for 5 in two overs.

He would play many times for MCC, including in one first-class fixture against Cambridge University where he enjoyed a useful partnership with fellow Somerset cricketer, Frank Phillips. He also represented Oxfordshire in Minor Counties cricket.

He was married in 1888 to Mary (née Rankin) and they had four daughters and two sons who survived into adulthood. As for his career in teaching, he left Warwick to follow in his father's footsteps and became proprietor of the College, Weston-super-Mare, in 1892. His stay there was shortlived because in 1895 he and his father went into partnership as joint-proprietors of the Oxford County School. Here, he played for

Thame CC with the *Bucks Herald* reporting on 'the brilliant batting of C. H. Hulls'. He had scored a quick-fire 50, ensuring victory over Pembroke College, Oxford, less than a minute before the scheduled end of play.

The County School was sold in 1898, at which point Charles Snr opted to help with the teaching at St Ives Grammar School (then in Herts) while Charles Jnr became proprietor of St John's College, Southend.

On 19 December 1912, having been apparently well the preceding week and having read the lessons at church, as he regularly did, he died of pneumonia at home in Southend at the age of fifty-one.

55
Crescens James Robinson
10 August 1885 v. Surrey, Kennington Oval

Crescens James Robinson

Born in Gloucester on 21 May 1864, Cres Robinson was a member of a wealthy family with business interests in Bristol. E.A. Robinson proudly claimed to be the largest buyers of paper in the British Empire. The Robinsons were far-sighted employers, concerned with the welfare of their staff.

Peter Roebuck refers to Cres as 'an unorthodox tail-ender who once kicked a ball to the boundary'. A batsman of modest talent who only ever bowled two overs, Cres was what every club needs: a rich supporter who is always eager to turn out, helping to avert a crisis when there is a struggle to find eleven men. It might be a slight exaggeration to call the Robinsons a cricketing dynasty, in that their perform-ances were generally of no great note, but Cres and his brother, Theo, represented Somerset, while other family members played for Gloucestershire. For many years the large, cricket-loving Robinson dynasty ran a team consisting entirely of family members. In 1891, a Robinson Family XI turned out against eleven members of W. G. Grace's family, at Backwell. The Graces notched up a total of 184, but the Robinsons fell short by 37 runs, despite 'a dashing innings of 67' by Cres.

Known as 'White Mouse' on account of his fair hair and

Cres Robinson – known affectionately as 'White Mouse'

Cres Robinson was an enthusiastic rather than an outstanding cricketer

slight frame, his best performance came late in his career, against Kent, with a hard-hitting (and totally unexpected) 55, when the tail wagged gloriously for twenty heady minutes. He retired from the county game in 1896, having chipped in with a grand total of 534 occasionally handy runs for the county in thirty-one first-class matches. Later in the same year, he was married to Clara Sidonie Reichel (née Herschel), a widow born in Dresden. They had no children. As one of twelve children himself, Cres had been obliged to explore new business ventures and was involved along with his brother, fellow Somerset cricketer, Theo, in running an oil seed crushing enterprise. He had retired by his mid-forties, suggesting that he was more inclined to enjoy his wealth than to accumulate more of it. He died on 8 June 1941 in Chelsea at the age of seventy-seven.

56
Edward William Page
10 August 1885 v. Surrey, Kennington Oval

E dward William Page

Born on 6 August 1864 in Bradford-on-Tone, Edward William was the son of a boot maker, John Page, and was brought up in nearby Wellington. A bright pupil who was able to rise above his working-class milieu, he became a pupil teacher at the Courtland Road School in Wellington before training as a teacher at St Luke's College, Exeter. He taught at Combe Florey, Pawlett and Williton National School before taking up his final appointment as headmaster of Datchet, Buckinghamshire, in 1900.

Edward had been married in 1888 to a Wellington girl, Ellen (née Bowerman), who was also a schoolmistress. They had no children and she was therefore able to pursue her career, but she died in 1919. Edward was remarried that same year to Lydia (née Wise), at the time a forty-seven-year-old spinster from Haringey. Lydia lived until 1931 and the year after her death, Edward was married in 1932 for the third and final time, to Frances Kate (née Brailey), fifty-one and a spinster at the time of her marriage to Edward, who was sixty-seven and clearly determined not to live alone. They honeymooned the following year in Cape Town, suggesting that whilst he may have loved his home comforts, Edward had retained a spirit of adventure. A niece recalled her holiday visits to 'Uncle Ted' in later life, remembering that he ran a strict household where regular visits to church were de rigeur and where her uncle was rarely about but 'always out doing good works'.

Edward Page was also a strict disciplinarian. He was known as 'Gaffer', while Ellen was referred to as 'Governess'. Never one to spare the rod, Edward would stand at the school gates at 9 o'clock each morning, cane in hand, ready to punish any laggards. An early entry in his school log book also adds that 'physical drill as a punishment is acting capitally'. At least some of the parents and guardians approved of his methods. One entry in 1904 reads: 'Gave Beard a thrashing at the request of his Grandmother'. He was just as peremptory in his dealings with his staff. One schoolmistress resigned after having been upbraided in front of the children for the way she taught them to read. Her replacement lasted six years before being reprimanded for having sent him a note without using headed paper and not having addressed him correctly as 'Dear Mr Page'. He bemoaned, very publically, the falling of standards and the introduction of modern methods of teaching. The school thrived under his leadership, as headmaster until 1926 and then for many years as manager (head of governors).

An enthusiastic club cricketer, Edward played initially for Wellington but continued to represent club sides close to where he was teaching. He was for a while captain of the Windsor and Eton club and finally settled for representing Datchet in his later years. In his only first-class game, Edward contributed 1 not out and a duck.

Also a useful rugby full-back, he represented Wellington and Williton. Indeed he seems to have been the leading light of Williton RFC in the late 1890s, given that at one time he was secretary, treasurer and chairman of the club, all concurrently.

He served as a Justice of the Peace for Slough and was for seventeen years a member of the Datchet parish council, taking on for a while the role of chairman. Also a warden of the parish church, he came to be referred to as the 'Father of Datchet', dying at the age of eighty-two at the King Edward VII Hospital in Windsor on 5 September 1946. He was survived by his third wife, Frances Kate, who died a mere two months later. The gates to the recreation ground were erected as a memorial to a man who was only fleetingly a part of Somerset cricket but gave much to the village of Datchet.

Edward and Ellen Page in 1896

57
Ernest George Murdock
10 August 1885 v. Surrey, Kennington Oval

6. f. Murdock

Ernest Murdock – head-
master of Christ Church
School in Clifton and a
successful club cricketer

Ernest Murdock was born in Keynsham on 14 November 1864. His father, Thomas, was a drill master and rifle instructor, training volunteers and styling himself a 'professor of calisthenics'. Given that in their early years Somerset were regarded as lacking in the batting and bowling departments but an above average fielding side, one wonders whether or not Thomas Murdock had influenced matters in any way.

Ernest decided on a career in teaching and taught for forty years at Christ Church Boys' School in Clifton. For the final thirty years he was the school's headmaster. A towering figure in the local sporting scene, he was a stalwart of Bedminster CC, opening the batting for many years and acting at various times as captain, treasurer and chairman of the club. He was also for a while chairman of his beloved Bristol City FC.

According to the *Western Daily Press* he batted in an 'unhurried, careful way' and he is also described as 'a useful bowler' at club level. His appearances for Somerset included two first-class fixtures in 1885 when he averaged a modest 8.33. Throwing in his lot with Gloucestershire in 1889, he made three first-class appearances for Somerset's neighbours in 1889, with an even more modest average of 2.50. He also took one wicket for Gloucestershire at a cost of eleven runs.

During the First World War he led the Athletes Battalion of Volunteers and was accorded the rank of major. A confirmed bachelor, Ernest Murdock continued after the war to be active in the community, particularly the sporting scene, and was playing cricket right up until the time of his death. He was devoted to his sister, Golinda, a spinster, and they resided together throughout their lives. Golinda survived her brother by some years and died in Worthing at the age of a hundred. Another sister, Beatrice, was married to Ernest's fellow cricketer, Ernie Hall, who also represented Somerset.

Ernest Murdock died at the age of sixty-one on 18 May 1926, at the start of the summer in which he had intended to retire as headmaster of Christ Church. He had been practicing in the nets - the first session of the season – at Bedminster CC's Clanage ground when, having returned alone to the pavilion, he collapsed and died from a sudden heart attack. At the inquest, the coroner for North Somerset, former county cricketer W. G. Burrough, was informed that among Ernest's last words were those to the Bedminster captain and former Somerset pro, A. E. C. (Bert) North: 'Bert, I can see them as well as ever, and they can't bowl the old man out yet.' He had for many years referred to himself as 'the old un' or 'the old man'.

Many mourned his passing, friends and former pupils thronged his funeral and funds were raised to ensure that a portrait of him and a memorial tablet would be placed in Christ Church School and annual prizes awarded to pupils in future years.

58
Edward Popham Spurway
20 August 1885 v. Hampshire, Southampton

Edward P. Spurway

Born on 4 April 1863 at Heathfield, Edward Popham Spurway followed in the footsteps of his father, becoming rector of the church and taking over the running of the family's cider business. His brother, Robert, also played for Somerset but pursued a military career. Their father, Rev. E. B. C. Spurway, had made a success of the cider-making business which would in time merge with Pallet's Cider to form the famed Taunton Cider Company based in Norton Fitzwarren. Spurway Snr's efforts at restoring the old church, on the other hand, are generally held to be an unmitigated disaster, a triumph of Victorian insensitivity with sixteenth century oak carvings being ripped out. The work, begun decades earlier, was completed in 1898 under the supervision of

E.P. Spurway – a rector and a successful cider-maker

Edward Popham Spurway, who approached the project with more of a sense of history, limiting his restoration to repointing the external walls. Indeed, local historians have every reason to be grateful to E. P. Spurway because the parish registers from 1698 onwards were 'carefully salvaged from a rubbish heap by the present respected vicar'.

He was educated at Charterhouse School, where he opened the batting for his school,

*Edward Spurway in the
Charterhouse XI*

and he went on to Trinity College, Cambridge. He first played for a Somerset XI in a friendly fixture in 1881, while he was still a schoolboy. A wicket-keeper, his only two first-class games – one in 1885 and another in 1898 – yielded an average of 6.50. Between his two outings, he had made regular appearances for a variety of club sides from Brympton to Taunton. He was also a regular with the Somerset Stragglers.

With his career mapped out at a young age, Edward stepped into his role as rector of Heathfield and manager of the cider-making business. Heathfield Cider had a wonderful reputation and was reportedly a favoured tipple of luminaries such as Queen Victoria and Viscount Melbourne. It is interesting to note that a brief obituary in the local press would make mention of the fact that he was a 'noted maker of Somerset cider, and won many prizes with it at the leading agricultural shows in the West of England', while little is made of his pastoral role. Perhaps this betrays the interests of the reporter, rather than offering a true reflection of Edward's life.

In 1889 he was married to Gertrude Mary (née Bagnall) in Pershore. They had six children together: five sons and a daughter. The three eldest sons would be killed in the war while the other two, Francis and Michael, would both play cricket for the county in the 1920s. Edward Spurway died at the age of fifty on 8 February 1914, his estate valued at £6,011 0s 1d, an assiduous accountant having resisted the temptation to round the figure.

59
George Eden Frederick Peake
24 August 1885 v. Surrey, Taunton

George Eden Frederick Peake

In one obituary, the Reverend Peake is described as 'much-esteemed' rather than, say, 'much-loved', suggesting a stiff formality. Certainly this ties in with his documented love of pomp and ceremony in the high church tradition. An explanation may lie in the fact that his father, also Rev. George Eden Peake, died in 1848 when George was only three. At the time of the 1851 census, he and his two brothers are listed as living in a cottage in Ruishton in the care of a servant and they would spend time residing with their grandfather, William Fisher, a landowner, and his wife, Jane.

Born on 6 March 1846 in Ruishton in Taunton, he graduated from St Mary's Hall,

Oxford, in 1871. His first preferment was the living of St John's in Bishops Hull. In 1874 George Peake suffered a career setback when the Bishop of Durham refused to allow him to take up the vacant position at St Oswald's, Durham, on the grounds of George's refusal to cease what were seen as papist or high church traditions such as the wearing of coloured stoles, the burning of incense and his insistence on turning his back on the congregation and facing the altar during the sacraments. There were clearly fewer such qualms when he was appointed rector of St Margaret-next-Rochester in Kent in 1878 or of St John's, Eastover, near Bridgwater, which heralded his return to Somerset. If he was not already part of the inner-circle, this status was secured by his marriage in 1881 to Laura Gertrude, eldest daughter of Rev. A. C. Ainslie, the founding father of Somerset CCC. Laura and George would have four daughters and no sons. While his wife and servants undertook childcare duties, George enjoyed himself as part of Rev. Ainslie's coterie of gentleman cricketers. Ainslie notes in his reminiscences that George Peake was one of the fellow clergyman who played alongside him as he established a team at Corfe. In his only appearance for Somerset as the county's final debutant in the pre-Championship era, George mustered a total of six runs in his two innings.

Rev. George Peake – son-in-law of Rev. A. C. Ainslie, the founding father of Somerset CCC

In 1887 he was offered the living at Holford (which contained no pulpit until one was erected in his memory in 1906) and then, in 1896, of Over Stowey. To this was added the income from being appointed an inspector of schools for the diocese of Bath and Wells. His final appointment was as the vicar of Brent Knoll, although he would not live to enjoy the appointment for long. The additional honour of being invited to accept a vacant prebendal stall in Wells Cathedral also came shortly before his death in his holiday home at St Columb, Cornwall, on 24 June 1901 at the age of fifty-five.

1891

"The promotion of Somerset to a place among the first class counties has been abundantly justified by results, the eleven having gone through an ambitious programme with great credit."

Bath Chronicle

Championship Position: 5 = of 9

Somerset had been invited back to the top table but they suffered a shaky start, including a humiliating defeat at the hands of Surrey, where the weather and injuries blunted their chances. Many thought that the team would once again fail to cling to their first-class status but there were some glorious victories once the under-graduates became available in the summer vacation. They enjoyed the sweet taste of revenge against Surrey and the joys of bowling out local rivals Gloucestershire for 25 at Cheltenham. Somerset managed a creditable fifth place in the table. Herbie Hewett had led a well-drilled side. Although overly reliant on flashes of brilliance from fast bowler Sam Woods, the elegant batting of Lionel Palairet and the skills on a sticky wicket of slow left-arm bowler Teddy Tyler, they were an exceptional fielding side. Gate receipts increased fourfold from the previous year and subscriptions rose by a third to more than 500. Recognising that bowling resources were spread thin, the club sent out a request to the eighteen affiliated club sides to seek out the services of a promising bowler as their pro. Their efforts failed to bear any immediate fruit.

60
Gerald Fowler
18 May 1891 v. Middlesex, Lord's

Gerald Fowler.

Gerald Fowler was born in Leytonstone on 27 July 1866 but his father, William, a successful barrister and for a while MP for Cambridge, soon moved the family to Moor Hall near Harlow. Gerald was brought up in some splendour along with his older brother, Herbert, who played for Somerset in the 'pre-Championship' days. The two of them were similarly built and smote the ball powerfully, in Gerald's case more often than not through the covers. Another brother, Howard, played cricket and rugby for Oxford University and was a rugby international with three England caps. Gerald's connections with Somerset began when he was educated at Clifton College (renowned as a breeding ground for young

Gerald Fowler – a Quaker and philanthropist but a punishing hitter

sportsmen) before he went up to Oxford. As a schoolboy he had enjoyed success as a bowler, not as a batsman. He had been invited to represent both Essex and Oxford, where he had continued to be used primarily as a fast bowler and lower order batsman. By the age of twenty-three he had become an occasional bowler, although he did twice manage five-wicket hauls in Championship matches, both in 1898. The high point of his batting career was his one and only first-class century when he shared an opening partnership of 205 with Lionel Palairet against Gloucestershire in 1895. He was one of W. G. Grace's five victims before Grace went on to rack up a score of 288, achieving his hundredth century in first-class cricket, all of which rather took the limelight away from Gerald in his moment of glory.

He was for many years captain of the Taunton cricket team at a time when most amateurs favoured the joys and variety of club cricket over net practice. A wealthy man, he made his living in the world of banking. Older brother Herbert had become a partner in the Fox & Co. bank in 1878. Within a year, the company's name had been changed to Fox, Fowler & Co. They have a unique claim to fame. The Bank Charter Act of 1844 had allowed provincial banks already in existence to continue issuing their own banknotes alongside the Bank of England. Banks formed after this date did not share the same entitlement. As the provincial banks were swallowed up, Fox, Fowler & Co (originally formed back in 1787 by the Fox family) was the last old bank

Fox, Fowler & Co. was the last provincial bank permitted to issue their own notes

standing. In 1921 they became part of the Lloyds Bank group and lost the right to issue their own notes.

Gerald Fowler oversaw operations in Taunton, keeping an eye on the finances of some of the players with more caution than when he batted. He put his numeracy to good use at Somerset, becoming their treasurer in 1896 and later combining it with the role of secretary. Married in 1899 to Ethel Ada (née Dewhurst), Gerald had no children and was a noted philanthropist, devoting his spare time to a number of local causes. He died of peritonitis at his home in Trull on 24 May 1916 at the age of forty-nine.

61
George Benjamin Nichols
18 May 1891 v. Middlesex, Lord's

George Nichols was born on 14 June 1862 in Fishponds, near Bristol. He had played briefly for Gloucestershire before joining his new county. Rumour had it that he had dropped one catch too many off the bowling of W.G. Grace, who had therefore instructed the county to dispense with his services. One in a long line of Somerset cricketers with literary aspirations, George Nichols was also a serial entrepreneur and a good all-round sportsman, who played rugby for Taunton in the winter months.

He was married in 1881 to Florence Enna (née Ball). In the following year, while bowling for East Somerset versus Wellington, he had the remarkable and near-perfect bowling analysis of 17 overs, 16 maidens, 10 wickets for 1 run. George had been hugely influential in helping Somerset to put together an irresistible case for inclusion in the Championship. In the previous summer, he had taken 79 wickets and contributed a hatful of runs at important moments. In one of Somerset's curtain-raisers for the 1891 Championship, he had raised expectations by plundering 311 not out from a shell-shocked Glastonbury attack. George Nichols was one of only three professionals on Somerset's books, the others being Albert Clapp and Nichols's great buddy Teddy Tyler. Although probably a better batsman than most of the amateurs in the county side, he was expected to earn his keep as a bowler.

A writer and a dreamer, he was a woeful fielder, though on occasions he proved a deadly medium-pacer. He could certainly never be accused of lack of effort and, with Somerset's bowling resources spread thinly, was seriously over-bowled. Nichols was at his happiest when writing or performing, though he tried his hand at a number of jobs, including running a gentlemen's outfitters and tobacconist's shop with Tyler in North Street, Taunton. In later years, with players hard to come by, he would be called on every once in a while by Somerset. If he was a shaky fielder in his prime, he was positively ponderous by the time he finally hung up his boots in 1899, frequently being barracked as he spilled catches or groped hopelessly as the ball sped past him.

George Nichols also offered up his services as a speech writer and he composed and took part in musicals and recitals, combining his two first loves when pulling together a team of performers (on both stage and cricket field) whom he called the 'Moonlighters'. His plays met with some success, though his greatest triumph is arguably the operetta *In the Days of the Siege*, where he was the librettist. Performed initially in Plymouth, it was then staged in Taunton where Nichols's commitment to the project had been the catalyst for the formation of the Taunton Amateur Operatic Society, which continues to thrive: a lasting legacy to a creative soul. He died in Dublin on 19 February 1911 at the age of forty-eight, one in a long line of Somerset players who were good cricketers and great characters, when the county might have been better served by having had great cricketers of good character.

G. B. Nichols – a useful all-rounder and a literary talent

62
Edwin James Tyler
18 May 1891 v. Middlesex, Lord's

Edwin J Tyler

Born in Kidderminster on 13 October 1864, Teddy Tyler, a slow left-arm bowler, caught Worcestershire's eye but they deemed him unworthy of a contract. Perhaps they were concerned about his action, which was regarded as suspect. Somerset thought

otherwise. A tall man at 6 ft 2 in, Teddy relied very much on length and flight rather than spin. His occasional quicker deliveries probably resulted from the bending of his arm. When the rules concerning questionable throwing actions were tightened in 1900, Teddy would find himself regularly being no-balled. His obituary in *Wisden* states that it was 'fortunate for him that he came out at a time when great laxity prevailed with regard to throwing'.

Capable of bowling non-stop all day, he put in a fair shift to earn his keep as a pro. Sam Woods noted that 'he, Nichols and myself were bowled silly'. He sent down nearly forty thousand first-class deliveries for Somerset before finally calling it a day and taking a well-earned rest in 1907. In 1895, he had joined the 'hundred club' with a mighty haul of 124 dismissals, including 10 for 49 against Surrey. He was rewarded with an England cap against South Africa in 1896 (on the 1895/6 tour), acquitting himself well with four wickets. Thereafter things fell away, but not until the turn of the century had his powers waned dramatically. He was no great shakes with the bat, but in the first published history of Somerset, F. S. Ashley-Cooper details a friendly game where Teddy was stunned by a blow from the first ball he faced and – perhaps rendered

E. J. Tyler – a major wicket-taker in Somerset's early years

unaware of his limitations by concussion – contributed 59 of the 68 needed for victory. Of the nine runs not attributable to Tyler, eight were extras. Such eccentricity also attached itself to his running between the wickets. Bill Roe recounted the time when, determined to give the strike to Roe, Tyler charged, head down, to the bowler's end, forgetting to play the ball, with the result that he was bowled, leaving his partner high and dry on 93 not out.

Married in 1890 to Blanche Annie (née Davis), Teddy had a sunny disposition and was loved by all. He threw himself into a number of business ventures including insurance sales, a travel agency, a spell as a pub landlord and his clothing and tobacconist's shop with George Nichols, though none of these seems to have been hugely productive. Perhaps he was too good-natured for the hard-headed world of business. Taunton School came to his aid, offering him the role of cricket coach and it was here that a future England captain, Jack White, came under his wing.

Teddy Tyler died in Taunton on 25 January 1917 at the age of fifty-two, one of the many Somerset cricketing outsiders who decided to stay put in the town that had adopted them.

63
Arthur Edward Newton
18 May 1891 v. Middlesex, Lord's

A. E. Newton

He was born in Barton Grange in Corfe on 12 September 1862. Arthur was preceded by a brother, Francis Murray Newton, who therefore stood to inherit the place, leaving Arthur to marry well. In 1891, at the age of twenty-eight, he was duly wedded to Mina, the sister of Cecil, later Admiral Hickley, who would play for Somerset. Sadly, their only child, Arthur Victor, died in action in Flanders in 1915.

Newton was often referred to as 'A.E.'. Eton and Pembroke College, Oxford, had instilled a stiff formality in him and he was thought of as old school and a cold fish. One of a number of wicket-keepers whom Somerset were fortunate enough to be able to call on in the early days, some said he should have played for England. Sam Woods probably got it about right when he said 'others may have been more brilliant, but never as consistent'. He was regarded as a tidy, nimble keeper and yet, as Peter Roebuck recounts, he was 'so clumsy that he could scarcely tie his own shoe-laces'. His batting was nothing to write home about but he had his moments, not least in the match against Gloucestershire in 1900 when he notched up his highest Championship score of 77.

A. E. Newton – he was still playing for Somerset in his fifties

Arthur Newton in the 1879 Eton XI

A. E. Newton had first appeared for the county as a seventeen-year-old in 1880. Throughout his career his appearances would be intermittent, his work as a land agent demanding a degree of travel. It is nevertheless a tribute to his staying power that his final first-class game was three days before the outbreak of war in 1914: a career span of thirty-four years. *Wisden* noted that in his final match he 'showed remarkable form behind the wickets for a man approaching the age of fifty-two'.

His letters reveal his unflagging energy. As well as organising matches long after most would have retired, A. E. Newton was still playing in them. *Wisden* reports that in his seventies, having cycled from his home in Trull to the County Ground, he effected five stumpings for the Somerset Stragglers. His was a charmed life, though not entirely without incident. A piece in the *Taunton Courier* in 1938 reports on his having been drawn into a dispute where a certain John Moore is accused of benefit fraud, having claimed four shillings to support his wife and children whilst being spotted moonlighting with some labouring work on Newton's house in Trull. The defence is centred on the fact that Newton describes him as an 'honest man' and that the only words Moore can read or write are the two that form his name. Moore concludes by apologising for his error and adding: 'I will pay back the money if I took it wrong.'

Without a whiff of scandal having ever sullied his own long life, A.E. Newton died in Trull on 15 September 1952, having spent the majority of his ninety years rooted in Taunton. In cricketing terms, he offers a remarkable example of longevity.

64
Samuel Moses James Woods
18 May 1891 v. Middlesex, Lord's

S ny woods

The press dubbed him 'Sammy'. Those who knew him addressed him as 'Mr Woods' or 'Sam'. He is undoubtedly one of Somerset cricket's most famous sons. Six feet tall and fourteen stone of pure muscle in his prime, he was a phenomenon who transcended the sport of cricket. His prowess and will to win were matched by his generous heart. Sam played the game and lived his life with fearless abandon. A sometimes erratic but penetrating fast bowler with an ungainly action, and an attacking batsman, he was also a superb close fielder. Born in Ashfield, Sydney, on 13 April 1867, he was sent to England in order to benefit from an education in the mother country. His parents had emigrated from Ireland and had made a tidy sum from part-ownership of a paper mill and some shrewd investments in land. The fortuitous Somerset connection was that Gilbert Burrington, bank manager of Fox, Fowler & Co.'s branch in Bridgwater, was appointed as young Sam's guardian. Sam would generously invite two of Gilbert's sons – Gilbert Jnr and Humphrey – to play for Somerset in later years.

Sam Woods – feted by the press and public, he combined superb athleticism and 'a mind supremely untroubled by examinations'

Sam first demonstrated his sporting prowess at Brighton College. He was accepted into Jesus College, Cambridge, entirely on the basis of sporting rather than academic ability. Stories of his lack of intellect are numerous and probably all apocryphal. On the basis of his performances at Cambridge, he was drafted into the Australian cricket team, for whom he played three times and he also made thirteen appearances as a wing forward for the England rugby team, some of them as captain. Later, he would be capped three times as an England cricketer. His exploits for Somerset are extraordinary and well-documented and on numerous occasions he proved the match-winner. Woods spent much of his youth playing sport, partying and relating anecdotes and very little of it applying himself to work or studies. In later life he

watched sport, drank heavily, continued to relate anecdotes and failed to apply himself. Appointed as captain after Hewett's departure, he led from the front and was an inspiration. But you can only win so many matches in this way. Captaincy demands considered strategies and disciplined application, both anathema to him.

Sam struggled to hold down any job for long. A couple of years as a bank clerk were not a success. Working for Hancock Breweries in Wiveliscombe and subsequently at the brewery attached to the George Hotel in Bridgwater, where he lodged, was prob-

S. M. J. Woods – a whole-hearted competitor with bat or ball

ably more to his liking. For all his generosity he rarely ever had to stump up for a round. Everyone wanted to show him their gratitude for the joy he had brought, which was why his waistline expanded in later years. He tried to join up for the war but was refused on the basis of his age and his rheumatism (which he blamed on having had to throw himself off a charging camel in Egypt and breaking his leg) but a friend secured him a commission with the Somerset Light Infantry depot near Taunton. He never saw active service. Chapman and Hall published his autobiography in 1925. A review asserts that he 'is still probably the best known man in the West Country', referring to 'a body that could breakfast off hot lobster and audit ale and then take all ten wickets, and … a mind supremely untroubled by examinations'. In later life, Sam resided in the George Hotel, in Taunton, owned by Somerset cricketer Ted Lock. In 1931, a specialist confirmed that he was suffering from cancer of the oesophagus. When he died on 30 April 1931 at the age of sixty-four, flags were lowered to half-mast as far away as The Oval. The Taunton streets were lined by the throng who mourned his passing. He had never been married. Why would he have been? He was wedded, for better or for worse, in health and then in sickness, to his beloved Taunton and Taunton's residents loved him with a passion.

65
Vernon Tickell Hill
18 May 1891 v. Middlesex, Lord's

Vernon Hill was born on 30 January 1871 in Llandaff, Cardiff, and would retain a Welsh lilt to his voice. The son of a Conservative MP for Bristol, he was educated at Winchester College and went up to Oriel College, Oxford. Only twenty at the time of his Championship debut, he would also play for Oxford University. One of that breed who bat left-handed and bowl right-handed (in his case, at fast-medium-pace), Vernon gained a reputation for wanting to hit every ball out of the ground, whether in the nets or in a match. He was a driver, not a slogger, with a large backlift, swinging the bat in a great arc. Noted for his arrogance and brusque manner, his overweening self-belief proved more often than not his undoing. He feared no bowler, regardless of their reputation. He even went as far as placing wagers on making a century, based on hope rather than previous form. On the one occasion this paid off, the bookie in question will have rued his rotten luck. That century was at Taunton in 1898, when he scored 116 as part of a record-breaking seventh-wicket stand of 240 with Sam Woods. Watching the two of them matching each other blow for blow

Vernon Hill – he hit the ball with 'amazing power'

must have been exhilarating. *Wisden* describes him as hitting 'with a power that was absolutely amazing'. In 1894, when Nottinghamshire were at the time hitting out ahead of a declaration, he came on as seventh change bowler and took 3 wickets for 1 run. It remains something of a mystery that he was not handed the ball more regularly.

He was married in 1901 to Gwynidd Blanche (née Llewellyn), the daughter of an MP. After retiring from cricket in 1912, he managed to talk his way into active service, despite being in his early forties. He served as a major in France and his troops might perhaps have had reason to be wary of taking orders from him, given that he seemed the sort of chap who might have led an ill-judged assault against a heavily-armed foe. Vernon Hill owned a dairy farm at Woodspring Priory, near Weston-super-Mare. He was also a magistrate, a churchwarden and a noted archaeologist. His autocratic manner failed to soften over the years. David Foot recounts in *Sunshine, Sixes & Cider* how Hill, having established that one of his staff was helping himself to some of the milk destined for the Great Western Railway, lined his employees up, loaded his gun and shot five bottles resting on a five bar gate before informing his staff that if the thieving continued, the culprit would suffer a similar fate. Having trained as a barrister, he was no doubt aware that he was stepping outside the law, but it did the trick. Vernon Hill clearly continued to chance his arm, long after he had ceased playing cricket. He died at Woodspring Priory on 29 September 1932 at the age of sixty-one. His brother, Eustace, also played for Somerset, as did his sons, Mervyn and Evelyn.

66
Frederic John Poynton
1 June 1891 v. Surrey, Kennington Oval

John Poynton – a 'steady bat' and a renowned physician. He recalls in his notes a confrontation with a member of the press who mocked the efforts of the Championship's newcomers:

I nearly committed homicide, for a pale, weedy pressman came up to me as I was walking into the pavilion, naturally downcast, and asked was this *really* a first class match? Up went my bat but the gentle Rev A P Wickham held me in check.

In 1933 John Poynton bequeathed his cricketing mementos and notes on a number of teammates to the Royal College of Physicians. Among the collection is a telegram asking him to play for Somerset against Surrey. It was sent on the day before play and exemplifies the chaos that had suddenly encircled the club, with Sam Woods unavailable through injury, the hard-hitting and experienced Bill Roe unable to make the trip and the Oxbridge undergraduates not yet on vacation. John Poynton answered the call but might have wished he had not bothered. The weather conspired against Somerset and they were trounced by the all-conquering men of Surrey. It was a rout and a humiliation with Surrey notching up 449 before the rain came and Somerset were twice bowled out for 37.

Born on 26 June 1869 in Kelston, near Bath, John Poynton was the son of the village's rector. Educated at Marlborough College, he went on to graduate from Bristol Medical School. A paediatrician who worked for many years at Great Ormond Street Hospital, he was considered the leading authority on rheumatism in the young. A shy man in the company of adults and possessed of an acerbic wit, he was entirely at ease with his young patients. He was also said to be cool in a crisis, as evidenced when a fellow passenger tried to commit suicide by disembowelling himself in a first-class lavatory on a train journey to Cornwall. Poynton stemmed the flow of blood, replaced the man's innards, and only then pulled the emergency cord to stop the train. The man survived.

John Poynton was deemed an excellent lecturer, a man of strongly-held views and a champion of his hospital. Although prone to feuds with any colleagues he thought dullards, his career was a success. He rose to become president of the British Paediatric Association. His book *Researches on Rheumatism* was considered the oracle and he remained an active campaigner in the field, credited with 'the establishment of special convalescent hospital schools for the better care of rheumatic children'. His private life was unhappy, ending in divorce in 1939 after years of separation from his wife, Alice Constance (née Campbell-Orde), to whom he been married in 1904 and with whom he had two children. Instead of devoting time to his family, he threw himself into all manner of pursuits. A pioneering motorist and aviator, he also sang in choirs and was perhaps too fond of whisky, describing his idea of hell as 'staying in a Scotch temperance hotel in Glasgow'.

Only available to play for Somerset intermittently, he also sometimes appeared for Lansdown, in Bath. *Wisden* describes him 'as a good steady bat, with plenty of confidence, and a fine fielder, usually taking cover point'. His last hurrah for the county was a non-first-class game against Glamorgan in July 1910, when, at the age of forty-two, he captained the side. Somerset won convincingly, though John Poynton only mustered two runs in total. He did, however, keep one of the match balls and later had it mounted on a silver ashtray, presenting it, along with his other mementos, to the Royal College of Physicians. He died in Weston, near Bath, on 29 October 1943 at the age of seventy-four.

67
Archdale Palmer Wickham
1 June 1891 v. Surrey, Kennington Oval

Archdale P. Wickham

Archie Wickham was one of the great eccentrics of the cricketing world. Writing about the Somerset match against Middlesex at Lord's in 1893, the reporter from *The Times* seems mesmerised by Wickham's appearance:

> *A peculiar picture presented itself at Lord's in the person of A. P. Wickham, the Somerset wicket-keeper standing with legs so far apart that his head just appeared above the wicket. He looked a queer figure even without his eccentric attire. He wore leg guards with black knee pieces. Above these were grey trousers and a black band or sash. A white shirt and a brilliant part-coloured harlequin cap completed his curious 'get up'.*

Born in South Holmwood, Surrey, on 9 November 1855 and a product of Marlborough College and Oxford, he had previously played for Norfolk (whilst a curate in Norwich). He began to play for Somerset after being appointed vicar of Martock. He was married in 1896 to Harriet Elizabeth Amy (née Strong) and David Foot writes that when Archie

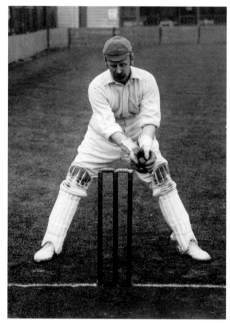

Rev. Archie Wickham demonstrated the art of wicket-keeping in his own inimitable way

was selected to play at the County Ground he would set off in great style in his horse and trap, with his wife, family and servants lined up to give him a rousing send-off. His style of wicket-keeping was as unorthodox as his attire. He kept his hands resting on his knees and took the ball disconcertingly late, showing wonderful reflexes. The technique seems to have worked. He held the record of the largest innings without conceding a bye (Hampshire's 672 for 7 declared in 1899) until he was finally knocked off that pedestal in 2002 by another eccentric but brilliant keeper, Jack Russell of Gloucestershire. Archie liked to unnerve batsmen by proclaiming Greek and Latin verse loudly. Some claimed he should have been considered for an England cap: the consternation that his unusual form of sledging would have caused the visiting Australians is perhaps the main argument in his favour. Wickham batted on 136 occasions but seemed to show little in the way of improvement over the years. One claim to cricketing fame says less about his skill than his appetite for the game. In 1901, when the Oxford University wicket-keeper, William Finlay, was injured, Archie volunteered to keep wicket for both sides. He remains the only person to have done so in a first-class game. As with his fellow Somerset keeper, Arthur Newton, Archie demonstrated admirable longevity, playing his last game at the age of fifty-one.

His three great passions were the church, cricket and lepidoptery. A Fellow of the Royal Entomological Society, he built up an impressive collection of mounted moths and butterflies which is now housed in the Natural History Museum, along with his copious notes on the subject. He served in a number of Somerset parishes, the last being East Brent, where he would live out his days, much-loved by his parishioners. Sadly, he became so beset by dementia that visitors such as his former teammate John Poynton found that Archie had no recollection of ever having played cricket. He died at the age of seventy-nine on 13 October 1935 and is buried in St Mary's church in East Brent. A stained glass window was placed in the church in his honour.

Archie Wickham – one of the eccentrics of the game whose three great loves – cricket, the church and Lepidoptera – are celebrated in a stained glass window at East Brent

68
Lionel Charles Hamilton Palairet
9 July 1891 v. Lancashire, Taunton

Lionel Palairet held his bat with the soft hands of a natural athlete. Historians of the club have described the way he 'persuaded' or 'charmed' the ball to the boundary. He also kept his head still and made his shots with the minimum of movement. In *The Jubilee Book of Cricket*, Ranji notes that Palairet gained the majority of runs on the off-side and suggests that this may have resulted from his having been coached by two bowlers with a consistent line and length. He and his brother, Richard, had in fact been coached privately by two professionals (Martin and Attewell), funded by the boys' father, Henry Hamilton Palairet, a cricket enthusiast who had played two first-class games for the MCC.

Lionel Palairet

Although Lionel was born on 25 July 1870 in Grange-over-Sands, Lancashire, his family were rooted in the West Country. His sporting prowess was clear from young age, though more as a bowler in the early days. He is credited with having taken seven

Lionel Palairet – regarded by many as the greatest stylist in the Golden Age of cricket

wickets in seven successive deliveries while attending Rev. Cornish's School in Clevedon. At Repton (where he was in the same team as C. B. Fry) and at Oriel College, Oxford, he continued to shine. Palairet was also a gifted runner and footballer. Somerset had every reason to be grateful for his presence. Over the course of a long career his batting average was in the mid-thirties at a time when the regular hazard of unplayable wickets depressed the figures of even the most resolute of batsmen. Seven times he exceeded a thousand runs in a season and he was regularly near the top of the national batting averages. His twenty-seven centuries included a top score of 292, against Hampshire in 1896.

L. C. H. Palairet – elder statesman of Somerset cricket

Many felt that Lionel Palairet should have enjoyed more than the two England caps he won in 1902, although his unavailability for touring matches (owing to work commitments) limited the options.

Married in 1894 to Caroline Mabel (née Laverton), he was employed as a land agent by Lord Devon and was regarded as fair and balanced both by his employer and the tenants. Although the local papers have numerous reports of disputes that he was called on to resolve, his job seems not to have been overly taxing, given that, having retired from cricket, he took up golf in a serious way, playing for Devon and arranging a Palairet Cup for competing golf clubs within the county. For a number of years he was president of the Devon County Golf Union which he had been instrumental in founding. Somerset CCC came knocking on his door, too, and he was their president at the time of his death in Exmouth on 27 March 1933 at the age of sixty-two. A photograph of Lionel Palairet was hung as a memorial in the old tearoom at the County Ground: a nostalgic reminder of Somerset's early, heady Championship days and a hint to batsmen of a more modern vintage as to how it should be done: a prompt as understated and elegant as the man himself.

69
Richard Cameron North Palairet
9 July 1891 v. Lancashire, Taunton

R. C. N. Palairet

Referred to as Dick, he was the younger of the two Palairet brothers. Born less than a year after Lionel on 25 June 1871, also in Grange-over-Sands, he, too, went to Repton,

Richard Palairet – but for an injury, he might have matched his brother's feats

where his batting average was far in excess of his brother's, and then to Oriel College, Oxford. Coached alongside his brother, he too showed the promise of greatness, starring at cricket, football and athletics (winning both the 100 yards and the mile at Oriel). Regrettably, he broke his knee whilst playing football at Oxford, with the result that his movements were restricted and he would never fulfil his rich potential. On leaving university he played less often for Somerset than his illustrious brother, dividing his time between cricket and business interests, where he worked alongside his father in what we might now call venture capitalism. The Palairets were no strangers to wealth and the reports in the *Western Daily Press* of Dick's marriage in 1899 to Emily Katherine, the daughter of Major Scobell of Down House in Redmarley, Gloucestershire, suggest eye-watering extravagance as more than a hundred members of the upper echelons of society descended upon the village.

The highlight of his cricketing career came against Sussex in 1896 with an innings of 156 in a second-wicket partnership of 249 with his brother, Lionel, who made 154 in what must have been a rare delight for the purists. After service in the war, from which he emerged with no debilitating injuries to add to his troublesome knee, Captain R. C. N. Palairet found his niche as an efficient administrator, becoming secretary both of the West Surrey Golf Club and of Surrey CCC. He was also joint-manager, along with Plum Warner, of the infamous Bodyline Tour of 1932/3. Dick Palairet was often regarded as brusque or arrogant, but some reports on the Bodyline tour suggest that he was one of the few Englishmen to have come out of the whole event still well-regarded by the Australians. He must have conjured considerable powers of diplomacy during the heated exchanges.

From 1939 until 1946 he was President of Somerset CCC, combining it for a while with the presidency of the East Devon Golf Club. He died at Budleigh Salterton in Devon on 11 February 1955 at the age of eighty-three.

70
Edward John Lock
9 July 1891 v. Lancashire, Taunton

Edward John Lock
George Hotel, Taunton.

Dismissed for a duck in his first Championship innings, Ted Lock managed to score 10 runs in the second innings. A local boy whose father owned the George Hotel in Taunton, this would be his top score in first-class cricket. Born in Taunton on 21 November 1868, he was twenty-two at the time of his Championship debut. He would follow his father, John, into the hotel trade, taking over the running of their hotel on Taunton's High Street. He also organised concerts and a report of one such event has him rendering the concluding song in a 'splendid tenor'. Ted would have had plenty of opportunities for singing (and drinking) as a regular member of the annual 'Moonlighters' tours – combining recitals and much inebriation with some entertaining cricket – led by the Somerset pros, George Nichols and Teddy Tyler. His name appears regularly in local reports playing for and, over several seasons, captaining Taunton, but he made only one other appearance for Somerset, in 1893, suggesting that he offered a last resort when the side were struggling to find eleven men. Writing in the *Taunton Courier*, H. J. Channon gives an insight into the Taunton captain's wristy batting style:

Ted Lock – an hotelier and a fine club cricketer

> *E. J. Lock was a stylish batsman, a good bowler and a very fine cover-point. He could score off the good length ball, had a sound defence on a sticky wicket, but what I remember particularly about his batting was the flicking of the wrist at the exact moment that is the secret of "correct timing". His leadership was admirable.*

Ted was married in 1901. He and his wife, Agnes Cowper (née Symington), would

Ted Lock appearing for 'Moonlighters'

have two sons and would run the George Hotel together for many years. Ted was also an active member of the Pickeridge Golf Club at Corfe and was a chorister at St Mary's church in Taunton for a total of seventy years, man and boy. He clearly took his singing very seriously given that he was also a member of the Taunton Madrigal Society and the Taunton Operatic Society.

A talented club cricketer and something of a character, these would have been sufficient grounds to have merited rather more than his two appearances for the county as the team struggled in later years. Ted Lock died in Taunton on 3 May 1949 at the age of eighty.

71
Joseph Arthur Gibbs
9 July 1891 v. Lancashire, Taunton

Born in Westminster on 25 November 1867 and educated at Eton, Arthur Gibbs graduated from Christ Church, Oxford. After two years in London working in the banking sector, he moved to Ablington Manor, in the Coln Valley, Gloucestershire, becoming squire of a small estate. Influenced in part by his devout Christianity, he demonstrated great benevolence to his staff and tenants. His mother, Laura Beatrice, would write that 'with all his tenderness of heart, he had a strict sense of justice and a clear judgement, and weighed carefully both sides of any question before he gave a verdict'. The countryside and the life of a squire proved much more to his taste than London had done and it was here that he was able to engage in his favoured pursuits of hunting, shooting, fishing, sport and – above all else – writing. His literary output included *The Improvement of Cricket Grounds on Economic Principles* (published in 1895), where he was able to combine his knowledge of cricket and monetary matters. His engaging description of life in the Cotswolds, entitled *A Cotswold Village or Country Life and Pursuits in Gloucestershire*, published in1899, proved his most lasting literary success. In the preface to the third edition (published after his untimely death), Laura Gibbs describes her son as 'one of those rare natures who combines a love of outdoor life, cricket and sport of every kind, with a refined and scholarly taste for literature'. In 1909, the newly installed organ at Notgrove parish church was dedicated to the

memory of Arthur and his brother, Stanley Vaughan Gibbs.
Had he not died young, he might in time have joined the
ranks of acclaimed cricket writers. As for his cricketing
output, it was unremarkable but by no means abject. He had
played twice during the 1890 season and acquitted himself
well. The match against Lancashire would be the first of five
first-class appearances and his top score would be his 75
against Oxford University in 1894. Sandwiched between
these efforts, he joined Lord Hawke's 1892/3 touring party
in Ceylon (Sri Lanka) and India, though he failed to make
much of an impression. A non-first-class innings of 178 for
MCC against Dulwich demonstrates that he was no also-ran.

Arthur Gibbs was able to keep cricket in perspective,
describing the idea of fellow amateurs turning out regularly
for three-day matches a waste of their wider talents and 'a
little overdone'. He was, however, also alarmed at the
advance of professionalism and it seems hard to reconcile
these two views. He died, tragically and unexpectedly, of
heart failure in Marylebone on 13 May 1899 at the age of
just thirty-one. He was not married. Only a month earlier,

*J. A. Gibbs – a cricketer
with 'a taste for scholarly
literature' and a successful
author*

he had written in his journals that 'you must influence for *good* if you write, and write
nothing that you will regret one day or think trivial'. It serves as a fitting epitaph and
a warning to all in the modern age of social media.

72
Ernest Dering Evans
20 July 1891 v. Gloucestershire, Taunton

Born in Clifton on 21 August 1861, Ernest Evans was the fifth son of a successful
tanner. His grandfather had owned a tannery in Ashburton, Devon, and his father had
continued in the business to the point that P & S Evans & Co, now based in Bedminster, had become a hugely successful enterprise. The tanning of leather was an unwhole-
some job, with young boys paid to collect excrement from the streets of Bedminster
and a process involving the handling of chemicals so toxic that workers generally
endured a short lifespan. They were at least reputed to be free of many infectious

E. D. Evans appearing for Clifton RFC

diseases, given that even rats eschewed the tanneries. Little wonder that the Evanses resided a safe distance from the works, enjoying the delights of Clifton. Ernest would follow in the paternal footsteps, becoming the owner of the Western Tanning Company of Bedminster and a director of his late father's business.

More successful as a rugby player than as a cricketer, Ernest was good enough to represent Gloucestershire at the game. He played for Clifton Rugby Club alongside an older brother, Harry Loft Evans, who would represent Scotland while studying medicine at Edinburgh University. During the 1881/2 season Clifton played their first floodlit match, installing four lights on poles lit by electricity from a steam engine. With floodlighting still very much a novelty, a crowd of 4,000 turned out to watch. It is reported that some players were confused and 'chased the shadow of an opponent rather than the man himself'. The match was abandoned when the lights failed.

The elder of two brothers who represented Somerset at cricket, he was already established in business and had a young family, having been married in 1883 to Margaret Maxwell Bethune (née Ogilvie), known as Mia. In his one and only game for the county, he came in at number ten and was bowled for a duck. Somerset only needed one run in their second innings to win the game and so his services were not required again.

He continued to develop the tanning business, alongside a brother, Parker. At the time of the 1911 census, he was living at Farley Coombe, Flax Bourton, in some luxury, with five servants at his disposal. After handing over the reins to the next generation, Ernest and his wife, Mia, divided their time between a holiday home near Lyme Regis and a main residence in Clifton. In stark contrast to his all-too-brief first-class career, he lived a long life, dying, back in his birthplace of Clifton, on 4 November 1948 at the age of eighty-seven.

73
Thomas Spencer
23 July 1891 v. Yorkshire, Taunton

Thomas Spencer

Thomas Spencer was born on 10 June 1850 in Fulham, the third child of a bank clerk who would rise to the level of bank manager. Thomas's first job on leaving school was that of a merchant's clerk, though he subsequently became a member of the London Stock Exchange. Married in 1877 to Alice Eliza (née Scott) and a father of three, his move to Somerset resulted from a decision to become a preparatory school teacher. He was for many years the principal of Naish House School at Wraxall and among his staff at different times were Wilfrid Young and Henry Martyn, both Somerset cricketers. On Christmas Day 1902, a major fire broke out, destroying much of the fabric of the building, with Thomas and his family obliged to lodge for a while at the local rectory. The changed circumstances acted as a spur and in 1905, at the age of fifty-five, having taught for approximately fifteen years at Wraxall, Thomas opted (along with his wife, Alice) to re-establish Naish House School in Burnham-on-Sea, continuing in the role of headmaster-proprietor well into his sixties.

Thomas Spencer a conscientious headmaster and club secretary

He only took part in three first-class fixtures and his main service to Somerset cricket was in an administrative capacity. He was instrumental in paving the way for Somerset's entry into the Championship when he and Herbie Hewett managed to persuade the County Cricket Council to dissolve itself, so that clubs could take control of the fixture list. Joint-secretary of the club with the charismatic Henry Murray-Anderdon, he yielded up the position to Sam Woods ahead of the 1895 season. Sam had no appetite for administration but was strapped for cash.

Thomas's modest career statistics suggest that he stepped into the breach in times of need. Sometimes he would go the extra mile to help the club. During the 1890 season, in the year before Somerset were accepted into the Championship, Staffordshire had arrived with only nine men. He and Cres Robinson had agreed to play for Staffs. Both had dropped catches. Both had blamed it on the sun. Somerset's captain, Herbie Hewett, had made hay while the sun continued to shine brightly. His 203 not out reputedly included a mighty blow that went through the window of a nearby cottage and crashed onto the tea table.

By the time of his death on 28 November 1933 at the age of eighty-three, Thomas Spencer had retired to Bishopsteignton in Devon.

74
Wilfrid Alec Radford Young
13 August 1891 v. Surrey, Taunton

W. a. R Young.

Wilfrid Young's father was for a while vicar of Chewton Mendip. Born in Brighton on 5 October 1867 and educated at Harrow School and then Selwyn College, Cambridge, Wilfrid had embarked on a teaching career when he appeared for Somerset. A right-handed batsman, he had represented Harrow three times in their annual fixture with Eton, but had failed to gain a blue at Cambridge. At county level, he managed to score 13 in the first innings against Surrey in a match which, against all expectation, Somerset would win, avenging their humiliation at The Oval, earlier in the season. These would be the only runs he would score in first-class cricket. His duck in the second innings was followed with a pair in his only other game, against Lancashire in 1893.

W. A. R. Young – thirteen runs were the sum total of his contribution

Married in 1895 to Edith Isabel (née Storey), he was by then a schoolmaster at Naish House, whose principal was Thomas Spencer, Somerset's joint-secretary and Wilfrid's fellow Championship debutant. Before long, Wilfrid opted for a change of career and a life in the clergy. Ordained in 1900, at the age of thirty-three, he would enjoy a long career in the Church of England. After time spent in Worcester and Rugby, he became rector of All Saints Church, Kimcote, Leicestershire, in 1907 and would remain there for forty years. The parish records show him active until the autumn of 1946. For forty years he noted assiduously the births, deaths and marriages, signing off each entry. Ironically, the entry for his death is incorrect: he is referred to as 'William'.

Wilfrid Young had died in The Rectory, Kimcote on 19 March 1947 at the age of seventy-nine, remembered by many for his pastoral care and by few for his deeds as a county cricketer.

Rev. Wilfrid Young – for many years the rector of Kimcote in Leicestershire

75
Edward William Ebdon
21 August 1891 v. MCC, Lord's

Edward W* Ebdon

Born in Bradford-on-Tone on 22 April 1870, Edward Ebdon was twenty-one at the time of his first-class debut. A wicket-keeper, he would be drafted into the Somerset team on two occasions as emergency cover, although the *Wellington Weekly News* reports that he had to decline other requests to step into the breach because 'scholastic duties would not allow'. As well as representing Somerset at cricket, he played in goal for the county at hockey and in 1906 was awarded an international cap in England's game against Scotland. A newspaper report of his goalkeeping display in a county game describes him as 'one of the best of custodians ... his saves at times were remarkably good'.

Edward Ebdon, who played for England at hockey

As was the case with two brothers who would also represent Somerset, he played his club cricket for Wellington, where he was the teacher at the Coram's Lane Elementary School. Boys of varying ages and mixed abilities would have been overseen by him in one classroom, requiring a level of concentration and multi-tasking on his part that would have made wicket-keeping seem positively relaxing. While living at The School House, he was married in 1895 to Bessie Amelia (née Culverwell), a 'fancy draper' and the daughter of a saddle maker. In 1902 he was asked by the Education Authority to take up a teaching post in the concentration camps in South Africa after the Boer War. He refused to go, though the decision seems not to have harmed his career. Later, he would take up the post of headmaster at Yatton Church of England School, where he stayed for many years, taking an active role in local events.

He was a member of Yatton cricket and hockey clubs, a Fellow of the Royal Geographical Society, an accomplished organist and conductor of the Yatton Choral Society. He also acted for a while as chairman of the parish council.

After retiring, he spent his remaining years living in Yatton, although his death at the age of eighty occurred in a Nursing Home near the Clarence Park cricket ground in Weston-super-Mare on 6 December 1950.

Lionel Palairet and Herbie Hewett are joined by W. G. Grace in celebration of their record-breaking first-wicket partnership against Yorkshire

1892

"We know of nothing in the history of the game to equal the rise of Somerset ... Last year it was a moot point whether Somersetshire should be admitted to first class cricket, but we fancy few will now ... find fault with the decision of the M.C.C. Committee."

Observer

Championship Position: 3 of 9

Somerset had pushed on. Herbie Hewett was magnificent – a superb captain and the leading run-maker in the country in a season blighted by wet weather. Hewett was the only man to top 1,000 runs that year and his haul included a double century when he destroyed the Yorkshire attack with some brutal hitting. Sam Woods took 90 wickets bowling very fast and erratically while Teddy Tyler returned figures of 9 for 33 against Nottinghamshire. There were no dissenting voices when *Wisden* later named Hewett and Lionel Palairet as two of their cricketers of the year. Most commentators were of the view that Somerset would soon be challenging Surrey for top honours. They were wrong. The 1892 season was as good as it would get. Some would argue that, 125 years on, their third place in their second season of Championship cricket remains their crowning achievement.

Coote Hedley, an amateur all-rounder, was the only significant newcomer.

76
Walter Henry Hale
2 June 1892 v. Surrey, Kennington Oval

Walker Hale

Wally Hale was born in the Temple area of Bristol, on 10 April 1870. He was registered at his birth as 'Walter Henry Heal'. At various times his father, John – a haulier and milkman, born in Tiverton – is recorded (along with the family) as 'Heal' or 'Hale'. The 1891 census has Wally (whose father has confusingly reverted to Heal on this occasion) listed as a 'Professional Cricketer', living in Bedminster. In 1893, he was married to Elizabeth Emily (née Denham) and together they would have three sons and two daughters.

Wally was clearly an able sportsman. Not only did he make a living as a cricketer but he was also a county-level rugby player. Indeed he has the rare distinction – reflecting Bristol's historical confusion as to whether it is aligned to Somerset, Gloucestershire or neither of the two – of having played for the two counties both at cricket and at rugby. In the winter months he played his club rugby as a forward for Bristol. When

Wally Hale – played for Gloucestershire and Somerset both at cricket and rugby

it came to cricket, it was Somerset who first called on the services of the young pro. He had been plying his trade with Shropshire, where he batted regularly at number three and opened the bowling with his slow right-arm deliveries. His haul of wickets was above average and he made decent scores. It is easy to see why Somerset were interested, though his eight matches for them were a disappointment. When Wally Hale and Somerset parted company he joined Burnley as a pro for three seasons in

Lancashire League cricket before Gloucestershire employed him. Between 1896 and 1909 he was called on by Somerset's neighbours on an ad hoc basis while he continued to play his club cricket at Knowle. He scored two centuries for Gloucestershire and topped the county averages in 1901. At Knowle, he undertook coaching duties, helping to develop the skills of some promising youngsters, among them Sydney Rippon, who would go on to play more than a hundred first-class matches for Somerset.

As well as earning money as a pro, Wally Hale was for many years a drainage inspector for the Bristol Corporation, who were clearly accommodating over his working hours, given the contribution he was making to the city's sporting scene. He died in Bristol on 12 August 1956 at the age of eighty-six.

77
William Ilbert Hancock
2 June 1892 v. Surrey, Kennington Oval

Born in Wiveliscombe on 10 April 1873, William Hancock would make a solitary appearance for Somerset. He was one of ten brothers. Between them, the Hancocks formed the core of a successful Wiveliscombe rugby team, with five of them (including William) representing Somerset, and two – Frank and Froude – becoming internationals. Froude played for England, the British Isles XV and the Barbarians. Frank played for Wales and is credited (while captaining Cardiff) with having introduced the idea of deploying both an inside and outside centre (where previously there was only one centre in the three-quarter line). An obituary in the *British Medical Journal* says of William that 'it is practically certain that he would have gained international honours in [rugby] football ... had it not been for an accident to the knee'. He also represented Somerset at tennis.

William Hancock – a member of a brewing dynasty who became a noted surgeon

The family had made their fortune from brewing beer, the company having its base in Wiveliscombe, where at one time they employed approximately half the working population of the town. Their beer was distributed far and wide, with further manufacturing facilities in Newport, Wales. With so many siblings, some of them had to move on from the family business. In William's case, he chose to become an ophthalmologist. After attending Dulwich College he worked at Guy's Hospital in London (which explains his availability to play at The Oval). At Guy's he captained the tennis and rugby teams. He qualified as a surgeon in 1896 and became a Fellow of the Royal College of Surgeons in 1898. In 1899 he was married to Margaret Hay Sweet (née Escott), who hailed from Langford Budville, not far from Wiveliscombe. They would have four children together. During a successful career, he worked at the Royal London and Royal Westminster Ophthalmic Hospitals. His death in Marylebone on 26 January 1910 resulted from a pulmonary embolism and thrombosis, four days after an operation for appendicitis. He was only thirty-six.

What of the man? He was spoken of as having been a good teacher and skilled surgeon, courteous and kind, especially to the children who came under his care. He is described in an obituary in the *British Medical Journal* as having a 'retiring disposition' and also as being 'a strong man in every way – mentally, morally and physically'. The praise is often fulsome in such notices but this one seems particularly heartfelt. He truly seems to have been the strong, silent type. William Hancock's first-class cricket career was by no means as successful as his medical career, given that his two innings for the county yielded seven runs. Perhaps we should be charitable and blame this on the knee-injury that had curtailed a promising rugby career.

78
Hugh Alexander Tapsfield
9 June 1892 v. Oxford University, Oxford

H A Tapsfield

A student at Magdalen College at the time of his appearance for Somerset, Hugh Tapsfield's father was at the time the rector of Nether Stowey. Hugh was born in Windsor on 31 January 1870, although his parents soon moved to Somerset, with Hugh becoming a boarder first at a school in Weston-super-Mare and subsequently at Bradfield College, where he played in the First XI. On going up to Magdalen, from where he graduated in 1892, he failed to make it into the Varsity side, though he had more success as a member of the Magdalen Football XI who won the Inter Collegiate Cup in 1891/2. In his only first-class cricket match he scored 0 and 1. In the opposing Oxford side who trounced Somerset were three players who would make sizeable contributions to the Somerset cause in the years that followed: Lionel Palairet, Vernon Hill and Frank Phillips.

Following his father into the ministry, Hugh Tapsfield's first curacy, between 1895 and 1897, was at Cheshunt in Hertfordshire. In 1897 he was married to Margaret Lillian (née Doxat). Never in one place for any great length of time, he served at St Andrew's, Westminster, at Byfleet in Surrey and at Lincoln Cathedral, where he was a priest-vicar.

From 1900, perhaps aware that he needed to offer stability for his family, his changes of role became less frequent. For six years he was a minor canon in St Paul's and then, from 1906 until 1911 he was the vicar of Bembridge on the Isle of White before he returned to the mainland and remained the vicar of Wootton St Lawrence near Basingstoke until 1920.

From 1920, he was an assistant curate for Weybridge & Hersham and was also appointed chaplain to the Metropolitan Convalescent Institute of Walton-on-Thames and chaplain to the Bishop of Guildford from 1929. In his later years he established a reputation as a fine golfer, representing Great Britain in the Derby Cup, the equivalent of the Ryder Cup, for seniors. Having retired to Byfleet, this remained his place of residence, although he died in the Shiel Nursing Home in Weybridge on 3 March 1945 at the age of seventy-five.

H. A. Tapsfield – a marginal Somerset cricketer (top) and a member of the Magdalen College XI, winners of the Inter Collegiate Cup in 1891/2 (above)

His appointments in the clergy had been many and various and one hopes his ministry was more of an inspiration to his congregations than his brief foray into first-class cricket had proved for the spectators.

79
Charles Edward Dunlop
9 June 1892 v. Oxford University, Oxford

C. E. Dunlop.

Born in Edinburgh on 25 June 1870, Charles Dunlop was living in Chew Magna at the time of his selection for Somerset, firstly against Oxford University and then, eleven days later, in his first Championship game. The 1891 census lists him as living with his mother, Amy. He was educated at Merchiston School, Edinburgh, and then at Wadham College, Oxford. Here he played cricket with or against the Palairet

Charles Dunlop – a headmaster who played once for Scotland

brothers and Vernon Hill (all of Oriel College and Somerset). He also appeared in a number of friendly fixtures in Somerset alongside Hill, during the summer vacations. After graduating he became a schoolmaster at Larchfield School, Helensburgh, in Scotland. Although he continued to represent Somerset in 1895 and 1897 he was only able to do so during the vacations. In 1897 he was married to Isabel Mary (née Ouless), a naval officer's daughter from Hampshire. He began to be beset by troubles in August 1901 when he purchased the Hermitage Boys' School in Lansdown, Bath, in partnership with a Mr Balshaw. Charles Dunlop appears to have been naive in his business dealings, putting in his wife's £900 legacy, which formed the bulk of the investment. Part of the deal was that he would take on the role of headmaster. With outgoings averaging £47 per week and income from fees of only £18 per week it soon became apparent that he had been duped. By July 1902, the partnership had been dissolved and Charles had been declared a bankrupt. He went to court to clear his name but was unsuccessful. His defence against the crime of continuing to trade while insolvent was based on two points. The first was his concern for the livelihood of his twenty-eight pupils (a mix of day boys and boarders) and his unwillingness to terminate their schooling until alternatives could be found. A second point, that 'the profession of a schoolmaster carrying on a school could not be held to be that of a trader because his chief asset was his brains' was dismissed by the judge. It is perhaps a reflection of Charles Dunlop's naivety that he should assume that trading required no brain power. The story became something of a cause célèbre and, aware that his reputation was in tatters, Charles gave assurances that he would attempt to pay off his creditors. He died in London on 21 August 1911 at the age of forty-one, the cause of death being given as heart failure. His father died in London the following month, offering a possible reason for Charles's presence in the capital.

He was a decent cricketer who played once for Scotland and forty-three times for Somerset, with an average of 16.50. The *Taunton Courier* describes him as 'one of the finest fielders of his day, and quite a useful batsman with a peculiarly original style'. *Wisden* confirms that 'he was an excellent fielder'. They could perhaps have added that he was either an unlucky or a very poor businessman.

80
Walter Coote Hedley
20 June 1892 v. Kent, Catford

W. C. Hedley

Sir Coote Hedley was one of that distinguished breed of cricketers who were knighted for their efforts, though in his case it had everything to do with his military career and nothing to do with his gallant efforts on behalf of Somerset. Born on the outskirts of Taunton on 12 December 1865, he was the son of a local magistrate who had retired from the army. Destined for a life in the military, Coote Hedley went to Marlborough College and then on to the Royal Military Academy at Woolwich. He joined the Royal Engineers as a surveyor and was involved in the Boer War, where he was directly involved in the conflict at Spion Kop, and the First World War, where he oversaw the mapping of the extensive and ever-changing trenches. In between, he took a prominent role in undertaking a survey of India from 1906 until 1908. He would retire from the army in 1920. Married in 1894 to Anna Susan (née Fellowes), he had three daughters.

He had represented Somerset during their pre-Championship days before brief appearances for Kent (where doubts were raised about his delivery as a fast-medium right-arm bowler) and Devon. He returned to the fray in 1892 as part of a Somerset team already growing in confidence. He was not just another well-connected amateur but someone who

W. C. Hedley – a military man and a useful all-rounder

brought all-round cricketing skills and athleticism, averaging 18.14 with the bat and taking 254 wickets at 20.77 apiece in 84 appearances for Somerset. He would go on fleetingly to represent Devon (again) and finally Hampshire, an indication of his peripatetic lifestyle. Hedley was also a successful rackets player and a scratch golfer.

Colonel Sir Walter Coote Hedley KBE, CB, CMG died on 27 December 1937 at Sunningdale, having just turned seventy-two. A tribute in *The Times* by Plum Warner speaks in glowing terms of Hedley's skill as a bowler and speaks of 'a charming man … whose gentle and delightful manner radiated happiness and ease wherever he went'.

1893

"They have fallen from their high position of last year ...
Too often, their cricket lacked the spirit of other years,
and especially was this the case with their fielding."

Western Gazette

Championship Position: 8 of 9.

Only four games were won. Herbie Hewett was again the leading batsman. With Sam Wood's powers as a pace bowler on the wane, Teddy Tyler stepped up to the plate with 98 wickets. Gate receipts were boosted by the visit of the Australians but the goodwill of supporters was tested when play was abandoned owing to rain, a decision that was reversed to avert a threatened riot. The *Bath Chronicle* noted its shame that Bathonians were failing to get behind the Somerset team, no doubt because of their disgruntlement that the headquarters were at lowly, bucolic Taunton. With no further costly improvements required for the County Ground, the club at last turned in a profit of £100. None of the three newcomers was of any great note, though Robert Spurway was the best of the bunch.

81
Robert Popham Spurway
25 May 1893 v. Sussex, Hove

R. P. Spurway.

A photograph of Robert Spurway at the crease has him looking like a player unschooled in batting techniques. But looks can be deceptive because here was a man who would record an undefeated first-class century and a 50 in his sixteen matches for the club. Born on 16 July 1866 in Heathfield near Taunton, his father, Rev. Edward B. C. Spurway, was an active supporter of Somerset CCC who had held the living at Heathfield since 1856 – a gift from a generous aunt. Proving that it is possible to serve both God and Mammon, Rev. Spurway had made a healthy sum of money by brewing cider, having taken on the business from the previous incumbent. In *The Farming of Somersetshire*, we are informed that 'the best sweet cider is made in the parishes of Kingston [St Mary] and Heathfield ... and may be kept for twenty years without losing its quality' (though this would have required supreme self-control on the part of the purchaser). The running of the family's cider-making business would fall to Edward Popham Spurway. Edward Jnr and Robert would both represent Somerset but whereas the elder brother, Edward, followed in his father's footsteps as a rector-cum-ciderman, Robert opted for a career in the army.

R. P. Spurway – the rumour that he died and was buried at sea was false

He was educated at Sherborne School and Haileybury College before training at Sandhurst and joining first the Worcestershire Regiment and then the Royal Scots (Lothian Regiment) where he rose to the rank of captain in March 1896. Not long after this he was seconded to the Army Pay Department, possibly as a result of health issues. Much of his life was spent toing and froing between England and South Africa and it was for Natal that he made his initial first-class appearance. Although the Spurway family were always ready and willing to help out Somerset, his appearances for the county were inevitably sporadic.

Married in 1896 to Kathleen Mabel (née Prall), a solicitor's daughter, their son was only two months old when Captain Robert Spurway died in Woolwich on 4 December

1898 at the age of thirty-two. Over the years a myth has been promulgated that he died of typhoid fever while aboard ship and returning from Natal. This is incorrect. The truth is far more prosaic. He died at home as a result of peritonitis. Team mate John Poynton states in his recollections that Spurway was 'a delightful man and a good cricketer, helping the county when in difficulty'.

82
Frank Bolus
15 June 1893 v. Yorkshire, Taunton

Born in Wolverhampton on 2 November 1864, Frank Bolus came down to Frome as a teenager and lodged with his brother and sister-in-law, Walter and Elizabeth, who ran a betting shop in the town. Frank and Walter both played club cricket for Frome and the younger man was spotted by Somerset, who employed him as a professional on an ad hoc basis, with ten appearances (and no great success) during the 1893 and 1894 seasons. An all-rounder at club level, he only ever bowled three overs with no wickets for the county and his average of 7.40 with the bat was modest. By 1895 any dreams of a career in county cricket were over and Frank became the landlord of The Angel Hotel in Frome, a less-than-salubrious backstreet establishment.

Frank Bolus – enjoyed more success as a landlord than as a cricket pro

Later, Frank became the landlord at the similarly 'cheap and cheerful' Granville Hotel in Hanley, Stoke-on-Trent. He managed the business with his wife, Sarah Ellen (née Smith), with whom he had two daughters. In a touching example of familial loyalty, Frank repaid the debt to his brother and sister-in-law when he gave house and home to the widowed Elizabeth Bolus, employing her as a barmaid. He died in Coventry on 15 September 1939, aged seventy-four. The picture of him, taken from a Somerset team shot, has him looking more or less as he was: a decent club cricketer and good pub landlord.

83
George Robert Wood
29 June 1893 v. Kent, Tonbridge

George R. Wood,

After a nervous start with a duck in his first innings, George Wood roared back with a half century in the second innings of the match against Kent. Sam Woods recounts in his autobiography that he had wired Rev. Wood asking him to step in when Lionel Palairet went down with appendicitis. The score of 52 should by rights have been higher. According to Sam, the Rev. George Wood had struck the ball high in the air towards a fellow cleric, Rev. William Rashleigh, whom Sam describes as 'a splendid bat but the worst fielder in Europe'. Rashleigh apparently 'picked it up on the long hop and chucked it up. The umpire gave my Christian out. Worst decision I ever saw.' George Wood played two more times for the county and his average of 16.80 over five innings is better than a great many Somerset batsmen.

Rev. George Wood – the victim of what his captain, Sam Woods, described as the 'worst decision I ever saw'

Born in Reading on 7 December 1865, he was brought up in Bromley, one of the eight children who shared the house with an impressive number of servants. After graduating from Merton College, Oxford, George followed his father into the ministry and was for many years the vicar of Almondsbury, near Bristol. He married Kathleen Ethel (née Brady) in 1900 and the couple would live in some comfort with their children and their band of servants and a governess. He lived for many years in Gloucestershire but at the time of his death on 3 September 1948 at the age of eighty-two, Rev. Wood was residing in Lyme Regis: unable, like so many others, to tear himself away from the West Country.

1894

"Somerset have three fine wicket-keepers in Mr Gay, Mr Newton, and the Rev. A. P. Wickham, but in the Canterbury match they were unable to secure the services of anyone of these."

Western Gazette

Championship Position: 6 of 9.

The quotation from the *Western Gazette*'s summary of the 1894 season reveals the ad hoc nature of cricket in a county overly reliant on amateurs. Herbie Hewett had departed to pursue his career as a barrister. Sam Woods was appointed captain. Sam was also given the job of joint-secretary in place of the quietly efficient Thomas Spencer, in order that his amateur status could be preserved. For all his virtues, Sam was ill-equipped for either role. Lionel Palairet now bore the weight of responsibility as a batsman and responded with a hatful of runs, conjuring many a majestic display. Teddy Tyler bagged nearly a hundred wickets. A low point was being bowled out for 31 by Lancashire at Old Trafford, though Somerset mustered six victories over the course of the season. There was earnest discussion about drawing Bath into the fold, though it was observed that the city needed to provide a ground fit for purpose. Having had to make further investments to offer spectators protection against inclement weather, the county ended the year with only 18s 10d in the bank.

The newcomers proved another collection of also-rans with the exception of occasional wicket-keeper Leslie Gay, who played four times for Somerset and once for England.

84
Leslie Hewitt Gay
14 May 1894 v. Middlesex, Lord's

Leslie HGay

He only played four times for Somerset but Leslie Gay earned fame for having represented England both at cricket and football. His only international cricket cap was in the First Test of the 1894-5 tour of Australia, in Sydney. Among his illustrious relatives was Sir Kingsmill Key, captain of Surrey. Perhaps Gay's elevation had something to do with his being well-connected, although he is described at the time as being an excellent wicket-keeper.

The son of a clergyman, he was born in Brighton on 24 March 1871 and educated at Marlborough College, Brighton College and then Clare College, Cambridge, where he gained blues in both his major sports. His appearances for Somerset were all in 1894. Although his links with the county were tenuous, his father had been the rector of Plaitford, in neighbouring Wiltshire. He was also a keen golfer who had played the game in Devon alongside Lionel Palairet. Another possible connection with the South West is provided by Julius Drewe, who had quickly built up a retail empire of Home & Colonel Stores, selling them in 1889 for an enormous sum of money. Drewe retired initially to Wadhurst Hall in Sussex and here the young Leslie Gay acted as his land agent. Drewe had cousins in Devon and before long would move there.

Leslie Gay – an international at football and cricket for whom the phrase 'living a life of gay abandon' was tailor made

Married in 1898 to Marguerite Dora (née Becke), Leslie Gay emigrated soon afterwards to Canada where he was for a while a rancher in Alberta. The couple returned to Hampshire for the birth of their first daughter, leaving her in the care of her paternal grandparents and a wet nurse. Never one to miss an opportunity, Leslie appeared for Hampshire, by then a first-class county. He and Marguerite had returned permanently to England by the time of the birth of their second daughter in 1905, with Leslie working once more as a land agent. The 1911 census reveals the couple now leading separate lives, Marguerite with the daughters in Exmouth and Leslie based in an imposing grace and favour residence in Boughton, near Northampton. Here he found plenty of time to indulge in his passion for sport and captained the Northampton Golf Club. At the outbreak of war he joined the 3rd Lancashires but by November 1915 was passed unfit for further active service owing to duodenal ulcers and varicose veins. He saw out the war in the Royal Defence Corps Headquarters, where he was promoted to the rank of major, a title he would retain in civilian life.

After the war Marguerite lived with her daughters near her family in Bedford while Leslie, describing himself as retired, decamped to Budleigh Salterton in Devon, where he lived in some comfort in a Georgian country house named Lee Ford as the companion of the owner, a young widow named Margaret Helen Cookson. Leslie became the guardian of her son, Richard. He remained an occasional cricketer, also playing golf at the local East Devon club and riding with the North Devon hunt. Margaret Cookson died in 1936, but Leslie continued to reside at Lee Ford until Richard sold the property in 1947. He spent the last three years of his life at the Belmont Hotel in Sidmouth, and finally a nursing home in the town, where he died on 1 November 1949 at the age of seventy-eight. He left his considerable estate to a daughter and not a penny to his longsuffering wife. Leslie Gay had enjoyed a hedonistic lifestyle – one might even venture to suggest one of gay abandon – unfettered by the cares or challenges facing the less well-connected.

85
Albert Harold Westcott
17 May 1894 v. Sussex, Hove

Born in Bridgwater on 6 November 1870, Albert Westcott was the son of a police constable. Indeed, the young Albert has the look of a village bobby about him, although he chose not to pursue that line of work. Instead, he tried out life as a solicitor's clerk, but soon forsook that to take up a career as a professional sportsman. He played his rugby and cricket for Bridgwater and although he was perhaps a better rugby player than a cricketer, professionalism was strictly prohibited in rugby. There is always the whiff of suspicion in such circumstances that a man's continued employment as a cricketer might have been linked to his importance to the rugby team. Certainly many of the same crowd tended to oversee the various sporting activities of a small town. On the rugby field he was deployed as what is now termed a fly-half, although he sometimes played as a full-back. In each case, his intelligent and effective kicking is often praised. G. A. Roberts informs us in *Somerset Rugby Football* that 'his place kicks are remarkably sure' and that 'he looks rather more than his 22 years, is 5 ft 9 in high and weighs 12 stone, being firmly built'. The Somerset team he played in were certainly more successful than their cricketing counterparts, with England internationals Hancock, Ebdon and Gamlin among their number.

Playing cricket for Bridgwater, he was regarded as a bowler who might on odd occasions notch up a decent score. One high point, reported in the *Gloucester Citizen* of 29 July 1902 was his 10 for 8 (in a game for Wellington, rather than Bridgwater) against Bishops Lydeard, although a market town versus a small village sounds suspiciously like a mismatch. When it came to Albert's six appearances for Somerset, this was neither the first nor the last time that Sam Woods (an eccentric and disorganised captain) would deploy a professional bowler more or less exclusively (and unsuccessfully) as a batsman. Sam Woods could be inspiring and exasperating in equal measure. Professionals such as Westcott would be obliged to bite their lips, take the money and depart.

Albert Westcott – a successful club cricketer who made little impression in the first-class game

At the time of the 1911 census he is still listed as a professional cricketer, living in Rowbarton at the age of forty with his wife Annie (née Williams), to whom he had been married in 1889, and their two sons. He was by then earning his keep primarily as a groundsman and coach. Perhaps it was with some reluctance that Albert finally returned to office work. Having moved to Salisbury, where he worked as a commercial clerk, Albert Westcott died in the infirmary at the age of fifty-eight on 6 February 1929 as a result of cancer of the liver and colon.

86
Henry Thomas Stanley
24 May 1894 v. Oxford University, Oxford

H T Stanley

H. T. Stanley – according to Sam Woods he was 'too fond of winning matches'

Although born in Hanover Square on 20 August 1873, Henry was brought up at Quantock Lodge near Over Stowey. A mock-Tudor home built on the grand scale by Lord Taunton, it had passed via the maternal line to Henry Stanley's parents. Hon. Mary Dorothy Labouchere was married to Edward Stanley, who became the local MP from 1882 until 1906.

Henry attended Eton and then Christ Church, Oxford, but failed to make it into the Oxford XI. Where most cricket-mad boys would delight in possessing a cricket bat, Henry had a cricket ground more or less his to use as he wished. It would be the scene of many a delightful coming together of members of the Somerset team. The 'Moonlighters' (the happy band led by Nichols and Tyler) would typically end their September tours at the ground. Sam Woods states in his autobiography that 'we used to have fine games at Quantock Lodge' but adds of Stanley that 'he was too fond of winning matches', hinting that the young host was something of a spoilt brat. Henry's coming of age party in 1894 is given a surprising number of column inches in the local press. Over a thousand members of their vast estate were invited and presentations were made to the young man.

The *Taunton Courier* deferentially records Henry's speech in full. He informs the assembled guests (safe in the knowledge that the vast majority of his partisan audience will never set foot outside the Quantock Hills) that 'I have been to Switzerland and other places abroad, but I do not believe there is any place in the world that can beat Over Stowey'.

The *Bath Chronicle* describes him as 'a batsman of the safe and steady school, his defence was of the soundest possible description'. Elsewhere, we are told that he was 'a rather unattractive batsman with a curious crouch'. His dour approach yielded an average of 16.08 in over fifty first-class matches for Somerset. After the 1899 season,

Lieutenant Stanley of the West Somerset Yeoman Cavalry left to take part in the Boer War. The golden child had the world at his feet. No doubt a period of military service followed by a political career had been mapped out. But on 16 September 1900, aged only twenty-seven, he was killed in a skirmish at Hekpoort, Transvaal. The letters of Corporal P. T. Ross were published after the war (in *A Yeoman's Letters*) and they contain a graphic account of how Stanley was shot in the head and continued to talk 'in a voice like that of a drunken man' before dying. Ross goes on to say that:

> *…in the garden of a Scotchman, named Jennings, by a murmuring, running stream, and beneath some willows, we laid him. By the side of the grave was a bush of Transvaal may, covered in white blossom, at the end were roses to come, and away back and front were the white-covered pear trees and pink-covered peach, perfuming the clear, fresh air, while on the sides of the babbling stream were ferns and a species of white iris.*

Perhaps the twenty-one-year-old Henry Stanley had been wrong. Maybe there were some resting places more beautiful than Over Stowey. Grieving for their son, the parents decided that there would be no more cricket played on the picturesque ground within their estate. It is reported that they planted trees in each of the recognised fielding positions.

87
Harry Walter Swayne
24 May 1894 v. Oxford University, Oxford

Harry Swayne was born on 3 March 1869 in Glastonbury, where his father, Walter Thomas Swayne, practiced as a solicitor. He followed his father into the profession, working in the practice. A regular in the Glastonbury club side, he was invited to play in the match against Oxford University and performed creditably with scores of 8 and 19 not out.

He was married in 1894, to Maude Isabel (née Harris) whose father was a captain in the Indian Army. Maude was the cousin of occasional Somerset cricketer C. H. Alison, whose father – Maude's uncle – was the Chief Constable of Somerset. The edge was taken off any celebrations owing to the death of Maude's father shortly before the wedding. Harry and Maude's son, Cecil, was born the following year. If the death of his father in 1898 was the spur for Harry to seek new opportunities, there is little

H. W. Swayne – a Glastonbury solicitor who joined the ranks of Somerset's one-match wonders. Three years before his only first-class match, Harry Swayne had opened the batting for a Glastonbury & District team who were put to the sword by a rampant George Nichols, who took five cheap wickets before plundering 311 not out from a demoralised Glastonbury bowling attack. In response to a total of 84, Somerset County & Ground amassed 656 for 8 before calling it a day. The one-sided encounter had no doubt bolstered Somerset's confidence ahead of the start of their first Championship campaign. Harry and his teammates would have found it a chastening experience.

doubt that Maude's connections with India shaped the decision for him to undertake legal work for the civil authorities in that country. His death in Pertapur, Mairwa, India, on 25 November 1911 at the age of forty-two, was sudden and unexpected. It would prove just one in a series of misfortunes to befall the men in Maude's life. In 1913, she was married to Edward Joseph Bull, an engineer, but he died in Chupra, India, in 1915. Maude retired to Burnham-on-Sea but in 1917 news would reach her that her only son, Cecil, had died of appendicitis in Quetta. Having already endured more than her fair share of tragedy, Maude lived a quiet life in Burnham-on-Sea until her death in 1940.

88
Ezra William Bartlett
11 June 1894 v. Kent, Canterbury

Ezra Bartlett's parents hailed from the West Country but work as a railway guard had taken his father to Doncaster, where Ezra was born on 26 September 1861, and then to Burton-on-Trent, where he was raised. Ezra came down to Taunton to take up a position as a telegraphist and clerk at the Taunton Post Office, though his behaviour was not always what his employers might have looked for in a conscientious and sober clerk. A scandal erupted in 1887, filling a fair few column inches of the local press when he 'was charged with having on 12th April 1887, unlawfully committed an indecent assault upon Martha Knight, wife of Frederick Levi Knight, Landlord'. Bartlett had been a frequent lodger at the Fleur de Lys Inn. On the night in question the landlord and landlady were overseeing the catering at an Easter Monday bash at the nearby Victoria Rooms. Bartlett arrived at the event at four o'clock in the morning and stayed until gone six o'clock. By the time he staggered back to the Fleur de Lys, Mrs Knight had collapsed on her bed, too tired to have bothered changing, and fallen sound asleep. Bartlett had entered her room and (unbeknown to Martha Knight, who had no recollection of events) begun to undress and molest her. After hearing the commotion, a servant burst in and saved what was left of Martha's honour. On arriving home, the enraged husband summoned the police, who arrested Bartlett. Two weeks in prison offered ample time for the young man to reassess the trajectory of his life and he made a full apology. We are informed that his solicitor stated that 'it was the act of a drunken man, and he was instructed by the prisoner to withdraw any imputations reflecting on the character of Mrs Knight', whereupon Frederick Knight (possibly with one eye on the prospect of future rent from his lodger) dropped the charge. A familiar tale, then, of a young sportsman fuelled by an excess of alcohol and testosterone into making unwelcome advances, but at least Bartlett had the good grace to show contrition.

The following year, he was married to Louisa (née Brown), a local girl. She was either a very forgiving lady or blissfully unaware of the events that had recently unfolded. Settling down to the more wholesome pursuits of clerical work and cricket, he was able to put the shameful episode behind him. Ezra was a successful club cricketer. An obituary in the *Taunton Courier* says that until his dying day he retained a bat to the back of which had been attached plaques presented to him when he had headed the averages for various club sides, including Norton Fitzwarren. His Championship career was less successful. In twelve first-class innings, he averaged 11.45.

Ezra Bartlett – employed for many years by the Taunton Post Office

He worked for forty years for the Taunton Post Office. He and Louisa had seven daughters, all of whom predeceased them. He remained a regular spectator at the County Ground. Ezra Bartlett died in Taunton on 16 March 1942 at the age of eighty, the whiff of shame over his roistering past having dissipated and not even a hint of it sullying his obituary in the local paper.

89
Edward Denison Compton
14 June 1894 v. Gloucestershire, Bristol

Edward · Denison · Compton.

He might bear a famous cricketing surname but his perform-ances were hardly worthy of the name. A duck and a 'did not bat' were all he had to show for his outing against Glouces-tershire and in seven innings for Somerset, he scraped together an average of 3.80. Edward Compton is one of a bewildering number of people who kept wicket for the county in the early years.

Born in Frome on 11 April 1872, he was the eleventh of seventeen children of Rev. Thomas Compton and his wife Emma. Edward was despatched at a young age to Chardstock College, then run by Henry M. Robinson, who styled himself 'Head Master of Chardstock College, Curate in Charge of Membury, Devon, Doctor of Divinity, Pembroke College, Oxford'.

E. D. Compton pictured as a young schoolmaster at King's School, Bruton

Edward Compton then went to Lancing College before returning to Somerset to take up a post as an assistant master at King's School, Bruton, where he spent his leisure time actively involved in sport. He played football as a centre forward for Bruton, netting nine goals in one match against Batcombe Rectory. He also starred for Bath and for Wells, scoring goals with great frequency and being selected to play for Somerset.

His achievements as a cricketer were less noteworthy, but he was nevertheless selected to play for Somerset. In 1893, he left Bruton to take a place belatedly at Keble College, Oxford, to study Modern History, winning a blue for football but not for cricket. His third-class degree was in all proba-bility an indication of time spent playing sport when he should perhaps have been studying.

Edward took up a teaching post at Summerfields School in 1896. Between 1896 and 1902 he appeared for Oxfordshire in Minor Counties cricket. He was married in

1900 to Annie Maud (née May) and three years later moved to St Leonards-on-Sea, Sussex, after being appointed headmaster of the newly-formed Summerfields Preparatory School, an institution that would gain a reputation as a place of learning for dukes and royalty, including members of the royal families of Monaco and Jordan. His appearance for Somerset against Sussex on 25 July 1907 (where he kept wicket at the age of thirty-five) is something of an aberration. Somerset were a man short. The county of his birth against his adoptive home. Would he step into the breach? Somerset were of course by then a hopeless case, but such is the appeal of the game of cricket, such is the allure of playing for your county, that he agreed to turn out for them. The headmaster reliving his schoolboy dream. He needn't have bothered as Somerset were hammered by Sussex by 9 wickets, within two days.

On retiring, Edward Compton became actively involved in local politics in Rye, Sussex, serving for many years as a councillor. He died there on 11 October 1940, aged sixty-eight.

90
David Linzee Evans
12 July 1894 v. Nottinghamshire, Trent Bridge

David Evans had played previously for Gloucestershire but the game against Nottinghamshire was his first for Somerset. The younger brother of fellow Somerset cricketer Ernest, he was born on 13 April 1869, in West Town, Somerset. As a boy, he attended Loretto School, Musselburgh, where another older brother, Harry Lode Evans (a Scotland rugby player who completed his medical degree at Edinburgh University) would have kept a watchful eye on him. The Evans brothers were part of a dynasty whose wealth came from the successful Bristol tannery business of P. N. Evans & Co.

On returning home, David Evans was soon given his first exposure to county cricket by Gloucestershire. The *Gloucester Citizen* informs us that at Loretto 'in 1887 he was spoken of as an uncertain bat and successful bowler, but in the following year he weakened in his powers of attack, but proportionately improved in batting'. He managed a 50 in only his second game for Gloucestershire. A reporter notes that the young man 'to whom Dr

D. L. Evans – hampered throughout his career by ill health

D. L. Evans

Grace has taken a fancy' may, through no fault of his own, have been the cause of a draw against Sussex because, as the paper put it, 'the Champion delayed closing his innings until the colt had got his half century' and Sussex survived by the skin of their teeth.

Married in 1895 to Grace Eleanor (née Harris), his happiest times were spent playing for the village of Flax Bourton alongside fellow Somerset players Theo Robinson and wicketkeeper Harry Chidgey. For many years he would be vice-captain and one of the mainstays of the club, turning in decent performances with bat and ball.

Having registered for Somerset, he played for them fifteen times. A top score of 60 and an average of 10.77 suggests that he was yet another good club player who could not make the grade at county level. He is described as a 'hard-hitting batsman' but he suffered from ill health for many years and would often leave for sunnier climes in the winter months 'and come back much improved'.

The *Western Daily Press* of 13 November reports that on 11 November 1907, David Linzee Evans had died in West Town at the age of thirty-seven. With the usual reluctance to give precise details, the paper states that 'lately his condition had given cause for much anxiety, and on Saturday last an operation had to be performed. Although this was successfully carried out, he had not sufficient strength to recover, and sank rapidly from exhaustion'. The definition of a 'successful operation' on the part of the surgeon is a generous one.

David Evans left behind a widow, three children and a Flax Bourton Cricket Club who felt his loss keenly enough to erect a plaque in the pavilion in which he had spent many happy hours of a life blighted by ill health but sweetened by the compensation of ample wealth and leisure time.

91
Percy John Ebdon
16 July 1894 v. Lancashire, Old Trafford

Percy John Ebdon

Born in Milverton on 16 March 1874, Percy Ebdon was one of three brothers who would each make fleeting appearances in the Somerset side. A talented all-round sportsman, he excelled at rugby. G. A. Roberts informs us in *Somerset Rugby Football* that Ebdon was 'a wiry, non-shirking forward, standing 5 feet 9¼ inches and weighing 12st 4 lb'. In 1897 he represented England twice – against Wales and Ireland. That came three years after his brief cameo for Somerset CCC.

In 1903 he was married to Nina Mary (née Gush), who worked in her father's drapery shop in Wellington. Percy had similarly followed in the footsteps of his father, John Ebdon, training as an accountant while working at Fox's Woollen Mills in Wellington, where he would spend the whole of his working life and would rise to the position of company secretary, retiring in 1939. The company was a major employer in the area and had a global reputation for quality, with celebrities and royalty numbered among their customers. It was a position of enormous responsibility for a local boy made good. He also became a director of the Wellington Building Society. His appointment during the Second World War as the fuel overseer for the Wellington district is an indication of his reputation for efficiency and tight control of the purse strings. The role required him to manage the allocation of licenses to coal merchants and to make daily decisions over increased fuel allowances for individuals who suffered 'altered conditions' or who had

Percy Ebdon found more fame as a rugby international than as a Somerset cricketer

taken on evacuees or refugees. He liaised regularly with the local press who urged the public to cut down on consumption, upbraiding those who left 'unscreened cinders' for the rubbish collection or had stockpiled coal. By his efforts, he managed to avert a crisis of fuel availability in the town.

Back in his distant past his employers had clearly been liberal in allowing him to pursue his sporting interests, which included playing as a hockey forward for Wellington and Somerset, as a rugby forward for Wellington, Somerset and England, and – perhaps least successfully – as a cricketer for Wellington and Somerset, where his two games for the county yielded 13 runs and an average of 3.25. As ever, his prowess as a rugby player would have been all that his friend Sam Woods would have required to draft him into the cricket team.

After a short but active retirement from business Percy Ebdon died in Wellington on 16 February 1943 whilst still in his role as fuel overseer. He was sixty-eight.

92
Thomas Wood
23 July 1894 v. Lancashire, Taunton

An accomplished musician – principally a violinist but also an organist – Tom Wood knew all about a stirring beginning and a triumphant finale, although his 11 runs in his one innings for his county hardly ranks as his finest entrance. Although born on 2 June 1861 in Leominster, Tom was brought up in Taunton where his father was a 'professor of music' and Tom and his three brothers all proved accomplished musicians. After a brief spell teaching in Seaton, he went on to become the music teacher at the Independent College (soon to be renamed Taunton School) whilst also acting as organist and choirmaster at St James's church. He had shown promise from a young age, having joined the choir of St Mary's church, Taunton, as a seven year old and in time had been made 'the leading alto'. In later years he put his considerable energy into various productions as a music master. Undaunted by a challenge, he oversaw perform-

ances by his boys of Handel's *Messiah* and excerpts of Mozart's *Requiem*, with staff being cajoled into taking part. Both were deemed a triumph by the local press. He is also credited with being the driving force behind the introduction of cricket at Taunton School. A report in the *Taunton Courier* sheds light on his unconventional methods:

> *He was not only a good player himself, but he was able to teach others in an extraordinary way. He used to take photographs of different poses and arrange them around his room; the boys were then brought in and had to stand in exactly the same positions as the men depicted on the photographs. He certainly turned out some very good cricketers in his time.*

He enjoyed consistent success with the bat for Taunton over a period of twenty years, often keeping wicket and occasionally bowling. A number of centuries are recorded and Taunton seem at times to have been overly reliant on him. Tom Wood also took part in the 'Moonlighters' tours, led by the amiable Somerset professionals, Tyler and Nichols. A typical itinerary has them visiting the seaside towns of Minehead, Porlock and Lynton before finishing the tour as guests

Tom Wood – a much-loved schoolmaster and a talented musician

of Henry Stanley at his father's private cricket ground at Quantock Lodge, Over Stowey. Great fun would have been had by all and we can be sure that Tom Wood brought out his violin and set aside any classical pretensions to perform some fiddling of a more rustic variety than he was accustomed to.

From the mid-1890s he took up temporary posts teaching music at Queen's College and King's College, both in Taunton. Then, in June 1902, the musician brought the first section of his life to a close and emigrated to South Africa. On 18 June 1902, he was the guest of honour at a meal hosted by the Mayor of Taunton. The list of attendees includes the great and the good of the town and the departing hero was presented with an illuminated testimonial, signed by 150 subscribers, together with 'a purse which had been knitted by a lady admirer, containing 40 sovereigns'. A rousing send-off for a man who had given much to the town and its grateful residents. While residing in Pretoria, he was married in Cape Town in 1911, aged forty-nine, to Arabella Clara Anna (née Deyns), known as Bella. In his new surroundings he continued to indulge his passions for music and cricket. At the age of sixty-four, he rode 100 miles through the Transvaal on his motorcycle to play in a match, scored 100 runs and then rode the 100 miles back home again.

He was still playing cricket at seventy-one when, on 15 March 1933, at Potchefstroom, Transvaal, he ran a single, reached the other end, collapsed and died instantly. The most dramatic of finales for an engaging, talented and energetic man.

Tom Wood keeping wicket for Quantock Lodge in 1891: behind him stands Tom Armstrong, the Notts professional

1895

"After many misfortunes, [Somerset] finished up in brilliant form, beating in succession Surrey, Yorkshire and Gloucestershire."

Western Times

Championship Position: 8 of 14

Five additional counties had joined the Championship – Derbyshire, Essex, Hampshire, Leicestershire and Warwickshire. It was typical of Somerset that late in the season they should win with ease against the county champions, Surrey, after some woeful performances earlier on. The nadir had been the match against Lancashire, when they were put to the sword by Archie MacLaren, who plundered a record-breaking 424 runs. Lionel Palairet continued to shine brightly with the bat and Teddy Tyler claimed 123 wickets and an England cap. High points included Tyler's 10 for 49 against Surrey at the County Ground and an opening stand of 205 between Lionel Palairet and Gerald Fowler against Gloucestershire at Bristol. Six wins and eight losses were recorded. George Nichols was granted a benefit match for his years of honest toil. He serves as a fine example of a Somersetshire cricketer: wholehearted and capable of stirring deeds at club level but rarely able to hit the heights at county level.

Among the debutants, Ernie Robson would give the county years of useful service once he had qualified by residency and Herbert Gamlin became a household name, though this was because he is deemed one of the greatest full backs ever to have played rugby for England.

93
William Barnett Sloman
13 May 1895 v. Cambridge University, Cambridge

William Barnett Sloman

William Sloman had been drafted into the side after an excellent performance in the trial match, where he scored an unbeaten century. The *Exeter & Plymouth Gazette* of 11 May 1895 furnishes us with the details:

> *The game may be described as an entire success, inasmuch as has been the means of discovering two good men who are likely to find places in the Somerset County team. These are {Jack} Bucknell, of Bedminster, and W Sloman, of Minehead ... Sloman, who played a very good and stylish innings for his 104, not out, in which he gave only one chance, and that on the boundary when he had made 89, will also play for Somerset against Cambridge.*

For many years, Sloman's trail has lain cold, though only through an error of transcription that has him as 'W. H. Sloman'. The man who played for Somerset was William Barnett Sloman, who would play his cricket for Minehead, Nichols and Tyler's 'Moonlighters', the West Somerset Licensed Victuallers and – on four occasions – Somerset. He was born in Minehead on 3 February 1871 and brought up among a family of inn keepers. His grandfather, William, and grandmother, Anne, had run the Horse and Crooks inn at Dunster and his father, Richard, and mother, Jane Amelia, had followed suit, running the Queen's Head Hotel in Minehead, while they raised their young family.

In 1878, when William was still only six, his father died and five years later, he lost his mother. In the intervening period, he had been admitted on 24 April 1882 to George Mildon's School at Alcombe, a mile from Minehead. William's older brother, Harry, would take the reins before long at the Queen's Head, assisted by William. The brothers would appear to have each inherited a half share in the busi-

W. B. Sloman – fast-tracked into the Somerset side after scoring a stylish century in the 1895 trial match

The Queen's Head, Minehead: painted in 1880, shortly after the death of William's father and later jointly-owned by William Barnett Sloman. The artist, Harry Frier, completed many watercolours of scenes around Taunton and Minehead and enjoyed commercial success, but died a penniless, homeless drunk. No doubt a few pints in the Queen's Head after he had packed his easel away will have contributed to his ruin.

ness. For a while William was obliged to work rather than play, but he would find time to pursue his interest in the game and be good enough to catch the county's eye in 1895, when he was twenty-four years old.

William Sloman was one of four debutants in the Somerset side who played Cambridge University. He continued the form he had shown in the trial match days earlier when he scored 48 in the first innings but in three further games, his scores fell away. He ended up with a batting average of 12.12 and took 1 wicket for 7 runs. Among his four games was the match against Gloucestershire – William's baptism in the Championship – won easily by Somerset, largely owing to a century by Sam Woods. George Nichols was dismissed in the first innings for the rare crime of 'hit the ball twice'. Nichols had apparently stopped the ball from spinning back onto his stumps and then in his confusion had set off for a run. Inevitably, it was W. G. Grace who had appealed.

In 1905 William was married to Tryphena (née Harper). The birth of their son on 12 Feb 1906 was announced in the local press. But tragedy soon struck. On 28 April 1906, months after his son's birth, William Barnett Sloman was dead at the age of thirty-five. The cause of death was tuberculosis. Poignantly, knowing that his death was imminent, William had drafted his will just three days earlier, leaving his share of the Queen's Head Hotel to his wife and son. And yet, within months the son (also named William Barnett Sloman) had died in infancy. Left to share the running of the hotel and perhaps displaying admirable pragmatism, Tryphena was married again within three months of William Snr's death.

His was a short life in which he had met with triumph and disaster and an even briefer career as a cricketer – initially one of great promise – where any triumphs and disasters paled into insignificance.

94
Alfred Graham Richardson
13 May 1895 v. Cambridge University, Cambridge

Alfred Richardson was born on 24 July 1875 in the Bedfordshire town of Sandy, where his father was for many years the vicar. Rev. John Richardson had previously lived in Clifton. Married to Ellen, they had had five children before she died in childbirth. Undeterred by this setback, Rev. Richardson was then married to Helen Graham (née Nash) with whom he would have a further ten children, including Alfred. Among Alfred's fourteen siblings, a stepbrother, Frederick Stuart Richardson, won renown as a prolific painter.

A. G. Richardson was poached by Somerset for one game but became a Gloucestershire player before leaving for South Africa

Educated at King's School, Canterbury, Alfred went up to Corpus Christi, Cambridge. He was invited to play for Somerset against his university. Somerset's claims on him were as valid as any other first-class county, given that his mother hailed from Cossington, in the north of the county. His scores of 40 and 35 were creditable, though neither his contribution nor a swashbuckling 180 by Sam Woods were enough to avert a heavy defeat. This would be his only game for Somerset as after leaving Cambridge, for whom he played twice, he threw in his lot with Gloucestershire, on the basis that his father had lived in Clifton for a number of years before becoming vicar of Sandy.

After graduating, he became an assistant master at Forest School, Walthamstow (better known in cricketing circles as the alma mater of England captain, Nasser Hussein). He played twenty times for Gloucestershire between 1897 and 1901, though he never hit the heights as a batsman.

In 1905 he left to become an assistant master at Grey College, Bloemfontein, remaining there until 1917 and playing for Orange Free State six times. Between 1917 and 1934 he was the headmaster at Umtata High School, in the Eastern Cape. He was married to a German music teacher there: they would have two daughters. The younger, who went by the moniker 'Kitten', became an inspirational English teacher and, later, headmistress of Victoria Girls' High School in Grahamstown.

Alfred Richardson died in Umtata at the age of sixty on 17 December 1935. Such was his popularity that the cathedral was packed to overflowing at his funeral service.

95
Ernest Robson
13 May 1895 v. Cambridge University, Cambridge

'Robbie' – adored by the Somerset supporters for the quiet way in which he gave his all for his adoptive county

Ernie Robson (often referred to in cricketing circles as 'Robbie') was born in Chapeltown, Leeds, on 10 May 1870 and would bring to the team some of that Yorkshire grit and capacity for unrelenting hard work that the county sorely needed. He would come to Somerset, already a seasoned pro at the age of twenty-five and would then serve the county for an astonishing twenty-eight years. He had started out playing club cricket and representing Cheshire between 1891 and 1893 before being taken on as a pro by Colne in Lancashire League cricket. Here, he caught Somerset's roving eye and they registered him. He played against Oxford and Cambridge Universities in 1895 (with no great success) but Somerset's faith was rewarded almost immediately when he made useful contributions with bat and ball in 1896.

Robbie was an undemonstrative man – many said he was very shy, although he came into his own on the stage when persuaded to set aside his pipe, put down his pint and sing in what the local newspaper called 'a pleasing tenor voice'. He was a competent batsman, who would score five centuries and forty-six 50s for the county. In 1899 he became the first Somerset pro to reach 1,000 first-class runs in a season. As for his bowling, he began his career as a fast-medium right-arm bowler but inevitably slowed over the years. His great asset was apparently his ability to maintain a relentless line and length. C. B. Fry wrote that Robbie had the knack of hurrying the batsman with the unexpected pace off the wicket.

The Somerset supporters adored him, valuing the wholehearted contribution of the man who came down to Taunton, made it his home and stayed playing for Somerset into his fifties. Robbie treated both triumph and disaster with equanimity, never ruffled and mustering the slightest of smiles when congratulated for a match-winning performance. For many years he managed the Frieze Hill Inn, on Richmond Road, Taunton, along with his wife, Mary Jane (née Jones), who hailed from Lancashire. It is indicative of how poorly paid the pros were that the club and supporters were regularly coming up with ideas to supplement their income: even running a pub still left Robbie and his family short. He was given two benefit years and supporters contributed in other ways. There was, for example, a collection of 210 shilling pieces when he scored a century against Surrey. Robbie's last season in county cricket – 1923 – proved a difficult time as he was losing a considerable amount of weight and looking 'exceedingly ill'. In May 1924, he was taken from his home in Taunton to Bristol Royal Infirmary where he was operated on to remove a cancerous growth. He was in fact riddled with the disease and died at the infirmary on 23 May 1924, aged fifty-four. The club and supporters rallied around and granted a benefit match to his wife that season. The *Taunton Courier*, recalling the sense of unruffled calm that he exuded, noted that 'his seraphic walk to the wicket was always sure to evoke a rousing cheer' and the *Western Daily Press* asserted that 'he was a man of fine character, and was much liked, not only by members of his own team but by those of other counties'. Ever a modest man, Ernie Robson would have mustered no more than a hint of a smile on hearing such praise.

For many years Ernie Robson made telling contributions with bat and ball

96
John Bucknell
13 May 1895 v. Cambridge University, Cambridge

The cricket archives have long recorded that Jack Bucknell played for Somerset on ten occasions. This is in fact incorrect. Jack only played for the county four times: three times during the 1895 season and once in 1899. The other appearances by 'Bucknell' – between 1899 and 1905 – were by his younger brother, Arthur.

Born on 7 June 1872 in Bedminster, Jack was the son of a solicitor's clerk. Tragically, Jack's mother died in 1879 at the age of twenty-nine and the boys would thereafter be brought up by their father. Jack became a schoolmaster while playing his club cricket for Bedminster. Invited to play in trial matches for Somerset in 1894 and 1895, he put together a compelling case for inclusion in the county side. The *Exeter & Plymouth Gazette* informs us that in the trial match of May 1895:

> *Bucknell of Bedminster ... a right-handed bowler with a medium pace, who can make the ball turn both ways, met with so much success and bowled so effectively that he has accepted an invitation to play for the county against Cambridge University.*

Jack Bucknell is described as 'strongly built' and a 'sound consistent bat with a strong defence'. Elsewhere he is reported to have been 'a capital slow-medium bowler who specialised in leg-breaks'. After joining Darlington CC in 1896 he was employed by Brechin for a year before returning to Darlington in 1898. There were further engagements with league sides – including Burnley St Andrews and Buxton – before he returned to Darlington in 1907 as an amateur and later became the club captain. Before his retirement, in 1913, he gathered together a hand-picked XI each year to take on Sir E. D. Walker's XI. In his team were a number of county players: Jack was apparently a well-known and popular in the first-class game.

At the end of the season he applied successfully for the role of professional cricketer with Darlington. One of 36 applicants for the job, his sponsors were Dr E. M. Grace and Sam Woods: such endorsements would have smoothed the path at his interview.

Four years later his brother, Arthur, enjoying success as a pro in the Midlands, was invited to play for Somerset. In July 1899, Jack's turn came to make his fourth and final appearance for the county. He made the trip down to Hull and the original scorebook, still in Somerset's possession, bears the name of 'J. Bucknell', although he appears in reports as 'Bucknell', suggesting that he received payment for this last appearance and the scorer is distinguishing between the two brothers. Jack failed to take a wicket, but was praised for the way he came in at number nine and held his own in a sterling partnership with Sam Woods in which Bucknell 'offered up serious opposition to the bowling'. Indeed, his batting was generally much sounder than Arthur's. In eight innings, he totalled 93 runs at an average of 18.60, boosted by his being not out in each of his first three innings. His highest score of 33 came against Oxford University. Jack took a total of 7 first-class wickets at 48.29 runs apiece, with best bowling figures of 3 for 93 against Cambridge University. He continued to be employed at various clubs as a pro, also appearing in the Durham county side. In 1905 he was married to Maria Thompson, one of the three daughters of Harry Thompson, who ran the Black Swan Hotel in Darlington and played Minor Counties cricket for Durham. For a while the newly-weds took over the running of the Waterloo Hotel, also in Darlington. His career was terminated by injury. The *Daily Gazette for Middlesbrough* announces on 1 May 1914 that:

> He has for a considerable time past suffered with an injured left knee which prevented him from playing for Darlington all last season, and this week it has been found necessary to amputate the leg … Mr Bucknell is progressing very favourably. He will, however, be a great loss to local cricket.

He died in Darlington on 5 March 1925 at the age of fifty-two.

97
Robert Bagehot Porch
20 May 1895 v. Oxford University, Oxford

Robert Bagehot Porch

Somerset continued to embrace amateurism and turn to the well-heeled members of society. Robert Bagehot Porch certainly fell into the category of the well-connected and wealthy Somerset amateur. Born on 3 April 1875 in Weston-super-Mare, he was brought up in Edgarley House, near Glastonbury, a house that would become inextricably linked with Somerset CCC when R. J. O. Meyer bought the place (renamed as Edgarley Hall) in 1945 and refashioned it as the Junior School for Millfield, home of an impressive number of future sportsmen, some notable Somerset cricketers among them.

Robert Porch came from a successful banking family, though he would pursue a career in teaching rather than finance. His grandfather Thomas Porch Porch (born Porch Reeves) had founded the enterprise that became the Glastonbury & Shepton Mallet Bank until it was bought by Stuckey's Bank of Langport (run by the Bagehot family) in 1835. They were later acquired by National Westminster Bank. Educated at Malvern College, Robert had made it into their First XI but his performances were not stellar. He went up to Trinity College, Oxford, but failed to gain his blue.

R. B. Porch, starting out as a cricketer (top) and photographed in 1961 (above), by then a venerable figure at Malvern College

Perhaps recognising that the snub would be all the motivation he needed, Somerset selected him for their game against the University in 1895. He scored 42 in the second innings. The momentum continued when he scored 85 not out against Essex. He might have had time to ponder whether county cricket was as alluring as he had been led to believe, though, as he stood in the field. Essex amassed a dispiriting total of 692. They were followed in the next game by Lancashire, who, with Archie MacLaren leading the charge, piled on 801. Perhaps Porch lost a little of his appetite for the game. He never managed to replicate his earlier successes and in twenty-seven first-class games between 1895 and 1910, his average slowly slipped to 15.46.

Malvern College also made calls on his time, given that he had gone back to his alma mater as a schoolmaster and would remain happily ensconced there for many years, known to generations of schoolboys as 'Judy' (a possible corruption of Punch and Judy). In 1919, he was married at forty-four to Kathleen Mitchell (née Hector), aged twenty-six, who had attended the Malvern College for Girls.

He loved his school and was appointed president of the Old Malvernians' Club. Unable to tear himself away from the place, he died in Great Malvern on 29 October 1962 at the age of eighty-seven. In his obituary, *Wisden* highlights the emphasis he placed on the importance of fielding. He is quoted as saying 'save six fours when the other side is batting and you have 24 to your name before you get off the mark, though it's not in the score-book'. Perhaps Archie MacLaren had been short-changed when he had only scored 424 off the Somerset attack.

98
Frederick Lewis Bishop Jennings
13 June 1895 v. Essex, Leyton

Frederick's grandfather, Thomas Jennings, ran a thriving tailoring business in Blagdon, just outside Taunton. Frederick Jennings, grandson of Thomas, was born on 18 March 1874 in Taunton. His mother – Sarah Jane – was unmarried. His biological father was almost certainly Frederick ('Fred') Underdown Bishop, the son of a carter, who had grown up knowing the Jennings family and attending school with them. Sarah Jane was a dressmaker and the census of 1871 informs us that she has 'hip disease', suggesting that she was markedly disabled. She would have been twenty at the time of the birth of Frederick Jennings, while the father would have been twenty-one.

Late in 1891, Fred Bishop and Sarah Jane were married in Poplar; perhaps a case of expediency, rather than a rekindling of any romance, helping to rid their offspring of the stigma of illegitimacy. Frederick Jnr trained as a teacher at University College, London. He lived with his mother – but not his father – in Poplar, London, where she continued to work as a dressmaker. Frederick was offered a job teaching at the Plashet Lane Council School in East Ham and he would remain there throughout his career.

By 1901, Frederick Jennings, still at the same house in Poplar, is listed as head of the house and a schoolteacher, with his 'aunt', Sarah Jane Bishop, living with him and still a dressmaker. Her husband was residing with his aged parents in Trull, working as a postman and gardener. Later, he became a farm labourer in Chard. He would in fact die in Taunton in 1922, suggesting that he never lived with Sarah Jane and Frederick Jnr.

Frederick played his club cricket in London and in 1895 took part in trial matches both for Essex and Somerset. In the Essex Colts v. Essex fixture at the end of April, things went badly. Absent for the first innings, he was dismissed by the fearsome pace bowler Kortright in the second innings. He was not alone. In that innings, Kortright claimed the impressive bowling figures of 13 for 21 as the seventeen men of the Colts were skittled out by the Essex eleven. Frederick Jennings was not alone in suffering at hands of Charles Kortright. Believed by many to be the fastest bowler of his generation, Kortright is rumoured to have 'sledged' W. G. Grace – a sore loser, ever ready to bend the rules to his advantage. Kortright supposedly asked loudly why Grace was headed back towards the pavilion, observing that only two stumps had been flattened and the third was still standing.

Two weeks later, back in the place of his birth for a Somerset trial match, he did himself more justice with a knock of 43 and the prized scalp of Lionel Palairet, whom he clean bowled. Somerset drafted him into the side for the away fixture against the Essex team who had just rejected him. This would be his only first-class game. The demon pace man Kortright bagged Frederick's wicket again in the second innings, leaving him with an average of 3.5. It had been a chastening experience for the schoolmaster, although, after having faced the bowling of the formidable Charles Jesse Kortright, handling a class of schoolchildren would surely have held no fears. The school log books confirm that Frederick was form master for a group of over fifty boys and that he had additional responsibilities as a history teacher, combining this at various times with supplementary subjects as various as geography and hygiene.

In 1921, at the age of forty-seven, he was married to Mabel (née Thompson), twelve years his junior. There to witness the wedding was his sixty-seven-year-old mother, Sarah Jane. Frederick and Mabel lived in Leytonstone for many years. His devoted mother, Sarah Jane, died in 1931.

After retiring from the teaching profession, he moved with his wife to Harrow, although he died at Boscombe on 21 December 1946, aged seventy-two.

99
Herbert Tremlett Gamlin
11 July 1895 v. Essex, Taunton

H. T. Gamlin – regarded as one of the finest of England's rugby full-backs

Born on 12 February 1878 in Wellington and a pupil at Wellington School, Gamlin was already well-built and an intimidating presence at the age of seventeen. He had also already represented Somerset both at cricket and rugby by that age, but it was as an England rugby international that he would find fame. He would represent his country fifteen times between 1899 and 1904. Herbert Gamlin had not taken up the game until the age of fourteen. Association football was the code of choice at Wellington School. Having not been coached in rugby, his methods were unorthodox. When it came to his 'long raking touch-finders' his schooling had served him well but when he caught the ball he did so away from his body, rather than hugging it as was normally the case. His huge hands and superb hand-eye coordination meant that he rarely dropped the ball. When tackling, he took opponents early by throwing himself towards them and 'smothering' both man and ball. Sam Woods said that Gamlin 'not only brought down a man *but shook him* [in the sense of leaving him shaken]'.

His tackling earned him the moniker 'Octopus'. In *Football: The Rugby Union Game*, published in 1925, Rev. F. Marshall states that 'Somerset provided England with their best full-back in Gamlin'. A description in the *Gloucester Echo* of the twenty-year-old Gamlin, selected for the game against Wales in January 1900, tells us that:

> *He is half an inch over six feet and weighing a little more than fourteen stone, and he is a teetotaller and non-smoker … A prodigious left kick, with a cat-like tackle.*

Even at the time of his death, people were still talking in awed tones of one particular performance against Scotland at Edinburgh in 1902. The Scots had overrun England, but on upwards of a dozen occasions Gamlin had tackled his man in one-on-one situations. With twenty-five minutes to go, England were somehow ahead, with two tries to Scotland's one. Scotland threw the kitchen sink at Gamlin but time and again he came to his side's rescue. England won the game 6-3: two tries to one. Even the most begrudging of the Scottish crowd must have realised that they had witnessed greatness. Very probably because of his prowess as a rugby player, he was offered employment at Devonport as a clerk and turned out regularly for Devonport Albion.

Herbert Gamlin had starred as a schoolboy bowler, with the high point being his 6 for 2 against Blundell's School. A right-arm off-spinner, he made his debut against Essex. In the following match, on 15 July 1895, he took the wicket of Lancashire's Archie MacLaren on a placid track at the County Ground, Taunton. Regrettably, MacLaren already had a record-breaking 424 runs to his name. As for his batting, Herbert managed two sets of pairs over his first two games. In his third and final game, he did at least cobble together seven runs.

He was married in 1903 to Olivia (née Lanyon) in Wellington but his work for the Admiralty would mean that his family would be brought up in Surrey. At the time of his death on 12 July 1937, in Pylford Bridge, Cheam, fifty-nine-year-old Herbert Gamlin was an 'official in the department of the Directory of Dockyards to the Admiralty'. His obituaries focus on his abilities as a rugby player rather than as a civil servant or cricketer.

100
William Robert Rutherford Smith
22 August 1895 v. Surrey, Taunton

William Robert Smith

William Smith hailed from Yorkshire. His father, John, had served for a brief while in the army before becoming a cricketing pro. In the modern age, when watching top-level sport is straightforward, given the media coverage and ease of transport, it is perhaps worth recalling that paying to see a local club side was the only option open to many, so that there was a wider and more equitable spread of income to be had among the raft of professionals. John Smith's career took him to places as far apart as Scotland and Wiltshire. He ended his cricketing journey as an umpire. Between his professional appointments, he squeezed in spells as a pub landlord in order to supplement his income. The most peripatetic of upbringings for his family and yet two of his sons – William and Douglas – caught the bug and became professional cricketers. Another son, Arthur, became landlord at the Golden Lion Inn, in Worcester.

William Smith was born on 23 April 1871 in Batley, where for a while his parents ran the Old Mill Inn. Their lives were not without incident. In February 1881, a dissolute named Charles Briggs, repeatedly gaoled for being drunk and disorderly and refusing to work despite having a sick wife and seven children to support, was given a sentence of four week's imprisonment with hard labour for stealing a clock from the Old Mill.

Trying his luck as a professional cricketer in Worcestershire, William worked for a while in the off-season as a drayman. Delivering barrels of beer was deemed preferable to serving the stuff to the drunk and disorderly. By the age of twenty he was turning out as a pro for the then second-tier county of Worcestershire.

William Smith during his time as the pro at Bath CC

He showed enough promise to attract the attention of Somerset, for whom he would play in six first-class matches, averaging only 6.25 with the bat and failing to take any wickets. For a while he became the pro at Bath. On moving to Wiltshire, whom he played for in Minor Counties cricket, he made his mark at a less elevated level than the County Championship, primarily as a strike bowler but also as a useful batsman.

His life as a child had been nomadic because of his father's preparedness to go wherever he must to earn a living. William chose a more settled life after having been married to Edith (née Crow), a Marlborough girl, in 1894. Four children came along, but then in 1904, at the age of thirty-five, Edith died unexpectedly and her aged mother moved in and helped out with the childcare. William played for Wiltshire until 1913 and then, after the war, stood as an umpire in first-class fixtures from 1919 until 1930, when he retired. He had spent forty years being paid for what he loved doing – being out on a cricket field. His married life was short but settled and happy and he had raised his children in the delightful town of Marlborough. Perhaps he failed to fulfil all his dreams but many would settle for less. He died on 23 December 1946, aged seventy-five, in Ewell Park, Surrey.

1896

"We have had many surprises during the present season,
but it is doubtful if any has equalled that experienced
by the victory of Somerset over Surrey."

Cornishman

Championship Position: 11 of 14

A pattern was emerging. While the likes of Surrey and Yorkshire added to their trophy cabinets, Somerset had to settle for the role of plucky underdogs building up a store of anecdotes and folklore with unexpected deeds of derring do. Once again it fell upon Lionel Palairet and Teddy Tyler to shoulder the burden with bat and ball, with Palairet in particular continuing his sparkling form, most notably when he scored an elegant but ruthless 292 against Hampshire. With only three victories, the county were becoming mired in mediocrity. Ron Roberts notes in his history of the club that the fielding, formerly a strength, 'became distinctly ragged'.

Of the new-joins, only Charles Bernard and Douglas Smith were equipped for the challenges of county cricket and both made useful contributions.

101
Douglas James Smith
7 May 1896 v. Gloucestershire, Bristol

Born on 29 May 1873 in Batley, Yorkshire, he was the younger brother of fellow Somerset cricketer, William. The two had spent their childhoods watching their father move from one form of employment to another, supplementing the wages he gleaned as a professional cricketer who never quite hit the heights, though he did represent both York-shire and Lancashire in his time. Douglas would play first for Worcestershire and then – between 1896 and 1898 – for Somerset.

He started off with some promising innings for Somerset, including a score of 62, but never bettered this. The *Glouces-ter Citizen* of 2 August 1897 gives us a clue as to why coun-ties such as Somerset needed to have club pros on call. It reports that 'Richard Palairet broke a finger last week, so that Douglas Smith found a place at the last minute'. Douglas was a wholehearted and popular cricketer, prepared to offer his services to any club, but it was at Yeovil, in 1898, a year in which he played both for the cricket team and for Yeovil Casuals FC, that the locals took him to their hearts. A report of the Yeovil CC celebrations states that 'the best average was obtained by Douglas Smith, the professional, to whom Mr Brutton [the team captain] referred in eulogistic terms for his good work during the last season'. After the speech 'various toasts were proposed, and some capital songs were sung', though Douglas was not there to join in, having already left to further his career in South Africa, where he was racking up some big scores for the Durban Institute. In a later incarnation, he stepped into the breach as a replacement umpire in the Fifth Test of the 1913-14 series between South Africa and England, his only game as an interna-tional umpire.

Douglas Smith starting out as an umpire (top) and still going strong in 1934

He took a liking to South Africa and was appointed cricket coach at St Andrew's

College in Grahamstown. Here he became a local legend, retaining his role for forty-five years. He remained a bachelor and also amassed sufficient wealth to leave a generous bequest of £2,200 to his beloved adoptive home. Ronald Currey relates the story in his history of the college.

One day, a few years before his death, Smith walked into a solicitor's office armed with a copy of the relevant sections of Rhodes's Will. His instructions to the solicitor must have surprised that worthy man. In effect they were these: "I am leaving all I have to St Andrew's. Take this Will and wherever the name of Cecil Rhodes appears cross it out and substitute 'Douglas Smith', and wherever he has written 'Oxford' cross it out and write 'Cambridge'."

The Douglas Smith Scholarship, offering one student each year a scholarship to Cambridge University, remains in place. A lasting memorial and a chance for others to make the most of their talents, as he did. He died in Grahamstown, the place he loved, on 16 August 1949 at the age of seventy-six, far away from his native Yorkshire.

102
Charles Albert Bernard
21 May 1896 v. Oxford University, Oxford

Born in Bristol on 16 February 1876, Charles Bernard was the third of six children of William L. Bernard, an architect, and his wife, Matilda. Charles seems to have had a thoroughly middle-class upbringing. Given that he would later play hockey for Old Redhillians, it is reasonable to assume that he attended Red Hill House School (although records of the institution are hard to find). If so, he would have been among the early intake of pupils to the new venture.

He was a naturally gifted man who followed in his father's footsteps and became an architect and chartered surveyor, based in Clifton. In his spare time he proved an accomplished hockey player. He was also an excellent golfer and played the organ in his local church in Clifton. Above all, though, he was a fine club cricketer who made sizeable scores for the Bristol Bohemians. His performances proved consistently good enough for Somerset to invite him to play for them. Where facing stiffer opposition proved too much for

Charles Bernard – a talented man who made the transition from club to first-class cricket with relative ease

many of Somerset's club cricketers, Bernard showed himself to be at home in elevated company. This no doubt resulted from his sound technique. The *Bath Chronicle* reported in 1899 that 'stepping out of club cricket into county matches, the new batsman at once accommodated himself to his surroundings'. He was, however, a poor fielder. Sam Woods says of Bernard that 'he was a bad catcher'. He played for the county thirty-three times and would have made many more appearances, had his work commitments allowed. He scored two centuries and eleven 50s, averaging 30.44. In 1901 he played his last game for the county, having made the decision to focus more single-mindedly on his career.

On 23 Sept 1903, he was married to Ethel Constance Temple (née Alcock), daughter of the rector of Hawling, in the Cotswolds. He continued to turn out for the Bristol Bohemians and regularly contributed runs. There was an hiatus in 1908: the *Western Daily Press* reports in March 1909 that 'it will interest many to know that Mr C. A. Bernard, who was unable to play last season owing to leg trouble, hopes to regain his place in the team this coming summer'. In later years, when he turned to interests other than sport, he was an active member of the Somerset and North Wilts Chartered Surveyors' Institution and he continued to be a church organist.

A man of many talents, he played his part for his county but would appear to have had a sensible and balanced view of life. Representing Somerset at cricket was not the be all and end all. He had a career to pursue and a wife and four daughters to provide for. He died in Clifton on 26 September 1953 at the age of seventy-seven.

103
Montague Alfred Sliney Sturt
11 June 1896 v. Cambridge University, Cambridge

Monty Sturt's father was a military man. Although Monty was born in Sunderland on 11 November 1876, Frank Sturt had moved his family to Taunton by the time his eldest son was ready for his schooling. Monty attended Taunton School, where he is described as having been 'a fine all-rounder' who bowled 'fast medium'. He was also a useful rugby player, turning out for Taunton RFC.

He became a clerk for the London County Council, living in Cricklewood with his wife, Ethel (née Reece), to whom he had been married in 1906. He was in the Public Control Department and she was an inspector, enforcing the Shop Hours Act. An early example of a 'career couple', they had no children and two positions of responsibility. Somerset retained contact with Monty while he played his club cricket in London and they called on his services for ten first-class matches over a fourteen-year period. He was unable to make much of an impression at county level and would only average 12.43, with a top score of 35.

During the First World War, he volunteered for the Army Service Corps and was mentioned three times in despatches for acts of courage, suggesting that, although overseeing supplies, he was at times close to the action. He reached the rank of major and was allowed to retain the title once he had returned to civilian life. After the war he resided in Devon where he played rugby for Devonport Albion and cricket for a variety of sides. In later life he resided in Dover.

He died in Buckland Hospital, Dover, on 16 January 1961 at the age of eighty-four.

Monty Sturt – seen in the colours of Taunton RFC and Moonlighters CC

104
Alexander Gould Barrett
11 June 1896 v. Cambridge University, Cambridge

Alexander Barrett lived a life of unabashed privilege. Born on 17 November 1866 at Moredon, a grand house near North Curry, he was the son of Major William Barrett of the 2nd Somerset Militia, whose family had for generations owned extensive land and properties in the surrounding area. His mother, Maria Herring (née Chard) was the sister of Colonel Chard who won the VC for his bravery at Rorke's Drift, in the Zulu Wars. Alexander attended Eton, as two older brothers had done, before he went on to Lincoln College, Oxford. He joined the West Somerset Yeomanry, a plaything for the rich, having been granted the rank of major before he resigned his commission in 1911. He would be known as Major A. G. Barrett for much of his life.

A keen cricketer, who often turned out for Somerset Stragglers, he played the game

A. G. Barrett, who hosted a match between his chosen XI and the Somerset Light Infantry for many years. He is photographed standing between his brothers.

primarily for enjoyment. One match at the County Ground in which he took part for Somerset Stragglers v. Somerset Clergy offered much excitement for the spectators when the Clergy amassed 453 in 215 minutes only for the Stragglers to respond with a score of 458 for 1 in a mere 122 minutes, Somerset cricketer G. W. Hodgkinson blasting 229 not out. Major Barrett's contribution was minimal.

From 1901 until the 1950s, A. G. Barrett's XI enjoyed an annual fixture against the Somerset Light Infantry and A. G. remained an enthusiastic participant, missing only two fixtures in the first fifty years of the tie – the years 1932 and 1933 – owing to a hunting accident that also led him to forego his role as President of Somerset CCC, a position he had held for two years. He made his only first-class appearance in 1896 against Cambridge University, scoring 6 and 0 in a game Cambridge won with ease.

174

He was married in 1909 to Dorothy (née Cartwright), a clergyman's daughter. They would have no children and the couple threw themselves wholeheartedly into charitable works, Dorothy directing her efforts primarily to the Red Cross and Alexander funding much of the restoration work at Pitminster Church, where he was a churchwarden between 1920 and 1945.

Already rich as a result of his allowance, Alexander outlived his older brothers and inherited the family estates. It was never necessary for him seek any work, given that the farms and properties he owned provided a substantial income which was supplemented by an extensive portfolio of stocks and shares. In 1946 he donated the 8.5 acres of Burrow Mump, near Athelney, and the ruined church of St Michael, to the National Trust, so that it could be used as a lasting memorial to the war dead of Somerset. He chose to live at Eastbrook House in Trull in the latter part of his life.

Dorothy predeceased him in 1948 so that on his death, his considerable estate was shared between his three sisters and their offspring. Among his nephews and nieces was Douglas MacDonald Stewart, a musician who composed a string of popular ballads in the inter-war years.

Major A. G. Barrett died in hospital in Taunton at the age of eighty-seven on 12 March 1954. He left the then considerable sum of more than £137,000. Not bad for a man who had never needed to work for a living and a more impressive statistic than any he had mustered with a cricket bat in his hand.

105
Harry Lindsay Somerled Macdonald
11 June 1896 v. Cambridge University, Cambridge

H L Macdonald

Born in Westminster on 2 August 1861, Harry Macdonald was a member of a family able to claim descent from the Norse warlord, Somerled (d. 1164) and from the Lords of the Isles. His parents were based in Caithness. The only son of Lt Colonel William Macdonald, who died of cholera whilst commanding the 93rd Sutherland Highlanders at Camp Jalozai (now in Pakistan) when Harry was only fourteen months old, he was brought up by his mother, Emma. He attended Charterhouse School and was commissioned as a second lieutenant in the Fife division of the Royal Artillery in 1879. By 1883, he had been appointed a captain in the 4th brigade of the Scottish division of the Royal Artillery. He was married in 1887 to Lilian Margaret Coke, the daughter of a wealthy civil and mining engineer who lived at Brimington Hall, Derbyshire. In

H. L. S. Macdonald –
raised in Scotland, he
became a pillar of the Bath
community in Somerset

that year, Harry resigned his commission (and would resign from the reserve of officers in 1892). Between 1889 and 1891, Harry and Lilian embarked on extended tours of Europe and his journals of their travels are now in the possession of the University of Edinburgh.

The married couple eventually set up home in Bathford, where they would reside for the rest of their lives. Harry became actively involved with both the Bath Athletic (Bath CC) and Lansdown cricket clubs, becoming in time a member of the Bath CC committee. He would also become a vice president of Bath Rugby Club. In 1896 he played his only first-class game for Somerset in a match against Cambridge University in which the county, struggling to conjure a full team, called up four debutants – Macdonald, McLean and Barrett – three of whom would not feature in first-class cricket again. He registered a duck and 22 not out.

Harry and Lilian had no children and perhaps as a result of this he was able to throw himself wholeheartedly into local politics. A staunch Conservative, he was at various times vice chairman of the Bath Rural District Council and member of Somerset County Council. During the war, he acted as a representative on the Military Tribunal, giving recommendations for exemption from service for men regarded as indispensable for farm work. From 1924 until 1934 he acted as chairman of the Weston (Bath) magistrates and was also an energetic chairman of the Bath and District Local Employment Committee whose aim was to help those struggling to find employment.

He died on 15 August 1936, at the age of seventy-five. We are left with an impression of a man whose background and the circumstances of his upbringing led him to be committed to a life of service to his adoptive community of Bath. Playing a sport he enjoyed for the county he had come to love would have been a source of pride.

106
Douglas Hamilton McLean
11 June 1896 v. Cambridge University, Cambridge

Douglas Hamilton McLean

Referred to by the rowing fraternity as 'Ducker', Douglas McLean was the son of Hon. John Donald McLean, a successful landowner and businessman who had emigrated to Australia at the age of sixteen and ended up as Treasurer of Queensland. John's wife, Mary (née Strutt) was a surgeon's daughter to whom he was married within days of her sixteenth birthday, while he was thirty-four. Douglas, one of five children who reached adulthood, was born in Sydney on 18 March 1863, but in 1866 his father was killed when he fell off his horse. His mother took the children to England in 1870 and, two years later, was married to another wealthy businessman, Thomas Platt, with whom she would have a further three children. Sadly, Thomas died in 1875, leaving Mary a wealthy widow in possession of eight young children and the family home of Stoberry House, near Wells. In 1883 she would marry another older man – Rev. Robert Gandall, the Clerical Canon of Wells – who left her widowed for a third time in 1887.

D. H. McLean – famed rower and occasional cricketer

Douglas was educated at Eton College, where, as Sir Leslie Ward (the cartoonist 'Spy') wrote in *Vanity Fair*, he proved 'an insubordinate little fellow' who 'took to the river and studied the theory of rowing with a strength and solemn industry that presently made him so proficient on it that he rowed in the Eton eight.' Indeed, no longer a 'little fellow', he had grown into a colossus by the time he rowed for the college. It was by no means certain that he would develop into the fine rower that he became, G. C. Bourne describing him as 'astonishingly clumsy in wrist and shoulder action'.

"Ducker" by Spy, Vanity Fair

At New College, Oxford, he was selected to row in the Varsity Boat Race on five occasions and in 1885 and 1886 was president of the Oxford University Boat Club. T. A. Cook tells a story in *The Sunlit Hours* that gives us a glimpse of McLean's life beyond the water, stating that at a performance of *Othello* in Oxford, Ducker was among the audience when he fainted and presumably brought proceedings to a standstill as his enormous frame was guided into the fresh air, a fellow undergraduate following the procession holding Ducker's gold spectacles that had become separated from his face during the fall.

Towards the end of his tenure, McLean was described as the outstanding oarsman among the participants in the Varsity boat race. Having travelled to India in 1887, his return was heralded with great fanfare, *Vanity Fair* stating that McLean was 'a born oar, and seems to row as well after his voyage from India as though he had been in the boat from the beginning'. Oxford were tipped as hot favourites. Alas, with Ducker seated in the important No. 7 seat and with Oxford looking well placed, his oar snapped. Fellow member of the crew, Guy Nickalls, relates the story in *Life's a Pudding*.

With the station in our favour and him out of the boat we could have won even then, but "Ducker" flunked the oncoming penny steamers and, instead of jumping overboard as he should have done, we had to lug his now useless body along, to lose the finish. That was disappointing.

In 1889, he was married to Eliza Mary (née Rocke), known as Mary. Appointed a JP, he offered his services as a rowing coach in his leisure time on a strictly amateur basis. It was a role in which he was regarded as outstanding. So much so that he would be invited back to oversee the development of the Oxford University crew. He also wrote a short treatise entitled *Oarsmanship*, which also appeared in a popular encyclopaedia of sport. Later, he collaborated in the writing of the book *Rowing and Punting*.

A popular character, unmistakable with his huge frame and bull neck but with his trademark pair of gold spectacles giving him a surprisingly studious air, Ducker was only an occasional cricketer. His presence at least gave some lustre to the Somerset team who had travelled to Fenners and lost heavily. Ducker mustered 13 runs, batting at No. 10.

In 1900 he volunteered for the Boer War. He was appointed a captain in the 69th Sussex Company of the Imperial Yeomanry and served for a while under the Military Governor of Pretoria but died of enteric fever in Johannesburg on 5 February 1901, aged only thirty-seven, proving that even the finest specimens of humanity can be laid low by a bacterium. A memorial service was held at Wells Cathedral. He is also commemorated on the Boer War memorial at Battle, East Sussex, and in Eton College chapel. Writing in the *Daily Telegraph*, John Edwards-Moss reported that Ducker 'was a man of absolute, uncompromising, unswerving rectitude – one of the most calm and unbiased judgement, yet of infinite tenderness, patience, sympathy'. These were the qualities that had made him an outstanding leader and coach, though not, unfortunately, on the cricket field.

1897

"Surrey's supporters received a severe shock on Saturday, when the leaders of the County Championship succumbed to Somerset and thus lost the chance of being at the head of the counties in 1897."

Whitstable Times

Championship Position: 11 of 14

Somerset won only three matches and yet, confounding everyone, they had thrashed the mighty Surrey home and away, with the result that Lancashire stole the Championship from under Surrey's noses. Twice it was Teddy Tyler who did the damage with his wickets. Some wags suggested that he should be granted the freedom of Manchester. Lionel Palairet had a moderate season, but captain Sam Woods, no longer the feared bowler of old, continued to make his mark as a batsman. Keen to swell the coffers, Somerset at last agreed to play at Bath, though spirits and gate receipts were dampened by the atrocious weather. Despite this inauspicious start, the committee felt that the experiment had been a success. The Bath Festival would prove an enduring part of the social calendar of arguably the most elegant of English cities. As with the Bath fixture, appearances at the August games at Taunton were dented by the rain. The county was now burdened with an overdraft of £124. There was talk of finding a number of wealthy donors. 1897 at least proved a good year with regard to the new-joins. Two professionals, George Gill and Monty Cranfield, and an amateur, Frank Phillips, would all make valuable contributions to the cause.

107
Montagu Henry Toller
17 May 1897 v. Yorkshire, Taunton

Monty Toller – a fine figure of a man and an Olympic gold medallist

A fast right-arm bowler and right-handed batsman, Monty Toller played at county level at both cricket and rugby. Also an England rugby trialist, he had a fine sportsman's physique: tall and broad-shouldered. His father was a solicitor in the firm of Bremridge & Toller (still active in the town of Barnstaple, more than a century later, as Toller Beattie). Born in Barnstaple on New Year's Day 1871, Monty was sent to Blundell's School, near Tiverton. On leaving school, he began playing cricket for Devon, his second game being for Gentlemen of Devon v. Gentlemen of Somerset, though he did little to impress the Somerset team, with Herbie Hewett and Bill Roe tearing into the Devon attack. He was eventually invited to play for Somerset but would only represent them in five Championship matches. Strangely, given that he would have been selected primarily for his bowling, he was only handed the ball for five overs in a first-class match against the Gentlemen of Philadelphia team, where he acquitted himself well enough with figures of 1 for 15. This anomaly may simply be indicative of the chaos that engulfed the team while Sam Woods was captain of the side.

In an England rugby trial match of 1895, Somerset cricketers P.J. Ebdon, M. H. Toller and H.T. Gamlin are standing 4th, 5th and 7th from the left

Monty Toller was also an enthusiastic club player and a leading light in the Devon & Somerset Wanderers who were touring France in 1900 when they were invited to take part in the Paris Olympics. The story is detailed in the pen portrait of his Wanderers teammate and fellow Somerset cricketer, Alf Bowerman. Both would play their part in securing the gold medal, though such was the farcical nature of the contest that the gold medal was not ratified by the Olympic Committee until 1912. Perhaps to ensure an even game, Monty did not bowl in the first innings. In the second, tearing in at a pace too hot to handle on a pitch of dubious standard, he bowled a match-winning spell of 7 for 9.

The cricket experiment was not repeated at subsequent Olympic Games, with the result that the Somerset pair, Toller and Bowerman, remain the only two county players to have won cricketing Olympic gold medals.

Back on home soil, Monty continued to practice as a solicitor in Barnstaple but his career took a new turn when in 1901 he married Mrs. Harriet Jones, who owned the Royal & Fortescue Hotel in the town. Harriet was ten years his senior and they would have no children. They managed the place together until 1913, when Monty left the running of the business to Harriet, who finally transferred the licence to a new owner in 1925. In the meantime, her husband had left for Brighton and was working once more as a solicitor, although he spent much of his time on the golf course. Thereafter, they appear to have led entirely separate lives. While Harriet remained in Barnstaple until her death at the end of 1944, Monty continued to reside in Brighton.

He had eased into retirement when he died on 5 August 1948 at Meon Beach, Titchfield, Hampshire, at the age of seventy-seven.

108
George Cooper Gill
17 May 1897 v. Yorkshire, Taunton

George Gill was born on 18 April 1876. At the time, his parents ran a drapery shop in Mount Sorrell, Leicester. His father, John Gill, was a professional cricketer who turned out for a number of club sides in Leicestershire and also represented the county on occasions in its early days as a second-class county. He chose to supplement his income in whatever way he could and took his young family first to Brecon and then on to Bridgwater, where for a while they ran the Golden Ball Inn. Outstanding success as a club cricketer for Bridgwater ensured that George soon became a regular county player, contracted to Somerset. A fast bowler who was no mug with the bat, he bowled off a very long run and, accord-

G. C. Gill – a whole-hearted all-rounder in the best Somerset tradition who bowled fast and hit the ball hard

George Gill – described by C. B. Fry as having 'tearaway pace'

ing to C. B. Fry, relied 'chiefly upon tearaway pace', though he was 'inclined to rely a little too much on the short-pitched, high-rising ball'. In his autobiography *My Reminiscences*, Sam Woods singles out 'Gill of Somerset' alongside the likes of Gilbert Jessop as one of the biggest hitters he had encountered and puts him in the category of 'fast-footed hitters'. His record for Somerset over ninety-three first-class games was a perfectly decent one, including a best bowling analysis of 7 for 65. George Gill opted to leave Somerset in 1902. The decision took the county by surprise. The *Taunton Courier,* whilst ruing the loss of Gill, was understanding over his 'reversion to his native shire', given that he had been offered an extended contract, more pay and that 'an opportunity presented itself to settle down in business with relations in Leicestershire'. For three seasons he played for the county of his birth (as did his brother, Ernest), his performances for Leicestershire having been broadly similar to those for Somerset, his highlights including one century and a 9 for 89. Having been married in 1908 to Ellen (née Skipper), he played league cricket in Staffordshire before the couple moved to Todmorden, where George was taken on as the club's pro for two years. Thereafter, he moved to a succession of clubs, being hired before the war by Boldon, whilst living in Sunderland and, after the war, his skills now in decline, as the Hylton Colliery pro in the North-East Durham Senior League. The Gill family would eventually return to Leicester, where George died on 21 August 1937 at the age of sixty-one.

109
Arthur James Hook
27 May 1897 v. Oxford University, Oxford

Born in Porlock Rectory on 12 February 1877, Rev. A. J. Hook was the seventh child – preceded by a brother and five sisters – of Rev. Walter and Mary Dyke Hook. He would only ever play two first-class matches for Somerset, the first against Oxford University in 1897 and the second in 1906, when he was fetched out of village cricket to make up the numbers when Hampshire visited the County Ground. In four innings he managed a respectable average of 14.33 while batting in the lower-middle-order.

Educated at Blundell's School, he won a scholarship to study maths at Exeter College, Oxford, where he played in the College XI alongside fellow Somerset cricketer Henry Martyn. After graduating, Arthur went into the ministry and was ordained in 1909. In 1912, he was married to Sylvia Charity (known as Cherry), daughter of Rev. R. H. Hart-Davis. His first curacy was at St John's, Glastonbury. Then in 1914 he became the rector of Hambridge. Although his excellent connections ensured the continued progress of his career, his true worth came to the fore when he became rector of St John's, Taunton, in 1920. The parish had been torn apart by strife. The previous incumbent, Rev. Reginald Wynter, had suffered 'depravation and ejectment', which is to say he had been sacked, because he 'had refused obedience to the Bishop of the diocese in the matter of the authorised service of Benediction'. Essentially, Wynter was 'high church' and was resistant to change. He was also a charismatic figure whose congregation joined in a mass walk-out, leaving only eight communicants. The new rector had his work cut out but rebuilt the crumbling fabric of the church, using his powers of persuasion to encourage patrons to dip into their pockets. A new altar was introduced and a church hall built. There were over a hundred communicants by the time he left in June 1927. His work was praised by Rev. Acland-Troyte (who happened to be his uncle), who told the assembled congregation that they owed their departing rector 'a tremendous debt of gratitude' for having come to them 'at a time of great distress. The parish and parishioners had undergone a kind of earthquake, and they were all at sixes and sevens.'

Rev. A. J. Hook – one of eighteen clergymen to have played first-class cricket for Somerset.

He left to become rector of Chardstock and then of Wrington. If he had hoped for an entirely quiet time, he was disabused of the notion when a fire broke out in the Wrington church tower in January 1945. The fire brigade were called and there was considerable damage to the structure but the sixty-eight-year-old Rev. Hook 'worked heroically in the successful efforts which saved the church'. Things were calmer once he was appointed rector of Stogursey, in the Quantock Hills. One footnote from this time is that in 1948 there was a forty-day drought, ended by torrential downpours.

The local paper subjected its readers to the excruciating details of precisely how much rain had fallen at each weather station, Holford topping the table with 2.40 inches in an hour. What is of note is that accountability for monitoring the weather stations rested with the clergy. Perhaps they were among the few citizens whose assiduity and integrity were beyond question.

Rev. Arthur Hook died on his eightieth birthday at Over Stowey on 12 February 1957.

110
Francis John Portman
27 May 1897 v. Oxford University, Oxford

Francis Portman was blessed with the sort of pedigree that had the Somerset committee licking their lips in anticipation but was cursed with the same inability to triumph on the first-class stage that dogged too many of the county's players. In the paternal line, his great-grandfather had been a property developer responsible for the prestigious Portman Estate and his grandfather was the 1st Viscount Portman. Francis's father, a fourth-born son, was the rector of Corton Denham, not far from Yeovil. On the maternal side, his grandfather was the 9th Baronet Mordaunt. Somerset's Osbert Mordaunt was his uncle.

Francis Portman – he supposedly 'ran himself to death racing with the kumars before breakfast'

Educated at Radley College, for whom he played in the First XI, he then went up to Christ Church, Oxford, and after graduating opted to become a teacher. He played twice for Somerset, on both occasions against Oxford, these being social occasions where Somerset appeared not overly concerned by the indignity of being regularly thrashed. He averaged 4.00 in four innings. His bowling was more successful, with his 3 wickets costing 22.66 each.

In 1901 he was offered the professorship of History at Government College, Lahore, and then in 1903 became an English master at Mayo College, Ajmer, India, known as 'the Eton of the East'. As well as teaching English, he also taught History and Political Economics. The last of these was an area of specialism at which he was at the forefront, compiling an unfinished book of his researches relevant to Indian subcontinent at the time of his death. He was in overall charge of cricket coaching throughout the college and was also the leading light at tennis, described in a tribute in the *Mayo College Magazine* as 'quite the best player we ever had'. There is also a description of his joining in with the boys in the 100 yard and quarter mile races, to encourage them. In short, he was seen as the role model of how a young Englishman should be. In *The Games Ethic and Imperialism*. J. Mangan writes that Francis Portman 'excelled in running, tennis, cricket, and racquets. Conscientious to a fault, he quite literally ran himself to death racing with the kumars before breakfast during the training for the school sports – an ill-advised activity for a European in the Indian climate.' Whilst this account contains a degree of poetic licence, it is certainly true that, having over-exerted himself, he was bed-bound and eventually overcome by the effects of typhoid, dying in Ajmer on 2 May 1905 at the tender age of twenty-seven. His loss was greatly mourned by staff and colleagues, who had found him an inspirational character.

111
Francis Ashley Phillips
10 June 1897 v. Sussex, Hove

Frank Phillips was born on 11 April 1873 in Monmouthshire. His mother, Anna Maria, was a surgeon's daughter. His father, who owned the Pontnewydd tinplate works, purchased the ailing Pontymister Tin Plate Company in 1880, borrowing £30,000 in order to add steel production. Things turned sour in 1893 when there was a prolonged strike over pay and within three years he was forced to sell the company. At the time of Frank's birth, his parents lived at Crumlin Hall, Mynyddyslwyn, a house designed by well-known architect Owen Jones 'in the Swiss style'. Frank was sent to Rossall School and then went up to Oxford University, where he won blues between 1892 and 1895. Somerset had spotted the young amateur and, given that his only county cricket had been for Monmouthshire, across the Bristol Channel, he was available and they called on his services. Peter Roebuck describes him as 'a forthright batsman whose defence was brittle'. But he was an accomplished player 'above the average' who made four centuries for the county, including a score of 163 against Sussex at Taunton in 1899. He averaged 24.52 over sixty-nine matches, between 1897 and 1911. Sam Woods wrote that 'F. A. Phillips

Frank Phillips – according to Sam Woods he was 'a wonderful hitter for his size, and a fine field'

was a grand bat … He was a wonderful hitter for his size, and a fine field.'

Frank's playing career was briefly interrupted when he volunteered for the Boer War but by the time he served in the First World War, he had already completed his stint in county cricket. He was married late in life in 1915 to Ruth (née Ives). In 1918, he was awarded a DSO 'for conspicuous gallantry and devotion to duty', when he 'set a splendid example of determination and resource to his men', having 'maintained a determined resistance against heavy odds'. After the war, now Major Phillips, he played some cricket in Worcestershire and Herefordshire.

His business interests included a directorship role with the Wolseley Sheep Shearing Machine Company and he and his family lived for a while first in the Welsh town of Builth Wells and then in Wormbridge, Herefordshire. In later life he was a JP and was appointed clerk to the Wye Board of Conservators. His role was to protect the Wye valley against industrial pollution and other despoilment. A trip down the Wye valley today suggests that his efforts were successful. Able to give the project the time and attention that he could never quite afford when it came to cricket, he has left a lasting legacy. He died at the age of eighty-one on 5 March 1955, by now residing in Breinton, Herefordshire.

112
Beaumont Cranfield
28 June 1897 v. Gloucestershire, Taunton

Monty Cranfield was born in the city of Bath on 28 August 1872 but brought up in Bedminster, where his father was the landlord of the General Elliot pub. Edward Beaumont Cranfield had originally been a cab proprietor in London but had left the capital and entered the hotel and pub trade in the West Country. His son, Monty, first came to the attention of Gloucestershire but W. G. Grace rejected him. Sam Woods informs us that 'Cranfield could do more with the ball than any bowler I ever saw, but you

cannot be a bowler if you ain't got a head'. In the right conditions he was deadly, but when things proved less favourable he had no alternatives to fall back on. As a result, his bowling figures show huge variation. C. B. Fry has left us with an account of Monty's bowling technique, describing how he tossed the ball very high but had a slighter quicker ball – still slow – that swung markedly in the air, forcing right-handed batsmen to play only leg-side shots. Fry comments that 'at times he has to have nearly all his fielders on the leg side'.

Regarded by some as an oddball, the public warmed to the little man, celebrating his eccentric ways. In his pomp, Monty sometimes proved a match-winner but once he had lost the ability to control the flight of the ball his haul of wickets fell away. He was still able to claim 563 wickets at 24.61 each over 125 matches. Surely even W. G. Grace would have conceded that he had been hasty in rejecting the young Monty.

Monty Cranfield – a match-winner whose ability to control the ball finally deserted him

His last match was in July 1908. Sadly, his retirement would prove shortlived. He was staying with his widowed mother by then, helping her with the running of the Old England in Montpelier, Bristol, a pub formerly run by Gloucestershire bowler Fred Roberts who had put up nets for W. G. Grace to practice his skills on a Sunday, a clever marketing ploy that had drawn hundreds of people to the pub to watch 'The Champion'.

Monty Cranfield died at home in Bristol on 20 January 1909 at the age of only thirty-six, having caught a chill while watching Bristol City play Southampton: a chill that turned out to be double pneumonia. He was dead within days. He had remained unmarried. A report in the *Western Daily Press* recalls that 'some of his best efforts … were achieved when the position was well-nigh hopeless'. At this time in their history the description fitted a fair number of Somerset's matches.

His brother, Lionel Lord Cranfield, also played for Somerset. A contemporaneous report informs us, in the language of the day, that a third brother, Percy, was the most gifted of three talented cricketers but was 'debarred from playing competitive cricket, owing to his being a cripple'.

1898

"They are joint holders of the 'wooden spoon' with
Leicestershire. Once, and once only, have they tasted
the sweets of victory, and for this they are indebted in a
measure to the wretched judgement of the Sussex batsman,
as well as to the pluck and energy of their captain,
Mr S. M. J. Woods ... The bowling has once again
proved terribly weak.'

Bath Chronicle

Championship Position: 13= of 14

Lionel Palairet was once more the leading batsman and Teddy Tyler the major
wicket-taker during a season in which the county's star continued to fade. A high
spot was a seventh-wicket partnership of 240 between Sam Woods and Vernon Hill
that would have emptied the bar, given their reputations as mighty hitters. At Bath,
against Hampshire, Ernie Robson bagged the county's first Championship hat trick.

Among the new recruits, John Daniell proved the most noteworthy. In time he
would take on the mantle of Sam Woods, leading Somerset CCC, though not necessarily always forwards. Another debutant, Harry Griffin, a bowler of humbler origins
than Daniell's, could have made a greater contribution, were it not for a questionable
bowling action and the fact that the county was too impoverished to pay for his services
more often.

113
Eustace Tickell Hill
26 May 1898 v. Oxford University, Oxford

The son of Sir Edward Stock Hill, MP for South Bristol from 1886 until 1902, Eustace, one of seven children, was the brother of free-hitting Somerset left-handed batsman, Vernon Tickell Hill. The brothers' middle name came from their mother, Frances Tickell, known as Fanny. Born in Llandaff, Cardiff, on 13 April 1869, Eustace attended first Rev. Cornish's School in Walton-in-Gordano, near Clevedon in north Somerset, and then Winchester College.

On leaving school, he was offered a commission with the 19th Hussars until the turn of the century, when he joined the 1st Battalion of the Gloucester Imperial Yeomanry, with whom he served in the Boer War as a major. He saw action at Wittebergen, Cape Colony and Transvaal before returning to England by 1904, the year he was married to Florence Muriel (née Bowen), daughter of Sir George Bevan Bowen of Llwyngwair, Pembrokeshire. The couple would have five children.

Eustace Hill – the brother of Somerset cricketer, Vernon, he played in only two first-class matches for the county

Having first played for Somerset in 1890, he appeared in two first-class matches: the 1897 and 1898 fixtures against Oxford University. His average of 17.50 is certainly more respectable than that of many of his teammates, suggesting some talent.

After resigning his commission in the army, Eustace ran a ship repairing business operating from the dry docks in Bristol, whilst living first at Winterbourne Park and later at Stonehouse Court, both in Gloucestershire. Having retired to Llansantffraed Court, near Abergavenny, he died on 11 January 1933 at Ruthin Castle, which had been converted into the UK's first private hospital 'for the investigation and treatment of obscure internal diseases'. He was sixty-three at the time of his death.

114
John Daniell
20 June 1898 v. Lancashire, Taunton

John Daniell – taking on the mantle of Sam Woods, he became the dominant personality in Somerset cricket for many years

John Daniell became the dominant personality in Somerset cricket for nearly thirty years, though not everyone believed he was a force for good. He had made his name as a rugby player before he developed as a cricketer. Born in Bath on 12 December 1878, he was educated at Clifton College and went up to Emmanuel College, Cambridge. He played rugby for Richmond and seven times for England. After his playing days he became an England selector and, for two years immediately after the war, President of the RFU. Some say that Sam Woods and John Daniell managed over the years to keep Somerset cricket afloat by begging, stealing and borrowing players with even the most tenuous of links to the county. Others lay the blame for Somerset's failure to leave the dark ages of amateurism on the two men, both outspoken and strong-willed leaders, in Daniell's case with a heavy dose of snobbery. There is probably an element of truth in both perspectives. Whereas Daniell's expletive-laden exhortations worked well in the febrile atmosphere of a rugby match, they could be intimidating or wearing in a county cricket game. Most of the team accepted his idiosyncrasies, knowing that he had the best interests of the club at heart. Some stood up to him. Jack MacBryan – never one to suffer fools gladly – was withering in his criticism of his captain.

John Daniell was an attacking middle-order batsman who occasionally promoted himself up the order. His average over 287 first-class games was a useful 21.78, including eight centuries. John Daniell believed in taking the fight to the opposition. Many of his finest interventions were as a fielder, where he took some brilliant catches as well as a number of painful blows while standing dangerously close to the bat, wearing his trademark homburg hat. No one ever doubted John Daniell's courage.

Not only did he serve as Somerset captain for thirteen seasons, plundering recruits wherever he could, but he also acted for a while as a selector for the England cricket team. There can surely be few men who could claim to have been international selectors both at rugby and cricket.

His family had built up their wealth with tea plantations in India and from the outset John showed little appetite for the business. After leaving Cambridge, he was taken on for a while as a schoolmaster by former Somerset player Bill Roe, at Stanmore Park Preparatory School. He taught there in two spells between 1901 and 1904. Among his charges was Hitendra Narayan, an Indian prince, whom he would later persuade to play for Somerset. Daniell also tried for a brief while to manage the tea-planting business in India, playing some club cricket while he was there, but he found it not to his liking and opted to pay a manager to run things and returned to England. Never motivated by money and never particularly well-off, he was married in 1910 to Manora Elizabeth Annie (née Garfath). He and his long-suffering family lived for a while in lodgings, first in Weston-super-Mare and then at the vicarage in Trull, but in 1928 he was persuaded that it would be sensible to buy a farmhouse in Holway Green, Taunton. He lived there, still involving himself in the twin worlds of rugby and cricket as an administrator until his death on 24 January 1963 at the age of eighty-four.

115
Cecil Spencer Hickley
11 July 1898 v. Hampshire, Bournemouth

Born in Somerset at Long Furlong House, Ashcott, on 22 January 1865, Cecil Hickley claimed direct descent from William the Conqueror. He was always destined – provided that he could learn to put one foot in front of the other without stumbling and eat his food from his silver spoon without drooling – to the reach the upper echelons of society. Once he had elected to join the navy, his eventual advancement to the role of admiral was well-nigh assured, but sport is the great meritocracy and those selected on the basis of status rather than ability will be found wanting. Hickley's average of 8.20 in his ten first-class innings for Somerset tells its own story. He had already played first-class cricket for Western Province when selected by Somerset but his record for them was no better. Although his status would have been enough to entice Somerset, the fact that wicket-keeper Arthur Newton was married to Cecil's

Admiral C. S. Hickley – his career in the Royal Navy was more impressive than his cricketing Curriculum Vitae

sister will have oiled the wheels. As for his naval career, Cecil Hickley was earmarked early for advancement with reports from senior officers describing him as energetic in his approach. He would command a number of ships in his time, though his qualities as a leader did not always go unquestioned. The *Dundee Courier* reported in 1903 that a stoker on HMS Pembroke named Charles Berdet Revell had been court-martialled for 'insolent behaviour' against Commander C. S. Hickley, his tirade including obscene language. The offender was given the arguably vindictive sentence of fifteen months' hard labour followed by dismissal from the navy. Never a thought that Hickley's style of management might have contributed to events. Honour had been restored to the well-bred officer. In 1909 Hickley, now captain of HMS Cochrane, was awarded the Royal Victorian Order. In June 1920 he retired one day after having been promoted from rear-admiral to vice-admiral (presumably to augment his pension). 1920 was a good year for him as he was also awarded a CB in the King's Honours List. Further promotion followed in 1925 when he was promoted to the rank of admiral within the Retired List. One cannot help but wonder how Stoker Revell's retirement would have compared, though it must be doubted that Cecil Hickley would have given the matter much thought.

His last Championship game for Somerset, in 1899, must have been a tedious affair for him as he and his teammates laboured long in the field while Surrey's opening batsman, Abel, amassed 357 not out. Hickley's appetite for the game was not quelled, though. For many years he organized an annual fixture between The Cadets and The Admirals at Dartmouth, though he continued to enjoy only very modest success as a batsman. He was married late in life in 1919 to a widow, Mrs Diana Susan Mostyn Ramsden (née Owen). At the time of his death on 1 May 1941 at the age of seventy-six, he was living primarily in Trull, near Taunton, although he also spent time at his Kensington residence, where his death occurred. His wife, Diana, arranged for a memorial to be placed in his memory on the west wall of Trull church.

116
John Francis Ebdon
14 July 1898 v. Gloucestershire, Bristol

J F Ebdon

Born near Milverton on 16 February 1876, John was the youngest of the three Ebdon brothers who played for Somerset in the early Championship years and the last to do so. Between them, they only mustered five appearances. The match against Gloucestershire was John's solitary Championship game for the county. The Ebdon brothers' father had been headmaster for many years at the Milverton Elementary School and was a keen rugby player who also 'shone at cricket'. A man of considerable energy, he lived until his ninety-sixth year.

John Ebdon played most of his club cricket for Wellington. He was also, along with his brother, Percy, an important member of the Wellington rugby team and represented Somerset at the game. Whether or not he might have been invited back by Somerset CCC is academic because he left to train as a teacher at Exeter, before graduating from the University of London. In 1923, he was married to Marjorie Mary (née Busher), a fellow schoolteacher who hailed from Abergavenny and taught at the County School for Girls in Dover. He was forty-seven at the time and she thirty-four,

John Ebdon – one of three brothers who made a combined total of five appearances for Somerset

and he had already been for a while a member of staff at Ilkley Grammar School in Yorkshire. A venerable institution, founded in 1607, the school had in the recent past moved to new, purpose-built premises and the governors had ambitious plans to expand. Ilkley Grammar inspired great loyalty on the part of its teachers. Five members (more than a third of the total contingent) of a staff photograph taken in the mid-1920s remained with the school until the 1940s. John Ebdon was still there in his late sixties, helping out during the Second World War. This must surely be deemed a good innings.

He died on 1 November 1952 at the age of seventy-six, at Scalebor Park Hospital in Burley-in-Wharfedale, not far from his adoptive home of Ilkley and something of a legend in that part of the world, though less so in the annals of Somerset cricket.

117
Harry Griffin
25 July 1898 v. Lancashire, Liverpool

Harry Griffin

Harry Griffin – known as "Joe", he was a useful bowler but his action was called into question.

Known among the cricketing fraternity as 'Joe', Harry Griffin was born at 41 High St, Street, in Somerset on 21 April 1873. Like the vast majority of residents of the town, Harry's parents and siblings were involved in shoemaking. Harry would also become a shoemaker. The town's shoemaking business had been the brainchild of the Clark family. Cyrus and James Clark had set up a company making rugs from animal skins. Noticing the amount of wastage from offcuts, James came up with the idea of making fur-lined slippers. They issued offcuts to outworkers each week and then paid their helpers each Friday when they returned the completed slippers. This side of the business expanded rapidly, with a number of innovations over the years. By the time of Harry's birth, William Clark, the son of James, was running Clarks Shoes. As Quakers, the Clarks were concerned for the welfare of their employees and built a school (which Harry would have attended) together with other facilities in the town such as playing fields. Harry was clearly a talented young cricketer, playing for Street over many years. A diminutive character with a look of self-belief about him, he was a slow left-arm bowler, capable of the odd useful innings at club level.

He had already been engaged as a pro by Todmorden in the Lancashire league when, after a trial match, he was invited to play for Somerset on a professional basis. In a bizarre turn of events – indicative of the chaos that captain Sam Woods managed to generate – the new recruit batted at number four and was not called on to bowl. In the following match, against Gloucestershire, he bowled a total of fifty-four overs and took nine wickets, including 6 for 40 in the first innings, though he was the eighth bowler that Woods called on, having tried seven others without success. The performance was, however, mired in controversy. The *Somerset County Gazette* tells us that

'Joe Griffin's delivery did not suit some of the players who expressed the opinion that it was not fair, but the umpires did not no-ball him for it. As has always been remarked by those who have played with him, it is certainly open to question.' Harry took further wickets against Lancashire and Yorkshire and after four games (three of which he had bowled in) he had claimed 14 wickets at 15.50 each.

Somerset decided not to utilise his services after 1899, either because they were unable to afford to take him on, given that they had offered a contract to A.E. Lewis, or alternatively because the rules on no-balling were tightened the following year (as Teddy Tyler found to his cost).

He was married in 1900 to Florence Beatrice (née Holley). Harry and his wife brought up a son and an orphaned nephew. After settling back in Street, Harry remained a central figure in their cricket in the following years. It was noted at Street CC's Annual General Meeting of 1908, where Harry was appointed as vice-captain of the First XI, that 'stress was laid upon the need for batting practice by the members, as the majority of matches last season were lost on account of weak batting'. Something similar could have been said of the county side, though it would be fair to add that the bowling and fielding were also below par.

A Street man through and through, having resided for most of his life in the town's High St, Harry Griffin died at the Bristol Royal Infirmary on 26 September 1938 at the age of sixty-five.

118
George Rupert Hunt
25 August 1898 v. Surrey, Taunton

With Somerset short of men for the fixture against Surrey at the County Ground, Taunton, they leapt at the opportunity to welcome a schoolmaster who happened to be in the area and bore all the right credentials. Importantly, he had been born in Bathwick on 23 March 1873 (along with a twin brother, Francis, who became a stock-broker). His father, Rev. William Hunt was the rector of River (near Dover) and George had attended Keble College, Oxford, where he had been an active sportsman. Between 1892 and 1895 he had played for the College XV and was appointed captain in his final year, during which Keble were unbeaten in inter-college matches. He was also a member of his college rowing eight and played for the Keble College cricket team and for Oxford University Authentics (the Second XI in all but name). His tutor's

George Hunt – a school-master who made one appearance for Somerset

report notes that he was 'in danger of making athletics the major work of life'. After graduating, he took up a teaching post at St David's School in Reigate.

A report in the *London Standard* of the match against Surrey informs us that 'the weather was in every way favourable and it goes without saying that the wicket was an excellent one'. There were runs aplenty but George was bowled for 1 in the first innings. With a draw already a foregone conclusion, the stand-in captain, Lionel Palairet, invited George to open Somerset's second innings, perhaps aware that the new man was unlikely ever to have another opportunity to experience county cricket. He made 3 before being caught by a young Surrey professional named Len Braund.

1898 was an eventful year for George Hunt, though hopefully his marriage to Mary Augusta (née Beavis) was more uplifting than his baptism in county cricket. Shortly thereafter he became a co-principal at High Croft School in Westerham, Sevenoaks. In 1905 he invested with two other business partners, the Gowrings, in another school, St Bede's, in Eastbourne. The school had opened its doors in 1895 with only four pupils and the Gowrings had purchased it in 1900. George Hunt had perhaps been offered the part share in the enerprise as part of his inducement to become the headmaster, but this was not a success: by 1909 the partnership was dissolved and he was teaching at Wootton Court School in Canterbury for two years. After a one-year spell teaching at King Edward VII School in Lytham, Lancashire, he headed back down to the South East and was a house master and for a while acting headmaster at Dover College. Essentially, he had been prepared to travel to wherever opportunities arose to further his career.

He died at the age of eighty-seven on 22 August 1960 at Old Burleston, Hampshire, seven years after his wife had died at the same address.

1899

"The cause of their ill success is not far to seek …
They had not at all a bad batting side, but they
were so weak in bowling that the prospect of
winning on good wickets was always remote."

Bath Chronicle

Championship Position: 13= of 15

This was a year for the batsmen with sunshine and bone-dry wickets. Worcester-shire joined the Championship, but it was Derbyshire who spared Somerset the indignity of a second successive wooden spoon. In the absence of Lionel Palairet, who had undergone an operation and would therefore miss out on the orgy of run-making, Sam Woods enjoyed an excellent season with the bat, with well over 1,000 first-class runs and a record sixth-wicket partnership of 174 with a youthful John Daniell against Lancashire at Taunton. Ernie Robson became the first Somerset pro to top 1,000 runs. Teddy Tyler was the major wicket-taker.

It was a season for records. Surrey gained some sort of revenge for their unexpected defeats of prior years, amassing 811 with Abel carrying his bat for 357 not out. When Hampshire put Somerset to the sword with a score of 672 for 7 at Taunton, Rev. Archie Wickham conceded not a single bye. The visit of the Australians and the gate receipts for the three days of £664 meant that Somerset were in the black again, though only just.

Although he would not technically qualify for Championship games until 1901, debutant Len Braund proved the greatest of all Somerset's pre-war pros. Among the other new-joins, A. E. 'Talbot' Lewis developed into a useful all-rounder and occasional match-winner who would serve the county well.

119
Albert Edward Lewis
11 May 1899 v. Yorkshire, Bath

A Lewis

A. E. Lewis – cricketing all-rounder, billiards player, businessman and goalkeeper

Tall and long-limbed, A. E. Lewis, a carpenter's son, was born in Bedminster on 20 January 1877. He came to be known as 'Talbot'. Peter Roebuck describes him as a 'careful, persevering cricketer rather than a dasher', a description that could equally well have applied to his fellow long-serving professional, Ernie Robson. Interestingly, they both also played professional football, Robson a compact, tough full-back and Lewis using his height and athleticism to advantage as a goalkeeper. Albert Lewis provided an early example of a "buy one get one free" offer, when Sheffield United sold Alf Common and him to Sunderland for what was regarded as the stratospheric price of £520. In less than a year, Common went on to command the first £1,000 transfer fee.

Lewis's career also included spells at Everton, Bristol City and Leicester Fosse. He is described in one report as 'a fine goalkeeper ... absolutely devoid of fear', the journalist also complimenting him on his sobriety when adding that 'Lewis is a life-long abstainer'.

As for cricket, in a career spanning 208 matches between 1899 and 1914, his nine centuries for Somerset combined with thirty-one 50s are testimony to his ability. In 1908 he scored 201 not out against Kent, demonstrating what he was capable of at his best. He showed his worth as a bowler, too, accumulating more than 500 wickets at an average of 23.17 with his medium-paced deliveries. He is described as having swing, pace and 'sharp break-back' that could take batsmen by surprise.

After the day's play, Talbot Lewis would often be found at a billiard table, where his skills were

'Talbot' Lewis – described by Peter Roebuck as 'a persevering cricketer rather than a dasher'

legendary and breaks of over a hundred were commonplace. He set up a sports shop –
part of the Sports Depot franchise – which he owned jointly with Somerset's former
groundsman, naming the shop 'Mettam & Lewis'. The range was extensive (and of
course included both cricket and billiards equipment). Talbot went on to develop other
business interests including the ownership of a billiard hall in Taunton together with
holiday bungalows which he let out, using them for his own escapes from the world
of business on occasions. Some writers have described Talbot as a notorious womaniser
in his younger days, also claiming that he remained a bachelor. Whilst it is impossible
to confirm how he spent his youth, he was undoubtedly married in 1933 to Lily
Attwood, who was forty at the time and remained his constant companion until his
death at Southmead Hospital in Bristol on 22 February 1956 at the age of seventy-
nine. He was by then a wealthy man, having risen from humble beginnings. For many
years he had given his best for the county. He had been popular with the supporters,
an extrovert who was considered good company. By way of comparison, his fellow
professional Ernie Robson, diffident and uncomfortable in the spotlight, was loved.

120
Arthur Bucknell
11 May 1899 v. Yorkshire, Bath

Arthur Bucknell

It was Arthur Bucknell's fate to have been consigned for more than a hundred years to
seeming oblivion in relation to the history of Somerset cricket. We should be grateful
to a keen autograph collector who asked the team to sign their autographs for him at
the fixture between Kent and Somerset in June 1899 and kept them for posterity.
Among the names are the eleven who appeared. Squeezed into the mix is the signature
of Monty Cranfield who, although he had appeared in the previous match, was unable
to play. The all-rounder Bucknell had been called up. Confusion arises from the fact
that two Bucknell brothers – Jack and Arthur – were both often referred to by their
surnames. Somerset player, Jack, had left for the North East in 1896, to take up a post
as a pro at Darlington, combining it with a career in teaching. It was Arthur whom
Somerset had called on, as evidenced by the autograph sheet. His name sits between
those of Ted Grant and George Nichols.

Born in Bedminster on 31 January 1877, Arthur had left school and was working
as a brewer's clerk. In an obituary, the tale is told of how he regularly went as a teenager
to the Gloucestershire ground where young men queued up to bowl in the nets to W.

G. Grace who offered half a guinea to anyone who dislodged the bails. Having been bowled three times in quick succession by young Arthur, Grace decided that enough was enough and suggested that he should become a professional cricketer. As with so much cricketing lore, the tale may be apocryphal. One of three talented brothers, all of whom managed to forge a living as pros, he cut his teeth with Bedminster but in 1898 and 1899 he was a pro at the famous Lansdown club. Here he gained a reputation as a successful fast bowler. The *Sheffield Evening Telegraph*, referring to the debut appearance, against Yorkshire, of 'Bucknell, the Lansdown pro' states that:

> *Bucknell deserved his place owing to his work with both bat and ball against M.C.C... in that he had four wickets for 28 and scored 41 not out, a pretty creditable dual performance. With Somerset so notoriously weak in bowling, his inclusion was quite justified. He is a fast bowler with a good free action.*

He played again in the match versus Kent in June 1899, where he was watched by our friend the autograph hunter. These were his only two appearances in 1899, although his brother, Jack, made an appearance in the game against Yorkshire, in Hull, recalled after a four-year absence.

Arthur was offered professional terms by Walsall, where the role was combined with that of a clerk working for a saddle manufacturer. He was then taken on by Bloxwich, with whom he became something of a local legend. Here he was joined by the oldest of the three cricketing Bucknell brothers – William Mitchell – who had previously played as a pro for Burnley St Andrew's in Lancashire League cricket. The *Walsall Advertiser* of 9 July 1904 is full of praise for the 'brothers Bucknell':

> *What a tower of strength this pair is to Bloxwich as all-round cricketers.*

In 1904, Arthur was called up again by Somerset, five years after his previous appearances. Given the length of the interlude, it is easy to understand an error on the part of the reporter for the *Derbyshire Daily Telegraph*, who states that 'against the South Africans, Somersetshire are trying a new professional from Bloxwich, named Bucknell'. It was a return to the fold for Arthur. Three more appearances followed in 1905. The *Somerset Year Book* of 1905 confirms his professional status by listing him in score sheets as 'Bucknell' but he is afforded the dignity of an initial – A. Bucknell – in the averages. Arthur Bucknell's record for Somerset is not a stirring one. He took 3 wickets for a total of 289 runs (and an average of 96.33). He amassed 51 runs at an average of 6.38. In Bloxwich, things were much rosier. Reporting on Arthur's

Arthur Bucknell, a talented pro who slipped unnoticed from Somerset's archives

benefit match against Wolverhampton, in August 1906, the *Walsall Advertiser* reports that:

> *... for several years {Bucknell} has rendered yeoman service to his club, and in large measure is the success of the Bloxwich eleven due to this clever exponent of the game.*

His career in Minor Counties was impressive, too: he racked up a total of 64 appearances for Staffordshire, between 1906 and 1914. In one of those games, on 11 and 12 August 1909, he lined up against his brother and fellow former Somerset cricketer, Jack, who was representing Durham. Staffordshire won the match by ten wickets, with Arthur claiming six victims in the game. Jack was not one of them. At the time, Arthur and his wife Elizabeth (née Short) ran the Crown & Anchor Inn, in Walsall, although they would only do so for eighteen months, perhaps tiring of maintaining order in what appears to have been a rough establishment.

Arthur Bucknell died in Walsall on 28 October 1922 at the age of forty-five. An obituary states that his end was hastened by a blow to the head by a cricket ball, but his death certificate indicates tuberculosis. His wife, Elizabeth, to whom he had been married as an eighteen-year-old, back in 1896, was at his bedside. The first detailed records of Somerset CCC, compiled by F. J. Gustard, were published in 1925 after the deaths of both brothers. Neither was around to challenge the error of omission when they were presumed to be one man. Subsequent publications have compounded the error. Arthur had been a hugely successful club and Minor Counties cricketer whose exploits for the county of his birth were less noteworthy and a man who was unaware that when he signed his name for an autograph hunter in Tonbridge, in 1899, he would be saving himself from the ignominy of being lost to Somerset's records.

121
Leonard Charles Braund
18 May 1899 v. Oxford University, Oxford

Len Braund – one of the genuine greats and a regular England international, he ended his days as a double amputee

He made his debut against Oxford University, but Len Braund's appearance in the Championship at Lord's in 1900 against Middlesex would spark an appeal on the part of his former county, Surrey, still smarting from the fact that he had been stolen from under their noses. Surrey had watched as he had developed in non-first-class games from a good player into a match-winner. They realised they had made a mistake in letting him go. Len had informed Surrey that he was leaving them for Somerset in 1898. On 1 June 1898 he took a room in Taunton, but had failed to take up residence until the September, perhaps because he had been too busy playing cricket. It was a technicality but the MCC upheld Surrey's complaint. Braund would not be allowed to appear until September 1900 (which meant the 1901 season at the earliest). Why would Len Braund wish to leave one of the top two counties for a bunch of also-rans? Perhaps he wished to be the leading light, taking on the mantle of Sam Woods. Something of a party animal, perhaps he enjoyed his visits to Taunton and liked the way some of the amateurs got on well with the pros and mixed with them socially.

Born on 18 October 1875 in Clewer, Windsor, Len had enjoyed a comfortable but unconventional middle-class upbringing. His father, John Braund, was a portrait painter who combined application with free-spiritedness.

Len made good use of his time over the summer of 1900, honing his skills by playing for London County under the watchful eye of W. G. Grace. He was also married that year to Ruth May (née Hancock), a bricklayer's daughter. He would play 281 first-class matches for Somerset and would represent England on twenty-three occasions. He would register twenty-five first-class centuries over sixteen seasons, his top score of 257 not out coming against Worcestershire in 1913. Although his natural instinct as a batsman was to attack, he knew how to dig in and defend on a sticky wicket. The fact that he carried his bat on at least four occasions is testimony to his doggedness and sound technique (as well as to the paucity of talent around him). His bowling was equally impressive, although the figures are marred by performances in later years. As a young man, he bamboozled opponents with his medium-paced leg-spin which, although sometimes erratic in line and length, could be deadly. Across his entire first-class career he took 5 or more wickets in an innings on eighty occasions; sixteen times he took 10 or more in a match. He exceeded 1000 runs in seven seasons and 100 wickets in four summers. Between 1901 and 1903, at the height of his powers, he completed the first-class double each season. Possessed of a big match temperament, he often saved his finest performances for the strongest opponents. Added to this, he was deemed one of the finest of slip fielders.

He was able to use his popularity to promote his Sports Depot outlet, in Argyle Street, Bath. Len and Ruth Braund lived above their shop with their four children. After his playing career, Len became a coach at Cambridge and a first-class umpire, officiating in 374 first-class fixtures and three test matches between 1923 and 1938. Following the amputation of both legs in 1943, he lived for a further twelve years, dying in Putney on 23 December 1955 at the age of eighty. He had not stayed rooted in Taunton as some of the county's greats had, in some cases fuelling the myths surrounding their own exploits. That was never Len's style. Perhaps this is why his achievements are not celebrated as much as they might be. But there is no doubting that this superb all-rounder – effective, rather than flamboyant – gave his all for Somerset and England.

Len Braund frequently proved a match-winner with bat and ball

122
Edward Grant
8 June 1899 v. Kent, Tonbridge

Edward Grant

Ted Grant was born on 16 June 1874 in the small village of West Dean, on the border of Hampshire and Wiltshire but the family soon moved to Widcombe, Bath. His father was a domestic gardener and the sons all left school at the earliest opportunity in order to earn a living: their occupations included carter, sawyer, baker and – in Ted's case – a domestic gardener, like his father. But Ted wanted to better himself and soon found a job as a waterworks inspector for the Bath Corporation, a position he would retain for many years. He was married to a local Bath girl and the 1911 census shows him and Annie living at Kingsmead Terrace in Bath, having been together for ten years. Both in their mid-thirties by this time, they had no children. Although his steady and happy life was not the sort to draw attention, he was an enthusiastic cricketer: a slow bowler, occasionally asked to bat up the order.

Ted Grant – associated with Bath cricket throughout his adult life

Ted Grant did enough in his club cricket with Bath to merit five games for Somerset over a two-year period. Things began well. For once, someone had briefed Sam Woods, and having selected a bowler, he opened with him. Ted rewarded his captain's faith, taking two Kent wickets for 19 runs, but he only ever took two more wickets for Somerset. He found his niche, though, in Minor Counties cricket, playing regularly for Wiltshire between 1903 and 1912. In one of his early games (against Monmouthshire, in August 1903) he took 6 for 9 including a hat trick and then went on to hit 32 not out. In the meantime, he was turning out for Bath whenever not tied up with Minor Counties cricket. Author David Foot recounts the story of the occasion when W. G. Grace came in and nicked an early delivery to the keeper. The Doctor refused to walk and, having subsequently crossed for a single, put his arm around Ted Grant's neck and asserted that had he hit it, it would have gone for four. Ted was not one to bear a grudge, but added it to a store of anecdotes that he would build up over a lifetime involved with cricket.

A report in the *Bath Chronicle* tells us that 'after being one of the mainstays of the bowling for a very long time … he is now a member of the Bath Club's committee, and scorer to the first team. He is often seen at the ground coaching the younger element.' In 1947 the same newspaper gives us a flavour of the veneration in which he was held after half a century and more of association with Bath cricket:

> *He is more than a perfect scorer. His advice given freely to any player has influenced in our club's favour many matches, and this over the period of the last 50 years. Long may he continue as our adviser and friend.*

In February 1950 he and fellow Somerset cricketer Henry Wood were made the first life members of Bath Athletic Cricket Club. Ted Grant loved his Bath cricket until the very last. He died on 12 January 1953 at the age of seventy-eight.

123
Henry Wildman Kettlewell
12 June 1899 v. Hampshire, Portsmouth

Henry Kettlewell was born on 20 July 1876 at Harptree Court in East Harptree and was educated at Eton before embarking on a military career. He played cricket for Eton for three years, primarily as a right-handed batsman and an occasional fast bowler. His one appearance for Somerset was in their fixture against Hampshire at the United Services Ground, Portsmouth. He batted in the middle-order and turned his arm for five overs without taking a wicket. He at least survived the second innings without being dismissed, his scores of 1 and 6 not out yielding an average of 7.

As for his military career, having been quickly promoted to the rank of second lieutenant, he was wounded in the Boer War but staged a full recovery. In 1903 he was married to Sheila Gladys (née Forsyth) while stationed in India. In 1916, whilst still active in the First World War, he inherited Harptree Court on the death of his father, William Wildman Kettlewell, who left estate valued at £89, 540 17s with the usual proviso that Henry's mother would continue to live in the family home. Henry in fact sold Harptree Court in 1920 and moved to nearby Harptree House. On his retirement from the army, Lt Colonel H. W. Kettlewell of the Shropshire Light Infantry went on a breathless round of public speaking engagements in the early 1930s. The titles of his talks suggest a nostalgic attachment to the past and they include dire warnings of the dangers of letting things slip, with titles such as *Disarmament, England's Green and Pleasant Land* and *Standards Old and New*.

Henry Kettlewell of Harptree House – cricketer and councillor

By the 1940s, residing at Harptree House, he involved himself in the minutiae of local politics, continuing to rail against falling standards. In one intervention, he upbraids the Clutton Rural District Council for the 'disgraceful condition of the Harptree Cemetery' and urges them to spend more money on its upkeep. Perhaps some members of the cash-strapped council might have felt tempted to suggest that he dipped into his own personal fortune but none dared venture their opinion. He is also reported as having a spat with Miss Rees-Mogg (a member of the political and journalistic dynasty) over the allocation of sugar for jam-making where a plucky Miss Rees-Mogg suggested that the retired Lt Colonel's decision to allocate all the sugar to the Women's Institute was an insult to the many women who wished to make jam but had no wish to become involved with an organisation as subversive as the WI.

Henry Kettlewell died at Harptree House on 28 April 1963 at the age of eighty-six, mourned by his family, though perhaps one or two councillors felt a sense of relief that their every move was no longer being watched.

124
Francis William Henry Cramer-Roberts
19 June 1899 v. Kent, Bath

F. C. Roberts, as he is referred to in the Somerset scorebook, was born on 7 April 1875 in Acton, Cheshire, one of six children, and attended first Mostyn House School in Cheshire and then Shrewsbury School, which he left in 1893. For a while he was an assistant teacher but in 1896 he enlisted at Liverpool with the Royal Marines Artillery, only to decide within a month that this was not the life for him. He joined the staff of The County School (now Wellington School) later that year, turning out regularly for Wellington AFC (as a centre forward) and the town and school cricket teams (as an outstanding all-rounder). Six feet tall, and with an athlete's broad shoulders, he was an imposing figure. Over four seasons at the County School he scored half the side's runs at an average of approximately 50 and took half their wickets at approximately 7 runs apiece.

He was invited by Somerset to a trial match before the call came to play against Kent at the Recreation Ground, Bath. In a drawn game, he acquitted himself well with the ball. A steady 0 for 6 in three overs was followed by an even more parsimonious 0 for 5 in five tidy overs. It was his woeful fielding – completely at odds with reports of his excellent fielding at club level – that was the talking point. He dropped catches at long-on and in the slips. The *Bath Chronicle*'s reports that 'F. C. Roberts, the Wellington recruit, cut a decidedly sorry figure in the field. Not only did he fail at fairly easy catches, but he might have stopped more than a couple of boundaries.'

A month later, in July 1899, he left his job as a schoolmaster at Wellington School and returned to the North, working for a while at the Edison Phonographic Co. in Manchester, before returning to The Wirral to help in his father's import and export agency, based in Neston. He had already appeared for Neston during the summer holidays, alongside his brother, Henry, and over the following seasons he played regularly for them, agreeing to captain the side in 1914.

Frank Cramer-Roberts in the 1893 Shrewsbury School XI (top) and at Wellington School, Somerset

In 1903, he was married to Mary (née Porter). He was twenty-eight and she was thirty-four. The 1911 census informs us that they had no children. Meanwhile, his cricket had gone from strength to strength. In *Fifty Years of Neston Cricket* by J. H. Gilling, we are told that:

> The club has had many fine cricketers, but … the best was Frank Cramer-Roberts, who from 1901 to … 1914 played one of the chief parts in Neston cricket. He scored twelve centuries, ten of them were not out, and in two successive seasons took over 100 wickets … He had played for Somerset and was always in demand.

Elsewhere, we are informed that he scored over 7,000 runs for the club and that after the war he left the area and 'up to 1938 … was still playing cricket in the South'.

During the war, having enlisted with the Household Cavalry but being released after eighteen days deemed unfit for service, Frank had joined the Army Pay Department and was appointed to the rank of lieutenant in 1916. For many years, he and his wife, Mary, lived in the village of Seale, Surrey, where Frank became active on the parish council. He died at home on 17 October 1945 at the age of seventy.

References in some sources to a 'Frederick Charles Roberts' having played for Somerset are incorrect.

Somerset XI in 1899. STANDING: G. C. Gill, G. S. McAaulay (Scorer), E. J. Tyler, H. T. Stanley, J. Daniell, E. Robson. SEATED: C. S. Hickley, W. C. Hedley, S. M. J. Woods, A. E. Newton, W. Trask. FRONT: G. B. Nichols

Somerset XI v. Sussex in June 1900. STANDING: G. S. McAulay (Scorer), E. Robson, W. Trask, E. J. Tyler. SEATED: V. T. Hill, L. C. H. Palairet, S. M. J. Woods, A. P. Wickham, G. Fowler. FRONT: G. C. Gill, A. E. Lewis, B. Cranfield

1900

"The action of Surrey in objecting to the qualification of Braund for Somerset is attributed by most people to spite, the Surrey folk being filled with chagrin at allowing him to pass from their county."

Bath Chronicle

Championship Position: 11 of 15

There were signs of improvement. Three sound amateurs – Phillips, Stanley and Hedley – were off in Africa quelling the Boers, but Lionel Palairet was back and scored nearly 1,000 runs. Under the tighter rules, Teddy Tyler began to be no-balled. His confidence was dented, but Monty Cranfield took on the mantle with 65 wickets. Astonishingly, two of Somerset's four victories were against the 1899 champions. Surrey had lodged an objection that Len Braund, whom Somerset had poached from them, had not actually moved into his residence in Taunton. Somerset were smarting. Surrey were twice defeated. It was perhaps a shame that there was not a little more needle in some of the affable West Country outfit's other matches.

Among the debutants, Oswald Samson made telling contributions with the bat, fast bowler Alfred Bailey put in some useful performances and wicket-keeper Harry Chidgey would continue to turn out for the county until the 1920s.

125
Oswald Massey Samson
14 June 1900 v. Oxford University, Oxford

O. M. Samson – a good county cricketer and an inspiring maths teacher

Born in Taunton on 8 August 1881, Oswald Massey Samson was the son of Charles Henry Samson, an architect, and his wife, Wilhelmina. Among the grand designs drawn up by C. H. Samson, the best-known was perhaps the Taunton Technical Institute, an imposing building completed towards the very end of the nineteenth century. A left-handed batsman and slow left-arm bowler, Oswald was educated at Cheltenham College. Drafted into the Somerset team as an eighteen-year-old for the match against Oxford University, he went on to graduate with a double first in maths from Hertford College, Oxford, where he gained his cricketing blue. After leaving Oxford he took up a teaching post at Rugby School and this limited his availability. For most of his career he was only able to represent Somerset during school vacations. Over the course of thirteen years he would play for Somerset in forty-five first-class fixtures, averaging 18.62 with the bat, including a century against local rivals, Gloucestershire. He was only used as an occasional bowler, claiming five wickets at 17.60 apiece, suggesting that he was perhaps underutilised.

Forsaking maths and Rugby School for the war effort, Oswald was commissioned as a second lieutenant in the Royal Garrison Artillery. In June 1917 he was promoted to the temporary role of lieutenant but on 17 September 1918 he died of his wounds near Peronne. The date of death on the Graves Registration Report Form is stated as 18 September, suggesting that he may have died during the night. His resting place is given as Plot 4 Row D in the local war cemetery, the bodies laid out with a mathematical precision that might have appealed to the former maths teacher. He was thirty-seven years old when he was killed. A prime number for a man still in the prime of life. He was never married. The Rugby School magazine, the *Meteor*, says of him that he was an 'inspiring teacher, resourceful in ideas for breaking the monotony of a lesson' and noted his infectious enthusiasm, talking of his 'unfailing good humour' and the fact that 'with a boy's outlook on life, he had a man's judgement'.

126
Alfred James Bowerman
21 June 1900 v. Lancashire, Taunton

Alf Bowerman was born on 22 November 1873 in Broomfield. A decent club cricketer who played for Bridgwater, he managed only eight runs at an average of 2.00 in his two first-class matches for Somerset. He has an unusual claim to fame, though, being one of twelve men (including only two county players) to have won an Olympic gold medal at cricket. The 1900 Paris Olympics comprised a hotchpotch of events. In the case of the cricket, the original intention had been to include teams from Great Britain, France, Belgium and The Netherlands, although the latter two pulled out. That left France versus Great Britain, or more accurately a group of ex-pats who had been working on the construction of the Eiffel Tower versus the Devon & Somerset Wanderers (comprising ex-Blundell's School pupils and players from the Castle Cary club) who happened to be on tour, promoting the game. These pioneers would later report that the French had proved too 'excitable' for cricket. The teams were scheduled to meet at the Velodrome de Vincennes. After some confusion over selection, it was agreed that both sides would be allowed twelve men. Among the twenty-four participants, only two – Alf Bowerman and Montagu Toller, who had both turned out for Somerset – were above-average club players. When the teams arrived, they were dismayed to find that there was nothing resembling a cricket square available. With tickets priced at an optimistic 1 franc for the best seats and 50 centimes for the second-class seating, fewer than 25 people would attend over the course of the two-day contest. Undeterred, the teams pressed ahead. At 5 o'clock on the first day, Great Britain (or 'England' as the poster has them) had been bowled out for 117 and France had responded with a total of 78. The teams agreed to suspend hostilities until the

Alf Bowerman – one of only two county players to have won an Olympic gold medal at cricket

211

following day. In the second innings, Great Britain declared at 145 for 5, Alf Bowerman top-scoring with 59. Thereafter, Monty Toller, bowling his fast-medium deliveries on an unplayable pitch, ripped through the opposition, taking 7 for 9. The gold medal position had been assured.

Alf Bowerman would play once more for Somerset in 1905. A timber merchant by profession, he had been married in 1895 to Frances Mabel (née Long). Later, having sold his business, he decided to take his wife and family to Australia, leaving for Brisbane in December 1912 to start a new enterprise there as a farmer. It is interesting to note that he had been taken to court by a turf accountant in 1910 for a gambling debt of £40, though there is nothing to say these two events are linked.

Alf then served in the First World War as a member of the Australian Imperial Force, enlisting in 1915 and being posted in the Middle East until 1919. His enrolment papers inform us that he was 5 ft 8 in tall and that by the age of forty-two he had 'iron grey hair'. He died in Brisbane, Queensland, on 20 June 1947, at the age of seventy-three, his record as a near-unique Olympian still intact. His death was perhaps linked to a fall the previous October, when he had fractured his skull while a resident of the Eventide Nursing Home. He was survived by his wife and children.

127
William Hyman
28 June 1900 v. Yorkshire, Dewsbury

Born in Radstock on 7 March 1875, Billy Hyman was a coalminer's son and one of five brothers. A gifted boy, he became a pupil teacher and then a fully-fledged schoolmaster in Bath, where he developed into a prolific club batsman. He also played football in the winter for Bath City FC and Somerset. In 1890, he was married to Margaret Emily (née Adams) and they would have two sons.

He was drafted into the Somerset side to play Yorkshire as a result of his success as a batsman at club level. The reports praised his superb fielding, with the *Yorkshire Evening Post* noting that the catch which ended Yorkshire's first innings involved Hyman's running twenty yards before catching the ball 'high up close to the spectators' before being 'loudly applauded' by a generous home crowd. The catch which dismissed Denton in the second innings is described as 'such a hot one that two fingers of the left hand were badly hurt, and he could do no more fielding on Friday morning, a substitute being found'. Meanwhile, he had a torrid time with the bat. In the first innings 'he was run out by Lewis, who in turn ran himself out'. The *Bath Chronicle* reports that in the second innings, unable to grasp the bat with his left hand, 'he was at the wicket for half an hour … exhibiting capital defence'. The newspaper notes that Sam Woods was 'very pleased with Hyman's display, and was anxious that he should remain in the team for the Lancashire fixture, but scholastic duties would not permit this'. Somerset did indeed stick with Billy and continued to select him as he became available. His appetite for runs in club cricket did not diminish. In July 1902, he managed to smite an astonishing 359 not out in 110 minutes for Bath against a Thornbury team captained by Dr E. M. Grace. 192 of the runs came in sixes, as testified by the scorebook, still in Bath CC's possession.

Billy Hyman would remain part of the Bath cricket scene for many years. A local reporter marvels at his free-scoring, stating that Hyman was 'rewriting the record books'. His performances for Somerset were muted but the county believed he had more to give and invited him to become a full-time professional for them in 1912, presumably reasoning that regular exposure at the county level would yield the desired results. Although he starred with a century against Sussex in 1913 in his home town of Bath, success was otherwise hard to come by and his thirty-eight first-class matches

Billy Hyman, who terrorised opposing club bowlers but scored only one century in the first-class arena

would yield precisely 1,000 runs at an average of 15.62. Sadly, Billy's wife, Margaret, had not been there to share in her husband's most notable innings for the county. She had died early in 1913.

In 1917, he was married again, to Winifred Nora (née Bunt), who hailed from St Austell in Cornwall. Billy subsequently left Bath to take up a teaching post in Walsall but was long remembered in the city he had served so well. He died at the age of eighty-three on 11 February 1959 in St Austell, his second wife's birthplace to which they had retired. The coalminer's son from Radstock had done well for himself, even if he had never quite made it as a county player.

128
Alfred Edward Bailey
28 June 1900 v. Yorkshire, Dewsbury

Alfred Bailey's birth was never registered but later documentation confirms that he was born in West Norwood in Surrey on 14 March 1871. In the 1901 census, the thirty-year-old Bailey gives his occupation as a 'Bricklayer and Professional Cricketer'. He is lodging in Lambeth along with his wife and their newborn son, who had been named John in memory of Alfred's father. John Bailey Snr was a bricklayer who had died in 1880, leaving his widow Eliza to care for Alfred and four siblings.

From 1891 until the middle of the decade, Alfred Bailey played for Surrey in non-first-class fixtures, but the county decided that he had no future with them. Determined to carve a career as a cricketer, he played professional club cricket, including a four-year spell with Ashton-under-Lyme in the Yorkshire League. His performances caught the eye of Somerset, who registered their interest and waited for him to qualify. An unspecified injury delayed his entry into county cricket and Somerset came to an arrangement with Rochdale that he should play for the club until such time as the county required his services, which they duly did for the away games against Yorkshire and Lancashire. There was much excitement in the local press, as Somerset felt they had unearthed a useful player.

Alfred Bailey who rose from humble beginnings to become a successful professional cricketer

We are told that 'Bailey is a medium pace bowler, breaks both from the leg and off, and on a sticky wicket is dangerous'. His first two appearances for the county proved disappointing and he stayed playing club cricket until 1905, when, having been invited back by Somerset, he produced some excellent bowling performances, including an 8-wicket haul against Middlesex. He began the 1907 season in splendid style, taking 8 for 46 against Yorkshire, but after this his returns were relatively modest and Somerset parted company with him later that season.

Alfred was then employed by the Dunfermline side as their pro from 1907 until 1909. Once again, he began brightly, with a return of 7 for 29 for his new club, which must have raised expectations to a fever pitch. On this occasion he did not disappoint, taking more than two hundred wickets in two seasons. He also made two appearances for Scotland. From 1909, he played for the Uddington club as their pro, but by 1911 he had ceased to be a professional cricketer and was running a tobacco and confectionery shop in Catford with his wife, Elizabeth (née Hunter), to whom he had been married in 1900. Their stay in Catford was shortlived. Alfred's brother, Fred, signed up for the Canadian Expeditionary Force in 1914 while a waiter at the Royal George Hotel in Moose Jaw, Saskatchewan. He lists Alfred as his next of kin and confirms that Alfred is living in Charlton, London. Alfred continued to earn a living as a tobacconist, moving to Swale, in Kent. An 'A. E. Bailey' – presumably him – is reported turning out for the Century Club as late as 1927, although he does not play a pivotal role, as might be expected of a man by then in his late fifties. He died on 1 August 1950 at the age of seventy-nine in Borden, Kent.

129
Harry Chidgey
2 August 1900 v. Gloucestershire, Bristol

Harry Chidgey

Harry Chidgey's parents owned the Angell Inn at Flax Bourton. Harry was born on 25 July 1879 and lived in the village or in neighbouring Backwell all his life. By the age of nine, he was already in the news after his cap and scarf were stolen from their peg at Flax Bourton school. On being alerted to the crime, the local policeman, PC Fox, cycled to Weston-super-Mare in pursuit of the culprits. A reporter noted that in their subsequent courtroom appearance the three thieves' heads were barely visible above the dock as they were given their sentences, 'the youngest to receive four strokes with a birch rod and the other two eight strokes each'. PC Fox was no doubt rewarded for his efforts with a pint on the house at the Angell Inn.

Harry Chidgey, a wicket-keeper who served Somerset cricket well for many years, once the county's fine group of amateur wicket-keepers was no longer available: he later officiated as a test umpire

At the age of eleven Harry passed the entrance exam to the highly regarded Merchant Venturer's School, Bristol, where he proved a promising young cricketer, playing for Flax Bourton at fourteen. His chance to represent his county came in 1900 but Somerset had a surfeit of amateur wicket-keepers and, with money in short supply, only called on Harry as a last resort. *Wisden* describes him as 'small, quick and neat' and Somerset would certainly come to be grateful for his consistent performances. From 1908 until 1919 he became a regular member of the team. Thereafter, his appearances became more sporadic until he was last called on in 1921.

His batting average of 6.91 with the bat in ninety-eight matches was modest but his one moment of glory came in 1909 when he appeared as nightwatchman and stubbornly held out the following morning for 45 runs, enabling Somerset, with further help from Len Braund, to glean an unexpected draw. Demonstrating the gulf between club and county cricket, Harry scored some free-flowing centuries for Flax Bourton. He became an institution at the club and in wider aspects of village life, serving for a while on the Rural District Council.

In 1925, he was added to the list of first-class umpires. The inhabitants of Flax Bourton were delighted when one of their own was asked to officiate in the Fourth Test of the 1926 Ashes series.

Harry's personal life was twice touched by tragedy. Early in 1902 he was married to Beatrice Louisa (née Horler), whose family hailed from neighbouring Backwell. Perhaps they had been childhood sweethearts. Together they managed the George Inn at Backwell. Then on 14 March 1909 Beatrice died at the tender age of thirty-three. They had no children. Harry was then married to Kate (née Abbott) in 1917 and her death in 1925 through pneumonia must have been a cruel blow, though he will have found comfort through the presence of their two young sons, Tom and Harry Jnr. He would also watch the progress of his nephew (his sister's son, A. E. Waters), a cricketer who represented Gloucestershire.

The affable local lad who never wished to stray far from his beloved village of Flax Bourton was prepared to trek around the country for Somerset, but home was where he loved to be and home was where he died on 16 November 1941 at the age of sixty-two.

1901

"… it was the manner of the successes over the great Yorkshire side of the early years of [the twentieth] century that really established Somerset as cricket's 'giant killers'."

Sixty Years of Somerset Cricket by Ron Roberts

Championship Position: 13= of 15

Another season in which runs came aplenty but too few wickets were taken. Lionel Palairet fell just short of 2,000 first-class runs, playing his part in three first-wicket stands in excess of 200. Monty Cranfield bagged over 100 wickets and Len Braund hit the ground running with over 1,000 runs and a useful haul of wickets. The standout performance was the astonishing defeat of the champions, Yorkshire, at Headingley. Between 1900 and 1903 a peerless Yorkshire side were only twice defeated, on both occasions by lowly Somerset. In 1901, trailing by 239 after the first innings, Somerset piled on the runs with centuries from Palairet, Braund and Phillips. Woods, Hill and Robson filled their boots, too. Somerset notched up a total of 630 and a demoralised Yorkshire collapsed, with Braund and Cranfield doing the damage. It was the talk of the county circuit. Sadly, it was one of only four wins. Consistency was not in Somerset's vocabulary.

Among the debutants, the charismatic wicket-keeper batsman Henry Martyn and the elegant Randall Johnson would prove the standout performers.

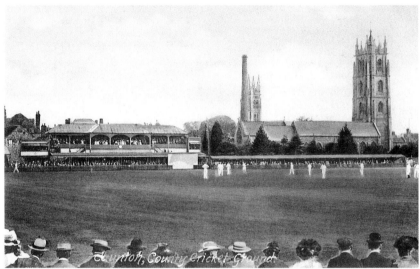

The County Ground, Taunton, at the turn of the century

Somerset XI in 1901
STANDING: H. E. Murray-Anderdon (Secretary), L. C. Braund, A. E. Lewis, E. Robson
SEATED: C. A. Bernard, A. E. Newton, S. M. J. Woods, L. C. H. Palairet, F. A. Phillips
FRONT: R. B. Porch, B. Cranfield

130
William Leslie Price
13 May 1901 v. Yorkshire, Taunton

The son of a woollen merchant, Leslie Price was born in
Taunton on 19 March 1881. He was educated at Queen's
College, Taunton, and embarked on a career as an auctioneer
after leaving school. A wicket-keeper and middle-order
batsman for Taunton CC, he also played in the position of
full-back for Taunton RFC, although only for a brief period
before he began to devote his leisure time to the newly-
formed Taunton Amateur Operatic Society, taking part in
their inaugural production in January 1900. The performance was of *In the Days of the Siege*, an operetta about Taunton
in the Civil War. The libretto had been written by Somerset
cricketer George Nichols and the operetta – already a success
at Plymouth two years earlier – 'attracted a large audience
and pleased the critics'. Among the chorus of cavaliers were
Leslie Price and fellow Taunton and Somerset cricketer, Ted
Lock. The *Taunton Courier* remarks that 'the choruses were
well rendered'. By 1904, Leslie Price had risen to the role of
one of the gondoliers in the eponymous operetta by Gilbert
and Sullivan. Also performing was Emelie Maude Polley,
whom Leslie Price would become married in 1906. They
would remain together until her death, forty-four years later.
It is surely no mere coincidence that one of their sons, Leslie
Gay Price, shares his name with the former Somerset and
England wicket-keeper.

*Leslie Price – his first-
match nerves curtailed his
county career but he
enjoyed many years as a
successful club cricketer in
Taunton*

With neither Newton nor Wickham available for the game against Yorkshire in
May 1901, Somerset gave the nineteen-year-old Taunton amateur, Leslie Price, his
opportunity. This proved a mistake. Writing in the *Yorkshire Post* 'Old Ebor' reports
that in Yorkshire's first innings Price dropped a straightforward catch and fumbled
an easy stumping. Furthermore, there were 35 extras in the innings. It would be
uncharitable to attribute them all to first match nerves on the part of young Leslie,
but the keeper must surely have been at fault for most or all of the 23 byes. Only one

bye was recorded in the second innings and so perhaps his nerves had settled. Yorkshire scraped home by one wicket. Price's errors had proved costly. Somerset had been denied a morale-boosting victory. He would never be selected again.

Leslie's career as an auctioneer was rather more successful. He rose to become a senior partner in the firm Greenslade & Co, whose offices were (and still are) in Hammett Street, Taunton. Leslie was also District Chairman of Auctioneers, overseeing arrangements in 1940 when an outbreak of the dreaded foot-and-mouth disease among sheep lasted for most of the year and had a majorly disruptive impact on Taunton's market days. He was still active as a senior partner and auctioneer for Gleenslade & Co in the 1950s. He died in Taunton on 6 February 1958 at the age of seventy-six. There would not have been many inhabitants of Taunton old enough to recall his three days as a nervous nineteen-year-old, fresh out of the Queen's College school team and suffering a baptism of fire in which he cost his county a victory and blew his chances of ever being selected to play again for Somerset.

<h1 style="text-align:center">131
Henry Martyn</h1>
6 June 1901 v. Oxford University, Oxford

Henry Martyn

Somerset had continued to scratch around for an amateur wicket-keeper capable of filling the shoes of the old campaigners, Archie Wickham and Arthur Newton. They must have felt blessed when Henry Martyn became available. Born in Lifton, Devon, on 16 July 1877, he was the seventh child of the rector of Lifton. At Exeter Grammar School he showed his early promise, playing for the school team for three years and captaining the side for one. Already strikingly tall at 'well over six feet', he gained a fearsome reputation as a competitor, insisting that the first team should meet for fielding practice each day. A former teammate recounted that some team members would be in a state of some terror as their tall, charismatic captain proceeded to 'flog the ball' at them. He was called up by Devon and on his debut, the day before his nineteenth birthday, came in at number six and blasted the Cornwall attack for 138 out of a total of 251 all out. Somerset took note and registered their interest. Devon had little or no prospect of hanging onto their brightest talent. At Oxford, he would play for the university for two seasons, with *Wisden* noting that 'it was obvious that a great wicket-keeper had been found'. Martyn combined fearlessness with a gift for showmanship. He was also unusual in wearing two pairs of gloves to allow him to take the ball at pace.

On occasions his fearlessness proved his undoing. Sam Woods relates in his autobiography that Martyn, full of unbounded optimism and prone to sharing his advice from start to finish in any game, was once hit full in the face by a bouncer from George Gill that removed two teeth. Woods ordered Martyn to hold his head still while he 'shoved them back into their sockets, they are still there, although a bit discoloured'. As a batsman he never held back. A reporter for the *Bath Chronicle* writes that 'the crowd used to sit up and take notice when he strode … to the crease to begin an

Henry Martyn – a charismatic wicket-keeper-batsman, tall and fearless

innings, which more likely than not, would be a display of vast muscular exercise of embarrassment to the widespread field'. Had he shown more temperance he might have improved on his average of 24.86 in seventy-four matches for Somerset, including a knock of 130 not out against the Australians in 1905.

After graduating, he had been taken on as an assistant schoolmaster by former Somerset joint-secretary, Thomas Spencer, who was principal of Naish House Preparatory School, based at the time at Wraxall. Henry decided, however, that a life in business would be more to his taste. Insufficiently wealthy to afford the hedonistic lifestyle of some of his teammates, his work as a commercial traveller at least allowed him some latitude to make himself available for Somerset during the season. But by 1906 he had to call it a day and focus on his career. He was married that year to Mabel Gunnora (née Gurney), daughter of the rector of Poughill, near Crediton in Devon. They had no children.

Henry served in the war as a second lieutenant but was withdrawn from the action owing to ill health. He was living in Dawlish at the time of his death on 8 August 1928, aged fifty-one. A man of Devon, he had possessed all the characteristics the Somerset supporters looked for in their players.

132
John Thomas
6 June 1901 v. Oxford University, Oxford

John Thomas

Jack Thomas – one of a happy band who enjoyed a lifetime of cricket with Bath CC

John Thomas, known as Jack, was born on 6 January 1869 in Wimbledon, the third of the five children of Champion and Mary Thomas. His father was at the time a railway clerk but soon moved to Wincanton when appointed the railway station master. An obituary in the *Bath Chronicle* entitled *A Pioneer of cricket in Somerset: Death of Mr J. Thomas* informs us that as a fourteen-year-old, Jack followed in his father's footsteps, joining the Somerset and Dorset Railway Service (at Templecombe). He worked his way up, becoming a 'Goods Rate Section Clerk' at the head office in Bath in 1894, eventually managing the department some years later. In 1898, aged twenty-nine, he was married to thirty-eight-year-old Emma Jane (née Dewey). They would have no children and she would predecease him in 1939.

He played cricket for thirty-five years in total, first for Wincanton and then for Bath. A useful club bowler, he once took 9 for 38 for Bath as the opposition racked up more than 200. He would only play three first-class matches for the county (including one Championship game against Sussex) and although he was handed the ball for a total of thirty-three overs, he only ever took one wicket at a cost of 130 runs, while his first-class batting average was 9.00. This latter statistic would have pleased and perhaps surprised Jack, who was regularly on the receiving end of good-natured banter from his Bath teammates over his often woeful performances with the bat.

He retired from the Somerset and Dorset Railway after forty-seven years of service when the company was taken over by the London, Midland and Scottish Railway in 1930. He was by then a widower. He died in his adoptive city of Bath on 20 August 1949 at the age of eighty. Jack Thomas had been a diligent man who had made the most of his talents.

133
Peter Randall Johnson
13 June 1901 v. South Africa, Taunton

P. Randall Johnson

Born on 5 August 1880 in Wellington, New Zealand, Randall Johnson was a great stylist. He batted with an elegance that prompted many to regard him as the natural successor to Lionel Palairet and he dressed immaculately, a silk cravat often around his neck and his whites with all the creases in the right places. Sometimes he would even turn up to a match in his top hat and morning coat. His father, G. R. Johnson, a barrister, had played for Cambridge University and Randall would represent first Eton and then Cambridge, where he played alongside Somerset's future captain John Daniell. The Somerset folklore has it that Daniell persuaded the committee to register Johnson as having been born in Wellington, without bothering to mention that they were referring to the city in New Zealand rather than the small town in Somerset. The story is apocryphal. Johnson's father owned Feniton Court in Devon and so no embellishment was required. (The anecdote has also been attached to Tom Lowry but he hailed from Okawa, so that we can dismiss that, too.)

Randall Johnson – regarded by many as the natural successor to Lionel Palairet

Johnson's batting inspires contrasting opinions. His teammate Jack MacBryan, perhaps motivated by jealousy, thought him an overrated popinjay. Peter Roebuck, writing in his history of the club, points out that over the course of 229 matches, Johnson's average was 25.82 – well short of greatness. That is the view of two batsmen dismissive of style over substance. Others regarded him with awe. Robertson-Glasgow talks of batsmanship 'comparable in style and fluency to that of Lionel Palairet ... Tall and graceful, Randall Johnson in play against fast bowling is something to remember'. Perhaps both arguments have some merit. It is certainly a fact that he was invited to tour Australia in 1911-12 but had to decline, owing to his work as a London stockbroker. Equally, the trajectory of his career shows a slow start, bogged down in mediocrity and a full flowering of his talent in 1908.

His 603 runs in the eight innings he was available included four centuries and he topped the national averages at 75.37. Thereafter he completed only the occasional innings of genius. He would score seventeen centuries.

He was married in 1905 to Kathleen Effie (née Hamilton-Gell), a clergyman's daughter from Clyst St Mary, with whom he had two sons and two daughters. As with a surprising number of people connected with Somerset cricket, she claimed descent from William the Conqueror. Had cricket been established in Somerset 900 or so years earlier, Somerset would no doubt have laid claim to the services of 'William the Bastard' and some captain he would have been.

He divided his time between the impressive Winslade House in Clyst St Mary, Devon, and his London base in Warwick Square, while he earned his living as a stock-broker. Randall Johnson was, for a while, a member of the MCC Committee. In later life, afflicted by arthritis, he required the use of a wheelchair, though he no doubt manoeuvred it with panache. He died in Sidmouth on 1 July 1959 at the age of seventy-eight. *Wisden* had it about right in reporting that he was 'brilliant rather than consistent'.

134
Hugh Ferguson Montgomery
13 June 1901 v. South Africa, Taunton

Although he sometimes wrote his middle name as 'Furguson' he is referred to as Ferguson on legal documents and on his memorial. He was born in Umballa, Bengal, on 6 May 1880 but his father became the rector of Halse, near Taunton. Hugh was educated at Marlborough College. A cousin of Field Marshall 'Monty' Montgomery, he opted for a military career.

A right-handed batsman, he played his first match for Somerset against the South African tourists in 1901, mustering only one run. Undeterred, Somerset invited him to play again a fortnight later in the fixture with Gloucestershire. The demands of his military career would mean that he would play in only twelve matches for the county between 1901 and 1909. His batting average was 13.27 and in addition he took three wickets but it was Montgomery's exploits as a soldier and the shocking manner of his death, that generated more headlines than anything he achieved as a cricketer.

In 1920 and by then a Lt Colonel, he was serving in Dublin as part of the British Army Intelligence Corps. On the instructions of the freedom fighter Michael Collins, twelve Irishmen known as 'the apostles' took the members of an alleged spy ring – the so-called 'Cairo Gang' – by surprise early on 21 November. Entering their various lodgings, they shot nineteen men, killing fourteen and wounding five. Not all were intended targets. Some, such as Montgomery, were in the wrong place at the wrong time. The group of spies seems to have been at best complacent and at worst incompetent. The fact that they were given their name as a result of their 'clandestine' meetings at the Cairo Café at 59 Grafton Street confirms that their activities were not as covert as they supposed. Certainly the Home Office Minister, Winston Churchill, had no sympathy for their plight, describing them as 'careless fellows who should have known better'.

H. F. Montgomery – the rector's son from the sleepy village of Halse, caught up in the bloody theatre of war

Montgomery was lodging in Pembroke Street when the gunmen broke in and executed their two intended targets – Major Dowling and Captain Price – but, coming out of his room on hearing the commotion, he was one of three further members of the military to be shot. It is possible that the assassins gunned him down with no intention to kill him, in order to make good their escape. Although seriously injured, he was rushed to hospital still alive. That afternoon, the British Army exacted brutal revenge with the shooting of fourteen people at the Gaelic Football match at Croke Park between Dublin and Tipperary. The English referred to the events as the 'Dublin Massacre' but it

was the name 'Bloody Sunday' that stuck. Lt Colonel Montgomery died of his gunshot wounds on 10 December 1920 at the age of only forty. He was buried with full military honours at Brompton Cemetery. His parents later unveiled a memorial to Hugh in the church at Halse, having already erected a tablet in memory of another son, Neville, killed in action on 21 August 1917.

135
George William Jupp
11 July 1901 v. Lancashire, Old Trafford

The son of a railway stationmaster, George Jupp was born in Axbridge on 30 October 1875, brought up in Clevedon and educated at Uppingham School. Although he was a marginal player for Somerset, the *Dundee Evening Telegraph* informs us that 'from 1894 until the war, Mr Jupp was a dominating personality in Scottish cricket'. He worked in the Edinburgh Office of Works, overseeing planning and the protection of listed sites. George was therefore only available to play for Somerset during brief vacations between the years 1901 and 1907 and averaged 11.00 in six innings.

It was a different story in Edinburgh, where he topped the Carlton CC batting averages in eleven of the twelve seasons between 1899 and 1910 inclusive, scoring twenty-eight centuries. He exceeded 1500 runs in the 1900 season and 'had a number of triumphs' as a bowler. One obituary states that 'he was for many years an automatic choice in representative matches' and – after praising him for his skill as a batsman and bowler – notes that 'his work in the field as a first slip is still spoken of by the older habitués of Grange Loan [Carlton CC's ground]'. He in fact made eleven appearances for Scotland between 1899 and 1912, his last innings – against Australia – resulting in a 50 and offering a tantalising glimpse of the talent Somerset had missed out on. N.

George Jupp – left Somerset and became a legend in Edinburgh

L. Stevenson provides us with an evocative account of George Jupp's charismatic approach to cricket in his book *"Play!" The Story of the Carlton Cricket Club*:

> *He could hit a ball as far as anyone I have ever known. He did so repeatedly. I recall, for instance, his fierce bombardment of the barrels in the courtyard of the Holyrood brewery. How the "railing crowd" round the High School enclosure, who were always appreciative of good cricket, used to look forward to the whirlwind batting displays of "Our George". I recall how, at Raeburn Place against Edinburgh Academicals, he drove a ball out of*

the ground, clean over the tram-lines, and through a window in the second flat of a Raeburn Place Tenement. I felt like going round and warning the other tenants to keep their windows open in case George, being in the mood, did it again. And at Grange Loan – well, it wasn't safe to hold a garden-party within a hundred yards of the ground while George Jupp was having his innings!

He was married in 1916 to an actress named Ethel Ritchie (née Armit) and clearly passed on his sporting prowess to one of his daughters – Nancy – who casually entered the Girls' Golf Championship at Stoke Poges, while aged thirteen and with little previous experience of golf. To her astonishment, she won the event. Speaking to a local reporter, she recalled that she 'was never very keen on the game'. George Jupp was more of an enthusiast and was often to be found in later life on the golf course at Longniddy, East Lothian. He retired from his role as Principal of the Office of Works in 1935 and, still living in Longniddy, died at the age of sixty-two on 6 July 1938. He was survived by his wife and two daughters, a celebrity in his adoptive home of Edinburgh, his amazing feats barely known about back in his native Somerset, whose supporters would have rejoiced in his exhilarating approach to the game.

136
Gilbert Burrington
11 July 1901 v. Lancashire, Old Trafford

Gilbert Burrington

For many years he was listed in the records as 'George Burrington', with the result that the story of his life – curtailed by the First World War – teetered on the verge of oblivion. Born in Bridgwater on 13 June 1879, Gilbert was the third child of Gilbert George Burrington and his wife, Amelia Frances. Gilbert Snr. was the manager of the Bridgwater branch of Fox, Fowler & Co Bank. He was also nominated as the guardian of the young Sam Woods when Sam's father returned to Australia. Sam lodged with the Burringtons during vacations and no doubt the young Gilbert would have idolised the dashing Australian sportsman. Along with his younger brothers, Humphrey and Harley, Gilbert Jnr was a boarder at King's School, Gloucester, where he is described as having been 'an avid cricketer'. After leaving school, he

Gilbert Burrington – a member of the XI who surprised everyone by beating the 'unbeatable' Yorkshire team in 1901, he died a war hero

lodged in Gillingham, Dorset, while he worked as a commercial clerk for a bacon wholesaler, but subsequent events suggest that he preferred the outdoor life. Between 1901 and 1902 he made three Championship appearances for Somerset as a tail-end batsman and enthusiastic fielder, his presence owing much to his sponsor, Sam Woods. He averaged 8.00 over his five innings for Somerset.

In the early 1900s he emigrated to Canada (as did younger brother, Harley). Gilbert became a deputy game warden in British Columbia while Harley became a cattle rancher in Alberta. Neither boy cut off their ties with England but they would both still have been in Canada when their father died in May 1908 and their widowed mother subsequently moved to Burnham-on-Sea, where she ran a guest house. Gilbert was back in the country in 1913 for his marriage to Marianne Emily (née Harries) of Tregwynt Manor, Pembroke, on 27 December.

In 1914, Harley enlisted in the Canadian Overseas Expeditionary Force. He died of neck wounds on 23 July 1915 at the General Hospital, Boulogne, after having been hit by a German sniper. We cannot know what motivated Gilbert to follow in the footsteps of Harley, but he enlisted with the 102nd Battalion of the Canadian Overseas Expeditionary Force on 16 February 1916. His details are revealed on his enlistment papers: his height of 5 ft 10 in, his grey eyes and brown hair. But he lied about his age, shaving off nine years. He was clearly determined to join up, whatever it took, despite that fact that he already had a child, John Harries Burrington. He landed in France on 12 August 1916 and his would prove a short war. Having played a decisive role in the recapturing of the Regina Trench at Le Sars in the Somme (for which he would receive a posthumous Military Medal for bravery and gallant conduct), he was killed on 21 November 1916 by a German shell while strengthening the newly captured trench. He was thirty-seven. The *Western Daily Press* of 27 December 1916 carries a brief obituary under the headline *A Former Somerset Cricketer Killed in Action*, noting that 'Private Gilbert Burrington, second son of Mr Gilbert George Burrington and Mrs Burrington of Westfield House, Bridgwater' was 'a keen and clever cricketer, having played for the county for several seasons'. He was buried at Albert, France, but the location of his grave has been lost: his name is recorded, though, on the Vimy Memorial in the Pas de Calais and also on a brass memorial erected by his grieving wife at Tregwynt Manor. A constant reminder of a life, a marriage and fatherhood cut short by war.

1902

*"... for years afterwards when West Riding babies were
unduly troublesome ... their mothers would say,
'You 'oosh or Len Braund will come and get you.' "*

From Sammy to Jimmy by Peter Roebuck

Championship Position: 7= of 15

The victory over all-conquering Yorkshire had everyone talking. It had been a virtuoso performance by Len Braund, who also completed a first-class (though not a County Championship) double. Lionel Palairet and Braund were the key batsmen. Monty Cranfield and Braund were the major wicket-takers. Palairet and Braund joined the England team. Gate receipts were up and it was announced at the AGM that 'the balance sheet was more in favour of the club than it had ever been before'. Life seemed a deal rosier than it had done in the preceding seasons. Spoiling the party was the unexpected departure of George Gill, poached by his home county, Leicestershire. Somerset had no doubt been enamoured with the idea of a strong quartet of all-rounders – Braund, Gill, Robson and Lewis – helping them to build on the relative success of 1902. In a case of the pot calling the kettle black, 'strong opinions were expressed by several present [at the AGM] that Leicestershire had not treated the Somerset Committee with the courtesy due them'. How quickly they had forgotten the manner in which they had lured Braund from Surrey.

COURTESY OF BARRY PHILLIPS

"Presented to LEN C BRAUND SOMERSET V YORKS JUNE 1902. SCORED 65 OUT OF 192. CAPTURED 15 WICKETS FOR 71 RUNS."

Of the debutants, only Percy Hardy made noteworthy contributions although the nature of his untimely death would evoke more headlines than his cricketing exploits.

137
Leigh Dunlop Brownlee
15 May 1902 v. Oxford University, Oxford

Leigh D. Brownlee

Writing to an autograph hunter, just a year before his death, Leigh Brownlee patiently explained the circumstances of his only appearance for Somerset:

I never played really for Somerset. These are the facts. I had been dropped from the Oxford XI in my second year when S. M. J. Woods, an old friend of mine, brought a Somerset side to play the 'Varsity. He gave me a place in his side to help me to get back to the Oxford XI, which I did eventually. This, of course, was not a County match, so I have no claim to have played for Somerset. It was later stated by a writer on cricket that I had committed the crime of playing for two counties in the same year, which was nonsense.

Leigh Brownlee – A Gloucestershire player who made a token appearance for Somerset

Brownlee clearly regarded this as a curiosity when set alongside his eighty-one other first-class matches, but, for the record, he scored 21 in his only innings for Somerset in a drawn game.

Born in Redland, Bristol, on 17 December 1882, Leigh was educated at Clifton College, where he caught the eye of Gloucestershire, for whom his father had played in two non-first-class games. William Methven Brownlee was a friend of W. G. Grace and had ghost-written Grace's autobiography in 1891. Leigh's brother, Wilfred, would also represent Somerset's neighbours. Leigh began well, scoring 66 against Somerset on his debut for Gloucestershire in 1901, the *Western Daily Press* reporting that he possessed 'batting ability quite out of the common' and talking of his 'brilliant cuts and off drives and occasional leg strokes'. He continued to appear for Gloucestershire during vacations while he studied at Oriel College, Oxford. Although never quite able to make his presence felt for the Oxford University XI, he was awarded blues both for cricket and golf. Back at Gloucestershire he had raised hopes to fever pitch in 1903, when, as one newspaper reports, 'a notable century was achieved by ... L. D. Brownlee, who on a wicket by no means easy scored 103 against Kent and took his side out of a difficult position. While this is the best thing he has ever done, the amateur had encouraged great hopes, for he has shaped like a good-class batsman, and the success should have a strong encouraging effect.' Alas, he would never quite hit those heights again and, from 1905 until 1909 made only irregular appearances while he pursued his career in journalism. Having begun by cutting his teeth by writing short stories for the *Bristol Observer*, with titles such as *"L.B.W" (A Cricket Story, wherein is related a Certain Miraculous Happening)*, he soon moved to work as a sub-editor on the *Daily Mirror*, living in Bloomsbury. Early in 1911, he was married to Ethel Mary Kynaston (née Herapath), a GP's daughter from Bristol. Leigh's career progressed sufficiently well for him to rise to the position of editor of the *Daily Mirror* from 1931 until 1934. He had taken on the role at a time when the paper was struggling and left the post when Lord Northcliffe sold the company. Thereafter he set up a Press and News Agency in partnership with William E. Owen, though the partnership was dissolved in 1936. After a career that had bound him to Central London, Leigh retired with his wife to the leafy suburbs and enjoyed many rounds of golf.

He died in West Hampstead (and not Clifton, as some records suggest) on 22 September 1955 at the age of seventy-two.

138
Frederick Percy Hardy
15 May 1902 v. Oxford University, Oxford

J.P. Hardy

Born in Blandford in Dorset on 26 June 1881, Percy Hardy was the son of a horse dealer and the second of eight children. He showed great natural talent as a young left-handed batsman and right-arm pace bowler, though the *Taunton Courier* adds that he was 'rather slow in the field'. On leaving school he was immediately drafted into the Dorset team and recommended to Surrey, where he was a member of the Oval Ground Staff in 1900 and 1901. In consecutive innings for the Colts he made 141 and 144 not out. Len Braund spotted him and quietly recommended to Somerset that they should register the youngster, given his West Country connections. Perhaps aware

of the flaws in Hardy's temperament that would later become apparent, Surrey made no issue of this. Whilst awaiting qualification, Percy appeared for Somerset against Oxford University and the Australians. An all-round sportsman, he would also play football for Somerset.

Struggling to make his mark as a professional cricketer, he was married in 1903 to Maud Mary (née Hawker), the bookkeeper at the London (later the County) Hotel in Taunton. Perhaps the signs were already there that Percy was a man with issues and maybe the club hoped that marriage would have a calming influence on him. It does not appear to have done so. A report in the *Taunton Courier* informs us of an altercation with the authorities when he refused to allow his son to be given the necessary vaccinations, seemingly through cussedness rather than any moral reasoning. Furthermore, his father-in-law would testify at a later inquest into Percy's death that 'drink made him by turns violent and depressed'. Percy had his bright moments but he was struggling – whether because of his fondness for alcohol or flaws in his technique – to make the impact he and Somerset had hoped for. 1910 was his best year. In a wretched season for Somerset, he was second only to A. E. Lewis in the county's batting averages, amassing 700 runs. In the final years before the war, he played primarily as a pro for the Imperial Tobacco club at Knowle, making only occasional appearances for the county.

Percy Hardy – a promising young batsman who met a sorry end in a toilet cubicle in King's Cross Station

There is strong evidence to suggest that by the beginning of the First World War, Percy and Maud were estranged. He had joined the West Somerset Yeomanry in September 1914, citing his mother, rather than Maud, as his next of kin and listing his address as the Princess Royal pub in Taunton. Six weeks later, he was hit by a car and suffered a ruptured kidney, rendering him temporarily unfit for service. He was discharged with a less than enthusiastic conduct rating the following March, returning briefly to the Princess Royal before moving to London, with *De Ruigney's Roll of Honour* stating that he joined the Lord's ground staff. Once fully fit, he was called up, re-enlisting in September 1915 with the County of London Yeomanry, though he never saw active service. He was found dead in a toilet cubicle at King's Cross Station on 9 March 1916, his throat cut, his demons slayed and his blood-stained knife beside him. It is assumed that he had been unable to face the prospect of the trenches. At the inquest, Sergeant F. J. Skoyles of the County of London Yeomanry described Percy as 'a strange man' and it was also noted that 'he had not been of sober habits for some weeks before he joined the Army'. A tragic end to a promising life turned sour. Dead at the age of thirty-four, with others left to clear up the mess he left behind. And the longsuffering Maud obliged to soldier on.

139
Colin Edwin Brown
15 May 1902 v. Oxford University, Oxford

Born in Stoke St Gregory on 12 October 1878, he was the son of a managing director of an oil cake company (whose business involved grinding the remains of seeds from which cooking oil was extracted, in order to make animal feed). Oil cakes proved not to Colin Brown's taste. Instead, he trained as a solicitor and practiced for a while in Bridgwater, also involving himself in politics as the Liberal agent for the town. A right-handed batsman and occasional bowler, he played club cricket for Bridgwater, who – along with many other club sides in the county – frequently featured guests from the county eleven and provided a number of amateurs for the Somerset cause, although club form rarely transferred to the more demanding environment of the Championship. First given an airing against Oxford University in 1902, he had to wait until 1905 for his further seven first-class fixtures, managing a batting average of 12.58 in fifteen innings and taking no wickets in his three overs. His best moment came in the fixture against Lancashire when, although he was twice dismissed by their fearsome pace bowler, Walter Brearley, he had reached his only 50 in the second innings. His efforts proved in vain as Somerset lost by an innings inside two days.

He was married in 1907 to Violet Primrose (née Butcher)

Colin Brown, who left Somerset to join a solici-tors' practice in Whitby

COURTESY OF BARRY PHILLIPS

233

in Devizes and they would remain together for eighteen years, living in Whitby, where they moved not long after their wedding, allowing Colin to practice as a solicitor there. Their marriage would end in acrimony when Violet Primrose proved too alluring to a married man who had been a friend of the Browns since 1909. The man named in their decree nisi was Arnold Herbert Walker, a motor engineer from Whitby. Brown reported that his wife's manner had changed after she stayed at Beverley and she later admitted to having enjoyed a liaison with Walker. Furthermore, a similar tryst had occurred at Salisbury. In more enlightened times, the wife is entitled to a share of the separating couple's earnings as a recognition of her contribution to the marriage. Not so in 1925. Brown was ordered damages of £1,500, presumably for loss of face. And for the crime of having fallen out of love with her husband and into the arms of a family friend, Violet Primrose faced a spate of lurid headlines in the newspapers about her infidelity.

His honour restored, his pound of flesh extracted, Colin Brown was married for a second time that same year. His new wife was Mildred Mary (née Bedlington), from Guisborough, Clevedon. One is left to wonder about possible hypocrisy. He continued to practice as a solicitor in Whitby and died in the town on 25 June 1936 at the age of fifty-seven, leaving his second wife and two sons (by Violet) his estate worth nearly £5,000, a sum which had been enhanced considerably by his divorce settlement.

140
Charles Hugh Alison
15 May 1902 v. Oxford University, Oxford

Charles Hugh Alison

Somerset made a habit of selecting extraordinary men who were ordinary cricketers. Hugh Alison offers a prime example. Born in Preston on 5 March 1883, he was one of four children of Charles German Alison, who later became Chief Constable of Somerset.

Educated at Malvern College, he went on to New College, Oxford, where he studied divinity (though he opted not to complete his degree). Hugh Alison represented Somerset twice against his old university and played in two Championship matches for the county. He would go on to play for Buckinghamshire in Minor Counties cricket but it was as a golfer that he shone. He gained golfing blues in 1903 and 1904 and also represented the Combined Universities on their tour of America. He was an accomplished player. In his book *Rub of the Green*, Bernard Darwin recalls a spectacular shot by Alison from the roof of a club house to halve a hole.

In 1906 Hugh Alison began working with the renowned golf course architect H. S. (Harry) Colt, who was designing the Stoke Poges golf course. Hugh was invited to become the first club secretary on a salary of £13 6s 8d per month plus an accommodation allowance., He was also taken on concurrently by Colt as a construction supervisor, cementing a life-long friendship. He began as an employee and among their commissions were new courses at Sunningdale and Wentworth, together with redesigns of Royal St George's and Royal Lytham & St Anne's. With business interrupted by the First World War, he joined the army as a captain, working in the ciphers unit. Soon after the war he re-established his connection with Harry Colt and together they designed twenty new courses and remodelled a further six in the USA. Their handbook on golf course architecture, first published in 1920, is regarded as a classic. Alison is quoted as saying that 'in planning a golf course there are no fixed rules ... and the variety which results is one of the greatest charms of the game'. By 1928 they were ready to set up a limited partnership, listed on the New York stock exchange, but the subsequent Great Depression meant that they had

Hugh Alison – a modestly talented cricketer but a highly successful golfer and golf course designer of world renown

to look further afield. Alison was handed complete control of the operation in the Far East and Australasia, where he gained a status approaching deity as a course designer. His many commissions included prestigious courses such as Kasumigaseki, Hirono and Kaiwana.

Business was interrupted for a second time at the start of the Second World War, during which he served once again in the decoding operation, though this time in the lower rank of lieutenant. After the war, his efforts were focussed on South Africa where he once again undertook a number of prestigious commissions. Although he was given an OBE for his work, the award apparently left him cold: he did his work for love (and no doubt financial reward) rather than for any honours. Hugh Alison died at the age of sixty-nine on 20 October 1952 in Cape Town, a year after the death of his great friend and business associate, Harry Colt. The world of golf afforded more column inches to his passing than the cricket writers mustered.

141
Frederick Marshall Lee
9 June 1902 v. Gloucestershire, Gloucester

Fred M Lee [signature]

Fred Marshall Lee – 'a gentleman who amused himself with farming in a small way'

The son of a successful merchant, Fred Marshall Lee was born in Paddington on 8 Jan 1871. Educated at Uppingham School and then Cirencester Royal Agricultural College, Fred was a serial entrepreneur who seemed disinclined to settle down in a house of his own and was never married. He was, however, blessed with a knack for making money. His greatest claim to fame is that he funded the earliest example of colour moving images, the creation of Edward Turner. A short reel, filmed in 1902 – using their patented method that entailed red, green and blue filters – was unearthed in 2012 at the National Media Museum in Bradford and includes images of the inventor Edward Turner's children. Turner was born in Clevedon, Somerset, and must have approached Lee for backing. They filed the patent in their joint names in 1899 and their application was accepted in March 1900. Fred is described on the application as a 'race-horse owner and financier'. Having played his part, Fred then sold on his interest in the project to the American movie mogul, Charles Urban. Lee had already moved on by the time the project suffered a major setback in the form of Turner's heart attack in 1903.

As a cricketer, Fred failed to generate runs as freely as he made money, but he was a sound technician who chipped in with some useful 50s and an average of 20.00 in over seventy-seven first-class appearances between 1902 and 1907.

A photograph of him gives us an impression of his sound technique. Uppingham School had coached him well. He had initially played on two occasions for Kent without success and qualified for Somerset through residency, living at Charlton Musgrove with his widowed mother and his brother, George, at the time of his selection. A description of his innings of 71 against Lancashire in 1907 talks of 'the majority of his runs coming from clean, hard strokes to the off'.

His life after retirement from county cricket was not without incident. The *Taunton Courier* of 3 March 1909 reports the court case in which he knocked down and killed a ten-year-old boy, Robert Sidney James, whilst collecting voters on election day in order to take them to the local polling booth. Lee rushed the unconscious boy to hospital in his 18/24 horsepower Swift, but all in vain. At the trial, he claimed that he was travelling at 10mph but other witnesses suggested he was speeding at 25 mph. He was exonerated. Asked to describe his profession he had replied that he was 'a gentleman who amused himself with farming in a small way'. There was no mention of cricket or venture capitalism. Fred Marshall Lee was living in Chard at the time with his brother. He remained there until his death at the age of forty-three at Wonford House Hospital near Exeter on 18 November 1914.

142
Samuel Gabriel Adams Ellis
12 June 1902 v. Lancashire, Old Trafford

Samuel Ellis

The *Western Daily Press* notes on 11 June 1902 that:

> *Local cricketers will learn with satisfaction that Somerset have at last recognised the ability of S. G. Ellis of Lodway, and have asked him to play against Lancashire next week. Ellis, who has been quite at the forefront of local cricket for many years, has always been a consistent and reliable bat, as well as a keen field. His many friends will wish him success in his first county match.*

For many years incorrectly listed as 'S. E. Ellis' in the cricketing archives, Sam Ellis was born on 5 April 1870 in Pill, Somerset, the sixth child of Thomas and Sarah Ellis. On leaving school, Sam worked as an office clerk in the Bristol Docks. He was thirty-two years old and residing with his stepmother, Florence, when he made his debut for Somerset.

He was later married to Marion Mabel (née Bryant), known as Mabel, the daughter

Sam Ellis – a hero at Lodway CC, he later became one of the forgotten men of Somersetshire cricket

of a retired local school teacher. At the time of their marriage both Samuel and Mabel were in their late thirties. They purchased a house in Knowle, where they lived with Mabel's parents (now in their seventies) along with the elderly couple's nurse.

As a club cricketer, Sam Ellis was a consistent performer over the years, his noteworthy contribution still fondly remembered in reminiscences of the Lodway team written as late as the 1930s. He was found wanting at county level, though, his first appearance for his county yielding scores of 0 and 5. He was not invited to play a second time, returning to club cricket and a career as an assistant accountant in Bristol Docks.

Having retired at sixty-five, Sam and Mabel moved to the coast at Portishead. This time, a younger brother of Mabel was invited to lodge with them. Sam Ellis died in Portishead on 26 March 1946 at the age of seventy-five.

143
Charles Oatley Bennett
12 June 1902 v. Lancashire, Old Trafford

C O, Bennett

Charles Bennett was a solicitor based in Bruton at the time of his Championship debut. Born in Ticehurst, Sussex, on 15 August 1872, Charles, whose father was also a solicitor, was brought up in Bruton. Educated at Haileybury College, he was a member of the First XI in 1889 and 1890 and was also an accomplished raquets player. He had become a solicitor after initially training to be a barrister. Charles was active in the local community, a member of the freemasons and a keen though never a sparkling batsman. Much of his cricket was played for Bruton and Wincanton, for whom he appeared as an all-rounder. In a match in 1894 he took five wickets in an innings while representing Hazelgrove and District against the Somerset Club and Ground side. As might be expected for a man who completed a number of decent but not outstanding innings at club level, Charles Bennett struggled in the first-class game, mustering an average of 5.00 in his four innings. His services were not called on again after the 1902 season.

He attempted to supplement his income as a solicitor with business interests. The prospectus for The Somersetshire Manufacturing Association, issued in April 1898, shows Charles Bennett and his father among the directors planning to raise a sum of £23,000 for the purchase of a number of companies in the region, bringing together the mining of raw materials and the production of bricks, tiles, pipes and lime. Reading between the lines, we are able to discern the connectedness of the business community and its links with Somerset cricket. The bankers managing the share issue were Stuckey's of Shepton Mallet (whose major shareholders included members of Robert Porch's family) and among the companies whose purchase was proposed was the Doulting Stone Company (of which William Trask was chairman). The newspaper reports do not reveal whether or not the venture was more successful than Charles Bennett's brief career as a county cricketer.

During the First World War, he served as a lieutenant in the Royal Flying Corps. He was never married and although he had returned to his roots, residing for a while in Burwash, Sussex, he was back in Bruton by the time of his death. For a long while he had suffered from epithelioma of the tongue, a debilitating problem that will have hampered his role as a solicitor. He died at the age of forty-eight on 23 May 1921 as a result of complications, three days after an operation in the city of Bath. A reasonable though not a prolonged innings: in life as in his club cricket. His nephew, Geoffrey Michael Bennett (son of Charles's brother, Philip) would represent Somerset on 109 occasions between 1928 and 1939 and more successfully than Charles had done, captaining the county on seven occasions.

Charles Bennett – a solicitor from Bruton whose record for Somerset CCC was modest: sadly he did not live to see his nephew, Michael Bennett, captain the county side

144
George Bernard Newport
3 July 1902 v. Gloucestershire, Bath

George Newport was born on 29 March 1876 in Muttom in the state of Tamil Nadu, India. His father was a teacher in a number of Indian missionary schools. George

attended the Non-Conformist Grammar School (Bishop Stortford), where he was something of a star pupil, playing the organ at school functions, winnings prizes for shorthand and matriculation, topping the batting averages and winning a place at Sidney Sussex College, Cambridge. He did not gain a blue at cricket but when he moved to Taunton School to take up the post of science teacher, he became active on the local sporting scene. He played as a wicket-keeper batsman for Taunton with some success. In the *Taunton Courier*, H. J. Channon writes of Newport's superb knock of 131 not out for Taunton Thursday in 1904 and reminisces about him elsewhere as 'a grand bat and in the first flight of wicket-keepers'.

He only ever played for Somerset on two occasions. In a close match, won by Gloucestershire, he registered scores of 11 and 16 and took three catches. He would perhaps have regretted turning out for Somerset two years later in another first-class match, a 12-a-side contest versus Oxford University in which he registered a pair, leaving him with a career average of 6.75 and four catches to his name. He also played football for Taunton Casuals and was good enough to be selected for the Somerset side versus Devon. He is named in a case where a timber merchant attempted not just to recover £5 4s 4d from the Taunton Casuals for non-payment but also (a trifle vindictively, perhaps) argued that the committee

G. B. Newport as a crick-eter (top) and as a member of the teaching staff at Taunton School in 1904

were all responsible and should be made to stand down. Among the committee members were George Newport and fellow Somerset cricketers Ernie Robson and Fred Marshall Lee.

George was married in 1910 to Helen Margaret Arundel (née Bell) and in the same year he left Taunton School to take up the position of headmaster at Crossley & Porter Schools, Halifax, where he would remain for thirty-one years until his retirement in 1941. As a headmaster, he was highly regarded and open to innovations, such as his experiment with dispensing with Saturday evening homework and replacing it with plays and orchestral practice. It is difficult to envisage that many of his pupils would have resisted that innovation. He retired to the West Country, living in Woodwater Lane in Exeter and dying at nearby Wonford Hospital on 12 July 1953, aged seventy-seven.

145
Cyril Alexander Highett Baily
24 July 1902 v. Surrey, Kennington Oval

C. A. H. Baily

Cyril Baily was born in Glastonbury on 17 July 1880. His
father and uncle ran the firm A. Baily & Co, at the time a
milling company. After leaving Bristol Grammar School,
Cyril was initially employed as a clerk. Like all good entrepreneurs, the family spotted a more profitable opportunity
and pursued it with vigour. Cyril would become the manager
of the Beckery Leather Works. The Baily family made sheep-
skin rugs, undersaddles and, from smaller offcuts of leather,
gloves (in particular boxing and wicket-keeping gloves) and
athletic equipment. They also followed the example set by
Clarks in nearby Street in building some model workers'
cottages at Beckery.

*Cyril Baily – he
was involved in the
manufacture of sporting
goods and a major
employer in Glastonbury*

He also found time for club cricket, regularly opening the
batting and bowling for Glastonbury and performing well
enough to be invited to play for Somerset. Coming in as a tail-ender, he scored 4 and
4 not out in his only match, against Surrey.

He married a Clifton girl, Dora (née Glass), in 1905. The business continued to
thrive and Cyril and his family moved to Newton, Hyde, Cheshire, presumably on
the basis that manufacture in the North West made more economic sense. He died on
21 September 1924 at the age of only forty-four, having been rushed to the Memorial
Hospital in Burnham-on-Sea. His mother was living at the time in Burnham and so
it is a reasonable assumption that he was visiting her. Although his involvement with
Somerset CCC had been negligible, Cyril Baily had made a notable contribution to
the county of his birth as a businessman and employer.

146
Oswald Walter Wright
24 July 1902 v. Surrey, Kennington Oval

Oswald Wright – a schoolmaster who played for Cambridge University and Somerset but never hit the heights

At the time of Oswald Wright's birth on 20 March 1877 in Maxton, Kent, his father managed the Diamond Brewery. Herbert Wright sold the business and moved the family to Dorchester, where he managed the Eldridge Pope Brewery in the employ of Alfred and Edwin Pope. The writer Thomas Hardy was a fan of his local brew, complimenting 'the most beautiful colour that the eye of an artist in beer could desire; full in body, yet brisk as a volcano; piquant, yet without a twang; luminous as an autumn sunset'. Not Hardy's finest piece of prose. Perhaps he was drunk when he wrote it.

Oswald was educated at Malvern College before following in his father's footsteps with a place at Cambridge, where he graduated from Selwyn College. He played two first-class games for the university as an opening left-arm bowler and tail-end batsman, taking one wicket in each match. Prior to this he had turned out for Gloucestershire's Second XI. After leaving Cambridge, he went into the teaching profession and Somerset called on his services while he was a schoolmaster at Walton Lodge Preparatory School, near Clevedon. With two ducks to his credit in his only match for the county, he joined the unhappy band of Somerset cricketers who never troubled the scorers. Oddly, given that he was a bowler, he only completed two overs, taking 0 for 6.

After leaving Walton Lodge, he taught for a while at Stone House School, Broadstairs, before becoming joint-headmaster of St Peter's School, near Seaford in Sussex in 1910. His fellow head was Geoffrey, the brother of John Hellard, who also played for Somerset. After a couple of years, Oswald Wright returned to teach at Stone House. He was there throughout and beyond the First World War, in which he did not serve. He died at the age of fifty-six on 19 December 1933 in the Montpellier district of Cheltenham. He was never married, leaving his estate to his elderly widowed mother, Jessie.

147
Gilbert Claude Vassall
25 August 1902 v. Surrey, Taunton

Known as 'Cheese', Gilbert Vassall joined the elegant Randall Johnson at the crease with Somerset requiring 65 to win and Surrey needing three wickets to record a victory. A more dapper pair of batsmen was never seen. With nerves of steel and a score of 27 not out, Gilbert saw Somerset home. This would be the pinnacle of his achievement for the county. *Wisden* stated in his obituary that Gilbert Vassall 'made few runs, and his fast bowling met with little success'. His performances at Championship level were indeed mediocre. Many would take pride in having turned out half a dozen times for the county of their birth, but for Gilbert Vassall it was a mere footnote in an extraordinary life. Born on 5 April 1876, he was the tenth of twelve children of the rector of Hardington Mandeville. Educated at Charterhouse, he proved an all-round sportsman and athlete who excelled in particular at football. At Oriel College, Oxford, he was president of the Athletic Union and captain of the University football team. An outside-right, he played during vacations for Yeovil Casuals (who would become Yeovil Town). A newspaper report states that on one occasion 'shooting with terrific force he broke the cross-bar with one of his shots'. Selected to play for England against Ireland in his final year at Oxford, he declined because the England game clashed

Gilbert 'Cheese' Vassall, whose appearances for Somerset were a footnote in an extraordinary and fulfilled life

with the Varsity match against Cambridge. Yeovil Casuals were thus denied the opportunity to claim an England international among their ranks. In 1904, he was a member of the amateur Corinthians team who humbled FA Cup winners Bury 10-3, confirming their status as one of the leading clubs in the country, despite their unpreparedness to take part in professional competitions.

On leaving university, he planned initially to enter the clergy but was never ordained. Having been married in 1902 to Rosa Mary (née Cotter), known as Mary, whom he had known since childhood, he took up a post as an assistant schoolmaster at the Dragon

Preparatory School, Oxford. He would stay for the rest of his working life, becoming co-headmaster. Among his claims to fame was that he had schooled a young John Betjeman in the elements of English grammar and composition. Gilbert's school plays were legendary and for many years he was the editor of the school magazine, *The Draconian*.

He was an inveterate organiser and according to *The Times* 'Vassall was largely responsible for the establishment of the Iffley Road Running and Football ground', this being the track on which Roger Bannister famously ran the first sub-four-minute mile. The report goes on to say that he also takes much of the credit 'for the introduction of the relay system into University and other athletics'. By 1906 he had ceased turning out on an occasional basis for Somerset but was still playing some football for Oxford City, who won the FA Amateur Cup that year. 'Cheese' Vassall appeared 6 times in the cup run, including in the semi-final, scoring 8 goals over the course of those matches.

Still teaching at the age of sixty-five, he died on 19 September 1941 at Oxford on the first day of the autumn term, seated in his chair, his young daughter on his knee. He was survived by his second wife Brenda Elizabeth (née O'Ferrall), to whom he had been married in 1929. *The Draconian* contained a number of warm tributes to a gentle giant who was clearly loved by his charges. *The Times* was as full of praise for the man as it was for his achievements:

He was the most modest of men, even-tempered, with a right sense of proportion as to the place of athletics in education.

Gilbert Vassall seems to have been universally liked and a man blessed with sporting prowess, the ability to help others to fulfil their potential and a flair for organization. His six games for Somerset are indeed a mere footnote.

Gilbert Vassall winning the long jump at Oxford in 1898 with a jump of 22 ft 5.5 in

1903

"The batting was better all round, but there was a falling off in the bowling ... In a wet season it was a little curious that the [bowling] figures should compare unfavourably."

Wisden

Championship Position: 10 of 15

It was noted at the AGM that the season had been 'about the worst on record as regards the weather'. The finances were equally moribund with a deficit of over £400, despite the county's guarantors having had to dip into their pockets. The Club and Ground matches, often a means of unearthing talent, were proving a financial drain and so a decision was made to end them. In a season of mediocrity, Somerset relied heavily on the batting skills of Lionel Palairet and the all-round performances of Len Braund. At least the county could still lay claim to a surfeit of well-regarded wicket-keepers. The newcomers were by and large a disappointment. Among them, Bert North of Bedminster was an honest pro asked to step into all-rounder George Gill's boots, but not given many chances to establish his claims and the Hon. Mervyn Herbert would bring some lustre to the team, though not many runs.

Somerset's fine amateur keepers – Newton, Wickham and Martyn – all played in 1903, though less frequently than the county would have hoped

148
Albert Edward Charles North
21 May 1903 v. Yorkshire, Taunton

a. E. North

In Bert North's debut game, the opponents were a weakened Yorkshire side. Selected as a pace bowler, he was for much of the time a bystander, contributing two runs and not being called on to bowl as Len Braund put on yet another virtuoso performance to destroy Somerset's opponents with bat and ball.

Bert was born in Bedminster on 20 December 1877. His father was a saddle maker and Bert was the eldest of five children, all of whom were still living with their parents at the turn of the century at 9 South Street, Bedminster. Bert began work as a draper's assistant but, having performed well as a fast bowler in club cricket, was trying to make it as a pro. He was married in 1903 to a schoolteacher named Eliza Maria (née Kelland) and perhaps at the time had visions of a rosy future in Championship cricket. But he was never able to hold down a regular place in the county side, despite a couple of gutsy performances – both against Gloucestershire: 4 for 47 in 1904 and 4 for 48 in 1908. He would also prove himself a doughty tail-ender, managing a score of 30 not out in 1908, when Somerset had been reeling against Sussex at 75 for 8.

It was Bert North's misfortune to have appeared at a time when Somerset were cutting costs and reluctant to invest in pros. He played his last match for Somerset in 1909, although he would twice be selected for Gloucestershire (who perhaps still harboured memories of his feats against them) but this was not the end of his playing days. Bert had first appeared for Bedminster in the late 1890s and would serve the club for the rest of his life. Over the winter months he would supplement his income with jobs such as that of a warehouseman, as recorded in the 1911 census. There are newspaper accounts of many fine performances for Bedminster. Teddy Spry, who played 89 times for Gloucestershire, recalled that he had never forgotten the experience of facing the young fast bowler Bert North, who removed his cap first ball and then 'laid out' Dr E. M. Grace. Another described how Bert would 'tear up to the pitch, swing his arm high up and let fly'. Bowling in tandem with his brother, Harold, he regularly skittled opponents out cheaply. Nor did he limit his exploits to bowling. During the period when Bedminster shared the Ashton Gate ground with Bristol City FC, he once scored a whirlwind 239 including 26 sixes against

Bert North – a Bedminster hero, never given the chance to prove his true worth at county level

Thornbury. Bert North was still making headlines for Bedminster CC as late as 1927 when, shortly before his fiftieth birthday, he took 3 wickets cheaply in the annual fixture against Bristol City FC before several hundred spectators. He had been captain of the club for many years and was also appointed club chairman following the death in May 1926 of the previous incumbent, E. G. Murdock, a Somerset player from the pre-Championship era.

Bert lived out his last days in nearby Knowle. He was still playing cricket up until the time he went into the Bristol General Hospital for an operation. He did not survive the ordeal and died at the age of fifty-five on

A. E. C. North of Bedminster CC, Somerset and Gloucestershire

the 4 June 1933: a Bedminster man through and through, and one who might have achieved even greater cricket success had Somerset shown some patience and perseverance.

149
Mervyn Robert Howard Molyneux Herbert
28 May 1903 v. Oxford University, Oxford

Mervyn Herbert was born on 27 December 1882 at Highclere Castle, Hampshire. He was the son of the fourth Earl of Carnarvon and his second wife: a late Christmas present for the couple who already had everything they could possibly have ever needed. The grandeur of Highclere Castle, the family's main residence, is enough to confirm the extent of their wealth and influence. The estate included a renowned cricket pitch and the stately home later became famous as the setting for the popular *Downton Abbey* television series. Mervyn's half-brother, the fifth Earl, would use a fraction of his wealth to fund the excavation of Tutankhamun's tomb. The family also owned Tetton House, in Kingston St Mary, which Mervyn would inherit in 1907. He was educated at Eton, where it is claimed that he was 'a dashing and attractive bat'. He played for Nottinghamshire against MCC as an eighteen-year-old schoolboy, impressing with a score of 65. A report at the time tipped him for future stardom, concluding the piece by noting that he was 'an attractive, clever lad with winning manners'.

Hon. Mervyn Herbert –
'a most lovable disposition'

He was a member of the Balliol College XI but failed to gain a blue. Five further Championship matches for Notts (1901 to 1902) yielded little in the way of success and in 1903 he played the first of his thirty-one matches for Somerset. His appearances were sporadic because of his role in the diplomatic service, which led to extended periods abroad based in British embassies. He registered scores of 55 and 78 in 1909, but these were his only half-centuries during a career in which he averaged 12.52 for Somerset.

He was appointed an attaché in the foreign office in 1907 and rose to the position of first secretary by 1919, serving in the British embassies in Rome, Lisbon, Cairo and Madrid. While first secretary at the embassy in Madrid he was married at the age of thirty-nine in 1921 to Mary Elizabeth (née Willard), the daughter of the American ambassador to Spain. The couple came to live at Tetton House, generating much excitement and 'the merry pealing of bells' as they moved in to the redecorated rooms that had been neglected in the preceding years. Mary Herbert took her role as lady of the manor very seriously, making appearances to give any number of worthy causes a boost. Her sister was the daughter-in-law of Theodore Roosevelt and her presence would have caused much excitement at the County Ground on her husband's occasional outings for the team.

Mervyn Herbert's death at the age of forty-six on 26 May 1929 was sudden and unexpected. Having visited Albania as a guest of honour, opening a public library (funded by his family) he was taken ill with 'malarial pneumonia' and died at the British embassy in Rome. A thoroughly decent man, who appears to have got on well with just about anyone, he was mourned by his family and the many employees on the family estate. His fellow JP, Sir Dennis Boles, paid tribute to him as 'a man with a keen sense of duty, full of common sense, and a most lovable disposition'. It mattered not a jot that he never quite made his mark as a cricketer.

150
Lionel Hugh Major
4 June 1903 v. Sussex, Hastings

Hugh Major was born in Burnham-on-Sea on 21 April 1883. He was the third son of Charles and Ellen Major. Charles was a brick and tile manufacturer with his business based in Bridgwater, one of a number of entrepreneurs who had benefitted from the plentiful supplies of clay and the ease of transport via Bridgwater Docks. The family moved to the village of Wembdon while Hugh was still young and he was sent to board at Hart House School, which had originally been based in Tregony, Cornwall, but had been re-established in the Manor House in Burnham-on-Sea when the original school burned down in 1893. On leaving school in 1902 Hugh worked alongside his father for eight years, learning the trade. He is recorded as having submitted patents in the UK and Europe as the family firm sought ways to add to their coffers. He was invited by Sam Woods to make his only appearance for the county in 1903. Sam was very active on the Bridgwater social scene and knew Hugh and his father well. Hugh had recently played for an S. M. J. Woods XI in Liverpool. Against Sussex he made scores of 6 and 11. Invited by his captain to bowl in Sussex's second innings, he took 1 wicket for 5 runs before Sussex knocked off the required runs.

In 1910, at the age of twenty-seven, he emigrated to Victoria in British Columbia to make his own way in the world. He left with no clear job to go to but immediately placed advertisements in the local paper, the *Daily Colonist*, seeking a position in brick and tile works and highlighting his experience in 'manufacture and management'. He was very soon managing an asphalt business in the Canadian town. Then in December 1912 he joined the 88th Regiment of the Victoria Fusiliers as a lieutenant. Meanwhile, he was very active in the local cricketing scene, playing for Victoria. One report of a match against Oak Bay in 1912 is headed *Major's Batting Was Feature* and reports 'a great innings' after 'L. H. Major came gallantly to the rescue' with a match-winning innings that included 'a magnificent on-drive to the north of the roof of the grand stand' on what the writer describes as a large ground.

In 1914 he was married in Christ Church Cathedral to Rose Fredericka (née Hole), who was residing at the time with her parents in the Mount Tolmie district of Victoria. Her father had been the vicar of Georgeham in Devon for many years and her late grandfather Dean Samuel Hole, famous in his lifetime, had been a noted churchman, author and horticulturalist. Hugh had by then already left his post in the asphalt manufacturing business and was listed as a financial agent. During the war he served as a Lt Colonel in the 2nd Battalion of the British Columbian Regiment . His involvement in active service was brief, lasting approximately one week. On 22 May 1915, at the Battle of Festubert, one of his fellow soldiers 'went mad and hit [Major] on the head with a rifle' after many days and nights of shelling. Already suffering himself from shell-shock and now concussed, Lionel was taken to hospital where it was reported that 'he has nervous manifestations', allied to memory loss . He would later embellish his war record and is described by one family member as 'a braggart'.

He was invited in 1917 to become a magistrate. Clearly a serial entrepreneur, he was running a Shell garage in Victoria by 1919 and hiring out a 7-passenger Lexington car.

Hugh eventually returned to the UK and lived for many years in Westbury-on-Trym. Still playing club cricket, he is recorded as having completed some decent knocks for the Optimists team, based in Bristol. His wife died in 1950. They had no children. Hugh was sixty-seven and still working, described as an engineer. In 1953 he moved to Exmouth where he set up a market gardening business. His wife's grandfather, Dean Hole, had been an inaugural recipient of the Royal Horticultural Society's Victoria Medal. Perhaps the granddaughter had passed on a love for the subject to her husband. Hugh was remarried in 1958 to his housekeeper, Winifred Irene (née

Palmer). He died at the age of eighty-two in Exmouth Hospital on 25 June 1965, leaving his estate to Winifred but being buried in Henbury in Bristol, alongside his first wife, whom he had been married to fifty years earlier. He had also asked that his service as a Lt Colonel in the 1914-1918 war should be recorded on his gravestone. He made no such request concerning his cricket career.

151
Humphrey Sandford Burrington
25 June 1903 v. Gloucestershire, Gloucester

Humphrey S. Burrington

Born on 5 April 1882 in Bridgwater, he was the son of Gilbert and Amelia Burrington. Along with his brothers, Humphrey seemed destined to become a pillar of the local community. Gilbert Burrington (the guardian of Sam Woods until he came of age) was the manager of the Bridgwater branch of Fox, Fowler & Co Bank. Humphrey's brothers, Gilbert Jnr (also a Somerset cricketer) and Harley would both be killed in action in the First World War. The brothers all attended King's School, Gloucester. Humphrey trained as a solicitor and practiced before the war in Bridgwater and Burnham-on-Sea. He played his club cricket in the area first for Bridgwater and later for Berrow. The local papers are hardly awash with his exploits, making it a safe assumption that his connection with Sam Woods had led to his being asked to play for Somerset on five occasions between 1903 and 1905. He averaged 10.83 and only ever bowled one over (in which he conceded ten runs) and so made no great imprint on the county game.

Humphrey Burrington – his father was the guardian of Sam Woods

In 1914 he enlisted as a private with the Somerset Light Infantry, rising to the rank of captain. On 21 March 1918 he was reported as missing in action at the Battle of St. Quentin. 21 March and the following forty-eight hours marked the time when the 6th Somersets were obliterated. After days spent enduring mustard gas attacks, the battalion was subjected to a ferocious artillery bombardment followed by wave after wave of German soldiers advancing through the fog. There were precious few survivors and Humphrey's family – already suffering from the loss of his brothers – must have feared the worst. Their joy must have been unbounded when it was confirmed that

Humphrey had in fact been taken as a POW and was repatriated in December 1918. After the war he became a partner in the firm of Chanter, Burrington & Foster in Barnstaple. He was never married. In later life, he became a keen golfer. The sea air and golf must have proved beneficial as he had reached the age of seventy-five when he died in Barnstaple on 15 April 1957.

152
Arthur William Sibbald Paterson
2 July 1903 v. Gloucestershire, Bath

Lt Colonel Arthur Paterson was a career soldier. Born on 28 February 1878 in Weston-super-Mare, he was the son of Major General Adrian Paterson, who had served in India. Arthur was educated at Malvern College before going up to Sandhurst. He had already completed an extended period of service as a subaltern in the Boer War when he began to appear on the local sporting scene. Clearly a fit young man, he shone as a hockey full-back for Weston-super-Mare and Somerset. Indeed, the *Bath Chronicle* makes no reference to his modest achievements as a club cricketer when announcing his selection for Somerset CCC but refers to him as 'an amateur well known as a hockey player in the West of England'. Arthur Paterson was also a useful rugby player, appointed captain of the Weston XV in 1904, though a transfer to India in that year put an end to any sporting ambitions back in his home county. In two matches for Somerset, he averaged 12.66 with a highest score of 19.

Arthur Paterson – a military man better known for his prowess as a hockey player rather than a cricketer

The 1911 census records him back on home soil, a captain in the Somerset Light Infantry and stationed at the Glamorgan Colliery Offices. Thereafter, he became an instructor at Sandhurst. He was attached to the Royal Irish Fusiliers during the war and fought at Salonika (now Thessalonika) before being sent to France. He was awarded a DSO in 1917. He retired in 1925 and joined the Army Reserve until 1933 when he was forced to leave at the age of fifty-five on the grounds of the age limit. In the meantime, he had immersed himself in the running of various clubs and societies and in local government while living in Burnham-on-Sea, bringing all his military experience to bear as chairman of the Burnham Urban District Council and acting as a JP. As chairman, considerable skills of diplomacy and leadership were called on, though he was at times accused of deploying dominerring tactics more suited to the heat of battle than the committee room. There seems to have been constant friction between the council (with a majority of residents favouring peace and quiet) and the Attractions Association who wished to improve Burnham as a tourist destination. Arthur Paterson was also called on to chair a stormy meeting about who should pay for the King's Silver Jubilee in 1935. Everyone seemed agreed on two matters. Firstly, that the celebrations were a good thing and no expense should be spared. Secondly, that someone else should foot the bill. He managed to steer the warring factions to a consensus.

He remained unmarried and, with no family commitments, he offered up his services as president of the Burnham Bowling Club, the local branch of the British Legion and the Burnham and District Boy Scouts. He was also a keen golfer and continued to be associated with the Somerset Stragglers cricket club.

Arthur Paterson died in Burnham on 13 November 1937, having given much back to the region in which he had been born, fifty-nine years earlier.

153
Frederick Thomas Coyle
10 August 1903 v. Kent, Taunton

Federick Thomas Coyle

Fred Coyle was born in Taunton on 25 July 1869. One of seven children of Thomas and Ann Coyle, he was raised as a Roman Catholic. For many years, Thomas and Ann ran a business buying and selling second-hand clothing in East Reach, Taunton. By the time of Fred's birth, the family were manufacturing coarse horse hair fabric, worn by many in the winter.

Fred Cole, who left Taunton to pursue his twin careers as a cricket pro and a retailer in Halifax

In 1891, now active in the business, Fred was married to Mary Philomena (née Colvin). at St George's Roman Catholic church, Taunton. By 1896, the couple had left Taunton, so that Fred could ply his trade as a professional right-arm fast bowler in the North of England. He played his club cricket in Northumberland and then Durham, representing Chester-le-Street from 1897 until 1900. He then moved to Halifax and opened a sports outfitter's shop, already up and running by the time he turned out for Somerset against Kent in his native Taunton. Such was the peripatetic life of the professional club cricketer that by 1904 he was contracted to Oldham. Announcing his appointment, the *Nottingham Evening Post* of December 1903 refers to him as 'an exceptionally good player all round'. Somerset remained in touch with Fred, who was a regular visitor to Taunton. His second and final appearance came in 1905. He took no wickets in his twenty-two overs for Somerset and averaged 14.00 with the bat.

Fred ploughed on with his club cricket while his family grew (to a total of eight children) and the retail enterprise continued to provide an income. Reporting on the forthcoming 1913 season, the *Yorkshire Evening Post* observes of the Kings Cross Club (in Halifax) that 'the inclusion of Fred Coyle in their ranks should do much to make their bowling strength more on an equality with their splendid batting'. Given that Fred would have been forty-four going on forty-five, we must assume that he was no longer bowling at full throttle. By this time he had joined two other sports outfitters – Joe Nicholls and J. T. Brown – and had become a partner in the company Nicholls, Brown & Coyle Ltd, with retail outlets in three sites across Halifax. The company would remain in existence until 1959.

His death at the age of fifty-six on 12 September 1925 was not unexpected. Three years earlier, diagnosed as having cancer, he had undergone a serious operation 'which while prolonging his life, could not eradicate the disease from which he was suffering'. His retail business had bound him to Halifax but the people of Taunton – particularly the Roman Catholic community – had not forgotten him. The *Taunton Courier* informs us in his obituary that he was 'a good vocalist and for many years a valued member of the Catholic choir at Halifax … [and] possessed a powerful bass voice'. We are told that on occasions he would return to St George's, Taunton, to sing and that one of his sons had become a Dominican priest while one of his daughters was a nun. A Requiem Mass was celebrated at St George's and 'prayers were asked for the repose of his soul'.

154
Percy d'Aguilar Banks
31 August 1903 v. Hampshire, Bournemouth

The son of a colonel, Percy d'Aguilar (or D'Aguilar) Banks was born in Bath on 9 May 1885. Educated at St Peter's, Weston (near Bath), before going on to Cheltenham College and then Sandhurst, he caught the eye of the Somerset committee with a score of 103 for

the Cheltenham XI in the annual Lord's fixture against Haileybury College in 1902 and followed this up with an innings of
131 for the Somerset Colts against a Somerset XI. Although
he was fast-tracked into the county team, his appearances
would be limited because of the demands of the military. He
would only ever play in seven matches and would never fulfil
his early promise, managing an average of 12.38. Percy
enjoyed more success as a polo player, playing for a Frankfurt
team that won three events in a tour of Germany in 1913.

Percy d'Aguilar Banks –
a fine young sportsman
and a war hero

Tragically, it was not polo on the agenda when the Germans
and British took on one another a year later.

In 1903 he had joined the Duke of Edinburgh's Wiltshire Regiment as a second lieutenant, and by 1912 had risen to the rank of captain, attached to the 57th Wilde's Rifles.
His involvement in the First World War was shortlived. At the age of twenty-nine,
Percy Banks was killed in action on 26 April 1915 at Ypres, having advanced to within
80 yards of the German line. The *Roll of Honour* provides us with a detailed description
of his final hours, giving a glimpse of the horrors encountered and the courage of the
combatants. He was leading a group of Indian soldiers, in the front line of the attack:

> *On crossing the first ridge the regt. came under an absolute tornado of fire of every
> description—shrapnel, machine-gun, rifle, and, last but not least, high explosive shells
> filled with asphyxiating gas … Still the attack was pressed to a point about 80 yards
> from the German trenches. Here Major Duhan, Capt. Mackie and Capt. Banks were all
> killed, as were also two of the Indian officers. Capt. Banks's orderly, a Sikh named Bhan
> Singh, had been severely wounded in the face early in the action, {but} in spite of this he
> insisted in following Capt. Banks till he {Banks} was killed. As soon as darkness set in,
> in the face of the appalling fire, and severely wounded as he was, his one thought was to
> bring back the body of his officer. Weak as he was from loss of blood, he staggered along
> carrying the body until he fell from exhaustion. They were both brought in, and Capt.
> Banks was buried near a farm house two miles north-east of Ypres. For this act of devotion
> and gallantry Bhan Singh received the Indian D.S.M. and later a Russian decoration.*

The tributes flowed in. Colonel Egerton wrote that 'we were all very fond of him
… and will feel his loss keenly'. A fellow officer spoke of Percy's 'great personal pluck
and power as a leader', adding that 'not the smallest detail relating to the men's comfort
was overlooked … they really had a father to command them. I've never seen any
native express such genuine sorrow at the loss of one of their sahibs'.

His mother was left to grieve the loss of her only child, but Kathleen Rosa Banks
was the feistiest of women. In 1949, two days before her 96th birthday some of the

details of her extraordinary life are reported in the *Bath Chronicle*. We are informed that she had introduced the game of badminton to England, setting up a club in Cheltenham, and that she designed and made six rugs that were accepted for use in the Ypres Memorial Chapel, where her son is remembered. As part of the Second World War effort, she coordinated the making and despatch of 5,000 knitted items for the troops. Percy had clearly inherited her charisma and – ironically – her never-say-die attitude to life.

155
Ernest Arthur Greswell
31 August 1903 v. Hampshire, Bournemouth

Ernest Greswell in a Stogumber XI (top) and in later years (above)

Ernest Greswell was born on 8 June 1885 in Madras, India. His father, William, had played in the 1875 fixture between Gentlemen of Devon and Gentlemen of Somerset that had been the catalyst for the formation of Somerset CCC. William Greswell had opted for a career in the civil service, which he combined with an investment in a tea plantation in Ceylon (Sri Lanka). By the time Ernest appeared for the county, William had settled back in his mother country as the rector of Dodington and an author. Ernest boarded at Repton between the ages of four and nineteen before going on to Hertford College, Oxford, where he gained a BA in Forestry. Although he had played for Repton, he never made it into the Oxford University team. First selected for Somerset while still a schoolboy, he represented them between 1903 and 1910. In twelve games he averaged 11.71 and as a slow right-arm bowler he only took two wickets at 44.50 apiece.

Ernest Greswell was married to Grace Lilian (née Egerton) in Rawalpindi, India in 1914. By 1916 he was working for the India Forest Service. He, his wife and their three children would return to England and live first in Oxford and then back in the Quantock village of Bicknoller on his retirement. He died on 15 January 1962 at the age of seventy-six at the Mount Royal Nursing Home in Minehead and was buried at Bicknoller. His younger brother, Bill, would also play for Somerset and would prove an outstanding cricketer.

1904

"Not much that is favourable can be said about Somerset's cricket in 1904 ... The best point about their play was that, unlike some of their rivals, they generally arrived at a definite result."

Wisden

Championship Position: 12 of 15

There was never any question of playing for a draw with Sam Woods at the helm. Wins were few and far between, although, against all expectation, they included the double over Surrey. Monty Cranfield was late out of the starting blocks as he recovered from illness and Len Braund suffered a severe blow to the wrist against the South Africans that hampered his performances, though the two managed over seventy wickets each. According to *Wisden*, Lionel Palairet showed 'undiminished brilliancy and grace of style' and A. E. Lewis at last began to fulfil his promise as a batsman, notably with his unbeaten century against Surrey.

At the AGM there was acrimony over the decision to play host to the Australians in Bath, in 1905. The traditionalists voted for Taunton, while the pragmatists were interested in maximising gate receipts. The pragmatists won the day. Any ill-feeling paled against the rancour that had brewed in relations with Surrey, from whom Somerset had poached Bill Montgomery.

The new-joins were essentially talented club-level cricketers. Hugh Poyntz – a career soldier only available on an occasional basis – was the best of the bunch.

A. E. Lewis in the throes of scoring 118 not out against Surrey

156
Gerard William Hodgkinson
12 May 1904 v. Oxford University, Oxford

(signature)

The archetypal cad, Gerard Hodgkinson was born in Clifton on 19 February 1883 but before long the family would move into their newly-built mock-Jacobean mansion, Glencot House, at Wookey Hole. The Hodgkinsons owned the paper mills there. This profitable business had been operating since 1610 but they had 'hit the jackpot' when the system of caves was discovered in the nineteenth century, generating enormous interest and spawning a highly lucrative tourist attraction. Gerard was packed off to Eton for his education, after which his father bought a farm – Burge Farm, at Bishops Lydeard – to occupy the son while he bided his time before taking over the running of the mill and the caves.

Gerard was married in 1907 to Florence Gladys Mabel Mackenzie-Ashton (known as Gladys), who lived at nearby Dene Court, Bishops Lydeard. The marriage would soon turn sour as a result of his wandering eye. By 1912, he had deserted his wife and a letter dated April 1913 pleading for his return is still extant. Gerard's response was sufficiently curt to prompt his wife to petition the High Court for 'a restitution of her conjugal rights'. The suit was abated when Gladys died after a major operation on 21 August 1913. Gerard had by now already begun a new life as a plantation owner near Nairobi.

Gerard Hodgkinson – the archetypal cad, he sued The Bodley Head over John Cowper Powys's thinly-disguised description of him in A Glastonbury Romance

The reason for the cooling of relations soon became public knowledge when Captain Lambton Jones-Mortimer of the Somerset Light Infantry petitioned against his wife, Sybil, on the grounds of her 'misconduct' with Hodgkinson. As early as 1910, Jones-Mortimer had asked his wife to end her 'association' with Hodgkinson but she 'went away frequently, and said that she had been to see her mother and friends'. The end, when it came, was brutal and irreversible. On 17 May 1913, Jones-Mortimer received the following letter:

This is just to let you know that by the time you get this letter I shall be on my way to

COURTESY OF THE ROGER MANN COLLECTION

Africa to join G. Hodgkinson. I hope that for the sake of all concerned you will divorce me as quickly and quietly as possible. If you should want further evidence you will find we stayed at the Waldorf Hotel together under his name on 21st and 22nd April – SYBIL

Fifty per cent of her requirements were met. The divorce was quick, though by no means quiet. Perhaps inevitably, Gerard soon turned his attentions elsewhere and he and Sybil parted. By this time, his nineteen appearances for Somerset were in the past. His last game had been in 1911. Only once would he score more than 50, when he reached a tantalising 99 not out against Gloucestershire in 1910. His exploits in the military were more heroic than those on the cricket field. He signed up to join the East Africa Mounted Rifles six days after war had been declared but later transferred to the Royal Flying Corps as a pilot. He became a lieutenant in 1917, having already been awarded the Military Cross.

He returned to civilian life after the war, initially in Africa, where he was married to Norah Beryl Record Shaw, in her early twenties. They would have a son, Colin, born at the Wookey Hole home in 1920. Gerard became both owner-manager of the Wookey Hole Caves and joint-master of the Mendip Farmers' Hunt, selling Glencot House but retaining control of the caves. In 1934 he sued The Bodley Head, the publishers of John Cowper Powys's best-selling novel *A Glastonbury Romance*. The leading character, Philip Crow, 'a man of the most immoral and most depraved character', was said to bear too many similarities to Hodgkinson for comfort. The judge upheld the complaint on the basis that 'Captain Hodgkinson … is quite a distinguished man … He has been a member of the Somerset County Cricket Club and has hunted with all the famous packs'. These factors were deemed of more relevance than the irrefutable evidence of his philandering ways. True to form, within a year, he took his twenty-year-old private secretary, Olive Treloar, on a four-month trip to Canada, where he appears to have had business interests. His wife, Norah, duly petitioned for divorce in 1936. Gerard would later marry Olive, almost certainly in Canada. Their daughter, Shiela, was born shortly before the outbreak of the Second World War, when Gerard was fifty-six.

He would re-join the air force in 1940, retiring in 1945 with the rank of wing commander and being awarded an OBE in that year's honours list. His son, Colin, would recall that his most vivid memories of his father were not of acts of paternal kindness but of a man decked out in splendid fashion for one of his regular hunting forays. Gerard Hodgkinson died at Wookey Hole at the age seventy-seven on 6 October 1960. He had been a well-known local figure though not necessarily loved by all.

157
Ellis George Whately
12 May 1904 v. Oxford University, Oxford

E. G. Whately's connection with Somerset was tenuous and based on his friendships with fellow Old Etonian Mervyn Herbert and the occasional Somerset cricketer Hugh Alison, who also attended New College and played alongside Whately in the 1904 fixture at Oxford. Also playing were two other debutants who would never appear again – H. G. Wheeler and G. D. Barne. This would be the last encounter between Somerset and a Varsity team until after the war. The teams and the public had lost their appetite for these meaningless encounters. Somerset were able after 1904 to focus single-mindedly on the Championship. Alas, to no avail.

Ellis Whately was born in Paddington on 27 July 1882, the son of a Scottish solicitor who was a partner in the firm of Ropper and Whately. Educated at Eton, he played for the First XI in 1900 and 1901 as a middle-order batsman and off-spin bowler, captaining the team in 1901. On going up to New College, Oxford, he was given every opportunity to establish himself in the Varsity team with twelve appearances for them but he failed to make his mark. He enjoyed modest success with the ball but his batting average was a woeful 4.55. His four appearances for Hertfordshire, where his parents resided in Harpenden, were similarly unsuccessful.

E. G. Whately as captain of the Eton XI (top) and a member of the Eton Ramblers club

On graduating, he joined his father's solicitors' practice based in Lincolns Inn Fields, his work interrupted by the First World War. He enrolled as a second lieutenant in the 5th Battalion of the Gloucestershire Regiment but was soon transferred to the 1st Battalion of the Hertfordshire Regiment Territorial Force. By 1917 he had risen to the rank of captain and was awarded the Military Cross. Later that year he was appointed as a deputy assistant to the Adjutant-General to the Forces. In 1918 he was awarded the rank of captain and brevet major. Removed to the reserve list in 1921, he relinquished his commission at the age of fifty, in 1932.

Future Somerset players Hon. Mervyn Herbert and E. G. Whately batting for Eton v Harrow in 1901

In 1918 he was married to Edith Winifred Rhoda (née Milburn), known as Rhoda, and they would have two daughters and two sons. On leaving the army and continuing his career as a solicitor, he lived at various times in Englefield and Chertsey. He died at the age of eighty-six on 4 September 1969 at his London residence in Cadogan Square, Chelsea.

158
Heneage Gibbes Wheeler
12 May 1904 v. Oxford University, Oxford

H. G. Wheeler

Born on 24 February 1870 in Berrow, where his father, Rev. William Hancock Wheeler, was the vicar from 1863 until 1881, Heneage's unusual Christian name - sometimes shortened to 'Henry' – was traditionally used on his maternal side. His grandfather, at one time physician to Queen Charlotte, had, for example, been known as Heneage. His second name, Gibbes, was his mother Margaretta's surname.

Heneage was an enthusiastic sportsman who took to football, where he played as a forward for Burnham and the Somerset XI. In addition, he was a well-regarded golfer who enjoyed some success in local tournaments. He played his club cricket for Bridgwater. Featuring as a middle-order batsman, he appears not to have been an outstanding player, though he made appearances for Somerset Club and Ground and Somerset Stragglers. He was also an occasional guest at the Quantock Lodge fixtures arranged by Somerset cricketer Henry Stanley. In his one first-class appearance he made scores of 3 and 5, batting at number eleven (of twelve players).

Heneage studied at the University of London and after graduating became a tutor. After this he taught at the venerable Bedford School but by the time of the 1901 census, he had become an assistant schoolmaster at Brunswick, a preparatory school in Haywards Health where Winston Churchill had been a pupil. In 1912 he opted for a change of career when he applied successfully for the post of Secretary of the Chamber of Commerce in Bombay at an important time when new docks had been built, although he returned to England the following year, on the death of his mother.

During the First World War he served as a captain in the Army Ordnance Department and rose to the rank of major in the Royal Flying Corps. It was a title that he would proudly bear for the remainder of his life.

After the war, Major H. G. Wheeler became a central figure in the Bexhill-on-Sea sporting scene, serving on the cricket, golf and football committees, his contributions being particularly noteworthy in the last of these. He was President of Bexhill FC for many years and the club's guiding light. His match reports, published in the local paper, are notable on occasions for the strength of his opinions. He also took delight in submitting articles such as his intriguingly entitled 'Leather', published in *Blackwood's Magazine*. Heneage was fifty-one and still residing at Bexhill-on-Sea when he was married to Florence Agnes (née Hayes), who hailed from St Louis, USA, and was the daughter of Joseph M. Hayes, a wealthy businessman. Florence was thirty-six at the time and the couple would have two children: Francis and Heneage Gibbes Jnr.

The family remained at the same address in Bexhill until Florence's death in 1959. When Heneage died on 4 August 1965 at the age of ninety-five, he had moved to nearby Brighton.

159
George Dunsford Barne
12 May 1904 v. Oxford University, Oxford

George Dunsford Barne,
Bishop.

The Right Reverend George Dunsford Barne OBE was born in Gordon Town, Jamaica, on 6 May 1879, although the family more or less immediately moved to Tiverton. His father, William Charles, a Devonian and originally in the military, died in Brussels in 1892, having bankrupted himself through investing in gold prospecting.

Playing alongside George Barne in his only first-class game were his cousin through his mother's second marriage, H. G. Wheeler, his golfing partner C. H. Alison, and Alison's friend at New College, E. G. Whately. With the Somerset team – twelve of them – filled out with these occasional cricketers, it was little wonder that Sam Woods's side were thrashed within two days. Barne managed scores of 1 and 9 not out

and he has the dubious honour of having played two innings in first-class cricket, both of them batting at number twelve.

Educated at Clifton College, George went up to Oriel College, Oxford, where he was a successful golfer, becoming a member of a Combined Universities golfing team that toured America, led by C. H. Alison.

After graduating, he was ordained in 1904 and was offered the curacy at Summertown, Oxford. In 1907 he was married to Dorothy Kate (née Akerman), whose father had previously owned a cement-making business in Bridgwater before he had moved the family to Burnham. George and Dorothy left for India when he was offered a position as a captain in the Simla Rifles, but within a year he had transferred to become a junior chaplain in the Bengal Ecclesiastical establishment. By 1912 he had been promoted to assistant chaplain and he returned briefly to England that year (when he guested for the Devon Dumplings cricket team). From 1912 until 1932, he was the principal of the Lawrence Royal Military School in Sanawar.

A former pupil, recalling his time there, describes it as 'a wonderful school' which accepted the children or orphans of the military 'from babyhood to mature adolescence'. 400 feet above sea level in the Simla Hills, it was established as 'an asylum from the debilitating effects of a tropical climate and the demoralising influence of barrack life'. Under the guidance of George Dunsford Barne it became 'one of the leading educational institutions in India'. He introduced the idea of

G. D. Barne – in the practical garb of an undergraduate golfer (top) and robes of office of a bishop

prefects and a house system, encouraged sporting fixtures and also brought in Cambridge examinations, while affiliating the school to the University of London. In short, he had attempted to recreate his own experiences at his alma mater, Clifton College.

He left to become the Bishop of Lahore, a position he held until 1949. A popular, much-loved character, he returned to England, where his last appointment was as the vicar of Harthill in South Yorkshire, although he died at the Royal Masonic Hospital in Hammersmith on 18 June 1954. Not a particularly wealthy man, he was survived by his wife, Dorothy Kate, who died in 1979. They had no children.

160
Hugh Stainton Poyntz
16 May 1904 v. Gloucestershire, Bristol

Colonel Hugh Poyntz DSO OBE was born in Nottingham on 17 September 1877. The sixth of seven children, his father was a retired major (Royal Marines) and Constable of Nottingham. His younger brother, Massey, also played for Somerset. The Poyntz brothers qualified for Somerset through residency at Gotham House, Tiverton, the family having moved there via Chelmsford, where William Poyntz had been appointed Chief Constable, following his stint in Nottingham.

Hugh was educated at Eastbourne College, which he left to join the 3rd Sherwood Foresters before joining the Bedfordshire Regiment, with whom he served in the Boer War in 1899. Promotion to the rank of captain came in 1907. In the meantime, he had played football whenever he could for Bridgwater Albion and The Army (whom he would captain in 1907). His thirty-seven sporadic appearances for Somerset came between 1904 and 1921. They yielded a batting average of 19.59. Only an occasional bowler, he never took a wicket for Somerset. He enjoyed his most productive period in 1908 when, as the *Bath Chronicle* notes, he 'gave reliable aid in the middle of the season ... though he had accomplished nothing sensational'. In 1909 he was married to Hilda Gwendoline (née Thackeray) in Bournemouth.

By 1912 he was back in South Africa and captaining Orange Free State. The *Luton Times* makes reference to him in 1913 as 'the noted cricketer, whose prowess with bat and ball we all know'. The observations are in connection with his performances in Bedford for the barracks team, where he played more of a starring role than he did at the more elevated county level. After temporary promotions during

Hugh Stainton Poyntz, who made useful rather than stellar contributions to Somerset's cause

the war and a period in 1916 when he was hospitalised, he was given the rank of lieu-tenant-colonel in 1921, having already been awarded a DSO. In the twilight of his military career, he became Master of the Duke of York's Royal Military School in Dover, a boarding school set up expressly for the children of the military. On retiring from the Army in 1936, he was awarded an OBE.

He died at the age of seventy-seven at Harestock Close, Winchester, on 22 June 1955, having done his bit for the family name.

161
Henry Wood
2 June 1904 v. Gloucestershire, Bath

Henry's father, Edward, had been a founding member of Bath Athletic CC. Born in Bath on 7 April 1872, Henry was a member of a close-knit family and remained for many years in the parental home, along with four sisters, two of whom were professional singers and the other two librarians. Henry worked in a bookshop in Bath. In later years he would take on the ownership of the shop. His other interests included singing, Methodism, rugby and cricket. A member of the Methodist choir from boyhood, he was also a member of Bath Operatic society. Although not a rugby player, he was 'a keen supporter of Bath rugby'. He was an efficient admin-istrator, appointed secretary of the New King Street Methodist Sunday School and joint-treasurer of Bath CC.

Henry Wood – a gentle soul and a man who adored his native city of Bath

Henry was part of a strong Bath side which included a number of occasional Somerset players in their ranks. A successful batsman at club level, he was asked on more than one occasion to take part in trials for Somerset, finally making his one appearance for the county in 1904. Coming in as a tail-ender, he remained unbeaten with a total of sixteen runs to his name. He was never given another chance to demonstrate how many runs he might have accumulated.

His beloved Bath club became embroiled in a dispute that had to be resolved by the MCC, while he was captain. In the August 1907 match against Gloucester, it became apparent that Gloucester's two run victory involved an injustice. The umpire had at one point signalled two byes but four runs had been allotted to the batsman.

When the inexperienced stand-in Bath scorer had pointed this out to his Gloucester counterpart, he had been told, the reports tell us, 'to "Shut Up"'. Only later had the timorous Bath stand-in spoken up. By the time matters reached a head, Henry was taking a break in Switzerland and it was left to fellow Somerset and Bath cricketer John Thomas to ensure that the result was confirmed as a tie.

Love came late for Henry Wood. In 1927 and at the age of fifty-five, he was married in Bath to Ethel Marion (née Neate), herself in her fifty-first year. In the last year of his life, he was made a life member of Bath CC along with fellow Somerset cricketer, Ted Grant. Sadly he did not have long to bask in the glory as he died on 1 December 1950 at the age of seventy-eight, following an operation. He was a man of Bath to his core, much loved and revered in the city to which he quietly gave so much of his time.

162
Ernest Napper Tandy
28 July 1904 v. Sussex, Bath

Napper Tandy found more fame as a military man than as a cricketer. Born in Axbridge on 13 May 1879, he was educated first at Tonbridge Castle Prep School (which opened its doors in 1891 but would last for only six years) and subsequently at Wellington College, where he played in the First XI. An enthusiastic rather than an accomplished cricketer, his two appearances for Somerset as a right-handed middle-order batsman yielded 25 runs at an average of 8.33.

On leaving school in July 1896 he had become a gentleman cadet at the Royal Military Academy, joining the Royal Artillery in 1898 as a second lieutenant. He fought in the Boer War and was mentioned in despatches. He was married in 1904 to Brenda Moncrieff (née Laing) at St George's, Hanover Square. He

Napper Tandy – an occasional cricketer who enjoyed a distinguished career in the military before becoming a leading light in the tobacco industry

© National Portrait Gallery

had achieved the rank of major by 1915 and by the end of the war, had been promoted to brigadier general and appointed Companion of the Order of St Michael and St George, an honour granted to those who 'hold high and confidential offices within Her Majesty's colonial possessions, and in reward for services rendered to the Crown in relation to the foreign affairs of the Empire'.

Having retired from the theatre of war in 1921, Napper Tandy remained on the reserve list until 1934, retaining the honorary rank of brigadier general and expending his considerable energy in a more indirect slaughter of the innocents through active service in the tobacco industry. In the 1920s, he became a company director, residing at the time at Gloucester Terrace in London. In 1935, the *Motherwell Times* announces that Brigadier General Tandy, chairman of the Tobacco Trade Association, is 'one of the outstanding personalities in the British tobacco trade, and his appearance at [an association] dinner is arousing much interest in tobacco trade circles'.

Napper was an ineterate pipe smoker, though this did not curtail his life unduly. He died on 6 May 1953 at the University College Hospital in St Pancras, a matter of days short of his seventy-fourth birthday. His wife, Brenda, survived him by some years. A resourceful woman, she was awarded the MBE in 1958 for her work as a member of the executive committee of the Officers' Families Fund. The two of them had built up an impressive collection of honours.

E. N. Tandy and his beloved
'Abdullah' pipe, drawn in
1947 by H. C. Iverson

1905

"The President expressed regret that the club had
had such a disastrous season, both from a
financial and a cricket point of view."

Bath Chronicle

Championship Position: 15 of 16

Northamptonshire had been invited to join the Championship. Len Braund topped the county's bowling and batting averages, supported by Ernie Robson, who was number two in both departments. With only one win, there was little to cheer about. *Wisden* noted, witheringly, that 'the eleven had a truly deplorable season', asserting that the 'one redeeming feature was the presence of H. Martyn', the county's flamboyant wicket-keeper. The fall-out with Surrey simmered on, though the MCC adjudged Somerset guilty only of a technical breach rather than any foul play, in poaching Bill Montgomery. There was a tail-off in support and, with an overdraft of approximately £700, the club was in dire financial straits. To add to their woes, the president, Sir Spencer Ponsonby-Fane, announced that the county had reluctantly agreed to pay the pros over the winter months, as other clubs did. The President expressed his firm personal view that this was an unfortunate turn of events and would encourage indolence. None of the debutants would make a lasting mark on the Championship, although Massey Poyntz would prove a loyal servant of the club, prepared in time to take on the captaincy when no other amateur seemed willing to do so.

163
Edward Stephen Massey Poyntz
1 June 1905 v. Gloucestershire, Bath

Massey Poyntz – 'the most affable of men': he would step into the breach and captain Somerset when their fortunes were at a low ebb

Another of the Somerset clique who claimed descent from William the Conqueror, Massey Poyntz was born in Chelmsford on 27 October 1883, at a time when his father was Chief Constable of Essex. The family moved to Gotham House in Tiverton, Devon, while Massey was a pupil at Haileybury College. He was devoted to his mother, Henrietta, and she was protective of him, reports suggesting that he was a man without guile, sometimes too generous for his own good. Affable but no great intellect and a keen rather than a gifted sportsman, Massey played his rugby for Bridgwater Albion (whom he captained for a while) and Somerset. He was also an enthusiastic hockey player and, in later life, a golfer.

It would be stretching things to call him a cricketing all-rounder, but he enjoyed the occasional success as a batsman and he bowled a little. A loyal servant of the club between 1905 and 1919, he achieved a batting average of 16.70 in 102 first-class matches. A piece in the *Western Daily Press* concerning an innings of 35 against Gloucestershire gives some insight into his limitations as a stroke-maker, stating that 'his one great scoring stroke is a late chop which is aimed to send the ball past point, and this was early crippled by specially placed fieldsmen'. Massey Poyntz only ever bowled during the 1911 season. Astonishingly, five of his eight career wickets were bagged when he came on as seventh-change bowler and took 5 for 36. His heroics were never repeated. His best service to Somerset was as a slip fielder with a safe pair of hands and as a captain, prepared to stand up and be counted at a time when the county's fortunes were at a low ebb.

Rev. Stancomb would proclaim at Massey's funeral that Somerset's popular captain demonstrated 'a combination of grim determination and a keen sense of humour'. With John Daniell taking temporary charge of his family's tea plantations, Massey Poyntz had agreed to lead the side. It was a thankless task, with Somerset destined to prop up the Championship table. Poyntz, an unabashed optimist, noted that it was down to 'a lot of bad luck that [Somerset] did not finish half way up the table instead of at the bottom'.

He signed up with the Bedfordshire Regiment when war broke out, joining his brother, Hugh, and enjoying rapid promotions until becoming a major. After the war, he would play for The Army against Cambridge University and would notch up his one and only first-class century. Away from the world of cricket, Massey Poyntz was involved in the drinks industry, in his early days as a hop salesman and then from 1922 as a director of Rigby & Evans Ltd, Bristol Wine Merchants.

Still based in Bristol, he died on 26 December 1934 at the age of fifty-one, while visiting the seaside resort of Minehead. He was never married. In his eulogy, the Rev. Stancomb stated that Massey 'never turned a deaf ear to an appeal for money' and 'was sometimes deceived', also asserting that he 'abhorred all forms of unfairness and cruelty, particularly in the case of animals' and 'never nursed grievances'. The hoary old anecdote was trotted out that, on being informed that he was wanted on the phone, as he shaped to leave the pavilion to bat, he responded: 'Tell them to wait. I shan't be long.'

Massey Poyntz, the most affable of men, deserves to be remembered for something other than descent from a Norman psychopath or for being the least successful captain in Somerset's history. Perhaps we should replicate his generosity of spirit and attribute the joke to him.

164
Arthur Samuel Sellick
12 June 1905 v. Middlesex, Lord's

Arthur Sellick was born in Gloucester on 20 September 1878, the sixth child of a carpenter. His life would revolve around cricket, which he would continue playing into old age, and his story would be one of constant financial difficulties. First spotted by Gloucestershire, he played for Somerset's neighbours in eleven first-class fixtures, averaging 18.42 but taking no wickets.

Whilst qualifying for Somerset he was married to Frances Olivia (née Richards), known as Olive, at Bath in 1904. Gloucestershire seem to have extracted more from him than Somerset, for whom he played on six occasions in 1905, averaging only 4.00 and taking no wickets. Arthur continued to ply his trade as a pro and in 1920 was turning out for Lansdown at the age of forty-one. His performances as a club cricketer were strong enough for him to be selected for Wiltshire over a sixteen-year period.

Arthur Sellick for whom cricket offered a buffer from the continuing threat of penury

He was appointed coach of Monkton Combe School in 1921while living in Trowbridge and this would set the pattern for the rest of his life. No longer able to demand payment for his services as a player, he took on a succession of coaching and groundsman roles. These included working for London Transport and for the BBC, maintaining their playing fields for a long period until his retirement in 1943. In addition to this, he was employed as an umpire in a number of first-class fixtures in the 1919 season. Always looking to find ways to earn enough to get by, he opened a sports shop in Trowbridge with his wife, but when they divorced – reports imply that this occurred in 1926 – Olive took over the running of the enterprise while Arthur tried his luck with a similar venture in Bristol (which quickly flopped, leaving him with debts of £300). In an acrimonious exchange at Trowbridge Court, Arthur applied for a reduction in his weekly maintenance payments from 35 shillings. His argument was that business was good for his wife, whereas he was now penniless and living with his two sisters in Bournemouth. With some probing, it was revealed that he had been taking advantage of the generosity of two ladies, Mrs Fricker and Mrs Sharp, who had been baling him out for some while. Olive's allowance was duly reduced to 25 shillings. Arthur would in fact live with Ellen Fricker until she died ten days before he did. She is refered to both as Fricker and Sellick in documents.

Still trying to scrape a living and relying on the generosity of his paramour, Arthur continued to play cricket. In 1934, he took more than100 wickets, including a 10 for 15 and notched up in excess of 1000 runs. We can safely assume that the level was rather lowly, given that Arthur was by now in his mid-fifties. His longevity is nonetheless impressive. A press report of 1946 describes the sixty-seven-year-old as 'very fit and still playing cricket', though he was still paying his 25s a week maintenance to his wife, who by now owned five properties in Bath. He made a further attempt to have Olive's allowance reduced, but she resisted. In the end, she had to settle for maintenance of 2s 6d per week.

Arthur Sellick died in Carshalton on 16 January 1958 at the age of seventy-nine. He had presumably hung up his boots by then and was still penniless.

165
Osbert Cautley Mordaunt
12 June 1905 v. Middlesex, Lord's

Osbert Mordaunt was born on 26 May 1876 in the family home of Gatcombe Court, Flax Bourton. He was a career soldier who joined the Somerset Light Infantry when he came down from Oxford University, embarking almost immediately for the Boer War. On returning unharmed to Somerset, he played for the county on fourteen occasions between 1905 and 1910. His batting average was only 5.66, with a highest score of 23, but he captured a total of thirty-seven wickets at 24.05 each, with his slow right-arm deliveries. Thirty of those wickets came in the 1907 season, including – in the match against Gloucestershire – an aggregate of 9 for 92 in the two innings.

He was married at thirty in 1906 to Constance Katherine (née Young). At this point he became a member of staff at Sandhurst. During the First World War he was chief signals officer to Lord Cavan in Italy and was awarded a DSO. Promotion followed in 1919 when he was given command of the School of Signals (which became the Royal Corps of Signals) until his retirement in 1924. During the Second World War, Colonel Mordaunt, as he had become, was an active member of the Home Guard. Although he played cricket for the Army, he was more noted for his horsemanship and was for a while a leading light in the Eridge Hunt Committee and the Eridge Polo Club in Sussex.

Osbert Mordaunt – a member of a cricketing dynasty, his county career was modest, although he enjoyed some success in the 1907 season

He died on 20 October 1949 at the age of seventy-three at Bells Yew Green, near Tunbridge Wells.

166
Alfred Ernest Yates Trestrail
19 June 1905 v. Lancashire, Taunton

The son of an industrial chemist, Alfred Trestrail was born in Somerset on 24 January 1876 at Hallatrow Court, owned by his uncle, Richard Sherring. He was brought up in Clevedon and went to school at New College, Eastbourne. He then graduated from Christ's College, Cambridge, before training for the legal profession and becoming a solicitor, practicing first in Clevedon, then Huddersfield and finally, for much of his career as a partner in the firm Moore, Trestrail & Blatch in New Milton, Hampshire. An all-round sportsman, he was particularly noted as a footballer, playing for Cambridge University, Crusaders FC and Bedminster FC. Between 1896 and 1900 he represented Somerset, whom he captained on several occasions. He also appeared for his county at hockey and lawn tennis. An obituary in the local press relates these feats but adds as an afterthought that 'he was also a good cricketer'. No mention is made of his one appearance for Somerset CCC. He in fact mustered seven runs in his two innings, caught no one and was not asked to bowl.

A. E. Y. Trestrail – a talented footballer who captained the Somerset county side, his cricketing career was less noteworthy

In 1915, he was married to Margaret Spiers (née Cunningham) and they would have three sons and a daughter. During the war he rose to the rank of major. Serving with the 10th Battalion of the Cheshire Regiment, he was invalided home in 1916 with trench fever, returning to France in 1918 and receiving a DSO for his bravery in capturing a German machine gun emplacement at Mouquet Farm. He was given leave in October 1918 in order to stand as a Labour MP for Torquay, having previously stood as a Liberal candidate at the local council election for Tiverton in 1910. Whilst on leave, he discovered a live German mortar (a *minenwerter*) among his surplus kit. How it came to be among his possessions is unclear, but recognising the danger he asked for help from a bomb disposal expert at the local military hospital (which was commanded by his father). The volunteer – Bombardier Hicky – proved not up to the task and was killed in the ensuing explosion, with Trestrail and his father suffering superficial wounds. The coroner's verdict was one of 'accidental death'. Regrettably, the election also went badly wrong, with only 4,029 votes cast for Major Trestrail and the Unionists retaining the Torquay seat with a healthy majority.

After the war, his life was centred around New Milton, Hampshire. He remained involved in local politics and was also president of the football and tennis clubs. He died at the age of fifty-nine on 5 February 1935. Having been confined to his bed owing to a bout of lumbago, he succumbed suddenly to a fatal heart attack. Alfred Trestrail's one appearance for Somerset was of little consequence when weighed against his many and varied achievements.

167
Ernest Shorrocks
19 June 1905 v. Lancashire, Taunton

Ernie Shorrocks was claimed by the war but, unlike many of his contemporaries, his life was not defined by it. A much-loved and admired science teacher and talented sportsman, he was born on 12 March 1875 in Middleton, Lancashire, and gained his MSc at Victoria University (later Manchester University). After a brief spell as a schoolmaster in the North – first in Manchester and then in Knaresborough – he came down to teach science at Queen's College, Taunton, and would stay there for nearly eighteen years. H. J. Channon, a pupil of his, would go on to be a teacher, journalist and writer. Channon was full of praise for the man who was everything a pupil could wish for in a teacher – inspirational, a successful sportsman and a wonderful person. Here is Channon writing in the *Taunton Courier* in 1949, reminiscing on those people who had shaped his life in one way or another:

> *In class his enthusiasm was infectious. He never paraded his cleverness but never deceived us with specious arguments. His chief concern was to encourage initiative and self-reliance in us, to get us to think clearly and to be painstaking and thorough. He had a sense of humour, {too} ... I am afraid we indulged in a little hero-worship ... but he was always so modest ...*

Ernie Shorrocks – an inspirational schoolmaster who lost his life in the First World War

275

Ernie played cricket and association football for Somerset and took part in county rugby trials. His failure to progress beyond a trial match and make the Somerset rugby team is perhaps explained in a newspaper report, written in 1902, stating that 'Shorrocks is very fast, but is comparatively new to rugby'. He was a successful club cricketer, described as 'a medium pace bowler with a length that tried any batsman's patience'. Furthermore, 'his slip fielding was a joy to see' and his batting 'as safe as a rock'. Would his abilities stand the test of Championship competition? In his one county match, against Lancashire, he was by no means out of his depth, coming away with 2 wickets for 30 and a batting average of 16.00.

After leaving Queen's he was for a little over a year a teacher at Huish's Grammar School in Taunton before he signed up for the Public Schools Battalion of the Royal Fusiliers. Ernie was killed in action in the Somme at the age of forty-one on 20 July 1916, while overseeing the clearing of a wood. His commanding officer, Captain Templar, wrote to inform Ernie's parents that their son had 'died fighting splendidly, and did wonderful works in reorganising the men'. More touchingly, a private in his platoon wrote to them, saying: 'Sergeant Shorrocks was not like an official over us, but a friend to everyone, and we all loved him.'

His name appears on the Thiepval Memorial. Ernie Shorrocks was never married but many mourned his passing. Some, such as H. J. Channon, never forgot their boyhood hero.

168
John Dowie Harcombe
19 June 1905 v. Lancashire, Taunton

This is a tale of two Harcombes: John and Joseph, the latter the younger by six years. Both were born in South Africa, the sons on Benjamin Harcombe, an engineer in the employ of Cecil Rhodes. The boys lost their father in tragic circumstances when he was killed in a mining accident whilst installing equipment in April 1896, with the result that they came to England from South Africa as youngsters. Joseph knuckled down, learned the fundamentals of farming on his cousin's farm in Wool, Dorset, and then left for Kenya, establishing a successful farming and plantation business. While not quite the prodigal son, John enjoyed himself for a few years while he pondered over an appropriate career before concluding that life on the Kenyan plantations might be no bad thing.

John Harcombe, referred to as Jack, had been born in Cape Town on 13 March 1883 and was sent to Taunton School, where he proved a valuable member of the cricket team. The school magazine notes in its report of the 1900 season, that he was the mainstay of the school bowling attack with his right-arm off-breaks:

> *J. D. Harcombe bore the brunt of the attack. On his day he was very effective ... His batting on occasions showed that he could if he would, but why not always?*

Jack came back briefly as a pupil teacher in 1902 before undertaking a four-year engineering apprenticeship with Easton and Bessemer.

The *Western Daily Press* reports in August 1905 that 'a capable batsman has been found in the person of J. D. Harcombe, a young Taunton amateur, who may be of considerable use to the county next season, if he can find time to play'. The writer's optimism had been heightened by the fact that over the course of his first three matches Harcombe had notched up a 3 for 51 against Lancashire and a score of 29 against Kent. Alas, he would not play again until 1914 and

J. D. Harcombe – after a bright start, his first-class career petered out

would only find time to appear in seven first-class fixtures for his county. He would average 7.60 with the bat and take no more wickets. Not quite the impact the reporter had hoped for.

In 1907 Jack left for Dayton, Ohio, in order to further his career as an engineer. He returned to England before the war, playing a solitary game for Somerset in 1914 before enlisting with the Somerset Light Infantry as a private. Having embarked for France in May 1915, he became a lance corporal in September, rising to the rank of temporary second lieutenant in the Devonshires in 1916. He returned from Tournai in November 1918, clearly exhausted and suffering from 'influenza, boils and carbuncles'. He was granted the rank of captain when discharged in July 1919. After the war he would play three more unproductive games for Somerset before moving to Kenya to join the coffee-growing and farming business of which his brother, Joseph, was a joint-owner. Harcombe & MacLachlan owned land in Koru and Ruiru and Jack lived on Ruiru Farm, Kenya, with his wife, Rose. He maintained his links with the South West, playing in friendly fixtures in the 1920s. He died in a nursing home in Taunton on 19 July 1954, having retired to Somerset with Rose less than a year earlier. He was seventy-one at the time. Jack Harcombe had been a modest cricketer who had raised hopes that he might deliver more for the county. The same could be said for many of the players who passed through the Somerset's metaphorical swinging doors at this time.

169
William Montgomery
13 July 1905 v. Australia, Bath

Bill Montgomery was born in Staines on 4 March 1878, the son of a linoleum designer and printer. He was a competent but not an outstanding performer who became the centre of an almighty row between Surrey and Somerset. He had joined the ground staff at The Oval in 1896 and hovered between Surrey's Second and First XIs from 1898 until 1904, never quite able to make his mark. In 1903 he was married to Hettie (née Platts). Perhaps this had been the spur to seek more secure employment. Whether Somerset were demonstrating subterfuge or mere incompetence is unclear, but they approached Montgomery and took him on as a pro for the 1905 season. They were taken aback by the venom of Surrey's response, with Surrey refusing to play Somerset – a position that would not change until 1908. The suspicion in many quarters was that Surrey were still smarting, having realised what an enormous error they had made in letting Len Braund depart for Somerset. Braund remained a great all-rounder, even if his skills as a bowler had begun to wane. If Somerset, for their part, felt that they had unearthed the next Len Braund, they were to be sorely disappointed. Bizarrely, Bill Montgomery – a bowler who could bat a bit – was barely asked to turn his arm, completing only twenty-nine overs in three seasons between 1905 and 1907 and taking 3 wickets at 35.66. His batting exploits were equally modest, with an average of 9.66 in twenty innings.

Bill Montgomery, whose presence in the Somerset side led to a major falling out with Surrey

The *Bath Chronicle* noted that after leaving to become a pro at Chippenham, Bill Montgomery subsequently 'decided to give up cricket as a means of livelihood, and has taken up a position as electrician in the North'. At the time of the 1911 census, he is based in the South again, living in Hertfordshire with his wife and two daughters.

He came back to cricket as a coach at Oundle School, Peterborough, where he worked for seventeen years, helping to hone the skills of many future county players including Reg Ingle, who would go on to captain Somerset.

Bill Montgomery had represented four counties: Surrey, Somerset, Cheshire and Hertfordshire. He died on 14 November 1952 at the age of seventy-four, still residing in Oundle, although his death occurred at the Memorial Hospital in Peterborough. Perhaps he had looked back with mild amusement, during his retirement, at the mayhem he had unwittingly unleashed as a young professional cricketer.

170
Thomas Richardson
13 July 1905 v. Australians, Bath

Yours truly
T. Richardson

Tom Richardson was a towering figure in Surrey's cricketing folklore but a mere bit-part player in the history of Somerset, for whom he came out of retirement to play one game. He was born on 11 August 1870 in Byfleet, Surrey, where his father, Henry, worked at the time as a domestic coachman, residing at Shrapnell Lodge. The nature of his father's profession and Tom's swarthy looks were perhaps the factors that led to a myth of his having been born in a gypsy caravan. Certainly his family had endured hardships, with a young Henry having to stay at the Uckfield Union Workhouse along with his sister, Rebecca, in the 1840s.

Tom Richardson – one of the all-time great fast bowlers, he was hauled out of retirement by Somerset for one game while he was a landlord in Bath

Soon after Tom's birth, Henry and Johanna Elizabeth Richardson moved to Hancock Cottages beside Mitcham Common and it is said that this is where Tom learned to bowl with great pace and accuracy.

It was an irony and cricket's good fortune that a man of superhuman stamina, arguably the most lion-hearted man ever to bowl in first-class and test cricket, was rejected by the army and the police as a result of a heart abnormality. Tom Richardson attracted many myths on account of his prodigious feats and his gypsy's looks but the truth of this story was borne out by the nature of his early death.

Neville Cardus deemed him one of the 'Six Giants of the Wisden Century', calling

him 'the greatest cricketer that ever took to fast bowling', adding that 'his bowling was wonderful because into it went the very life-force of the man'. Coming in off a long run and delivering the ball with an intimidating leap and with great speed and accuracy rather than variation, his achievements were legendary. At the height of his powers in the four years between 1894 and 1897 he took in excess of 1,000 wickets. Able to bowl flat out in searing heat for many hours, he was a phenomenon, a force of nature. In total, he took 2,104 first-class wickets and 88 test wickets in 14 appearances for England.

If his appetite for bowling was insatiable, it was matched by his consumption of beer. Prone to putting on weight, he became embroiled in a losing battle to retain his fitness and went into decline. That having been said, he was still capable on occasions of being a matchwinner and delivering 100 wickets in a season. Surrey terminated his contract in 1904 and he was by then a shadow of his former self.

Tom had been married in 1895 to Edith Emma (née Cheesman) but the marriage only lasted until 1902, with Tom being given custody of the children. He later lived with a 'housekeeper' named Emily Birch who had been a manageress of a railway refreshment room (or café) in Kingston-upon-Thames. Emily helped Tom in his later years in the running of pubs.

At the time of his call-up by Somerset for the match against the Australians, he held the license of the Wine Vaults on York Street, in Bath, and was woefully short of fitness. He was a man to draw the crowds, though, and the spectators hoped for a miracle. Alas, on a benign track, the batsmen made hay. Warwick Armstrong hit a triple century for the visitors and Henry Martyn saved Somerset faces with a fearless assault on the Aussie bowlers that left him on 130 not out when the match ended in a draw. Tom took no wickets for 65 runs.

He and his partner Emily moved to Richmond where, from 1907, they ran 'The Prince's Head', a pub on The Green. Tom's physical exertions, his excessive drinking and his heart disorder all caught up with him on 2 July 1912 when he suffered a heart attack at the age of forty-one in an open field named Les Mollienes, whilst on a walking holiday at St-Jean-d'Arvey, in Chambery, France.

171
Arthur Ernest Boden Freeman
3 August 1905 v. Sussex, Bath

There were heartfelt tributes to 'Old Ernie' when he retired in 1935 and again when he died in 1948. They tell of a man loved by generations of Bath schoolchildren. Those children would have found it hard to believe that the frail old man they beheld was 'one of the fastest bowlers and hardest-hitting batsmen in Somerset in his day'.

Ernie Freeman was born on 15 October 1871 in Iron Acton, near Chipping Sodbury. His parents were for many years the master and mistress of the school in Yate.

Ernie qualified as a primary school teacher at the Taunton Wesleyan School (Queen's College) and then took up a post as assistant master at the Walcot Council School in Bath in 1894. He would remain there for twenty-four years.

In 1894, the world must have seemed a wonderful place for young Ernie Freeman. He had been appointed to a permanent teaching job and in a Gloucestershire trial match, he clean bowled W. G. Grace, bowling at a hostile pace. It is not clear why he and Gloucestershire took matters no further. Perhaps a career in teaching promised more security for him. By 1905 he had gained a good reputation as a pace bowler and big-hitting lower-order batsman. We may well wonder why a man selected for his bowling was not handed the ball. To offer the case for the defence, Sussex were bowled out cheaply, with Sam Woods deploying four known bowlers. Woods then went out and hit a swashbuckling 125

Ernie Freeman – 'one of the fastest bowlers and hardest-hitting batsmen in Somerset in his day', he was a much-loved school-master

before the weather intervened and the game petered out into to a draw. In other circumstances, Sam might perhaps have used his new bowler. Coming in at number ten, Ernie made 3 runs in his only innings. That was the end of his adventure.

On 1 January 1895 he was married to Elizabeth Luiscote (née Silvester), with whom he would have six children. He went back to ply his trade with Bath and would do so until in time he donned the umpire's coat. The *Bath Chronicle* of 1929 announces the change:

> *Mr Ernest Freeman, who is skipper of the Bath 'A' cricket team, is giving up play at the end of this season ... In his heyday, he was one of the lions of the Bath first team. As a bowler and hitter he gave long years of wonderful service to the club. Some of the biggest smites ever seen at North Parade have come from his bat, and some of the most sensational bowling performances have been attained by him. 'Ernie' is popular on and off the field.*

For twenty-four years he had been assistant master at Walcot. There followed a further seventeen years in a similar role at West Twerton Council School. It must have seemed to the children of Bath that 'Old Ernie' had been in his post for ever. It probably appeared that way to him, too. He died in Bath on 30 November 1948 at the age of seventy-seven, opening the floodgates to all those warm tributes, his fleeting appearance for his county a mere flash in the pan in a long, fulfilled life.

Somerset XI in 1905.
STANDING: G. S. McAulay (Scorer), A. E. Lewis, A. E. Newton, H. S. Poyntz, L. C. Braund, A. S. Sellick. SEATED: C. E. Brown, F. M. Lee, S. M. J. Woods, C. E. Dunlop, H. Martyn. FRONT: B. Cranfield

1906

"Somerset did not do anything brilliant, but ... they improved
a great deal upon their deplorable record of 1905."

Wisden

Championship Position: 11= of 16

This was the year when Sam Woods finally handed over the captaincy. A talismanic figure in his prime, his spirit might still have been willing but the body was weakening. The greater blow was the announcement that Henry Martyn, described at the AGM as 'the most brilliant wicket-keeper in England', would no longer be available. Martyn was the only Somerset man to top 1,000 first-class runs in the season. A great loss. Randall Johnson had shown flashes of brilliance and among the bowlers, Braund, Lewis and Bailey had shared most of the wickets. Of the newcomers, only Lionel Cranfield looked likely to make any impact at county level. Alas, his timing was awry. He was sacrificed as the club announced that they had reached a crossroads. They had lost over £900. The committee had concluded that the pros were to be culled and the county would become predominantly an amateur county in order to balance the books. 1906 was therefore a watershed year in which Somerset consigned themselves to the status of also-rans for the foreseeable future. Lionel Palairet was asked to take on the captaincy. Lord Devon graciously agreed that his employee would be made available throughout the forthcoming season.

*Lionel Palairet (l) who took over the
captaincy from Sam Woods (r) in 1906*

Somerset XI v. Yorkshire at Bath on 27 August 1906
STANDING: *C. J. Bowring (non-playing), E. Robson, O. C. Mordaunt, H. S. Poyntz, A. E. Lewis,
H. E. Murray-Anderdon (Secretary)*
SEATED: *P. R. Johnson, F. A. Phillips, S. M. J. Woods (non-playing), L. C. H. Palairet, H. Martyn*
FRONT: *A. E. Bailey. L. C. Braund, F. M. Lee*

172
Lionel Lord Cranfield
17 May 1906 v. Warwickshire, Taunton

Lionel Lord Cranfield

Lionel Cranfield was born on 11 October 1883 in Brixton, London. His father was a cab proprietor at the time. Edward Beaumont Cranfield soon took the family to Bristol, where he became an hotelier and licensed victualler. Lionel first tried his luck as a cricketer with Gloucestershire. Having already benefitted from his brother Monty's wicket-taking abilities, Somerset registered their interest and in 1905 Lionel completed his qualification by playing as a pro for Wells, who funded his wages through voluntary subscriptions. He enjoyed a hugely productive season, taking more than two hundred wickets at 8 runs apiece. A report states that 'he has an easy, yet deceptive delivery, breaks both ways, and sends down an occasional fast one which always takes a lot of playing.' A good all-round sportsman who played as a fly-half and full-back for Bristol RFC, he was never really given the chance he deserved by Somerset. He played in four first-class matches and was only asked to bowl thirty-two overs, taking 2 wickets in total for 57.50 runs each. Lionel left Somerset and plied his trade in Lancashire League cricket. The *Wells Journal* notes that 'it was a matter of surprise that Somerset should have allowed him to go after a totally inadequate trial.'

L. L. Cranfield – successful for many years in Lancashire League cricket and 'an inspiring character'

Having been married in 1906 to Maud (née Hicks), an accomplished artist whose works were exhibited at the Royal Academy, he settled into his new environment, proving an enormous success and employed by various clubs over many years: Crompton, Heywood, Middleton and finally, in 1930 at the age of forty-six, Enfield. Gloucestershire had come calling again and he made a number of appearances for them. His career was interrupted by the war, when he joined the 4th Lancashire Fusiliers as a lance corporal. He was gassed but staged a recovery while posted for a while to the Labour Corps. After returning to the fray, he was severely wounded. In the confusion, Maud was informed that her husband was dead. It is reported that when he arrived back home unannounced and still in a terrible state some months later, Maud fainted at the sight of her husband, whom she had believed she had lost.

Writing in *Cricket in the Leagues*, John Kay cites Lionel as an inspiration and relates that he managed to juggle league cricket with his retailing business. Kay also notes that Lionel deserves credit for rebuilding Middleton CC after the club had 'suffered much through the ravages of war'. Lionel in fact managed two florist's shops with Maud concurrently: one in Middleton and another in Heywood. These ventures allowed him the luxury of turning down offers from wealthier league clubs. His loyalty was in turn rewarded with visits to the shop by supporters. After finally retiring from league cricket, Lionel took up the post of assistant coach at Eton College. Somerset might have missed an opportunity, but cricket in general benefitted from a talented, hardworking pro and an inspirational coach.

He died in Sale on 17 May 1968 at the age of eighty-four, having had the quiet satisfaction of seeing his son Lionel Montague (known as Monty) play for Gloucestershire.

173
James Maxwell
17 May 1906 v. Warwickshire, Taunton

Jimmy Maxwell was born in Taunton on 13 January 1883, the tenth child of a travelling draper named Thomas and his wife, Sarah. Their fortunes fluctuated, not helped by the fact that customers occasionally defaulted on their monthly payments for goods. Thomas was in the courts on a number of occasions with clear evidence that he was something of a hothead. He was held in contempt of court at Chard in 1891 for 'grossly insulting His Honour Judge Paterson'. The children were brought up as chapel-goers (perhaps owing to the maternal influence) at North Street Congregational Chapel, with Jimmy being sent to the local Independent College which became Taunton School, attended primarily by the children of Non-Conformists. The new arrival would have been welcomed during perilous times when the former headmaster had plunged the school into a crisis by leaving in 1894 to set up his own school, taking more than half the

"Cranfield, the Heywood pro, played a lively tune, taking 6 Milnrow wickets and scoring 84." Rochdale Observer, *July 1914*

pupils and several staff members with him. By 1899 there were only 70 pupils and Jimmy had been made captain of the school football team, rugby having been abandoned in 1896 because of the shortage of numbers. He was also a leading light in a Cricket XI that included fellow Somerset players E. S. Goodland, J. D. Harcombe and C. G. Deane. The school magazine tells us that:

> *Our season was most successful ... Goodland and Maxwell with the bat, Harcombe with the ball ... We shall be sorry to miss Maxwell from our team next year.*

H. J. Channon refers to Maxwell's propensity to try to bowl too fast and to sacrifice caution with the bat, calling him 'a fast, hostile bowler, not over accurate, but his whole action of delivery was the acme of concentrated endeavour. He was a fierce hitter.' Jimmy played ten first-class matches for Somerset, primarily as a tail-end batsman and pace bowler. His batting average of 16.72 was better than might be expected of a lower-order batsman. Having left during the 1906 season he met with some success as a pro at New Brighton in Lancashire League cricket, returning to the Somerset team for the 1908 season and taking 5 for 63 against Lancashire at Liverpool. Thereafter, he was employed

Jimmy Maxwell – 'a fast, hostile bowler, not over accurate'

as a pro by Swansea and also represented Glamorgan on a number of occasions, turning in some excellent performances that merited him a place in a South Wales side that played the South Africans in 1912. Married in Taunton in 1907 to Violet Thornett (née Telling), he had two children. He was supplementing his earnings with his own travelling draper's business until he was declared bankrupt in 1914. The causes of failure are given as 'heavy trade expenses, rates and taxes, and insufficient capital', which would appear to cover most aspects of business.

Thereafter he returned to the fold to work for his father, Thomas, in Taunton. Thomas was determined to keep his business going during the war and at various points, he was obliged to reapply for certificates of exemption for his sons. In the end, Jimmy was required to sign up and duly received his War Medal. Jimmy Maxwell's career as a professional cricketer had come to an end and he focussed instead on his business interests and the less onerous demands of club cricket. He died in Taunton on 27 December 1967 at the age of eighty-four.

174
Henry Hurl Humphries
21 May 1906 v. Sussex, Bath

Hurl Humphries – a strongly-built left-handed batsman with a superb throwing arm

Known as Hurl, he was born on 8 September 1885 (not 1879 as some references state) in Warkworth, Ontario. He had strong connections with both Canada and Bath. His father (also Henry Hurl Humphries) hailed from Ontario but his mother, Catherine, was from a Bath family involved in the manufacture of coach bodies. Returning to Bath as a young man, Hurl would make the city his home, although Canada had shaped his interests. He was involved, for example, in exhibition matches of 'rink hockey' and would return to his homeland on occasions, such as when he played for the Combined Canada/USA team versus Australia in 1913.

Hurl was married in 1918 to Alice Mabel Amor, known as Mabel, the sister of fellow Somerset cricketer Stanley Amor, for whom he worked as a builder's foreman. Mabel was an active member of the community, involved in a number of fund-raising activities and a leading light in the Oldfield Park Women's Pleasant Monday Evenings club.

Nearly 6 feet 1 inch tall and a strongly-built left-handed batsman, Hurl was comfortable either in the middle-order or opening the innings. He played for Bath alongside his brother-in-law, who captained the team for many years. Hurl had his moments, such as his 'brilliant century' (118 not out) against Weston-super-Mare in August 1933, when he was forty-eight years old. Hurl and Stanley were both still playing in 1938, when 'Hurl Humphries made a welcome return to the Bath ranks'. His Somerset career reads as: one match, no runs, no balls bowled and no catches. He did, however, make a telling intervention by throwing down Cox's wicket when the Sussex batsman was allegedly 'halfway down the pitch'. Cox was neither the first nor the last batsman to be caught unawares by the man John Ruddick, a chronicler of Bath cricket, described as 'the fastest thrower I have ever seen'. Hurl would seem to have been blessed with both a fine throwing arm and a serendipitous piece of nomenclature.

He died in Bath on 12 October 1964 at the age of seventy-nine. Sally Milsom writes of her 'Uncle Hurl' as 'a very special man who played an important role during my childhood' and one can picture an affable, avuncular figure: a great bear of a man and adored by his young relatives.

175
Richard Bethune Fripp Selwyn-Payne
28 June 1906 v. Hampshire, Portsmouth

Born in Rangoon on 18 September 1885, his middle (maternal) name was Fripp and not Tripp, as sometimes stated. With an impeccable military background and a mother who had been born in Staplegrove, Taunton, Richard was a shoo-in to the Somerset side. Both of his grandfathers had been prominent in the military, rising to the rank of colonel and his father had served in the Somerset Light Infantry before becoming a major general on the General Staff. Educated at Malvern College, Richard was commissioned into the Somerset Light Infantry in 1907. His was called up for Somerset's match at the United Services Ground, Portsmouth, where

Richard Selwyn-Payne, who made only one appearance for Somerset

Hampshire were twice skittled out by Len Braund. The *Taunton Courier* explains that 'R. S. Payne is studying at one of the Southsea Army Colleges, and his opportunity … arose through sudden illness preventing P. R. Johnson from playing.' Coming in at number ten, he was 15 not out overnight, but despatched in the first over of the following morning. With the weather having turned, Hampshire's fate was sealed.

Although this was his only game for Somerset, he would make occasional appearances for Wells and later for Exmouth. In 1914 he was promoted to temporary lieutenant and transferred to the Motor Machine Gun Service, operating machine guns mounted on motorcycles. He had risen to the rank of captain when he retired from the army. Thereafter, he would enjoy a quiet life in Exmouth in South Devon, living with his mother, Clara, until her death in 1945 and spending much of his leisure time playing golf or bowls. He died in Exmouth on 1 February 1949, aged sixty-three. He had remained unmarried.

176
William George Burrough
23 July 1906 v. Warwickshire, Edgbaston

W. G. Burrough – known
in club cricketing circles as
'the Wedmore Express'

Born on 22 July 1875 in Clun, Shropshire, William was the son of a rector who for many years held the living of Eaton Bishop, near Hereford. The extended Burrough family had made their fortune manufacturing gin, most famously the Beefeater brand. One of William's brothers, Francis, would become joint-managing director of James Burrough Ltd. William spent most of his adult life in Wedmore practicing as a solicitor. In 1906 he set up the practice of Burrough & Crowder with Alec Crowder, who would also play for Somerset. The two men ran their business from space rented in a stationery shop belonging to William Pople, Burrough's future father-in-law.

At club level, the two of them formed a formidable duo, with Alec Crowder a prolific run-maker and William Burrough an intimidatingly fast bowler known as the 'Wedmore Express' but also capable of scoring the occasional century. In 1906 William made four appearances for Somerset and – used primarily as a bowler – took seven wickets at 49.14 each, while contributing a total of 40 runs at an average of 5.71. The statistical record does not tell the whole story. The *Wells Journal* records that 'had Somerset's fielding been up to standard, several Warwick wickets would have fallen to [Burrough]'.

He was married in 1907 to Lilian (née Pople), a music teacher in Wedmore. The couple would have two sons, one of whom – Herbert Dickinson 'Dickie' Burrough – would play for Somerset over a twenty-year period. Within a year of his wedding,

William had set up the Wedmore Electric Light & Power Co., a successful enterprise which ensured that Wedmore became one of the earliest adopters of electricity in Somerset. Having served its purpose, the firm would finally be wound up in 1928.

He was a lieutenant in the Wedmore Volunteer Corps during the First World War and must have seemed a ubiquitous presence in the village in the years that followed. The untimely loss of his bosom friend Alec Crowder would be a huge blow to William, but he continued to put his considerable energies into the development of Wedmore. He became a partner in a new solicitors' practice of Burrough, Pulliblank & Horner with offices in Wedmore and Cheddar. Still a leading member of Wedmore CC, he was also a keen footballer and later president of Wedmore AFC. William's wife, Lilian, had died in 1919, aged forty-one. He was married for a second time in 1921 to Dorothy Ethel (née Tate). In later life he took up golf and was also a member of the bowling club and a keen tennis player. For a while chairman of the parish council, he held a number of directorships of businesses and charitable organisations. He was also a coroner for North Somerset.

When he died in Wedmore at the age of sixty-four on 30 December 1939, he left an enormous gap in Wedmore society. He was survived by his second wife and four children.

Wedmore CC. William Burrough sits with his hands on a teammate's shoulders: fellow Somerset cricketer, Alec Crowder, sits beside him, fourth from the left

1907

"There is no disguising the fact that the outlook for
Somerset in the immediate future is far from hopeful."

Wisden

Championship Position: 14 of 16

The finances perked up when a successful pre-season bazaar raised over £1,000.
Lionel Palairet bemoaned the fact that his team had 'quite lost that spirit of
playing together which was the secret of success in the old days'. Perhaps it had escaped
his attention that part of his remit as temporary captain was to engender team spirit.
Len Braund topped the county's batting averages with a modest 28.36. A. E. Lewis
claimed 82 wickets. Albert Trott of Middlesex chose the game against Somerset at
Lord's as his benefit match and had the misfortune to take four wickets in four balls
followed a short while later by a hat trick, bringing the game to a premature conclusion
and impoverishing himself in the process. Bertie Bisgood's startling debut in June led
the county to believe that they had found a replacement wicket-keeper batsman as
talented as the much-missed Henry Martyn. They had not. The two new pros, Bert
Whittle and Bill Montgomery – by then qualified by residency for Championship
games – proved a disappointment. Somerset's diplomatic efforts to build bridges with
Surrey bore fruit with an agreement that fixtures would be resumed for the 1908
season. Surrey had perhaps accepted that Bill Montgomery had been no great loss to
them and that an increasingly enfeebled Somerset side presented the opportunity to
gain valuable Championship points.

177
Albert Edward Mark Whittle
9 May 1907 v. Yorkshire, Taunton

Albert Whittle

Continuing their search for affordable talent, Somerset alighted on Bert Whittle, an all-rounder who had notched up one century, a dozen 50s and a couple of five-wicket hauls for Warwickshire. Coming into his own as a pro for Olton, near Birmingham, he enjoyed a remarkably successful benefit match for Olton versus Yardley in 1901, notching up an unbeaten century and taking all 10 Yardley wickets for 51 runs.

Bert had been a late developer as a county player but had enjoyed a flowering of his talent in 1904 and 1905. After that his form had fallen away. Somerset were able to claim Bert for their own because he had been born in Bedminster on 16 September 1877. He was one of six children brought

Bert Whittle of Warwickshire and Somerset, who enjoyed only limited success for the latter

up by their mother, Bertha. She worked as a charwoman in order to keep the family together after the death of her husband when Bert was only two years old. Married in 1903 to Frances Clara (née Cradock, later spelt as Craddock), known as Clara, Bert had only moved to the Midlands when offered a trial by Aston Villa FC.

Nicknamed 'Bonner', he totalled 867 runs in twenty-nine matches for Somerset at an average of 18.84 and captured only eight wickets at 51.25. Having played regularly until 1908, he only reappeared for three matches in 1911. When he parted company with Somerset, he was running a grocery store with Clara in Bedminster. They had five children at the time, all of them nine or younger, and with the pressures of running a business and so many mouths to feed, Bert suffered a nervous breakdown. He was committed to the Dorset County Asylum in Charminster. Bert died in the asylum on 18 March 1917 at the age of only thirty-nine, the cause of death given as ulcerated colitis. Clara was obliged to survive alone until she was remarried in Bristol, though not until 1922.

178

Charles Gerrard Deane

27 May 1907 v. Sussex, Taunton

C. G. Deane.

Buster Deane – a larger-than-life character and 'a man of fine physique' who succumbed to fever in India

Known to his friends as 'Buster', Charles Deane's life was lightened by moments of comedy but ended in tragedy. Reporting on a match between Exeter and Torquay on 11 July 1914, the *Western Times* states that Deane was 'in quite his best form'. We are told that, in making his match-winning 117, 'he hit with perfect freedom all around the wicket, his play being attractive to watch'. He was finally caught off the bowling of fellow Somerset cricketer, Ralph Hancock. If metaphorical clouds were gathering over Europe, they failed to dampen the spirits of the men playing cricket that day. Five months later the war would have claimed the lives of both Deane and Hancock.

Born in Oakhill on 8 March 1885 and educated at Taunton School, Charles Deane is described in the *Western Mail* as 'a man of fine physique'. He played football for Torquay and Devon as a centre-half and was a decent rugby and water polo player. His father was a general practitioner who had 'married well' and the son was able to enjoy a pampered lifestyle. He was never married.

Wisden notes that 'he was a good batsman and a fine field'. He played thirty-six times for Somerset between 1907 and 1913, averaging 11.95 with the bat and taking eight wickets at 25.75 each. This is in stark contrast to his performances for Torquay where he chalked up a number of centuries. As was so often the case, the gulf between club and county cricket proved too great.

Buster Deane was a larger than life character. In 1910, we gain an insight into his batting in the *Sheffield Evening Telegraph*. The report relates, in light-hearted vein, how Deane had made a rod for his own back by having the temerity to hit a soaring six off the great Yorkshireman, Hirst. The ball could not be found, with the result that Hirst was handed a replacement that proved more to his liking. Deane was soon heading back to the pavilion, having been bowled 'neck and crop'. An accompanying cartoon makes play on Deane's having dumped the master out of the ground.

In a piece in the *Western Daily Press* of July 1911 entitled *Deane and the Dog*, we hear that Deane:

> ... *hit the ball to square leg, and the ball was bounding along to the leg boundary at a pretty brisk pace, when an Irish Terrier ran from amongst the spectators and 'retrieved' the ball to the – it must be assumed – entire satisfaction of Huggins. The dog, with much tail-wagging, laid the ball at the feet of the nearest fieldsman, and trotted back proudly to its master.*

Deane puts Hirst into Bramall Lane

An undoubted case of being dogged by ill luck.

The *Western Daily Press* states that 'C. G. Deane is one of the army of [Somerset] cricketers who, upon dismissal for a moderate score, leaves behind the impression that he ought to have done better. He is a stylist and this morning he had the bad luck to play on to a ball he had carefully watched'. More misfortune. Perhaps Private Deane should have heeded the warning signs when he signed up with the 5th Battalion of the Devonshire Regiment. On 14 December 1914 and aged only twenty-nine, this 'man of fine physique' succumbed to the grip of fever at Multan, in India. His name is included on the memorial to the fallen at Karachi, Sindh. Bad luck had visited him one final time and no one was laughing now.

179
Edmund Parris Paul
3 June 1907 v. Lancashire, Bath

With Somerset's fortunes continuing to bump along at rock bottom, their temporary captain, Lionel Palairet, would call on six different wicket-keepers during the 1907 season, including three – Newton, Wickham and Palairet himself – who boasted a combined age of 133. At least Edmund Paul offered some relative youthfulness, having been born in Taunton on 4 February 1882. His father (also Edmund) ran a bakery and confectionery business with a shop on Station Road, Taunton. E. Paul & Co would continue to be part of the Taunton retail scene for three generations, latterly run by two generations of Cunnebers, who had married into the family.

Edmund Paul was educated at Huish's Grammar School in Taunton, leaving the school in a blaze of glory. He had dived into the River Avon and dragged a drowning boy to safety while enjoying a leisurely cruise in August 1898. He was presented with

E. P. Paul – left his family's bakery and confectionery business in Taunton to pursue a teaching career

a bronze medal by the Royal Humane Society.

Where two of his sisters had chosen to follow their father into the confectionery trade, Edmund opted for a teaching career and it was while a schoolmaster in Taunton that he played regularly for the town as a wicket-keeper batsman. H. J. Channon, the tireless chronicler of Taunton cricket, wrote: 'I shall never forget the crisp cutting of E. P. Paul'. He played four times for Somerset between 1907 and 1910. On the third occasion he was not the keeper, it being well within the bounds of possibility that two wicket-keepers had been selected mistakenly. The honour fell to Harry Chidgey. As if to atone for the error, Edmund Paul was invited to open the batting in his final match, though this did nothing to boost his average of 4.62 over his eight innings.

He disappeared from the scene when offered a teaching post at Brentwood School in Essex, where he played both cricket and football, though all thoughts of sport stopped for a while when he broke his knee-cap whilst playing for Brentwood FC against Old Foresters. The newspapers report that Old Foresters graciously agreed that Brentwood should be allowed to field a substitute, an innovation that would have to wait another fifty-one years before the authorities deemed it accepted practice. He continued to teach at Brentwood School for many years before retiring to Taunton. Three sisters had predeceased Edmund and his brother, Frederick, who both took up residence in the old family house. Neither of the brothers was married. In retirement, Edmund took time out to travel extensively to destinations such as South Africa and Australia. He died in Taunton on 24 April 1966 at the age of eighty-four, leaving the considerable sum of £79,000, accumulated from inheritance rather than through his career as a teacher.

180
John Alexander Hellard
10 June 1907 v. Worcestershire, Bath

John Hellard's father was a partner in the firm of solicitors, Bewes & Hellard. Born in Stogumber on 20 March 1882, John boarded at King's School, Canterbury, having won both junior and senior scholarships. He was a member of the Rugby XV and the Cricket XI. A future as a successful solicitor seemed assured when he was admitted in 1906. His father had also been a land agent for the estates of Nettlecombe Court and Halsway Manor and a director of the Seaton & Beer and West Somerset Industrial Railways. John would look overseas to advance his career, though not before he had made two appearances for Somerset – one in 1907, the other in 1910 – in which he totalled 18 runs at an average of 6.00.

J. A. Hellard – forsook his career as a solicitor and lost his life in the First Battle of The Somme

After cutting his teeth as a solicitor in his father's firm, he left for Colombo, in Ceylon (Sri Lanka). At the outbreak of war and until 1915 he was a member of the Town Guard there, but was eager to serve in Europe and joined the 3rd Battalion of the Somerset Light Infantry as a provisional second lieutenant. He went to France in May 1916 attached to the 1st Battalion, but his would be a short war. On the morning of 1 July 1916, in the First Battle of The Somme, he and his colleagues left their trenches, advancing towards the German line at a slow trot. They were soon forced off course by heavy machine gun fire and found themselves trapped and sitting targets. They were mown down in their hundreds. Such was the carnage that it would be some while before the bodies could all be found and not all of them identified.

The date of death inscribed on his gravestone is 2 July 1916 but this is incorrect. He in fact died shortly after 7.30 am on the morning of 1 July 1916, as confirmed in a letter sent by Corporal George Hibbard (retained by the War Office and seemingly never acknowledged). Hibbard states that: 'On Saturday 1st July ... I saw Lieutenant Hellard hit through the head by a bullet. He dropped beside me. I crawled to him [but] he was dead.' A bright young man of only thirty-four. Buried with a headstone shared with an unnamed soldier at Serre Road Cemetery in Beaumont-Hamel, not far from where they fell. He was unmarried, his parents and siblings left to grieve. The date of his death is wrong but at least we have the bare bones of John Alexander Hellard's life story. The man buried with him has not been accorded that dignity.

181
Bertram Lewis Bisgood
20 June 1907 v. Worcestershire, Worcester

COURTESY OF THE ROGER MANN COLLECTION

Bertie Bisgood – a wicket-keeper batsman who announced his arrival with a brilliant debut

Bertie Bisgood came in a blaze of glory. An amateur club cricketer from Glastonbury, he was recommended to Somerset's beleaguered captain, Lionel Palairet, as a wicket-keeper batsman who might play a part in arresting the county's continuing decline. In the game against Worcestershire, Palairet opted to keep wicket himself, placing his faith in the newcomer's batting skills. In the first innings Bertie scored 82, shepherded by the experienced Len Braund, who made a century. In the second innings, he scored a measured and unbeaten 116. The *Sheffield Evening Telegraph* refers to a 'startling debut' and adds that 'should his achievement of scoring 198 for once out not be a flash-in-the-pan, he will prove a rare fine capture for Somerset, who, since H. Martyn has dropped out has needed greater strength in batting and wicket-keeping. Bisgood is clever in both departments.' His scoring strokes were mostly off-drives. Perhaps a limited repertoire of shots ensured that bowlers soon learned how to bowl to him. He certainly failed to come anywhere near capturing the form of his debut until he scored 116 and 78 not out against Gloucestershire in 1914 – almost a mirror image of his debut – leaving the club to wonder what might have been. He played in sixty-seven first-class matches for Somerset. Strip away his two outstanding performances and we are left with little of substance.

Born in Glastonbury on 11 March 1881, Bertie was the seventh child of Roman Catholic parents and educated at Prior Park, Bath. In August 1905 he was admitted as a solicitor and became a partner in the firm Hatchett, Jones, Bisgood, Marshall &

Thomas. Later, he would opt for a career as a stock broker. Bertie served in the First World War as a second lieutenant in the Royal Garrison Artillery before enjoying a last hurrah for Somerset in the Championship in 1919, followed by three non-Championship fixtures.

He enjoyed success as a badminton player and as an accomplished golfer, with a number of his exploits detailed in the local press. In 1922 he was married in Kew to Mrs Dorothy Ursula Harvey (born Cundall), whose first husband had served in the Indian Army. She already had a son and Bertie and Dorothy would have a daughter together. Jeanne Bisgood was born in Rich-

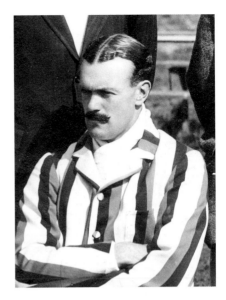

mond in 1923 and became an international champion golfer, eventually becoming President of the Parkstone Golf Club, as her father had done, before her. Bertie continued throughout his life to be a devout Catholic, donating a substantial amount of his wealth to the Roman Catholic Church. He was made a Knight of the Order of St Gregory the Great by the Vatican and Bertie and his brother, fellow Somerset cricketer, Eustace, donated two houses to the cause in East Sheen in 1938, so that a church could be built there (although not until 1953). He retired from the Stock Exchange and moved to Branksome, near Canford Cliffs in Dorset, where he helped to bring about the establishment of a church. He died in Branksome on 19 July 1968 at the age of eighty-seven.

182
Vivian Henry Bruce Majendie
29 August 1907 v. South Africa, Bath

Vivian Majendie played his debut game for Somerset against the South Africans in 1907 and the first day went satisfyingly well. He had been chosen as a wicket-keeper but top scored with 28, following this up with a tidy performance behind the stumps.

Vivian Majendie – 'his first appearance for his county was a highly creditable one'

A report informs us that 'for an hour he played the bowling with confidence and skill, and as he kept wicket – catching two and stumping two – his first appearance for his county was a highly creditable one.' In his one and only Championship game, he deferred to wicket-keeper and captain, A. E. Newton. He kept wicket in the second innings, effecting two more stumpings, but had no great success with the bat, leaving him with a first-class average of 13.75. He was an accomplished player, capable for example of scoring a big hundred for Devon Dumplings against the Somerset Stragglers but with insufficient time to develop his game.

Born on 20 April 1886 in Ipplepen, Devon, he was the son of the rector, who was one in a long line of clergymen. Vivian Majendie, however, enjoyed a hugely successful career in the military, passing out from Sandhurst in 1904 and being commissioned into the Somerset Light Infantry in 1905. He served in Southern Nigeria and India before taking on the role of commanding officer of the 1st Battalion of the Somerset Light Infantry in the First World War. His *History of the 1st Battalion over the Latter Half of the War* was published in 1921. Meanwhile he had been married in 1916 to Evelyn Margaret Dickson (née King).

After various promotions through the ranks he was appointed General Officer Commanding of the West Lancashire Territorials and was made Colonel of the Somerset Light Infantry. In 1941, Major General V. H. B. Majendie CB DSO was made General Officer Commanding of Northern Ireland, where he welcomed the first wave of thousands of American troops. The film reel of an appeal to the men of Northern Ireland is still in the possession of the Police Museum of Northern Ireland. Majendie looks and sounds the part of the archetypal GOC, urging the men of the Province to avoid complacency, to see Hitler as a threat and to join the fray. He was appointed President of the War Office Regular Commissions Board in 1943, before leaving the army in 1946.

Vivian Majendie retired to Radlett, Hertfordshire, and died in nearby Watford on 13 January 1960 at the age of seventy-three.

183
Ralph Escott Hancock
29 August 1907 v. South Africa, Bath

P. E. Hancock.

Born in Llandaff on 20 December 1887, Ralph was the only son of Francis (Frank) and Mary Hancock, members of the Wiveliscombe brewing dynasty. At the time of Ralph's birth, Frank was overseeing the company's factory in South Wales, playing rugby for Cardiff and Wales.

Ralph was brought up in the family home of Ford House, near Wiveliscombe, passed down to his father. Educated at Rugby School, he would prove an excellent rugby forward who played regularly for Somerset, as his father and uncles had done. The *Bath Chronicle* tells us that 'as a cricketer, he was a useful bat and took many wickets in club games', his main club side being Wiveliscombe, although he sometimes turned out for Somerset Stragglers.

Ralph Hancock – 'he was a useful bat and took many wickets in club games'

His county cricket career yielded only modest results. His first appearance was against the South Africans in 1907 and he would play his ninth and final game in 1914. He was only used for seven overs as a bowler, but without success. He averaged 12.11 with the bat, the high point being the match against Sussex in 1913, when his scores were 28 and 34. That was also the year in which he was married to Mary Hamilton (née Broadmead), a clergyman's daughter from neighbouring Milverton. Ralph had opted for a life in the military. On leaving school, he had joined the 1st Battalion of the Devonshire Regiment. By 1911 he had been promoted to the rank of lieutenant.

COURTESY OF THE ROGER MANN COLLECTION

His involvement in the war was shortlived. He would be awarded the DSO for his actions on 23 October 1914 when he 'displayed conspicuous gallantry in leaving his trench under heavy fire and going back some 60 yards over absolutely bare ground to pick up Corporal Warwick, who had fallen'. Such fearlessness begets awards but is a recipe for a short life. His DSO would be awarded posthumously with the dreaded words 'since killed in action' appended. The *Western Morning News* of 23 December 1914 contains an eye-witness account by Private Andy Burgoyne detailing events over the six days that culminated in Ralph Hancock's being shot on 29 October 1914 in Festubert, La Bassée, France, aged only twenty-six.

His body lies in an unknown grave ('at a point running North and South through Festubert' according to a letter to his wife from the War Office), though Ralph is remembered in memorials, including the oak panel in the church of St Andrew in Wiveliscombe, where he is named alongside the other fifty-four men from the small town who lost their lives in the First World War. The family also donated a new altar in memory of their only son. The extent of his inherited wealth was such that his wife, Mary, would want for nothing financially. This was doubtless no consolation to the newly-wed, left clutching the DSO medal (still in the possession of the family) and a few precious memories.

1908

"It was plucky of J. Daniell, after a prolonged absence in India, to come home and undertake the responsibility of captaining a team with such a paucity of material to call on."

Bath Chronicle

Championship Position: 16 of 16

A wretched season was briefly lit up by the brilliance of Randall Johnson, who arrived late and scored 603 runs in four matches. Len Braund put in some redoubtable performances with the bat, including a fourth-wicket stand of 199 with Sam Woods at Southampton that stirred memories of past glories. A. E. Lewis and Ernie Robson plugged away with the ball but Somerset only mustered two wins all season. The nadir was being bowled out for 33 by Lancashire at Liverpool. Support was falling away at the Taunton matches and the gates at Bath, although greater, could not stop another annual deficit. Somerset had lost their way and the guarantors had run out of patience. The debutants were, with one notable exception, not up to the mark. The one outstanding prospect was Bill Greswell but it summed up Somerset's ill-fortune that their match-winning swing bowler would only be available for a short while before the family's business interests in Ceylon would demand his attention. Cricket in the county was at a low ebb, teetering on the brink of collapse.

Somerset XI in 1908.
STANDING: *E. S. Goodland, E. Robson, A. E. Lewis, A. E. M. Whittle, H. Chidgey, B. Cranfield*
SEATED: *H. S. Poyntz, L. C. H. Palairet, J. Daniell, S. M. J. Woods, L. C. Braund*

184
Alexander Jeffries Crowder
11 May 1908 v. Lancashire, Bath

Alec. J. Crowder

Alec Crowder was born on 22 October 1874 in Anerley, at the time in the county of Surrey but subsequently incorporated into the district of Penge, in Kent. His father was a member of the legal profession and would become a high court judge and chancery master. Educated at Berkhamsted School, Alec became a solicitor. He was already showing talent as a cricketer, with trials for Surrey. In 1906, having been married to Mary Christina (née Cockburn), whom he met whilst training as a solicitor in Brighton, he moved to Wedmore to become a partner with William Burrough in the firm Burrough & Crowder. These two men were great friends and pillars of Wedmore society. Both were active sportsmen and great organizers. On the field, Burrough, the fast-bowling 'Wedmore Express' and Crowder, the prolific batsman, transformed Wedmore into a near-invincible village side. Alec proposed that in order to keep the team fit during the winter months they (or rather he) should form the Wedmore Hockey Club of which he became captain and secretary. According to the *Wells Journal*, he was an 'adept and enthusiastic player' who 'infused a good deal of life into the game and was ... a scorer in most matches' The experiment clearly paid off on a personal level with Alec racking up four centuries (two of them unbeaten) for Wedmore, the following season.

Alec Crowder was a prolific run-maker for Wedmore. Crowder (r) and William Burrough (l) are seen above in the Wedmore Hockey XI. The business partners and great friends were invariably seated together in team photographs

In 1908 he was drafted into the Somerset team, but proved unable to replicate his club form, scoring 44 runs in his three matches at an average of 7.33. The *Wells Journal* informs us that 'Crowder preferred the less strenuous local game and after two or three games in county cricket returned to make centuries for the Wedmore Club'. It is easy to understand why a successful solicitor, comfortable in his own skin and with no need to prove anything to anyone, should prefer smiting the ball to all corners of club grounds to the alternative of playing a bit-part in three-day county games. A forty-one verse poem of dubious quality entitled *The Sports of Wedmore*, submitted to the *Wells Journal* in 1908 by J. Merriman, includes verses in praise of the village's cricketing solicitors.

Of Burrough, he writes:

> Now there's one man can sling 'em in quickly,
> As our foes have found out to their sorrow ;
> Now, who makes the sticks somersault thickly ?
> W.G. No. 2, surnamed Burrough !

His paean to the prowess of Crowder is no less fulsome:

> Then at batting, one named A. J. Crowder,
> Can't he pile it on thick when he's smiting ?
> With his sixes he makes 'em cheer louder,
> And it all *looks* as simple as writing.

During the war, Alec served as a lieutenant in the Royal Garrison Artillery. His was not the most glorious of war records but it should be borne in mind that he was forty-three when he signed up. Never asked to serve abroad, he was soon moved to a desk job in Leeds owing to rheumatism, aggravated by the cold and damp conditions. His medical report asserts that he was 'only suited for sedentary work and should not live in a hut'. After the war, the rheumatism appears not have had any effect on his success as a club cricketer, which continued right up until the 1920 season, when he

Wedmore CC. Somerset cricketer W. G. Burrough is seated in the centre: beside him, leaning forward, is A. J. Crowder

registered a score of 109 not out against Blackford. By then, Alec Crowder had become captain of the Cheddar Valley Golf Club. He and William Burrough were enjoying success off the field, too, earning enough through their practice to be generous bene-factors to the church and – in the case of Burrough – purchasing land for playing fields. But then Alec departed for Ferring-by-Sea, Sussex, where 'the lamentable death of A. J. Crowder' on 5 June 1922, at the age of forty-seven, left his wife and family mourning their loss but comfortably provided for. The cause of death was given as *encephalitis lethargica* or 'sleeping sickness', a widespread problem in the years after the war, particularly among Caucasian men.

He had proved one of the many who excelled at the club level but not in the more demanding first-class game. In Alec Crowder's case, you suspect that Somerset would have been more vexed and disappointed than he ever was.

185
Stanley Long Amor
11 May 1908 v. Lancashire, Bath

Stanley Amor was a dominant presence in Bath for many years and sufficiently so that the *Bath Chronicle* featured on its front page photographs of his marriage to Mabel Isabel (née Christopher) on 8 July 1914. Stanley, known by many in sporting circles simply as 'Skipper', was born in the city of Bath on 22 July 1887. He was the grandson of Jacob Long, who had established the firm of Jacob Long & Sons, Building Contractors, of whom Stanley would become a joint-managing director, overseeing many major projects in the city. A successful businessman, he also became a director of Bath & Portland Stone Firms Ltd and later a member of the board of Wessex Associated News Ltd (who owned the *Bath Chronicle*). For the majority of Batho-nians, his fame rested on his commit-ment to sport in the city. As young as fifteen, he had represented Somerset

Stanley Amor on his wedding day (left) and executing a lofted drive in the Bath CC nets (right)

307

at hockey and he would play for and later become chairman of Bath Rugby Club. But it was as a wicket-keeper batsman and captain for thirty-five years of Bath (with players such as Henry Wood or John Thomas standing in in his absence) that he would be most revered, finally stepping down in 1930. Over much of that time, his brother-in-law, fellow Somerset cricketer Hurl Humphries, was a teammate. In Stanley's final season as captain, the Bath side had remained unbeaten. A fine way to depart the scene.

S. L Amor – a worthy recipient of the cognomen 'Skipper'

Stanley played on twenty-six occasions for Somerset and although his contributions with the bat were limited, he proved perfectly capable of keeping at county level, with a total of 26 catches and 21 stumpings. 'Skipper' may have hung up his boots in 1930, but right up until the 1950s he remained active on sporting committees, referred to as Captain Amor after his service in the First World War in the Royal Flying Corps (later the RAF).

He died in his home city on 7 August 1965, aged seventy-eight. If ever a man was worthy of the rank of captain it was Stanley Long Amor.

186
Edward Stanley Goodland
28 May 1908 v. Worcestershire, Taunton

Edward Stanley Goodland

Born in Taunton on 22 September 1883, Stan Goodland was one of the sons of Edward Goodland, who owned a coal merchant business. Their main yard beside the River Tone was no more than a lustily struck six from the County Ground. The family controlled the supply of coal and maintained a huge fleet of delivery vans, with depots close to a number of railway stations. Stan never showed any interest in dirtying his hands with coal – his elder brother having been groomed to take the reins – and would make his living in the sale of finer goods. He was educated at Taunton School, where he proved a success at sport, captaining both the football and cricket XIs on occasions. At the 1899 Sports Day, he 'won his events in really excellent style, particularly the hurdle race'. The school magazine mourned the hole left in its batting on his departure. On leaving school he went up to London where he took his first steps in learning the ropes of the jewellery and fine antique trade at the Goldsmiths & Silversmiths Co., Regent Street. Coming back to Taunton, he utilised his new-found skills as a partner in an established fine jewellery business, which was renamed Franklin, Hare & Goodland.

Stan was also active in the Mary Street Chapel (to which his father was a major benefactor), taking on the role of Sunday School teacher. He was an assured public speaker and a leading light in the Literary and Debating Society, whose meetings were held at the chapel. He was also a member of the Taunton Amateur Operatic Society. Given that he took on some leading roles, we can assume that he was no blushing violet.

The *Western Daily Press* begins its report of Stan Goodland's debut match with the headline *A Promising First Appearance*. We are informed that he 'showed promising form for a man new to county cricket, making most of his runs on the off-side'. He had in fact made 42 not out, but this was another false dawn for Somerset. Stan would play four times in total for the county during the 1908 and 1909 seasons. In five further innings he would amass only five more runs.

Soon afterwards he became engaged to a fellow member of the Operatic Society, Rose Lydia Goodland, who happened to be his cousin. Sadly, she died of consumption less than two months before their scheduled marriage. Stan refused to let the setback dull his zest for life. He was a man of ideas, ambition and energy. We know this because the local papers outline plans for the proposed Taunton Festival in August 1914 that he played a large part in orchestrating. There would be dramatic productions, a band performing each day, a flower show, whist drives and various sideshows which 'should bring in a goodly harvest of coppers'. All of it designed to rescue Somerset cricket from its moribund state, although the Kaiser would of course put the kibosh on the Taunton Cricket Festival in the years that followed.

Stan Goodland – 'showed promising form for a man new to county cricket, making most of his runs on the off-side'

Stan found a new love interest in the form of Elsie (née Hyde). His regular correspondence with Elsie would sustain him through the horrors of war. His letters to her are detailed in the book *Engaged in War – the Letters of Stanley Goodland*

E. S. Goodland in later years

1914 – 1919. He had joined the Somerset Light Infantry and would rise to the rank of major, serving in the Persian Gulf, Mesopotamia, Palestine and Egypt. He was awarded both the Military Cross and the Croix de Guerre and remained a reservist until 1933. He also became a director of Mallet & Son, who had offices in Bath and New Bond Street. Married to Elsie in 1920, he played an active role in civilian life. For many years, he was president of the Taunton School Old Boys' Association. He died at the age of ninety in the Quantock village of Bicknoller on 12 January 1974.

187
Marwood Mintern Munden
9 July 1908 v. Kent, Dover

Mintern Munden was born in Ilminster on 13 June 1885, the son of a medical practitioner. Educated at Crewkerne Grammar School, he went on to study medicine at Guy's Hospital, qualifying in 1911 and setting up a practice at Chalford, Gloucestershire in 1912, the year in which he was married to Alice Muriel (née Archer).

Mintern Marwood of the Royal Army Medical Corps

Their happiness at the birth of their son would turn to grief in March 1914. Their child was quite literally smothered by affection when the family dog, who was enormously fond of the infant and inseparable from him, found its way into the boy's bedroom and lying on the cot, inadvertently suffocated him. Mintern Munden had made his three first-class appearances for the club in 1908 and it is safe to assume that his reputation as a medic was greater than his fame as a cricketer. His five innings yielded an average of 6.20 and a top score of 11.

Dr Munden joined the Royal Army Medical Corps in 1916, serving with the 89th Field Ambulance and the 2nd Battalion of the Royal Fusiliers and gaining a Belgian Croix de Guerre for his efforts in helping to evacuate and treat wounded Belgian soldiers. Returning to civilian life, he hit the local headlines. Not for heroism but as a co-respondent in a divorce case involving Elsie Hack. The headline in the *Hull Daily Mail* is startling to modern eyes in its misogyny.

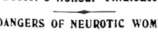

Doctor's Honour Vindicated.

DANGERS OF NEUROTIC WOMEN,

The jury were treated to the missives from 'Bunny', as Mintern had signed his letters off, to Mrs Hack, who had confessed to her husband that she and Mintern had engaged in an adulterous relationship between spring 1914 (shortly after the death of Mintern's son) and 1917. Mintern would have been struck off if found guilty and denied the allegations. His correspondence reveals a young man wrestling with his sexual urges, rather than an out and out 'bounder':

My darling old Billie Cheerio,

... I cuss myself to think how near we went. Still it was your fault you darling old girl. You sort of put me on my honour. We are pals, and I trust we shall remain as we always were, no more and no less true pals. It is possible for two opposites to keep pals provided they control themselves. Anyway, we have succeeded so far, and somehow, you know, darling, I feel like being stuck up about it. At the same time I could cuss at the opportunities missed.

For all that he was adjudged to have controlled his base urges and was exonerated, it is easy to imagine much grovelling in the Marwood household once Bunny's letters were in the public domain.

He would be called upon to testify in some difficult cases – such as when Mrs Constance Gibson found a dead body in the suitcase of her unmarried servant in 1928 and Dr Marwood opined – perhaps tempering medical knowledge with a dose of humanity – that he had every reason to suppose that the baby was stillborn. When off-duty, Mintern Marwood continued to play club cricket for many years, including a spell as captain of Stroud CC. He was also keen on hunting and fishing for prey that were unlikely to bite back in the way that Elsie Hack's aggrieved husband had done.

He died on 8 March 1952 at the age of sixty-six in Eastcombe, Gloucestershire: flawed – as we all are – but a doctor who had done much more good than harm.

188
William Territt Greswell
3 August 1908 v. Middlesex, Taunton

Athletic News referred to Bill Greswell in 1909 as 'the most brilliant cricketer of last season's wonderful Repton XI', the school having produced that year five county cricketers. The article relates how, through inventiveness and application, Bill found a way

Bill Greswell – a seriously good cricketer who took the art of swing bowling to new heights

to impart prodigious swing to a cricket ball in both directions. It also noted that Somerset had managed no more than to delay his father's decision to send the 'tea-planter-to-be' off to learn his trade. Witnessing the twenty-year-old's century and nine-wicket haul at Lord's against Middlesex would have been a bittersweet experience. Bill was a seriously good cricketer. In another age he might have opted for a successful career as a professional. It was to be Somerset's loss that he would only ever be available as and when his work commitments allowed. Over a twenty-two year period from 1908 until 1930 he made 115 appearances for the county, many of those when he was past his prime, and yet he took 454 wickets at 21.57. In the 1912 season he took 132 first-class wickets at 17.78, leaving Somerset to rue what might have been. His in-swing was exaggerated through an extraordinary action where he leaned back at something in the order of a 45 degree angle. Nor was he a mug with the bat, averaging 15.48 during his career for the county.

Born on 15 October 1889 in Cuddalore, India, Bill was brought up in the Quantocks. His father, originally a high-ranking civil servant, had settled for the life of a Somersetshire clergyman, local historian and author. Educated at Repton along with his older brother and fellow Somerset cricketer, Ernest, Bill was obliged to leave for Ceylon (Sri Lanka) and manage the family tea plantation after his successful inaugural season.

Whilst in Ceylon, he excelled at a number of sports including cricket, football, hockey and athletics. There are slight variations in the statistics although the differences are not material. According to S. P. Foenander, official recorder to the Ceylon Cricket Association and writing in 1925, Greswell took 1071 wickets there between 1909 and 1924 at less than 8 runs apiece. He would surely have longed at times for the stiffer challenge of first-class cricket in England. Bill was twice married. His first wife was Gwendoline Doris Rose (née Marshall), with whom he had two sons before their marriage ended in divorce. Subsequently, he was married at a register office in London to a niece of Somerset cricketer A. E. Newton, Rachel May (née Sadler). They had a son and daughter together.

He retired from county cricket in 1930 in order to focus on business. An investment in the rubber industry encountered problems, severely affecting Bill, who suffered depression and a nervous breakdown. When he succumbed to a further breakdown while serving in the Home Guard during the Second World War he underwent electro-convulsive therapy. In retirement he served on the local Rural District Council and was President of Somerset CCC between 1962 and 1965. He died in Bicknoller on 12 February 1971 at the age of eighty-one.

189
Edwin John Leat
13 August 1908 v. Kent, Taunton

Edwin John Leat

Edwin or, in cricketing circles, John Leat was born on 24 April 1885 in Wellington, Somerset. His father was a solicitor's clerk. Educated at Wellington School, John became a pupil teacher there at sixteen, a relatively common occurrence for bright pupils capable of supporting schoolmasters in helping younger pupils and often their first step toward a teaching career. He joined his father in playing for Wellington CC and headed the batting averages in 1904 with 'a fine average of 45.33' although this fell away the following season. In 1906 he spent a year as an assistant schoolmaster at the Stoke Road School in Slough before undergoing two years of qualification at Exeter Training College, for whom he played cricket, including annual fixtures against his old Wellington team. On returning to Buckinghamshire, he taught at the Chalvey National Schools and played for the county. Also in the Buckinghamshire side on occasions was C. H. Alison, who had earlier played for Somerset, but would become more renowned for his achievements as a golf course designer.

E. J. Leat – 'a good sportsman and an ideal soldier'

J. E. Leah.

He sometimes signed himself for autograph hunters as J. E. Leat

In June 1915, before he left for the war effort, John Leat was married to Winifred Emily (née Young), an elementary school headmaster's daughter from Slough who worked as a Post Office clerk. He joined the Oxford and Bucks Light Infantry in November 1915 and was commissioned as a lance corporal in the 2nd battalion of the

Dorsetshires. Like so many other optimistic newly-weds, John Leat would be killed in action, in his case at age of thirty-three on 8 June 1918 near Beaumont-Hamel, France. Reporting his death, the *Bucks Herald* describes him as 'a good sportsman and an ideal soldier'. His name is included on the memorial at Poziere.

Winifred was seven months pregnant when John died. Her letter to the War Office survives. Bringing to life the uncertainty for those left grieving the loss of soldiers missing in action, she states:

I am told there is no trace of his body and yet if he had been a POW I think I would have heard by now as I know he would have done his utmost to get a letter to me. I hope in the event of his body being found and buried I may be informed as it would be some slight consolation to know he had been properly buried.

Their son, Edwin George, was born on 14 August 1918. Winifred was 100 years old when she died in Hillingdon on 17 May 1985. She never remarried and no doubt in all those years, a day never went by without her recalling her brief time with her husband.

The statistics in relation to his Somerset career – 18 runs over two matches and an average 6.00– suggest mediocrity at the first-class level but the trajectory of his career speaks of an excellent teacher and no doubt a loving husband, lost in a senseless and violent conflict.

1909

"Things turned out far better than anyone had dared to hope."

Wisden

Championship Position: 11 of 16

Somerset had arranged to play only sixteen matches, the minimum number required to qualify for the Championship, in order to reduce their losses. They won four of them. Bath hosted four games (including the visit of the Australians) but the *Bath Chronicle* bemoaned the 'cold, inclement weather' and noted that many Bathonians resented having to part with 6d in order to secure a place on a bench – not even a seat.

Daniell and Braund doggedly led the fight with the bat. Lewis and Robson were the principle wicket takers, supported by Bill Greswell, who was considered by *Wisden* 'a loss to English cricket' when he departed for Ceylon. There was a sprinkling of stardust in the final game of the season when Prince Narayan – real life Indian royalty – who had already made an appearance for Somerset against Australia, was allowed to field as a substitute against Middlesex, owing to Lewis's injury. Also in the field for a while was Middlesex's Trott, whom the opponents had graciously loaned when Len Braund had wandered from the ground caught unawares by Somerset's batting collapse.

Of the new-joins, the professional Bertie Morgan proved blessed with a fine bowling arm but his effectiveness was blunted by alcoholism. Somerset had begun to plunder the local schools for burgeoning talent. Some of the boys would be lost to the war. One lad from Taunton School, John Cornish White, made very little impression at first but would become a mainstay of the club for many years and an England captain.

190
Frank Douglas Howarth Joy
10 May 1909 v. Yorkshire, Bath

J. D. H. Joy

Frank Joy – his brief career with Somerset was curtailed when he went back to his native Yorkshire to teach in Aysgarth

Frank Joy was born on 26 September 1880 in Southfield, Hessle, Yorkshire. The son of an oil merchant, he was educated at Winchester College and New College, Oxford. He represented Oxford University at athletics (in the long jump) but failed to gain a cricketing blue as a left-arm fast-medium bowler. He chose teaching as a career and began by working as a tutor for the children of the Rajah of Dhar, in India, before progressing to the Central India College. In 1908 he was instrumental in helping The Europeans to win three first-class matches in India, taking a total of twenty-eight wickets. In 1909 he returned to England and Somerset grasped the opportunity to select him for eleven matches between 1909 and 1912, his appearances restricted by his teaching commitments. His best bowling performance was his 5 for 44 against his native Yorkshire and his total haul of 29 wickets at 35.27 apiece compares well with many of the bowlers Somerset turned to. He averaged 9.72 with the bat. His career with Somerset was curtailed when he was employed by Aysgarth Preparatory School in Newton-le-Willows, Yorkshire.

Frank Joy was married in 1914 to Mona Constance Annabel (née Anderson) days after he had signed up with the King's Own Scottish Borderers as a second lieutenant. He left the unit in January 1915 in order to undergo an operation to remove cartilage from his right knee, following problems with synovitis, sustained in the trenches. Returning to France in June 1915 as the camp adjutant at Carcassonne, he was deemed only fit for light duties. Promoted to the rank of captain in 1917, he was discharged in 1920. After his war service he was appointed the headmaster of Aysgarth School and remained in the post for a number of years. He retained his links with Winchester College, in Hampshire, turning out for Old Wykehamists during the 1920s. He retired to Hampshire where he became active in local affairs, including a spell in the 1950s as chairman of the

Hampshire Planning Committee.

He died in Winchester on 17 February 1966 at the age of eighty-five. The *Western Daily Press* notes, in reference to his Somerset cricket career, that 'on one or two occasions he did well'. In his life as a whole he had done well on rather more occasions.

191
Leonard Cecil Leicester Sutton
17 May 1909 v. Hampshire, Southampton

Leicester Sutton was born on 14 April 1890 in Kingston, Jamaica. He spent his early years there while his father ran a plantation in Mandeville, arriving in England in 1904. Educated at King's School, Bruton, he shone as a schoolboy cricketer and played for the First XI for an impressive five years. In the latter years he opened both the batting and the bowling, developing into a fine player under the watchful eye of his schoolmaster, Percy Vasey, who would play one match for Somerset. Leicester was a left-arm pace bowler and according to the school magazine 'a good hard-hitting bat with plenty of strokes, notably an excellent off-drive, a magnificent shot just behind point, a good late cut and a fine powerful pull'. Clearly an all-round talent, he also

Leicester Sutton, who played in his school First XI for five years

played in the football and hockey teams for four years. He was invited to play for Somerset at the age of nineteen. At 5 ft 8 in and weighing in at twelve stone, he was a well-built lad and impressed when he made 30 in the second innings of his debut game. Regrettably that would be as good as it got. In seventeen matches he averaged 7.12. He only ever bowled one over, taking 0 for 6.

He decided on a career in estate agency. After a spell working in Bath and shortly after playing his last game for Somerset in 1912 he moved to Canada where he worked in a real estate business in Toronto. He signed up for the war at the end of 1914 and arrived in France the following October. Perhaps it was a mercy that he took leave for a week at the end of April 1916: a week in which he could taste civilian life before plunging back into the horrors of war and meeting his end on 3 June 1916, aged only twenty-six. He lies in an unknown place in an unmarked grave. His school magazine, *The Dolphin*, gives an account of his army experiences:

Harold Hippisley and Leicester Sutton – boyhood friends, future county cricketers and brilliant all-round athletes who would both lose their lives in the First World War within a matter of a few years

During the war he served with the 4th Canadian Mounted Rifles, declining a commission on joining because he desired the experience of a private's life and again on reaching France because in this case acceptance would have meant leaving his unit at the critical moment. He rose to be Sergeant and at last applied and was accepted for a commission in the 3rd Dorsets after a considerable spell of active service, but the end came before his papers were completed. On June 2nd, 1916, he was very severely wounded by shrapnel at Zillebeke, a singularly desolate and forbidding locality not far from Ypres. Carried to a German dug-out he was as well treated as circumstances would allow, and remained conscious and cheerful for a time. Next morning he died in the presence of Corporal White of his regiment.

His name is included on the Menin Gate Memorial at Ypres as is that of his good friend, Harold Hippisley, another old boy of King's School who played cricket for the county.

There is poignancy in a boyhood blessed but an adulthood so short that it is defined by a brief county cricket career, an even briefer clerical career and – briefest of all – a bloody war that claimed him.

192
Bertie Francis Morgan
17 May 1909 v. Hampshire, Southampton

Bertie Francis Morgan.

Bertie Morgan was born on 6 December 1885 in Finsbury Park, London, and began his working life as a stonemason. He came to Somerset's attention when he was taken on as a pro by the Imperial Tobacco team in Knowle, for whom Percy Hardy also played at various times. Both would prove troubled men who drank more than was good for them (or indeed for those around them). In Percy Hardy's case it would lead to a life foreshortened by suicide. In Bertie Morgan's case it has been suggested that it led to a Championship career cut short.

Married in 1908 to Clara Annie (née Fairweather), a domestic servant from Edmonton with whom he would have three children, he put in some good all-round performances for the Imperial team. He was considered both a productive batsman and useful left-arm fast bowler at club level, but things went awry when he was invited to play for the county. Peter Roebuck summarises Morgan's brief cameo by informing us that 'alas, he was a difficult man with a fondness for ale and free speech'. Bertie and Somerset parted company after six matches. His batting average had been a paltry 5.72 and he had taken only two wickets for 175 runs. For a while he returned to being a stonemason in Wood Green but he must have missed the life of a professional cricketer because he reappeared before long as a pro playing for a variety of teams in Lancashire League cricket, returning to stonemasonry during the winter months.

Bertie Morgan – according to Plum Warner, he could have played for England 'had he not been such a rover'

Bertie Morgan during his time as Billingham Synthonia's professional

From 1913 until 1924 he performed well enough to play Minor Counties cricket on a frequent basis for Staffordshire, while he plied his trade at club level. Announcing that Werneth Central had engaged him as their pro, the *Lancashire Evening Post* describes him as a 'medium to fast left-hand bowler and a hard hitter'. His reputation continued to grow. By 1924, the *Derbyshire Times & Chesterfield Herald* informs us that 'one of the best-known League professionals in the country, Morgan has had considerable experience with Staffordshire and also the Lancashire and Central Lancashire Leagues'. He switched to spin bowling after an accident in 1924, continuing to lead the bowling attack for other club sides in the area before moving across the Pennines to play for Billingham Synthonia in County Durham. He was still regularly topping the bowling averages for the club well into the 1930s. In 1937 his benefit match against Darlington was a wash-out and he chose the match against Blackhall as an alternative, managing a hat trick on the day, a rare feat at the best of times but especially laudable for a man of fifty-one. No less a judge than Plum Warner claimed that Morgan could have played for England 'had he not been such a rover'. Clara and the children had remained in Wood Green whilst Bertie spent his summers playing cricket and when he was done with the game he returned full-time to the life of a stonemason.

He died in Billingham on 25 February 1959 at the age of seventy-three. His longsuffering wife Clara was clearly a survivor. She died in Haringey in 1977 in her ninetieth year.

193
Trevor Coleridge Spring
20 May 1909 v. Lancashire, Bath

Trevor Coleridge Spring

T. C. Spring – more readily associated with Devon cricket, he played only eight times for Somerset

On three occasions, Rev. H. C. Spring of Alwington in Devon would receive news that a son had died. First to go was Geoffrey in the Boer War, then Harold, who had died of fever, and finally Major Trevor Coleridge Spring, who died as a result of septic poisoning suffered in Singapore some years earlier. The Rev. Spring must have wished that his sons had followed him into the ministry.

Trevor Spring had been born on 6 February 1882 while his father was a chaplain in Bengal, India. After moving to Devon he was educated at Blundell's School, before embarking on his distinguished military career. He joined the Somerset Light Infantry as a reservist and served almost immediately in the Boer War. He received his commission in the regular army in September 1902, when he was appointed a second lieutenant in the Hampshire Regiment. For a number of years he was an officer in the Territorials and then a general staff officer at the Tyne garrison. He became involved in the field during the First World War and was promoted to the rank of major in 1917, the year in which he was awarded a DSO. After the war he was appointed a brigadier major in the Territorial Army and then in 1922 was appointed General Officer for the Straits Settlements. He suffered septic poisoning in his head while in Singapore and this would trouble him for the remainder of his life.

For a number of years he had represented Devon at cricket. His appearances for Somerset, once they had persuaded him to change his allegiance, were limited to a combined total of eight matches in 1909 and 1910 in which he averaged only 8.85 and bowled only fourteen overs, though he did take 3 for 59 against Middlesex in 1910. He was married that year, to Gwladys (née Griffith), a police constable's daughter from Flintshire, with whom he would have three children. Later, he would register his only first-class century for The Army against The Royal Navy.

The *Exeter & Plymouth Gazette* informs us that he 'caught a chill in his head when attending a football match at Winchester' while stationed at the Hampshire Regiment Depot and that he decided to have an operation. He died of complications on 13 March

1926 at the age of forty-four. He was buried three days later back in Alwington, outlived by a father who had endured the deaths of his three sons.

194
John Cornish White
20 May 1909 v. Lancashire, Bath

Born in Holford on 19 February 1891, Jack White was a member of a farming family and brought up near Stogumber. Taciturn and doggedly determined, he demonstrated the cussed contempt for adversity needed to glean profit from a hill farm or success in the cauldron of an Ashes test match. He is surely the greatest of all Somerset-born bowlers, though there was little in his first couple of seasons for the county to suggest that he would become a major force in English cricket through much of the 1920s and 1930s. Educated at Taunton School, he had the good fortune to be coached by former Somerset and England cricketer, Teddy Tyler. He was also blessed by the presence of a village cricket pitch on his father's land, enabling him to spend hours honing his craft. Drafted into the Somerset team as an eighteen-year-old, he took one wicket in 1909 at a cost of 90 runs. By 1910 he was dropped by Somerset. Undeterred, Jack worked on his technique and came back in the two seasons before the war as a successful wicket-taker. In 1914 he was married to Agnes (née Mortimer), from a Devon farming family and during the war they worked the land.

Jack White – established himself as the mainstay of the Somerset bowling attack for many years and is regarded as one of the greats of the game

The post-war years saw the flowering of his talent. For fourteen successive seasons he took well in excess of 100 wickets at a consistently parsimonious average. Twice – in 1929 and 1930 – he completed the double of 100 wickets and 1000 runs. He was accused by some of hogging the bowling in later years, though most Somerset supporters were grateful to him for carrying the weight of responsibility on his own shoulders. His teammate Raymond Robertson-Glasgow felt that Jack

White had the ideal temperament for a slow bowler.

I never saw him excited, though sometimes he would go a little redder when an important catch was missed off his bowling, and he would mutter: "The trouble with that cock is that he's fast asleep."

He imparted very little spin and relied on varied flight and 'liveliness off the pitch' in the form of a quicker delivery or one that bounced unexpectedly high. He may have been assisted by the fact that he was an expert at picking at the seam at a time when this could be done with impunity. He was a firm believer in fair play, though, and it is said that he never appealed unless he was certain that a batsman was out. He played fifteen times for England, five times as captain, taking 49 wickets and – perhaps most significantly – having an economy rate of 1.97 runs per over, attributable to the fear he engendered in batsmen, rendering them reluctant to attack him. The zenith of his career came at the age of thirty-seven when he bowled 124 overs in the searing heat of Adelaide in the Fourth Test against Australia, taking a total of 13 wickets in England's unexpected 12-run victory over the old foe. It was described as 'an historic feat of endurance and skill' for which he was feted by the national press. He applied himself as doggedly to his batting as he did his bowling. Considered a natural number eleven in his early years, he developed into a useful batsman. His average grew with the passing years and his centuries all came in the latter part of his career.

J. C. White – gentleman farmer and England cricket captain

He retired from cricket at the age of forty-six to focus entirely on farming. Perhaps Somerset had hoped and even begun to believe that Jack White could keep on going for ever.

In later years he lost the sight of an eye in a shooting accident. He died at the age of seventy on 2 May 1961 at his home in Combe Florey, at the foot of his beloved Quantock Hills. He was at that time president of the club he had served so well. Gates were installed at Somerset's County Ground as a memorial to him, with his initials engraved on them. A symbol of the club's gratitude for the 2,166 wickets he had taken. His widowed wife, Agnes, was there to witness the ceremony. Never a great one for displays of emotion, Jack would have been mildly embarrassed at all the fuss. J. C. White always let his actions do the talking. The statistics speak volumes of his greatness.

195
Hitendra Narayan
10 June 1909 v. Australia, Bath

H Narayan of Cooch Behar

Hitendra Narayan was born on 1 July 1890, the youngest son of the Maharaj of Cooch Behar in Bengal. He was tutored by Somerset captain John Daniell, who was trying his luck at that time as a schoolmaster. We can safely assume that Daniell's lessons involved cricket coaching as well as the 'three Rs' as he prepared his young charge for his secondary education. At Eton, Prince Narayan would display some prowess as a sportsman, winning the junior high jump and becoming runner-up in the junior long jump. He went up to Pembroke College, Cambridge, but failed to gain a blue. Not that this would have dampened the enthusiasm of the Somerset committee. When you are losing most of your matches, why not do so with some panache and include real life royalty in your ranks?

Hitendra Narayan – tutored as a boy by Somerset captain, John Daniell: the presence of Indian royalty brought lustre to the Somerset cricketing scene

In 1908, Hitendra Narayan was even discussed in the Houses of Parliament after he had hit and injured a pedestrian while driving his car in Sturminster Marshall, Dorset. The issue was that although his main residence was Piccadilly, 'as a foreign Sovereign Prince he was not liable to the process of British

In a photograph of the sons of the Maharaj of Cooch Behar, Hitendra is seen standing on the right

law'. He had agreed to attend any legal proceedings only on the basis that it was understood that he was immune from prosecution. The victim's local MP had questioned whether or not such a ruling should remain on the statute books in the future. The report contains no evidence of any changes to the law.

From 1908 until 1910 he lit up the Taunton social scene while he first qualified for and then played for Somerset. Whilst staying at Taunton he guested for Somerset Stragglers and made various other appearances in club cricket. With an eye for the glamour attached to any association with him, the Taunton Harriers Athletic Club and the Taunton Holy Trinity Cricket Club both invited him to become a vice president. He graciously condescended to do so. He was not a hugely successful batsman at club level although he performed outstandingly well in a drawn game between Somerset Stragglers and Devon Dumplings in 1909 when he scored 104 and 103 not out. There was surely an element of deference on the part of the reporter when the *Nottingham Evening Post* reported in 1909 that 'he continues to score heavily in local cricket'. Having played for Somerset against the Australians in 1909, he represented the county on three occasions in 1910, but with no performances of note and a total of 45 runs at an average of 6.42.

The novelty had worn off by 1911 and he had left. It had all proved a letdown after the initial excitement on his arrival. Hitendra Narayan served in the First World War as an honorary lieutenant and was injured on the Western Front. He survived, but only until he died of influenza in Darjeeling on 7 November 1920 at the age of just thirty. In his history of the club, Peter Roebuck rather unkindly includes Narayan in his 'litany of incompetents' although this perhaps acts as a counterbalance to some of the fawning accounts of his ability as a batsman. Of particular note is the large proportion of stumpings he endured, suggesting that he was rather more cavalier in his treatment of bowlers than his abilities allowed. Perhaps he had been listening too carefully when coached by John Daniell, who was never one to adopt a half-hearted approach to any confrontation.

196
Eustace Denis Piers Bisgood
19 July 1909 v. Kent, Gravesend

Eustace D Bisgood

One game at Gravesend reads as a depressing little entry in the record books, more so when we read that Eustace Bisgood managed a duck and a score of 6. All in marked contrast to his younger brother Bertram's spectacular debut that had yielded nearly two hundred runs. Born in Glastonbury on 6 February 1878, Eustace was brought up at the police station on Benedict Street. His father was the Deputy Constable of Somerset, an Irishman brought over by the recently appointed Chief Constable who had made the decision to place his trusted colleagues in key positions. John and Emily Bisgood brought their children up as Roman Catholics and Eustace and Bertie would remain devout adherents in adult life, the two of them combining to donate two houses in East Sheen so that a church could be built there.

Eustace was already thirty-one and a stockbroker when he made his only appearance. He played club cricket for Merton in Surrey, along with two older brothers, Edward, a stockbroker, and Gerald, a solicitor. He also turned out for Hampstead Nondescripts, whom he captained for a number of seasons, leading their annual two-week tour of Devon, the highlight of which was the fixture against the Devon Dumplings. Included in the Nondescripts team was Dr Reginald Ingram, who would make two appearances for Somerset.

Eustace finally tied the knot in 1924 at the age of forty-six when he was married to Florence (née Taylor). He lived to the age of eighty after retiring to Sidmouth, where he died on 4 March 1958.

Eustace Bisgood appearing for Nondescripts (top) Eustace Bisgood in later years (drawing by Felicity Jewell, for Devon Dumplings CC Jubilee Book) *(above)*

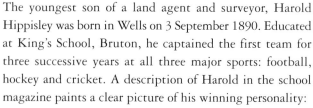

197
Harold Edwin Hippisley
23 August 1909 v. Worcestershire, Worcester

Harold Hippisley, who played county hockey and cricket in his teens but was killed in action at the age of twenty-four

The youngest son of a land agent and surveyor, Harold Hippisley was born in Wells on 3 September 1890. Educated at King's School, Bruton, he captained the first team for three successive years at all three major sports: football, hockey and cricket. A description of Harold in the school magazine paints a clear picture of his winning personality:

> *Essentially a trier, he never knew what it was to be beaten and was never satisfied with anything short of his best. The peculiar charm of his personality will be readily recalled by all who knew him here: modest and unassuming, healthy in mind as in body, cheery and equable in temper.*

He was still only eighteen when invited to play cricket for Somerset having already establishing his reputation as a hockey player where 'he was a splendid forward and scored

prolifically for the Weston-super-Mare team' as well as representing Somerset and the Western Counties. In his first innings for the county he came in at number nine and hit 40 not out. That would prove the highpoint of what had looked to be a promising career. A damning pattern was emerging of mismanagement of bright talent, of youngsters failing to build on early success.

Having left school in 1909, Harold went to the Royal College of Agriculture in Cirencester for three years. After graduating, he was awaiting news over his application for a post with the Board of Agriculture when he answered his country's call. Another delay ensued as he stayed at home awaiting news from the War Office. With the benefit of hindsight, the *Bath Chronicle* would describe what followed as 'a pathetic circumstance'. We are told that 'on Tuesday 4 August 1914, he received his orders and a special marriage licence was obtained the same evening', whereupon he was married the following day to Ivy Gwendoline (née Cooper) and left for France later in the day. This is in fact a romantic myth, as Harold and Ivy had been married at Portsmouth Register Office on 18 October 1913.

Harold fought at Mons, at the Marne and the Aisne 'without receiving injury'. His last letter home was sent on 12 October, bearing the news that he had received orders to march north. Second Lieutenant Hippisley of the Gloucestershire Regiment was killed in action on 23 October 1914 in the defence of Langemarck, blocking the road to Koekuit. He was only twenty-four. Harold and his men had been gunning down the hapless Germans in their hundreds when he was hit. In an eye-witness account of the details we are informed that:

> *The bullet struck the middle of the forehead. He was attended by his servant, Private Brown, who was under the impression that if he kept the brain from oozing out of the hole he would be all right. After a time he was convinced that the wound was fatal and that his master had no chance. He then divided his time between the parapet, where he would fire a few rounds, and then return to Lieutenant Hippisley. Between his concern for his master and his desire for revenge on the Germans, he seemed to have gone crazy.*

Harold Hippisley's commanding officer, Lieutenant-Colonel Lovett, wrote: 'I need hardly say how popular he was amongst everyone, and how deeply we deplore his loss.' He is commemorated on the Menin Gate in Ypres. In May 1914, in his last cricket game back at Bruton, he had scored 99 to ensure victory for the Bruton Nomads over his old school. He had left the sporting arena on a high. Five months later he was shot dead in a godforsaken hell-hole. The golden boy who had been destined for success was gone.

Somerset XI in 1910, captained by Massey Poyntz. The pros are on their feet and the amateurs are seated. STANDING: L. C. Braund, B. F. Morgan, F. P. Hardy, A. E. Lewis, H. Chidgey, E. Robson. SEATED: B. L. Bisgood, T. C. Spring, E. S. M. Poyntz, M. R. H. M. Herbert, J. C. White

1910

"... in the depressing season just concluded ...
it is idle to deny the causes of the want of success –
inefficient batting, and worse bowling."

Bath Chronicle

Championship Position: 16 of 16

It is hard to imagine a more dispiriting season for the players and supporters. Somerset sat at the bottom of the table. There was not a single victory and most of the defeats were decisive, notably the game at Bath against Lancashire, who declared at 286 for 2 and still won by an innings and 58 runs. The captain, John Daniell, was absent for much of the season, through injury. Not a single century was registered and A. E. Lewis topped the bowling with 77 wickets. The fact that the huge decrease in payment for professionals had led to a profit offered no consolation. There were promises of a 'nursery' paying promising young pros as an investment for the future and there were strong calls for Championship fixtures to be held at Weston-super-Mare where the gate receipts would be greater than at Bath or Taunton.

Although an interesting and varied bunch, the newcomers were never likely to impose themselves on the county game. The best of them was the professional fast bowler, Charles Taylor.

198
Hervey Robert Charles Tudway
9 June 1910 v. Hampshire, Aldershot

Hervey Tudway – raised in Wells, he was wounded at Ypres and lies buried in Boulogne

Hervey Tudway's life was one of privilege, but it would be cut short by the war like so many of his generation. The Tudways had their roots in Wells. Hervey had been brought up at Milton Lodge, where his father began work on the spectacular gardens which are now open to the public. The family was also blessed with a London residence in Berkeley Street, where a team of twelve servants saw to their needs.

Previous generations of the family had spawned Members of Parliament for the city of Wells, having made good through the misfortunes of generations of slaves, with the Tudway wealth having been derived from their sugar plantations in the West Indies. On his mother's side, his grandfather was Sir Frederick Hervey-Bathurst, a Conservative MP who had bowled for Hampshire and MCC. Born on 23 September 1888 in Westminster, Hervey was sent to Eton, where he won the school fives in 1907 but failed to make it into the First XI.

Wisden states that Hervey Tudway 'played frequently for the Household Guards' and this was enough of a recommendation for him to be added to the team sheet when Somerset travelled to Aldershot to pit their wits against Hampshire, with the twenty-one-year-old possibly stationed there at the time. He did better than many of Somerset's fleeting guests, scoring 6 in each innings. But that was it. By July 1914 he had set sail for South Africa, expecting to embark on a long and illustrious military career. On arrival, news reached him that war had broken out in Europe and he was obliged to head back home. Fast-tracked to the rank of lieutenant, he was thrust into action and was wounded on 10 November in the First Battle of Ypres, where most of the officers of the 2nd Grenadier Guards lost their lives. Hervey died eight days later on 18 November 1914 in the No. 13 General Hospital in Boulogne at the age of only twenty-six. He lies buried in the Eastern British Cemetery, where the sheer volume of graves affords a small glimpse of the desolation wrought by the conflict. It is clear from subsequent correspondence that Hervey's father, Charles Clement Tudway, was devastated by the loss of his only male heir. In a letter to the War Office, he requests the return of his son's uniform as a memento of his dead boy. Perhaps the presence of Hervey's four sisters ameliorated the pain.

A plaque was placed in Hervey's memory in Wells Cathedral, the exquisite mediaeval building that his childhood home overlooked. A more uplifting sight than the cemetery where he lies buried in Grave No. 775.

199
Reginald Edward Tierney Ingram
11 July 1910 v. Kent, Tunbridge Wells

Reginald E Ingram

He is referred to in the county scorebooks as 'Dr R. Ingram'. For many years it has been incorrectly assumed that he was Dr Peter Robert Ingram, born in Chapel of Garioch, Aberdeenshire. Reginald Ingram, also a medical practitioner, was in fact born in West Brompton, Kensington, on 22 January 1869. He was the son of Colonel Matthew John Tierney Ingram, a prominent Roman Catholic and a distinguished military man who was at one point Master General of the Royal Ordnance Corps. Reginald's parents hailed from Limerick, Ireland, and he was one of twelve children. He qualified as a doctor in August 1895 and was married on 15 August 1896 to Ella Ogilvy Erskine Jackson, the daughter of a major-general. Marriage seems not to have tamed Reginald's wilder instincts, given that he was fined £2, as was a brother, Malcolm, for having been caught skinny-dipping in The Serpentine in July 1900 and having been chased, whilst entirely nude, by a fully-clothed Police Constable 74 A, who cornered his quarry 'within fifty feet of the Royal Humane Society's Receiving House'.

What of his connection with Somerset? As early as August 1899, we are informed that Dr Ingram, playing alongside another brother, Walter, 'was responsible for the downfall of eight batsmen for only 38 runs' in a game for Yeovil against a Somerset County & Ground side containing Braund and Robson. Perhaps this had lodged long in the memory of his victims. Later, he came on annual August cricketing tours with the Hampstead Nondescripts. Indeed, the annual tour to the West Country, preceded by a small number of warm-up matches in London, was the raison d'être of the club. Based for a fortnight in Sidmouth, their fixtures were against Devon club sides, but a further connection with Somerset was a match against J. B. Challen's XI in North Devon. Cecil Braithwaite's *Happy Days with Rod, Gun and Bat* contains a brief account of the Hampstead Nondescripts. The author describes Dr Ingram as an all-rounder, but the doctor enjoyed more success as a bowler. In the 1908 season he was the club's leading bowler with 34 wickets at 9.00 runs apiece. Although generally described as Dr R. Ingram, a report on the Nondescripts v. Devon Dumplings match of 1908 in the *Exeter & Plymouth Gazette* lists him as R. E. T. Ingram, leaving no room for doubt about his identity. He also appeared occasionally for Incogniti while they were captained by former Somerset player Col. Cleveland Greenway. When asked to step into the breach and help Somerset out at Tunbridge Wells and then The Oval, Reginald Ingram was forty-one years old and by then he is described in the *Dundee Evening Telegraph* as a 'left-hand slow to medium bowler'. In the event, he bowled 21 overs, took no wickets and scored a total of 16 runs at an average of 4.00. He was not called upon again.

He resided in Warwick St in the City of Westminster, where his surgery was also based and he remained there throughout his adult life, though without his wife. There is every reason to believe that Reginald and Ella lived separate lives after the birth of their children, although, as Roman Catholics, divorce would have been out of the question. Neither seemed cut out for the strictures of married life. Having borne three children into the world, only two of whom survived, Ella carved her own career as an actress, poet and playwright, using the stage name of Miss Ella Erskine. She established a fine reputation for her acting and writing skills. Her plays, four of which were published as *The Brownie and other Short Plays*, are described by one reviewer as 'bright and witty'.

During the war, Reginald served with the County of London Royal Army Medical Corps and was promoted to the rank of temporary captain in June 1918. Whereas Ella was widely photographed, Dr Reginald Ingram appears to have adopted a lower profile. He died at the age of sixty-three on 13 November 1932, bequeathing his estate to a sister.

200
Charles James Taylor
11 July 1910 v. Kent, Tunbridge Wells

Charles James Taylor

He is referred to erroneously as 'W. H. Taylor' in a number of sources but Charles Taylor signed himself in the 1911 census as a 'Proffessional [sic] Cricketer', giving Somerset as his employers. Outside the cricket season he resided in Witton, Birmingham, along with wife Beatrice Maud (née Davis) – to whom he had been married in

1905 – and their four children, one of whom was born after the 1911 census.

Born in Bedminster on 8 June 1881, his father was a timber sawyer, whose work soon took the family to the Midlands. Charles developed into a useful right-arm fast-medium bowler – tall, tough, long-limbed and good enough to play three times for Warwickshire, with a record of 9 wickets at 28.55. Released by Warwickshire, he had been taken on by Neath as their professional when Somerset expressed an interest in the man born in the county and he was duly called on at a time when the county's bowling desperately needed shoring up.

Charles James Taylor – a hardworking pro, he served Somerset well but was deemed surplus to requirements and went on to enjoy a number of successful years in Staffordshire cricket

He would play a total of eighteen first-class matches over the 1910 and 1911 seasons. At club level he was exceptional and consistently among the wickets. At county level his record was a reasonable one, with 52 wickets for Somerset coming at 32.76 apiece. His 5 for 62 against Lancashire and 6 for 82 against Kent show that he was capable of penetrating spells. Although he took more wickets than any other bowler in what proved a woeful 1911 season for the county, his services were dispensed with. He was now thirty and Somerset had opted to reduce the cost of the pros, favouring investment in young, up-and-coming players. Charles moved to Leek, where he played in the North Staffs League. A history of Leek informs us that in 1912 'the club engaged the services of a noted Somersetshire professional, who had done good service for that County as a bowler, in the person of C. J. Taylor.'

Over many years, Charles Taylor consistently topped the averages for Leek Heathfield and then a merged Leek side, regularly taking approaching 100 wickets a season at an impressive single-figure average. He represented Staffordshire on a number of occasions between 1921 and 1932, by which time we can assume that he had slowed considerably, though what he had lost in pace he had gained in guile. His son, Fred, would follow in his father's footsteps and became a useful pace bowler, representing Warwickshire and Staffordshire. Charles died in Leek on 25 August 1960 at the age of seventy-nine.

201
Humphrey Forman
11 August 1910 v. Worcestershire, Taunton

Humphrey Forman

Ayres's Cricket Companion singled out the seventeen-year-old Humphrey Forman as destined for great things, noting that 'his style is attractive, his patience commendable, and his defence excellent. With perseverance he might also become a decidedly effective slow bowler.' Born in Repton on 26 April 1888, Humphrey was the son of Arthur Forman, a theologian and schoolmaster at Repton School. His mother was Eleanor (née Pears), the headmaster's daughter. For a schoolmaster to dally with the headmaster's daughter is career suicide but to marry her is surely an astute career move. Arthur Forman was well-known in cricketing circles, contributing an annual report on public schools cricket to *Lillywhite's Annual*. He was an imposing figure and his duties at Repton included that of cricket coach. Among his charges were C. B. Fry and the Palairet brothers but Humphrey never quite reached the heights of those alumni.

Snippets of anecdote lead to the view that Humphrey had an engaging, easy-going manner. Educated not at Repton but first at Laleham School, near Staines, and then Shrewsbury School. He then went up to Pembroke College, Cambridge, appearing for the university (by then as a fast bowler) in one first-class match, against Kent. He went on to become a schoolmaster in Bury St Edmunds and it was while a teacher

Humphrey Forman pictured as a promising teenager

there that he played for Somerset. His father had died in 1905 and his widowed mother had moved (with some of her offspring) to Minehead. On his annual trips to visit the family during the Summer vacations, Humphrey played for Minehead alongside his brother, Thomas, who was now a master at Shrewsbury School. In July 1909 Humphrey had impressed with a score of 48 and a six-wicket haul against Taunton Deane and had scored 86 and taken 6 for 31 against Devon Dumplings the following July. He was invited to play for Somerset against Worcestershire that August, the local press describing him as 'H. Forman of Minehead', adding that he was 'a bowler who has appeared with success in local cricket'. He took one wicket for Somerset for a total of 88 runs, made 4 runs in two innings and never appeared again. If Humphrey was as easy-going as we suppose then that will not have bothered him unduly.

Prior to the war, he was offered a role as a schoolmaster at Stanmore Park School, run by former Somerset cricketer Bill Roe. In 1917, Humphrey's sister, Rosamond, married Geoffrey Fisher who was by then headmaster of Repton and would go on to become the Archbishop of Canterbury. Regrettably, Humphrey had been unable to attend the wedding of his sister and Fisher, being indisposed. He had signed up for the war effort. He was promoted to the rank of lieutenant, attached to the 3rd Battalion of the South Wales Borderers in April 1915. He was wounded and captured by the advancing Germans in May 1915. He has left a detailed handwritten account of the event. He remained a prisoner of war, held at Halle and Furstenburg POW camps until his repatriation on 18 November 1918. The Imperial War Museum has retained a collection of his photographs of his time as a POW and so we know that he was allowed some creature comforts. Never married, he emigrated to teach at King's College, Bangkwang (a suburb of Bangkok) where he died on 21 May 1923 at the age of only thirty-five.

Arthur and Eleanor Forman (front) in 1890. Behind them are Old Reptonians Richard Palairet (seated centre) and his brother, Lionel (standing centre)

202
Humphrey Seymour Ramsey Critchley-Salmonson
15 August 1910 v. Sussex, Bath

Somerset thought they had unearthed a precocious talent when they heard of the exploits of young Humphrey, captain of the Winchester College XI. A tall, long-limbed schoolboy with a long run-up, a 'windmill action' and a fearsome turn of pace, he was terrorising most of his peers. He was born in Preston, Weymouth, on 19 January 1894, but his parents had moved to Minehead. In a match between Somerset Boys and their Wiltshire counterparts, the young prodigy was upstaged by a fifteen-year-old named John MacBryan, who, by dint of a near-faultless technique and a dogged refusal to yield his wicket, saw off Humphrey. Somerset called on the services of both boys, although it would be MacBryan who would go on to greater glories on the cricket field. Humphrey and Somerset would find that an approach that struck

Humphrey Critchley-Salmonson – tall and long-limbed (top); Humphrey Critchley-Salmonson savouring the delights of country house cricket (above)

fear into the hearts of callow schoolboys did not quite pass muster against men of county standard.

Playing two matches in each of the 1910 and 1912 seasons, the first as a sixteen-year-old, he took a total of five wickets, although he would return again between 1924 and 1928, taking that tally up to twenty-four wickets at 29.25. His best innings with the bat came against Hampshire at Bath in 1924, when he scored 66. The *Bath Chronicle* talks of 'some remarkably powerful strokes'.

His limited availability resulted from time spent in Argentina, where he was trying to build his fortune and where he was married in 1922 to his first wife, Valerie Francisca (née Scott) in Buenos Aires. He found time to play cricket there, including a return of 5 for 43, in an Argentina v Brazil game, a fixture more readily associated with football. His business and sporting activities were curtailed when he was commissioned as a second lieutenant in September 1913 and promoted to lieutenant in December 1914, in the 1st Scots Rifles. For a while he acted as a recruiting officer in Scotland. He would retain his links with the country, playing in the early 1930s as part of Lord Carnegie's XI in their annual tour of South Scotland.

His wife Valerie filed for divorce in 1929 on the grounds of Humphrey's adultery with Phyllis Dorothy Compton, who bore the title Lady Chichester. Theirs was more than a mere dalliance, given that they were married in 1930. As an aside, the divorce papers inform us that Humphrey was manager of the Greyhound Racing Association at the time. The newly-weds settled for a while in the Bath area and he turned out for Bath CC on a number of occasions, also joining Sir Julien Cahn's XI on a tour of Argentina.

In 1935, Humphrey and Phyllis moved to Lyndhurst but their marriage fell apart and he moved to Chagford, in Devon. He carried on playing cricket until the outbreak of the Second World War when he was appointed a flight lieutenant. In 1944, Humphrey was married for a third time, to Beryl Gwynifred Martin. The couple lived for five years in Bristol before they retired to Payhembury in Devon, where Humphrey died on 24 April 1956 at the age of sixty-two, leaving his estate to his third wife.

1911

"The gates were the worst in history of the club, but the truth is that the team did not play well enough to draw spectators."
Gerald Fowler, Treasurer and former player

Championship Position: 16 of 16

Somerset managed one victory in what proved another dismal season. The idea of a 'nursery' for young pros had been abandoned when the man who had agreed to fund it – Henry Murray-Anderdon – fell ill. The longsuffering guarantors, now smaller in number, dipped into their pockets to the tune of £1 17s 6d apiece to keep the club afloat. Randall Johnson topped Somerset's batting averages but was rarely available. He was followed by A. E. Lewis who was blighted by injuries. Charles Taylor was the principal wicket-taker, though his haul of 38 wickets was not much to write home about. *Wisden* observed that John Daniell had 'led the team with unflagging spirit, but at times he must have found the task disheartening'. The report adds that 'the outlook for Somerset is cheerless'. *Wisden* could not have known that three new recruits – Jim Bridges, Tom Young and Jack MacBryan – would all make significant contributions to the cause in future years.

Randall Johnson (seen in later years) must surely be among a small minority of cricketers who have flayed a Middlesex attack whilst wearing a cardigan: he was Somerset's leading batsman in 1911

203
James Bridges
11 May 1911 v. Hampshire, Southampton

Jim Bridges – summoned many great performances over the years

Although he styled himself 'J. J.' and for a while 'J. F.', he was in fact plain James, known as Jim. References to 'James John Bridges' are erroneous.

Jim Bridges was born in Timsbury on 28 June 1887 and his was an upbringing far removed from that of any of the amateurs who graced the County Ground. His father was a boot and shoe maker and his mother an occasional corset maker, when the demands of motherhood allowed. By the age of thirteen, Jim was working down the mines as a wagoner, pulling Mendip coal through narrow seams. This was unpleasant work and over them all lurked constant fear: as recently as 1895, an underground explosion at the Upper Conygre pit had claimed the lives of seven miners and four pit ponies.

Once he had grown into a willowy young man, Jim ceased working down the mines and tried his luck as a male nurse in London, where he was married in 1910 to Annie Margaret (née Connell), known as Margaret, with whom he would have seven children. He was also proving a useful club cricketer. When word reached Somerset that he qualified for them by birth, the county seized their opportunity and drafted him into the side for the fixture against Hampshire. Thus began a first-class career that would see him serve Somerset for many years as a pro and then, in the final few years leading up to his retirement from the game in 1929, as an amateur. In that time he would take 685 wickets at an average of 25.59, summoning many great achievements, including forty-five 5-wicket hauls, but never quite achieving greatness. David Foot tells us that 'his action was high, his in-swing calculated, though too many catches went down off him'. Peter Roebuck writes that 'given a more phlegmatic personality, he might have risen to the heights, but ... his fuse was short'.

Somerset bowlers have made a habit of being on the receiving end when landmark achievements are being posted by batsmen. Jim Bridges entered the canon when Jack Hobbs matched W. G. Grace's haul of centuries, but he did snare Hobbs for 101 (although it is well-documented that Hobbs often sacrificed his wicket after completing a century, to allow others to bat).

A tail-ender, his finest hour as a batsman came in 1919 against Essex at his home ground of Clarence Park, where he also played his club cricket for Weston-super-Mare. Sharing a last-wicket stand of 143 with Holland Gibbs, he was left stranded on 99 not out.

Jim's family were based for much of the time in Brentford, Ware and Edmonton. He was possessed of a strong work ethic both on and off the field. For a while he ran the Clarence Hotel in Weston-super-Mare. David Foot writes that this became a favoured watering hole of visiting cricketers, but Jim soon returned to the South East, working as a coal delivery man in Enfield. He was living in Hackney at the time of his death on 29 September 1966 at the age of seventy-nine. Jim Bridges was grafter who had given his all.

204
Charles Ross Lyall
18 May 1911 v. Yorkshire, Taunton

Born on 3 October 1880 in Calcutta (now Kolkata) in India, Charles Lyall was the youngest of seven children and destined for a peripatetic life in the military. He did, however, have strong connections with Taunton and would settle there in later years. Graduating from the Royal Military College in 1900 as a Queen's Cadet, he became a lieutenant in 1902. In 1904 he resided for a while with his parents at Netherclay House in Bishop's Hull near Taunton, his father having retired there from a senior role in the Indian Civil Service. Charles became part of the Taunton sporting scene, playing both rugby and cricket for the town.

C. R. Lyall – played for Somerset at both cricket and rugby

His appearance for Taunton RFC as a three-quarter was much anticipated after his performance in a trial match (although it was delayed after he suffered a cycling accident) and he soon graduated to the Somerset rugby team. He also played for Taunton at cricket and opened the batting for the Somerset Stragglers team but before long his commitments had drawn him away. He would, however, retain links with the town both via his parents and through Dorothea Gertrude Iles (the daughter of a local

Charles Lyall

surgeon) to whom he was married in the cathedral at Calcutta in October 1906. Dorothea's family lived at Shuttern House, which backed onto the town's Vivary Park. They would have three children – Ailsa, who was born in Taunton while her parents were residing with the Iles family in 1911, and David and Rodney, both born in India. Charles's brother-in-law, Dr Alfred Iles, would later become the mayor of Taunton.

Charles Lyall played for Somerset on two occasions in 1911, making a total of 55 runs, having only been dismissed twice. His military career continued to progress seamlessly, with a promotion from captain to major with the 36th Sikhs in 1916, while he served as a recruiting officer. After a posting in Mesopotamia he became an instructor at the Central School of Musketry before a spell in Waziristan, after which he was promoted to lieutenant colonel in 1924. He retired from the Indian Army in 1933 and took up residence in Haines Hill, Taunton. He was still living there at the time of his death at the age of sixty-nine on 4 June 1950 in hospital in Basingstoke.

205
Henry William Saunders
17 July 1911 v. India, Taunton

Henry William Saunders

Harry Saunders was born on 28 June 1883 in the village of Pusey (then in Berkshire) but his parents moved to Weston-super-Mare while he was still young. His parents, John and Clara, ran a guest house in Weston for many years. In the 1911 census, John (by then a widower) proudly describes his son as a 'Certificated Assistant School Master' employed by Somerset County Council.

Harry's first sporting breakthrough at county level had been in 1908 when he played rugby for Somerset against Gloucestershire. In 1910 the *Western Daily Press* describes Harry the cricketer as 'a Weston player with a reputation as a hitter' and goes on to report a 'merry display', where 'what he lacked in defence he made up in the whole-hearted manner in which he went for the bowling'. They were describing an appearance for a Somerset XI against G. L. Jessops XI and the lusty blows formed one half of a partnership with fellow Somerset batsman, Manek Bajana. Harry first turned out in a first-class match for Somerset in 1911 in their fixture against the Indians. The local newspaper reports show that he regularly made a contribution as a Weston player though rarely went on to build a big innings and had established a reputation as a useful left-handed batsman. But he would have to wait until 1914 for his baptism in Championship cricket as a thirty-one-year-old. Harry might have regretted his call-up, given that – with a pair – he joins that unhappy band of Somerset players who mustered not a single run in their Championship careers. It is unfair, though, to regard him as a no-hoper. He was a very good club cricketer who came to his county's aid and had the misfortune to bat on a howler of a wicket in a low-scoring game in which Alonzo Drake took fifteen wickets for Yorkshire for 51 runs. Drake clean bowled Saunders on both occasions. That was the beginning and the end of his Championship career, although he would play against Oxford University in 1921 and 1922.

He was married in 1911 to a local girl, Florence Marion Maud (née Pottenger), and continued to be part of the fabric of Weston-super-Mare for many years. In his memoirs, Somerset's Bill Andrews tells us how, having moved to Weston as a twelve-year-old, he was taught by Saunders, who 'was apt to talk more about sport than lessons he was taking'.

Harry Saunders – 'what he lacked in defence he made up in the whole-hearted manner in which he went for the bowling'

When Bill announced to his former teacher in 1930 that he had handed in his notice at a solicitor's office to take up a role as a professional at East Coker (ushering in a long and successful career with Somerset) Harry Saunders apparently informed him that he was 'off his head'. Perhaps his opinion had been shaped by his own experience of Championship cricket. Harry was a positive influence on a number of young lives. For thirty-five years he remained a schoolmaster at the Walliscote Road Council School. He was a leading light in the Evening Continuation School, set up to further the education of young men and he was also on the committee who organised Somerset's annual cricket festival at Weston-super-Mare. In later years, he became a keen angler in whatever leisure time was left. He never reached the age of retirement but died at fifty-eight in Uphill near Weston-super-Mare on 24 April 1942.

206
Albert Henry Howard Southwood
14 August 1911 v. Kent, Taunton

Howard Southwood – 'a man of simple dignity and kindness'

Howard Southwood was a modest man who gave his all for the town he loved and lived in for nearly eighty-three years. Born in Taunton on 19 July 1882, his father was the porter at the Taunton Poor Law Union Workhouse. His mother continued her job as a dressmaker after her marriage and was well into her thirties when she had her two children. On leaving school, Howard worked as a clerk in a solicitor's office but he would decide in time that this was not the life for him. As a fellow councillor would say in later years 'he wisely deserted the law for a more remunerative appointment'. A committed member of the Baptist chapel in Silver Street, he would rise to become a successful businessman, but one with a heart, and a mayor of Taunton more concerned with doing good than he was with the trappings of office. He is described as being 'always in sympathy with the underdog'. Another colleague described him as 'a man of simple dignity and kindness' who was 'prepared to fight a lone battle'.

He was a successful club cricketer, essentially a batsman but one who could bowl well enough to be considered an all-rounder. In the 1920s, he would captain the Taunton Saturday XI for some years. H. J. Channon tells us in the *Taunton Courier* that:

> *Howard Southwood's presence in the team inspired confidence. He took full advantage of loose balls and scored his runs gracefully and quickly. It was a sheer joy to watch his on-side strokes. His bowling and fielding were as good as his batting.*

His calm and thoughtful but steely demeanour clearly manifested itself in every walk of life. Certainly he would not appear to have been overwhelmed by the prospect of county cricket, averaging 16.00 in his three matches for Somerset.

Married to Eleanor Maynard (née Latcham) in 1909, Howard decided that the life of a clerk in law was not for him and founded a firm of auctioneers and estate agents based in East Street, Taunton: Howard Southwood & Co.

342

In 1928, when the county set up a knock-out competition for the Under 25s with eight districts competing for the cup, each district proposed a captain who was over twenty-five and Taunton chose Howard Southwood, knowing that he would prove a good mentor. He became a town councillor in 1934, before being elected to the role of mayor in November 1947. He was at the time sixty-five years old and a hugely popular choice. In his acceptance speech he noted that a woman whom he had known all his life and who was now a hundred, had remarked on hearing of his appointment: 'Young Howard Southwood? Isn't he a bit young to be the mayor?' Howard and his wife, Eleanor, brought their combined wisdom to the role and after retirement they continued to live in the town.

He died on 13 July 1965 at the age of eighty-two. He had done his bit for the town he loved: quietly and more calmly than some of the local legends, but he was no less of a hero for that.

207
Archibald Young
24 August 1911 v. Worcestershire, Worcester

Born in Bathwick on 6 November 1890, Tom, as he was known, truly belongs to the late 1920s and early 1930s when he finally came into his own as an all-rounder who shored up the batting and bowling. Between them, he and Jack White would keep Somerset afloat. As a measure of his importance to the county, in seven seasons out of eight between 1925 and 1932 he was either the number one or number two run-maker and between 1930 and 1933 when John Daniell's successor as captain, Jack White, took the trouble to find out that Young was actually a fine off-spin bowler, he was one of the top two wicket-takers in three seasons out of four. Indeed, of all the accusations of mismanagement that can be piled at the door of John Daniell, this error of judgement was one of his greatest. It is perhaps a sad reflection of his view that professionals were a blight that had to be borne and that they should only speak when spoken to.

Tom Young had arrived on the scene as a young pro with Lansdown in Bath. In the winter months he played as a goalkeeper for Bath FC. A slight figure, sickly since childhood, he was nevertheless a cut above the ordinary club cricketer. Already inclined to struggle through ill health, life became considerably harder for him when he was the victim of a gas attack from which his lungs never recovered, while serving in

Tom Young – a loyal servant of Somerset cricket

France. He was a cussed fellow and always one to overcome adversity, forthright to the point of being considered irascible, though perhaps few understood the considerable discomfort he was forced to endure. His infirmity could have driven a lesser man into his shell but in Tom Young's case it was the spur that drove him. Without a constitution that could take to quick singles, he went on the attack as a batsman. Unable to run around in the outfield, he became a fine slip fielder. Limited in the pace he could bowl, he developed into a fine off-spinner. Triumph was eked out of the disaster of his weakened lungs but this could not have been the case but for his innate ability and courage. His moodiness and irritability would sometimes pucker into impish humour as he lifted the ball over cover point's head or slashed it through the slips for another four and made some jocular aside intended to inflame the opposition. In 310 matches, he scored eleven centuries for the county. His batting average was 25.40. He took 388 wickets at 25.58 and held onto 218 catches. Somerset understood his worth. When his benefit match in 1930 proved a two-day wash-out that earned him only £100, the club stepped in and raised £750. The committee also offered help when it became clear that he needed hospital treatment in 1936. But, cussed and determined as ever, he wanted to die at his home in Bath, with his wife Violet Mary (née Dabner) to whom he had been married in 1922. His death on 2 April 1936, a little more than two years after his last county game, was not unexpected but it still came as a shock that one of Somerset's great stalwarts had died at the age of forty-five.

208
John Crawford William MacBryan
28 August 1911 v. Lancashire, Bath

[signature]

Whereas most cricketers might rejoice in having received an England cap, Jack MacBryan bemoaned his ill-luck in laying claim to being possibly the only player in test history not to have batted, bowled or even to have fielded the ball during his international career. Born in Box on 22 July 1892, he was the eldest of five children of a medical practitioner who owned a lunatic asylum at Kingsdown House. At the age of ten, the loss of his mother hit Jack very hard. His relationship with his father would always remain frosty. Educated at St Christopher's Preparatory School in Bath, he went on to Exeter School. He developed a sound and attractive technique built around 'footwork, science and application'. Jack took pride in the fact that his style of batting comprised well-judged and well-timed strokes rather than the flamboyance associated with many of his fellow amateurs and he made it perfectly clear that he regretted being in a team he regarded as a shower led by a buffoon in the shape of John Daniell.

Jack had wanted to follow his father into the medical profession but was pushed towards the military. He made his debut for Somerset while on leave from Sandhurst and acquitted himself well. On reaching the age of twenty-one, he immediately resigned his commission and opted to study medicine at Bart's. But then the war intervened, with Jack spending much of it in POW camps, though, as an officer and the son of a doctor, he was treated well. After the war he went up to Jesus College, Cambridge. He gained his

Jack MacBryan – a fine craftsman frustrated by the amateurism that prevailed in Somersetshire cricket

cricketing blue there. A keen sportsman, he would also represent Somerset at golf, rugby and hockey. He also won a gold medal as a member of the Great Britain hockey team at the 1920 Olympics in Antwerp. His shoulder was dislocated during a fractious rugby game for Bath against Pontypridd and thereafter he was able neither to throw the ball nor to play a drive with any great force in the arc between cover point and mid-off. He adapted admirably, mastering the late cut and on-drive to near-perfection. He gave his all despite his obvious disdain for the Somerset set-up, topping the batting averages every year between 1922 and 1926. His 8372 runs for the county at an average of 31.00 in 156 first-class matches included sixteen centuries. In 1924, he was invited to play for England in the Old Trafford test against South Africa in place of Jack Hobbs, who had been dropped after turning down a request to tour Australia the following winter. There were fewer than three hours of play and his international career ended swiftly when Hobbs relented.

Jack MacBryan spurned close friendships and was unhappy in his personal life. Married to a chorus girl named Myra (née Thompson) in 1928, she soon tired of his caustic tongue and they separated. Having set up as a stockbroker, he never managed to make the sort of living he would have hoped for. At the age of eighty, he found himself in penury after a stockbroking partnership with two others had failed spectacularly. He would see out his days living in lodgings in Cambridge, spending much of his time completing complex embroideries of his own design – a skill he had developed while a POW. He died in Cambridge on 14 July 1983, just short of his ninety-first birthday.

1912

"In a county like Somerset it goes against the grain to depend upon professionals, but unless we raise a considerable sum to ensure this, Somerset will go downhill still further."

Vernon Hill, former player

Championship Position: 14 of 16

The writing was on the wall. A loss of over £700 was at least partially rectified by calling on the guarantors. The treasurer was of the view that Somerset cricket was in danger of imminent collapse. A 'shilling fund' was launched in the form of a raffle, intended to ensure the county's continued survival. In another season of mediocrity, the arrival of Manek Bajana added some quality though not enough backbone to the batting and Bill Greswell made a welcome return to the fold, proving the principal wicket-taker. Of the new recruits, only Bajana and Bruce Hylton Stewart, the son of a Bath clergyman, could be regarded as county-level cricketers.

Bill Greswell, who returned in 1912 and took 132 first-class wickets at 17.78 apiece

209
Manek Pallon Bajana
6 May 1912 v. Sussex, Hove

An article in the *Western Daily Press* gives notice of Manek Bajana's arrival in an invitation game between a Somerset XI and G. L. Jessop's XI:

> *An Indian from the same neighbourhood as Prince Narayan is a fine cricketer … He is not the same type of batsman as the Prince, but he appears to be sounder in defence, and, moreover, he has a greater variety of strokes.*

Manek Bajana – a favourite with the Somerset supporters, known affectionately as 'Pyjamas'

The combination of condescension and fascination with these exotic arrivals from the far-flung parts of the British Empire is of course typical of the time. Born in India on 14 September 1886, he was touring England as part of an All India team in 1911 and began with a pair against Surrey. He had found his feet by the time he came to Taunton, scoring a free-flowing 108 out of his side's 196 in their first innings and creating the platform for their victory. His suggestion that he would be interested in a spell in county cricket was leapt upon by Somerset as no county had registered him. Blessed with inherited wealth, he was able to play as an amateur, although he was involved for a while in an antiques and art dealership in London, perhaps in an attempt to supplement his income.

The Somerset supporters took to him, referring to him fondly as 'Pyjamas' and appreciating his approach to the game. The newspaper reports reveal that he tended to take the game to the bowler with his stylish, firmly-hit strokes. His positivity was not always a source of success. Between 1912 and 1920 he played in fifty-one matches, scoring two first-class centuries for Somerset, both in his final season. Although his career average was only 20.71, he proved a valuable addition to a very weak side. Indeed, in 1912 – his first season – he scored more first-class runs than anyone else. The fact that he did so having amassed only 635 runs speaks volumes about the moribund state of Somerset cricket.

During the war and after his departure in 1920, Manek Bajana played for Indian Gymkhana. He continued to do so until the 1926 season. He maintained his links with this country and it is clear from the photographs of him that he was fond of adopting the mannerisms and dress of an English gentleman, reflecting the mutual fascination between the two cultures. He was staying at Bethnal Green at the time of his early death at the age of forty on 28 April 1927. He had been an exotic and fondly remembered addition to the ranks of Somerset cricketers and one who made a greater contribution than many at a time when the county was foundering.

210
Elliot Dowell Tillard
27 May 1912 v. Gloucestershire, Taunton

[signature: E. D. Tillard]

Elliot Tillard was born on 22 July 1880, in Cheltenham. His father, Charles, was a classics teacher at Cheltenham College who had played cricket for Surrey. His mother was the daughter of Rev. Dowell of Blakeney in Norfolk. Elliot was educated at Great Malvern School and his parents had moved to Bathford after Charles's retirement, thus providing his connection with Somerset.

A career soldier, Elliot joined the Royal Engineers as a second lieutenant in 1899 and was promoted to lieutenant in 1902, the year in which he was stationed in India before he then served in Somaliland. By 1906, he was back in the UK for a while, finding time to play for East Gloucestershire, although he was near the bottom of the batting averages and well down the bowling averages, and this for a team not noted for outstanding success. Here is what the *Gloucester Echo* says of them:

E. D. Tillard, who rose to the rank of Lt Colonel but failed to hit the heights as a cricketer

> The {1906} record is not a flattering one, but, as is well known, the East Gloucestershire club play the game to get real enjoyment out of it and they can never be accused of sacrificing the best traditions of sport for the mere sake of a win.

The same might have been said of Somerset, but it is perhaps a surprise that Elliot managed to perform much better with the bat for them than he did for East Gloucestershire, with an average of 15.00 in his sixteen innings for the county, all during the 1912 season. Regarded as an all-rounder but not deployed as a bowler to any great extent by the county, he did manage a best first-class bowling analysis of 6 for 40 while playing in India later in 1912. He continued playing occasional first-class cricket on the Indian sub-continent until he was forty-seven.

In 1914 he was married in India to Molly (née McNeely), from Donegal. The following year and now a major, he was stationed in East Africa, where he oversaw the construction of a number of bridges that allowed the flow of supplies, calling on a combination of ingenuity and the hard work of his men. Among the more interesting prisoners taken was a grey parrot who had been taught to say, in a near-flawless Teutonic accent, 'Gott Staff England' and 'Hoch der Kaiser' (which translates very loosely as: 'Stuff the English' and 'Three Cheers for the Kaiser'). The bird proved too bright for its own good when it quickly learned to mimic the sound of the 'fall in' whistle at full volume. Soon tiring of downing tools and standing in line, the company agreed to 'supress' the bird.

Elliot Tillard was awarded the DSO in 1917 and continued his progression until reaching the rank of lieutenant colonel. After his retirement, he and his wife lived in Bathford but also had a property at Batworthy-on-the-Moor, near Chagford. He died on 19 February 1967 at the age of eighty-six in Flexbury, Bude.

211
Biron Howe House
27 May 1912 v. Gloucestershire, Taunton

Biron House was born in Curry Rivel on 18 December 1884 and was brought up above his father's corn merchant's business at 30 High Street, Taunton. Educated at Huish's Grammar School, his first employment was not in the family business but as a draper's assistant. His father, Francis Trivitt House, must have been either short of capital or determined that his children should learn to stand on their own two feet financially. Whilst working in the retail trade, Biron played for a variety of local sides. He generally opened the batting and performed well enough to be taken on by Chard as a professional wicket-keeper batsman. By this time, his father had opted for the life of a gentleman farmer and the family were living at Langaller House near Creech St Michael.

While playing for Chard he was asked to step in and appear for Somerset. He did so on only three occasions and managed a total of 30 runs in four innings, including a 19 not out in his very first knock, when he came in at number eleven. It is typical of Somerset that an opening batsman should come in as the last man and sadly predictable that he should perform well in his first game, only for his batting to fall away. Equally typical is that in his next match the recruit should find, much to his surprise, that John Daniell had summoned two professional wicket-keepers. Harry Chidgey was given the nod on this occasion, although Biron kept once more in his final game.

Biron House – a wicket-keeper batsman: severely wounded in the war, he never fully recovered from his injuries and was given a send-off described as 'semi-military in character'

During the First World War he served with the West Somerset Yeomanry, first in Gallipoli and then in Palestine where, in Gaza, as the *Taunton Courier* informs us:

> *. . . he was severely wounded by the bursting of a shell which killed five of his comrades. His life was despaired of, but he made a remarkable recovery after an eye had been removed.*

He was subsequently promoted to sergeant and helped to manage a POW camp once he had recovered sufficiently from his wounds. He returned to civilian life in May 1919.

After the war he came back to live with his parents at Langaller House, though he never managed fully to recover his health, dying at home at the age of forty-five on 3 June 1930. His funeral was led by a former army chaplain, Rev. H. L. Walker and is described as 'semi-military in character', reflecting the fact that he had effectively died of his war wounds. The vicar himself, having delivered his eulogy, proceeded to play the last post. Biron House was never married. Perhaps it is no coincidence that having lost a wife and a son, his father also gave up the ghost later that same year.

212
Bruce de la Cour Hylton Stewart
17 June 1912 v. South Africa, Bath

His middle name is sometimes given as 'de la Coeur', but 'de la Cour' is the correct spelling (confirmed on official documents) and nor was there a hyphen in his surname,

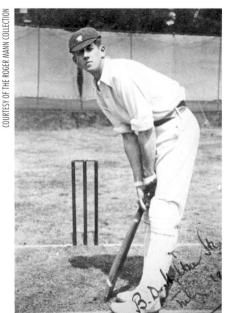

Bruce Hylton Stewart – a dashing all-rounder and a music teacher

though he is generally named as 'B. D. Hylton-Stewart' on scorecards. He was born in New Brighton in Cheshire on 27 November 1891. His father was a minor canon at Chester Cathedral at the time but was soon appointed the rector of Bathwick. Bruce attended Bath College before going up to Cambridge University. Two of the brothers were very musical and both accomplished organists. Charles became organist first of Rochester Cathedral, then Chester Cathedral and finally of St George's Chapel, Windsor. Bruce became a schoolmaster. He taught briefly at The Leys School before being offered the role of director of music at Haileybury College where he remained until the early 1930s. He then accepted a similar post at Marlborough College.

In 1915 he was married to Mary (née Thorneley), the daughter of a Cambridge tutor. Mary died of pneumonia in 1935 and Bruce was married in 1937 to Margaret Helen (née Campbell), the daughter of the rector of Wilton. He made his first appearance for Somerset in unusual circumstances when Harry Chidgey was struck in the eye early in the game against South Africa and a full substitution was allowed. The *Yorkshire Evening Post* tells us that 'he is a tall young gentleman and bowls right-arm medium ... with some break from the off'. He was in fact a bowler who could bat well enough to be considered an all-rounder. In his first season he returned the astonishing figures of 5 for 3 against Worcestershire in a devastating spell of 2.2 overs. Having announced himself on the scene, he would only manage one other five wicket haul. He came into his own as a batsman in 1914 with a century and a 91.

The *Bath Chronicle* explains the circumstances of an innings against Gloucestershire, where the umpire controversially instructed that Bruce should be recorded as 'retired hurt':

> In the Bank Holiday match between Somerset and Gloucestershire ... B. D. Hylton-Stewart {sic} was struck on the head by a fast bumping ball and fell on to his wicket. Thereupon rose the question as to the mode of his dismissal. No appeal was made but for the sake of the score book the umpire was asked his opinion. He ruled that as the batsman had finished his stroke the credit of the wicket should not go to the bowler.

The 1914 season would be his last, because he had taken up the offer of his first teaching post at The Leys School in Cambridge. He had proved a useful all-rounder and would go on to play cricket for Hertfordshire.

Bruce Hylton Stewart died in Marlborough on 1 October 1972 at the age of eighty.

213
Norman Hardy
11 July 1912 v. Northamptonshire, Northampton

Born on 11 March 1892 in Norton Hawkfield, Norman Hardy became a popular and widely-respected member of the Bristol social scene, often referred to as 'Our Nor'. He left school and became a grocer's apprentice working for the firm of H. H & S. Budgett of Nelson Street, Bristol, who ran a significant wholesale business supplying groceries to independent retailers. He rose through the ranks to become an important member of the management team, his service broken by the war, which he volunteered for at the earliest opportunity as a private with the British Expeditionary Force. He was made a sergeant in 1916 and was twice severely wounded, first in the head and then with bullet wounds to his right forearm and left hand. Each time he recovered sufficiently to re-join the fray.

He played his club cricket at Knowle. A fast-medium bowler, he was also good enough to have earned a place at club level as a batsman. He would play for Somerset on eleven occasions between 1912 and 1921. His batting average of 14.08 included a highest score of 38 in a valuable last-wicket stand with Jack White. His bowling

Norman Hardy – 'Our Nor' was a fine athlete and a popular figure in the Bristol area

return of 34 wickets at 21.97 is highly respectable and included a 4 for 22 against Surrey in 1919 (crowned with a spell of three wickets in four balls). But he is remembered in Bristol for other reasons.

Each year, football teams within the top two divisions of the Bristol Downs League compete for the Norman Hardy Cup. On 17 November 1923, he had been playing for St Andrew's against St Nicholas, at Fishponds, when, having already scored a goal, he felt ill and was led to the changing room to recover. He had partially changed when he collapsed and died of a heart attack. He was only thirty-one years old. Perhaps his war wounds had contributed to his untimely death. There was an outpouring of grief in Bristol sporting circles and, in his honour, the Norman Hardy cup was inaugurated: it is still competed for, a century later.

Norman Hardy was never married and still lived with his mother in Knowle at the time of his death. Cricket was his first love. Only twenty when he first played for his county, he was almost certainly good enough to have played for them more often had his work commitments allowed it. But the truth is that he was happier playing with his club mates at Knowle and uneasy in the company of the more aristocratic element among the Somerset team members. The *Western Daily Press* informs us that:

> *Not only was he a fine bowler, but when he liked he could make runs, and his free hitting was always an attractive feature … Bristol has lost a splendid example of British manhood, and sporting circles a keen supporter and wonderful ornament.*

Hugely popular in his short lifetime, fondly remembered long after his early death, Norman Hardy carved his own little slice of immortality in the form of a piece of silverware coveted by the many Bristolians following in a fine tradition of club competition.

214
Arthur Albert Brinkley Pape
25 July 1912 v. Northamptonshire, Bath

Arthur Albert Brinkley Pape

In his only appearance for the county, Arthur Pape bagged a pair and did not bowl. His record is by no means unique in Somerset's history. Born on 30 July 1890 in Fairford, Gloucestershire, he was the son of a railway station master whose job obliged the family to move first to Wellington and then to Ilminster.

Tall and slim, Arthur played cricket as a young man for Bradninch as a middle-order batsman. He also played football for Ilminster as a striker. At the time of his debut he was a trainee with the civil service but he did not remain in Somerset for long, moving before the war to the village of Castle Eden, near Hartlepool. Here he was employed by W. J. Nimmo, who owned the Castle Eden Brewery. Nimmo was a very wealthy man who indulged his passion for cricket by playing for Castle Eden and serving on the Durham CCC committee for many years. Arthur worked as a brewery clerk and his employer was happy to release him as necessary to play cricket, including representing Durham Pilgrims – a nomadic side who drew on the pool of county players in the manner of Somerset Stragglers. In 1921, Arthur played for the Durham county side.

He enlisted in the war effort in December 1916, rising from the level of private to that of quartermaster, undertaking clerical work and remaining in England. At the end of hostilities he returned to Castle Eden, captaining the cricket team for more than ten years, from the start of the 1920s and generally opening the batting. Later he became both secretary and treasurer of the club. If W. J. Nimmo perhaps failed to land himself a stellar cricketing talent, he most certainly secured the services of a loyal employee who retained his association with Castle Eden throughout his adult life.

Arthur Pape in the Caste Eden CC team

COURTESY OF DURHAM COUNTY COUNCIL (Ref: PPP Cast006)

Arthur Pape was forty-six when he was married to Ellen (née Hewitt) in 1937 but he did not live long enough to enjoy any retirement, dying in hospital in Hartlepool on 11 August 1945 at the age of fifty-five.

Somerset XI in 1912.
STANDING: E. Robson, J. Bridges, A. E. Lewis, H. Chidgey, L. C. Braund,
M. P. Bajana
SEATED: L. C. L. Sutton, E. S. M. Poyntz, J. Daniell, W. T. Greswell, J. C. W.
MacBryan

1913

"The most surprising event of the season in Somerset
cricket has been the wonderful development of
J. C. White as a bowler."

Bath Chronicle

Championship Position: 16 of 16

To the relief of many, the 'shilling fund' had exceeded all expectations and raised nearly £500. It had been announced in January 1913 that the club would not now be disbanded, but would remain part of the Championship for at least another year. Perhaps those paying their shillings were dismayed to hear that, having paid off their debts, Somerset would not be investing in a new intake of professionals. Unsurprisingly, the performances on the field showed no improvement. Massey Poyntz agreed to take on the captaincy for the season, though he was absent at times through injury. There were two wins, both against Derbyshire. Somerset were back in their familiar place, propping up the Championship. Jack White was at last beginning to demonstrate his true worth as a slow left-armer and topped the county's bowling averages with a decent haul of wickets. Len Braund enjoyed a return to form with the bat. With the passing of time it has perhaps been forgotten how perilously close to exiting the Championship Somerset were and what an important role the local boy White played in ensuring the county's survival.

Five new players were called on. None of them was up to the mark.

215
Percy Walter Vasey
19 May 1913 v. Yorkshire, Bath

P. W. Vasey

'Peter' Vasey appearing for King's School, Bruton

P. W. Vasey as a hockey player

Not overly fond of his given name, Percy Vasey was known as 'Peter'. He was born in Highbury Park, London, on 29 July 1883. His father, George, was variously a schoolmaster and clergyman. After attending Merchant Taylor's School in London, Peter graduated from St John's College, Oxford. After leaving Oxford he was appointed assistant schoolmaster at King's School, Bruton, where he played an active role in the development of the school's cricket and hockey. He was assisted by the school's professional coach, 'Tommy' Bowring, a local Bruton boy who also played for Somerset. His pupils included Somerset players Harold Hippisley and Leicester Sutton.

Peter Vasey served in the war as a captain in the Dorsetshire Regiment and then the Manchester Regiment. After being invalided home, he returned to France with the 1st Battalion of the Dorsetshires, only to be invalided home again in August 1916 to spend a month in hospital recovering from paratyphoid. He seems not to have returned to France on this occasion and was more fortunate than a number of his pupils, who had died in action.

After the war he remained for many years a schoolmaster. In 1939 he was turning out for Somerset Stragglers against King's, Bruton, still evidently a competent club cricketer. In an exciting match, with the school chasing a score of 178, he was handed the ball for the final over, with King's looking set for victory. He took four wickets in five balls and the match ended in a tie. In the innings as a whole he had taken 6 for 24. His only game for Somerset back in 1913 had been less impressive. Not asked to bowl, he scored 13 runs in total in his two innings.

Peter Vasey died in Crediton on 11 September 1952. He was sixty-nine and was never married. It is safe to assume that he had spent many more hours in his retirement mulling over the loss of his star pupils who had played for the county than he ever did over his own three days playing for Somerset.

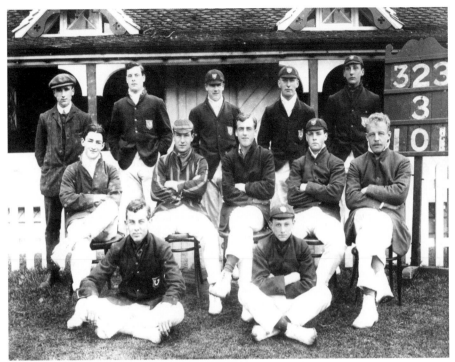

In a strong King's Bruton side of 1909, Somerset players Vasey, Hippisley and Sutton are seated in the centre, while fellow Somerset cricketer, the school coach and groundsman, C. J. 'Tommy' Bowring, stands in his suit on the left

216
Lancelot Edward Seth Ward
26 May 1913 v. Kent, Catford

His name appears sometimes as Launcelot, although he was generally known as Seth Ward. Born on 7 August 1875 in Apsley, Hertfordshire, he was the son of Rev. Percival Seth Ward, vicar at the time of Apsley. Educated at Felsted School in Essex, he opted for a military career, joining the Oxfordshire and Buckinghamshire Light Infantry in December 1897 and serving in India before being seconded to the King's East African Rifles in 1902. At the outbreak of the First World War he was in overall command of the British Forces in East Africa and played a crucial role 'with limited materials [and] aided by a slice of luck' in keeping the German forces at bay until reinforcements arrived in the shape of the 29th Punjabis, led by Colonel J. M. Stewart.

After returning home he served on the Western front. By now a lieutenant colonel, he was promoted to the rank of temporary brigadier general. Twice he was wounded and on six occasions he was mentioned in despatches. On 1 January 1918 he was awarded the bar to add to his DSO, a rare accolade granted directly by King George V. He has left his personal recollections of the war with the Imperial War Museum. In his papers he details the hurdles overcome in wresting East Africa from the Germans at the start of the conflict and how this was followed by a transfer to England in 1915 to train new recruits for deployment in France. He also outlines the preparation for various battles including among others the Somme, Ypres and Amiens.

His cricketing exploits were less heroic that his soldiering would prove to be. His school magazine, *The Felstedian*, gives us some idea of his abilities. As a footballer he was described as a fine forward with plenty of pace but slow in 'taking and making a pass'. As for his cricket, his performances were mediocre. A report describes him as 'a left-hand bat with splendid driving power on the off, but uncertain, owing to his extreme weakness on the leg-side'. (He is erroneously described as a right-handed batsman in later sources.) His credentials as a Somerset man are unclear. Fellow officer Elliot Tillard is likely to have effected an introduction and Seth Ward had also appeared for Free Foresters alongside a number of Somerset players. His one Championship game for Somerset yielded a 0 and a 3. Two further games, one against Cambridge University and another against Oxford in 1920, were barely more successful. He averaged 3.60 with the bat. His appearances for the MCC and All-India were more fruitful though certainly not stellar. After retiring from active service, he served between 1924 and 1929 as aide de camp to Sir Charles Bowring, Governor of Nyasaland (now Malawi), a man entirely unrelated to C. J. Bowring, who made his debut for Somerset a month after Ward.

Planning for life beyond the military, Lt Colonel Seth Ward CMG DSO had purchased a tea plantation in Nyasaland but he died in Lambeth on 27 August 1929 at the age of fifty-four after a lengthy illness, his dream snatched from him before he embarked on his new venture. An obituary in *The Times* informs us that he was never married. The newspaper describes him as 'a keen cricketer'. Keen he may have been, but all his achievements of note were in the military sphere. His Somerset career had been as ill-starred as his tea plantation business in Nyasaland.

217
Charles James Bowring
30 June 1913 v. Yorkshire, Bradford

Charles James Bowring

C. J. Bowring is not the man listed for many years in the cricketing archives. Born on 15 July 1887 in Bruton and christened as James Charles, his father was a plumber, Charles Henry Bowring, who became the landlord of the Crown Inn in Bruton but died in 1893 when young James Charles was only five years old. Two years later, his mother, Emma, was married to Thomas James, a carpenter from Bruton, a widower with two young children of his own, and young J. C. thereafter adopted the name 'Charles James', retaining his original surname. In 1902 he left school to become the assistant groundsman at King's School, Bruton. The head groundsman was Harry Smart, who was married to Bowring's older sister the following year. After eleven years in the role, Harry and his wife left for his native Nottinghamshire, where he found employment as a miner.

C. J. Bowring – known as 'Tommy', he was the coach and groundsman at King's School, Bruton

Having been sent off for a year in 1907 to further his education as a groundsman and coach, Charles became the cricket pro and coach at King's School, Bruton. A popular figure, he was known to everyone as 'Tommy'. Chosen to represent Somerset as a batsman, Tommy Bowring only managed an average of 6.00 in seven innings. His bowling figures were rather more impressive with 3 wickets at 8.66 apiece. His best performance came against Kent. Randall Johnson, standing in as captain, had given Bowring his chance. With nothing at stake, he handed the ball to the professional who was struggling to make his mark. Tommy Bowring didn't disappoint, with a return of 3 for 24 in a little over five overs, while Kent were hitting out before declaring. The *Wells Journal* felt moved to explain that the anomaly was not a result of the usual Somerset chaos:

> As Bowring, who is the professional at Bruton School, was the sixth bowler tried
> against Kent on Friday, and then captured three wickets for 24 runs, the pavilion gossips
> – some of them, at any rate – were wondering why he was not tried earlier, but he was

included in the Somerset side for his batting, and when he was given a turn with the ball the Kent men were "having a go". Hence his success. Bridges in this innings could only get one wicket for 63, whereas in Kent's first knock he claimed six for 44. He was suffering from a sore heel. Hence his failure.

In 1915, Tommy was married to Maud (née Cole), a domestic servant who worked in neighbouring Castle Cary. He was employed by King's School throughout his working life, remaining their groundsman until his retirement in May 1958. Still living in Bruton, he died less than a year later on 16 January 1959 at Summerlands Hospital, Yeovil at the age of seventy-one.

218
Leslie Phillips Marshall
30 June 1913 v. Yorkshire, Bradford

Writing about Leslie Marshall in the *Taunton Courier*, H. J. Channon informs us that:

He broke all kinds of records at school, won the Public Schools hurdles in 1912 and 1913, but though he went up to Cambridge, a wound in the leg received during the war prevented him from winning the "blues" which he would probably have gained otherwise.

Born in Madras on 25 January 1894, Leslie was sent as a young boy to Taunton School, where he flourished both academically and at sports, captaining the football and cricket teams. As a young boy, he and a friend had played single-wicket together utilising every spare moment of leisure time, using a flagpole as a wicket and keeping a record of every run. His dedication yielded results. He was a regular scorer of centuries for Taunton in club cricket and on one occasion made 213 for them. Another article in the *Taunton Courier* gives us an insight into his technique:

The Dr lets few chances of scoring go begging on the leg side. His grip of the bat is interesting. The left wrist is held with the back of the hand facing the batsman and he finds it very effective.

First selected by Somerset at the age of nineteen in 1913, he was obliged to delay completion of his degree owing to the war, but graduated from Cambridge and qualified as a medic. He made eleven appearances for Somerset over an eighteen-year period, his last game – against the New

Leslie Marshall – a fine club cricketer and a much-loved G.P.

Zealand tourists – proving something of a swansong, with Leslie executing cover drives that 'were a treat to watch' and registering his highest first-class scores of 29 and 37 while 'batting in his beautiful style', albeit a style that had yielded an average of only 8.52. He also bowled four overs in his county career, taking one wicket at a cost of sixteen runs.

He was married in 1931 to Catherine Mary (née Hext), also a qualified doctor. They lived for a while on Staplegrove Road, Taunton, before moving to Blagdon Hill, where they resided for the remainder of their lives. Alongside his work as a GP, Leslie found time to be a leading light in the Rotary Club and was for a while president of the Taunton School Old Boys' Association, officiating at a number of functions. Catherine was no less energetic, overseeing the local branch of the Association for Mental Welfare and acting as a medical officer for the Red Cross.

Dr Leslie Marshall had arrived in Taunton as a bewildered little boy, but had succumbed to the town's welcoming embrace (as so many other Somerset cricketers have done) and made it his home. He died there at the age of eighty-four on 28 February 1978, a much-loved former GP who had given an enormous amount back to the place he loved, and the last surviving player to have represented Somerset before the First World War. His wife, Catherine, another of the town's adoptees, died three years later.

A photograph of 1912 shows the Marshall brothers, Leslie and Alan, as members of the Taunton School football team, with Leslie (the captain), holding the ball and Alan beside him, clasping his hands together: also in the team (player standing furthest right) is L. H. Key, who would play for Somerset after the war

219
Hubert Frederic Garrett
28 July 1913 v. Northamptonshire, Bath

Hubert. F. Garrett.

Hubert Garrett was born in Malvern, Melbourne, Australia, on 13 November 1894. He was the son of Edward Thomas, who had emigrated from Ipswich, and Norah (née Hunter-Brown). The date of birth is nine years later than has for many years been held to be true, adding to the poignancy of what followed. He had played for two years in the Melbourne Grammar School XI, starring both as a batsman and a leg-break bowler. An accomplished athlete and academically gifted, he came over to England to study at Queens' College, Cambridge, and although he failed to gain his blue, he returned some excellent bowling figures for H. D. G. Leveson-Gower's XI in June 1913. There was little to connect him with Somerset, beyond his friendship with Somerset cricketer Bruce Hylton Stewart. Hubert was staying in Bath in July 1913 and it is likely that he was the guest of the Hylton Stewarts. Perhaps Somerset were confident that with the blessing of an influential figure such as Leveson-Gower no questions would be asked over the matter of registration. Here is how the *Bath Chronicle* outlines the eighteen-year-old Hubert's brief adventure with the county:

Hubert Garrett – a promising youngster, his end was sudden and brutal

> He came into the side with a reputation as a "googly" bowler but did not do remarkably well in that role in that he bowled 140 overs, his 14 wickets costing 36.28 runs apiece. Mr Garrett was at Cambridge with Mr B. D. Hylton-Stewart {sic} but did not get his blue.

There were further rumours – false, as we now know, though they persisted for many years – that his father was Tom Garrett, the noted former Australian all-rounder who had played in Australia's first ever test match in 1877.

Hubert's connection with Somerset began and ended in 1913 and had therefore been severed before he volunteered for the war effort with the 9th Battalion of the East Yorkshire Regiment and was quickly promoted to rank of lieutenant, arriving in Gallipoli on 31 May 1915. Three days later he was attached to the 1st Battalion of the Royal Dublin Fusiliers and his platoon was immediately sent to the forward trenches. One wonders what the battle-hardened Irishmen made of the fresh-faced twenty-year-old leading them. He was killed the very next day, on 4 June 1915, in the third Battle of Krithia, near Achi Baba, although he was not immediately confirmed as dead and his remains were never recovered. Ordered to take possession of what was believed to be a deserted trench, Hubert led his men over the parapet, whereupon 'three machine guns opened fire from the supposedly unoccupied trench with murderous effect'. An eye-witness account by Captain R. A. Gordon Cane describes how 'our men were simply mown down', adding that Hubert was one of three platoon commanders who had not returned but could not be proven to be dead. The letter adds that Garrett's 'gallantry was remarked upon by several eye-witnesses'. Hubert had endured a short and violent war in which he had been doomed quite literally from the moment he put his head above the parapet. Another life – that of a talented and hopelessly optimistic man, barely more than a boy – snuffed out. The absence of absolute proof that Hubert had died in the carnage led to years of anguish for his father, Edward, who was still writing to the War Office as late as 1918, seeking confirmation as to whether or not Hubert had been found.

Somerset XI on 19 May 1913 at Bath.
STANDING: H. E. Hippisley, J. C. White, F. P. Hardy, G. S. McAulay (Scorer), E. Robson, H. Chidgey, J. Bridges
SEATED: L. C. Braund, J. Daniell, E. S. M. Poyntz, P. W. Vasey, M. P. Bajana

1914

" ... it is once more difficult to find cause for gratification over anything done by Somerset."

Wisden

Championship Position: 15 of 16

There was much to look forward to at the start of the season. In an early example of global branding, a Somerset Society was set up in Kuala Lumpur. The members sent £24 to boost the county's coffers. There were also to be three festival weeks: Bath, Weston-super-Mare and Taunton. In the case of Taunton, the August fixtures would be supported by a number of fund-raising events which it was hoped would create a carnival atmosphere. While lauding the Weston experiment, the *Yorkshire Post* bemoaned the fact that the wicket was unfit for county cricket, although Alonso Drake, who took 10 Somerset wickets in an innings, was probably not complaining. Nor were the Somerset committee, given that nearly 200 members had enrolled from the Weston area. It was a disappointment that the mood of optimism was not matched by improved performances on the pitch. Any vestiges of sunny positivity were of course extinguished by the declaration of war with Germany. Len Braund was again the leading run-maker and Jack White enjoyed another fine season with the ball, well supported by the indefatigable Ernie Robson.

Among the debutants were the Rippons, identical twins who between them would contribute useful runs, much confusion and plenty of folklore.

220
Albert Dudley Eric Rippon
9 May 1914 v. Surrey, Kennington Oval

Enter the Rippons. Dudley's lower parting is often the best way of distinguishing the identical twins. As at their birth, Dudley preceded Sydney into the world of county cricket.

They were born in Bayswater on 29 April 1892 and moved to Radstock at a young age, attending King's College, Taunton. They were already demonstrating their prowess as cricketers as schoolboys, Dudley at the time a wicket-keeper batsman and Sydney a batsman.

H. J. Channon gives us a first-hand account of having been struck by them as fourteen-year-olds:

> *I first saw the brothers Rippon open the innings for King's College ... Two small boys, twins, aged 14 years, Dudley Rippon (major) and Sydney Rippon (minor) came out to give King's a good start ... When they were in the scoring was very slow, but their solid defence wore down the bowling. They had a complete understanding in running between the wickets.*

On leaving school they lived with their guardian, Margaret Ellis, in Bath. Dudley tried his luck as a clerk for a gun manufacturer, but before long opted for a career in journalism, first with the *Bath & Wilts Chronicle* and later with the *Daily Chronicle* and *Illustrated Sporting & Dramatic News*. He quickly made a name for himself as a Bath crick-eter. For a while, Sydney played his cricket separately at Knowle, but once they were both together at Somerset,

Dudley Rippon – a dependable batsman whose confidence deserted him after his experiences in the First World War

confusion was rife. They often took to wearing either a tie or a belt to distinguish between them, although they were quite prepared to partake in practical jokes to confuse scorers, umpires and opposition. In his first season, Dudley twice carried his bat, including a superb knock of 105 not out against Sussex at Bath. Later, against Yorkshire, he top scored in both innings and took five wickets, though Somerset still lost by an innings in less than two days. It had been an impressive first season for the young amateur. But then the war intervened.

Dudley joined the Horse Transport section of the Army Service Corps but was very badly wounded at Gallipoli. He was never the same man again and was given an honourable discharge with a Silver War Badge and the rank of lieutenant. The war had been hard enough, anyway, but being separated from his twin for the first time in their lives made matters doubly traumatic, even though they kept in touch with regular letters to one another.

He was married in1918 to Agnes Mary (née Webb) in Kensington and he took up county cricket again, his highpoint being a score of 134 against Essex. But then, during the match against Sussex in 1920, he went into meltdown. Having been run out for a duck in the first innings after a rare misunderstanding with Sydney, he was unable to face the prospect of batting in the second innings and had to be taken to a local hospital, still clearly suffering from the delayed effects of his war experiences. Perhaps it is a coincidence or perhaps a response to circumstances, but twin brother Sydney knuckled down and scored a century in the first innings and then carried his bat for 19 runs in the second innings while his teammates crumbled around him. Dudley had completely lost his appetite for county cricket and never appeared again, leaving his brother to fly the family flag while he, Dudley, focussed on his life as a journalist. He died in Wallingford on 16 April 1963, aged seventy, the first twin to arrive by a matter of minutes and the first – by a matter of three years less three days – to depart.

221
Philip Palmer Hope
9 May 1914 v. Surrey, Kennington Oval

The son of a bank manager, he was born on 10 February 1889 in Hartlepool and educated at Sherborne School. His parents had settled in the West Country. Philip emigrated to Canada in 1907with the intention of becoming a rancher but he returned to England in 1910, shortly before his father's death. He remained in the area and became involved in the Bath sporting scene, appointed captain of the Bath rugby team in 1913. He was also selected to play rugby for Somerset. Given the qualities required for such a role, it should perhaps come as no surprise that he seems to have been fearless to the point of recklessness. The first concrete evidence of this comes in a court case of

1914 when he killed a pedestrian, fifty-nine-year-old Jeremiah Lambern, while apparently speeding on his motorcycle. Although his story differed from that of the witnesses, he was absolved of any blame by the judge. His elevation to the Somerset cricket team soon followed and, used primarily as a middle-order batsman, he made useful contributions between 1914 and 1925, including a highest score of 77 against Essex in 1921.

During the war, his fearlessness continued to be manifest, while he worked as a dispatch rider. In a letter, he informs a friend:

> *I'm at present living in a 'dug out' and at the approach of a shell we all dive for our burrows like rabbits ... I have just got another bike, a shell and horse between them knocking the {previous} bike to blazes. Luckily I was not on it at the time.*

In 1915, in another narrow escape, Philip was driving a motor car when a German shell crashed through the bonnet, also removing his passenger's arm and knocking him unconscious. He was taken to a nearby cellar until he regained consciousness. He made a full recovery and after the war he carried on where he had left off, captaining Bath RFC and turning out for Somerset at cricket.

P. P. Hope – the fearless captain of Bath RFC

In 1921, he was married to Sophie Millicent (née Harker). The *Bath Chronicle* reports a minor tragedy at the time in the Hope household, informing us that Philip was involved in a crash and that his dog, Caesar, was killed while riding in his master's sidecar. Philip Hope was unhurt. Another narrow escape for the fearless Mr Hope, while carnage beset those around him. In 1922, he and Sophie left to start a new life in Canada but they would return after three years. Perhaps Sophie was too frail for the hard life of managing a ranch, given that she died of a stroke in May 1929 at their home in York Terrace, Clifton. Later the same year he was married again, to Katherine Edna (née Armstrong). The couple lived in Torquay, with Philip working as a rep for White House Distillers. He spent much of his time playing cricket for Bovey Tracy or amusing himself on the golf course and sailing around Brixham and Torquay. Their marriage ended in divorce with both parties remarrying. Philip's third wife was Olive Marion (née Norton). He lived for the remainder of his life in Bristol and died in the city on 19 May 1962 at the age of seventy-three.

222
Arthur Ernest Sydney Rippon
21 May 1914 v. Surrey, Bath

Sydney Rippon – an identical twin 'of sensitive, highly-strung and eccentric disposition'

The Rippon twins began their careers as Somerset players at more or less the same time, but it was Sydney – a fortnight later to the party – who would enjoy much greater longevity as a cricketer. Born on 29 April 1892, they are characterised by Peter Roebuck as 'identical twins of sensitive, highly-strung and eccentric disposition'. Whereas such eccentricity led to Dudley's abrupt exit from county cricket, Sydney was able for a longer period to channel his oddities into eking out every last drop of his talent. Raymond Robertson-Glasgow says of Sydney that 'he loved to make an affair of the act of batting; he did much bat-twirling in the Jack Hobbs manner, and resorted to Swedish exercises between the overs, and, to the disgust of the bowler, even between balls'. The Somerset supporters would fondly cheer his unusual antics. Both brothers showed great powers of concentration and a dogged determination not to yield their wicket lightly, only rarely cutting loose. Sydney proved a reliable opening batsman and an occasional match-winner, most notably against Glamorgan in 1922 when he led an unexpected victory charge, scoring 102 not out. His six centuries were evenly spread and his career average of 21.77 tells a tale of a workmanlike batsman rather than one touched by genius.

Separated from his twin during the war and serving as a second lieutenant in the Royal Fusiliers, he was wounded at the Somme and then contacted meningitis. Like Dudley, he was honourably discharged with a Silver War Badge in 1917.

Perhaps it is appropriate that a man who quietly went about accumulating his runs with resolute attention to detail should have spent his working life as a tax inspector for HMRC, but it must be hoped that some of his eccentricities never spilled over into the workplace. Of particular note were his sudden flashes of indignation, if he ever felt he was being criticised or mocked. Guy Earle, the most generously muscled among the Somerset amateurs, would be called on to intervene, sitting on Sydney if necessary until the storm had passed. On one occasion, Sydney was pressed into action by Somerset while on sick leave from the Civil Service, adopting the assumed name of 'S. Trimnell' (his grandmother's name) in order to hide his identity. The truth will out, of course. The local reporters referred obliquely to the fact: how could they not, when he had the 'misfortune' to draw attention to himself with noteworthy contributions of 92 and 58 not out. His immediate boss was forgiving.

The Rippon Twins: Dudley (l) and Sydney (r)

Somerset called on his services as late as 1937. He was bespectacled by then and had lost some of his prowess but he remained as eccentric as ever. His son, Geoffrey Rippon, took pride in watching his father and no doubt the father was proud of the son as Geoffrey rose through the political ranks and played his part in the UK's entry into the Common Market. After his retirement, Sydney would regularly entertain Somerset players at the Civil Service Club when the team played in London.

He died in Surbiton on 13 April 1966 at the age of seventy-three.

223
Edgar Cedric Ball
11 June 1914 v. Hampshire, Bath

Cedric Ball was a fine figure of a young man, standing 6 feet 3 inches tall and with a powerful, athletic physique. He was born in Kew on 11 Jan 1892, although his parents were both Bristolians. Edgar's father, Edward William, had played three times for Gloucestershire but with no great distinction. Three innings had yielded three ducks. The father's work as a land surveyor and auctioneer had taken the family to Surrey but they were living in Clifton by the time Cedric was eleven. He attended Clifton College, where he stayed until he was sixteen. At school he proved an excellent all-round sportsman and a successful left-arm opening bowler. When he was selected first for Devon and subsequently for Somerset, he was used as an opening batsman, not as a bowler. He was a keen rugby player – representing the successful Clifton XV – and

one explanation for the change of emphasis would be the possibility of an injury that limited his bowling: his army records certainly refer to scarring on his left forearm. His three first-class matches and six innings for Somerset yielded an average of 5.83.

He emigrated as a young man to Regina, in Saskatchewan, Canada. Here he worked in a clerical capacity for a farming family (who hailed from Scotland) until he enlisted with the Canadian Expeditionary Force which comprised volunteers for the war effort. He arrived back in Europe at the beginning of April 1918, serving in France and then being discharged in April 1919. He had endured a short but very active war. Cedric stayed for two years in Bristol, residing with his widowed mother and occupying some of his time by playing rugby for Clifton. Then in 1921 he was off back to Saskatchewan where he found employment as a clerk while playing the occasional game of cricket against touring sides, most notably an Australian team that included Bradman.

E. C. Ball – an imposing presence on the rugby field, he emigrated to Canada

He was married to Violet Mayo (née Magee) and the couple remained in Canada. For the final eighteen years of his working life he was employed in a clerical capacity by the Federal Government. He was living in Vancouver and already a widower by the time of his death on 15 May 1969 at the age of seventy-seven. His son was there to witness Cedric's losing fight with cancer that had spread from the lungs to the brain and was coupled with acute bronchopneumonia.

224
Arthur Herbert Bezer
11 June 1914 v. Hampshire, Bath

Arthur Herbert Bezer

Arthur Bezer was born in Bath on 20 October 1875. He spent the whole of his life based in the city and became something of a local celebrity. Drafted into the Somerset side as an emergency measure in their fixture against Hampshire at the Bath Recreation

Ground, he managed scores of 0 and 1 and bowled two overs without taking a wicket. His one appearance is but a footnote in a life of service to cricket. His first employment was as a cabinetmaker's apprentice, working for the widely renowned firm of Messrs. Norris & Co, but he was advised to seek the open-air life 'for health reasons'. He applied for the job of professional groundsman at Bath in 1893 when he was eighteen and would stay with them for forty-six years. He was a useful all-rounder at club level, regularly picking up wickets as a first-change bowler and capable of big scores, with some centuries to his name. But it was for his skills as a groundsman that he would become famed. The challenge for Arthur was twofold. Firstly, he had to live with the fact that Bath were at times fielding a total of five sides, all requiring pitches to be prepared. Secondly, as evidenced by court cases, he had to cope with vandalism. In one case, 'five lads' were brought before Bath Juvenile Court in November 1935 for having smashed seats and inflicted damage on the pitch. Vandalism is nothing new.

Married in 1904 to Helen (née Moore), Arthur continued in the role of groundsman long after he had given up playing the game and is consistently described as a much-loved figure. By the early 1920s, benefit matches were being held to supplement his income. This became a regular event. The *Bath Chronicle* states in 1929 that:

Arthur Bezer – a popular figure who was Bath CC's groundsman for many years

> *"Bezer's Benefit" at North Parade is one of those hardy annuals which the public never tire of supporting. The Bath Cricket Club Groundsman … is a popular figure … and visiting sides, no matter how important, declare without hesitation they have never seen a ground kept better or wickets more consistently good.*

Tragedy struck in Bath on 11 July 1944. At the age of sixty-eight, Arthur arrived home at 9.45 pm carrying 'a raincoat, umbrella and four library books' but tripped on his raincoat at the top of a flight of fifteen stone steps. His wife found him unconscious at the bottom of the stairs. He was taken immediately to hospital but died of a brain haemorrhage. His obituary concludes:

> *He had a genius for preparing wickets. He was called in by clubs all over the West for his advice. As a player he was a very good all-rounder – a useful change bowler and a determined bat.*

A memorial fund was set up within a month of his death and quickly reached the then substantial sum of over £250. Until her own death in 1957, Helen Bezer continued to be helped out with an annual benefit match in her late husband's honour. His experience of county cricket had been brief but Arthur Bezer had been a celebrity in his own back yard.

225
Alan George Marshall
6 July 1914 v. Sussex, Hove

Alan Marshall – who became inextricably linked with his beloved Taunton School

Alan was one of two brothers who qualified for Somerset through residence as pupils at Taunton School. The 1901 census tells us that at the age of five he was the youngest boarder at the school, having been born in India on 17 April 1895. The presence of his seven-year-old brother, Leslie, must have offered some comfort to him. Taunton School took their cricket very seriously, having employed coaches such as ex-Somerset bowler Teddy Tyler and the former Sussex all-rounder, Jesse Hide, in order to boost performance. The Marshall brothers were model pupils, bright and talented at sport. Alan is reported as having been an excellent schoolboy cricketer, playing for the First XI for five years, scoring 689 runs at an average of 53.00 and taking 47 wickets at 14.30 apiece in 1914. Twice in his schoolboy career – in 1910 and 1911 – he took all ten wickets in an innings, on both occasions against local rivals Queen's College, who must have been glad to see the back of him.

He joined the Royal Navy in 1915 but was on active service only for a short while, spending most of the First World War in administrative roles. After the war he went up to Sydney Sussex College, Cambridge, graduating in 1921 and returning to his old school as a teacher of natural sciences (later chemistry) with additional responsibility for games. The teaching of economics was added at a later stage. His outstanding exploits as a schoolboy cricketer were never repeated at the more demanding level of Championship cricket. A willing servant of the club, he would represent Somerset in forty-five first-class matches between 1914 and 1931, achieving a top score of 37. His bowling figures read as ten wickets at 33.30 runs apiece. A club cricketer who was readily available, one of his great virtues was adaptability. During the 1929 and 1930 seasons when Somerset were struggling in the absence through illness of their wicketkeeper, Wally Luckes, Alan Marshall and Frank Lee shared wicket-keeping duties, as testified by Marshall's nine stumpings.

Alan spent his final ten years as deputy headmaster (then termed second master) of Taunton School. A tribute to him in the school magazine after his retirement speaks warmly of his life of service, noting also that he had been president of the Old Boys' Association for three years (a role also undertaken by his brother, Leslie). The tribute informs us that:

> *It was as far back as 1900 that two small boys came to Taunton, both of them destined to become leaders in their school days, and after to serve the School, one as Medical Officer, and the other on the School Staff ... Under {Alan's} coaching the games took on a new life and the prestige of Taunton on the rugby ground and on the cricket field leaped ahead and has never looked back ... {He was} kindly, just, utterly straightforward and intolerant of anything shady, but beloved and respected by all who came in contact with him.*

By the time of his death at the age of seventy-eight on 14 May 1973, he had retired to the village of Pettistree, near the Suffolk coast. He was never married. Instead, he was wedded from the age of five to Taunton School and to a life in sport.

Alan Marshall (r) with his brother, fellow Somerset cricketer, Leslie (standing left)

226
Frederick Cecil Banes Walker
9 July 1914 v. Kent, Gravesend

His name was not double-barrelled as is often incorrectly assumed. As was the case for so many young men of his generation, Cecil Banes Walker is defined by the photograph of him in military uniform. But for the war, he would have followed his father

Cecil Banes Walker – one of fourteen Somerset cricketers who died in the First World War

into the business world. He was born in North Petherton on 19 June 1888. His father, Harry, had moved from the Lincolnshire town of Alford, not far from Skegness. Having decamped to the South West, Harry became managing director of the brewers and pub owners *Starkey, Knight and Ford.* Something of an eccentric, Harry Banes Walker apparently used often to ride to work from North Petherton to Bridgwater on his horse and adopted a relaxed style of management, as likely to be reading *Sporting Life* and planning his next trip to the races as directing proceedings.

Cecil worked for a while at the Ashton Gate (Baynton's) Brewery but his career would prove short-lived, as would his involvement in the war. He enlisted as a private with the 4th Battalion of the Gloucestershire Regiment on 2 September 1914, the day after war was declared, suggesting a rare enthusiasm for the cause. Subsequently commissioned as a machine-gun officer in the 3rd Battalion of the Devonshire Regiment, he had been serving in France for two months when he was killed on 9 May 1915 during the futile attempt to oust the Germans from their trenches at Aubers Ridge, Fleurbaix. 10,000 British and Indian soldiers were killed, wounded or taken prisoner. A letter from the War Office confirms that he was buried at the appropriately named La Trouble, two miles south of Fleurbaix. He was only twenty-six years old.

The *Bridgwater Mercury* informs us that Cecil was educated 'at Mr Coplestone's School in Exmouth and afterwards at Tonbridge' and that he was 'an enthusiastic cricketer'. He played his club cricket for Bridgwater and Long Ashton, appearing for Somerset five times during the 1914 season. *Wisden* describes his batting style as 'aggressive' and his approach appeared to succeed against Hampshire when he scored 40 runs. His average over ten innings was 19.11, so that any pyrotechnics at the crease must generally have been brief. A capable hockey player, he represented Gloucestershire at the sport. In a life cut short by the war, these remain his crowning achievements. He was not forgotten by his former colleagues. A war memorial in honour of former Clifton rugby players was erected in 1931 and subsequently moved to the entrance of Cribbs Causeway shopping park. It includes the name of Cecil Banes Walker.

227
Walter Frank Quantock Shuldham
27 July 1914 v. Sussex, Hove

Walter Shuldam was born on 17 June 1892 at Stoke House, in Stoke-sub-Hamdon, where his family managed a fruit farm, notable for a fine crop of apples. He attended Marlborough College and although he played cricket for the school, enjoying some fine moments, including a quick-fire 151 against an I Zingari XI, it was as an athlete that he shone most brightly.

Here is what a local report says, in April 1911:

The most outstanding feature of Marlborough College Sports ... was the performance of W. F. Q. Shuldham, who won practically all the events open to the whole school, those secured being the 100 yards and 200 yards, the quarter- and half-miles, the long jump, the hurdles, and the steeplechase.

W. F. Q. Shuldham – a talented athlete who performed outstandingly at Marlborough College

This must have been an exhausting though exhilarating couple of days for the talented eighteen-year-old and serves as a reminder that even players with a modest record of success at county level cannot be dismissed lightly. A right-handed batsman, Walter Shuldham's Championship career straddled the First World War, with only six appearances over a ten-year period. His eighty-one runs in nine innings yielded an average of 9.00. His swansong in first-class cricket was a couple of games against the MCC, who were touring India and Ceylon (Sri Lanka) in 1926. He fared only marginally better in these two outings.

Given that the family fruit farm continued to thrive, he clearly enjoyed more success in that domain than he did as a cricketer, although his career as a professional soldier came first. He was commissioned into the West Somerset Yeomanry as a second lieutenant in 1914 and by the end of the war was an acting captain in the Indian Army.

He was married in 1920 to Doris Elizabeth (née Haggard). In 1930 he was seconded to assist the Maharaja of Jaipur in the administration of matters of state. He was promoted to the rank of major on 19 May 1933. On retiring from the army, Major Shuldham took the reins at the family fruit farm and played his part in the local political scene, acting as magistrate and taking up the one-year ceremonial post of High Sherriff of Somerset in 1954.

He died at the age of seventy-eight on 7 February 1971 in Stoke-sub-Hamdon. The business he managed continues to thrive as an organic soft fruit farm, still run by the Shuldham family.

W. F. Q. Shuldham, the 227th and final first-class Somerset debutant before the onset of the First World War.

Afterword

Somerset cricket had more or less stood still since they had gained first-class status in 1882, thirty-two years earlier. And yet they were still standing. The committee continued to espouse the values of amateurism. The teams had comprised many larger-than-life characters and on occasions a brilliant cricketer had been unearthed. Any triumphs had been infrequent and unexpected. Slow scoring was anathema to many of the players, with success measured more in sixes struck than victories gained. The longsuffering supporters had been entertained and exasperated in equal measure. But few if any of them would let go of a faint hope – some would say an entirely unrealistic hope – that one day they might, by some miracle or other, win the County Championship.

For four years there was something more important than cricket to occupy everyone. Fourteen Somerset cricketers would lose their lives in the First World War. As *Wisden* would note in 1918, 'the immediate outlook is not very hopeful, as it may be a hard matter to get together a team of adequate strength'. They had been saying something similar before the war. In the event Somerset would surprise everyone with a moderately successful season in 1919.

Index of Somerset Cricketers 1882-1914

Order of debut appearance shown in brackets.
Page reference for each player's biography is also given.

Forman, H. (201) 334

Fothergill, A. J. (5) 26

Fowler, G. (60) 107

Fowler, W. H. (1) 20

Fox, H. (8) 30

Fox, H. F. (6) 27

Freeman, A. E. B. (171) 281

Gamlin, H.T. (99) 166

Garrett, H. F. (219) 364

Gay, L. H. (84) 143

Gibbs, J. A. (71) 124

Gill, G. C. (108) 181

Goodland, E. S. (186) 308

Grant, E. (122) 204

Greenway, C. E. (22) 49

Gregg, T. (33) 65

Greswell, E. A. (155) 256

Greswell, W. T. (188) 311

Griffin, H. (117) 194

Hale, W. H. (76) 132

Hall, H. E. (43) 82

Hall, H. G. H. (10) 32

Hancock, R. E. (183) 301

Hancock, W. I. (77) 133

Harcombe, J. D. (168) 276

Hardy, F. P. (138) 231

Hardy, N. (213) 353

Hedley, W. C. (80) 137

Hellard, J. A. (180) 296

Herbert, M. R. H. M. (149) 248

Hewett, H. T. (47) 86

Hickley, C. S. (115) 191

Hildyard, L. D'A. (25) 53

Hill, E. T. (113) 189

Hill, F. J. (17) 42

Hill, R. E. (16) 41

Hill, V. T. (65) 114

Hippisley, H. E. (197) 326

Hodgkinson, G. W. (156) 259

Hook, A. J. (109) 182

Hope, P. P. (221) 368

Hotham, F. W. (24) 52

House, B. H. (211) 350

Hulls, C. H. (54) 97

Humphries, H. H. (174) 288

Hunt, G. R. (118) 195

Hylton Stewart, B. D. (212) 351

Hyman, W. (127) 212

Ingram, P. R. See Ingram, R. E. T.

Ingram, R. E. T. (199) 331

Jennings, F. L. B. (98) 164

Jewell, W. J. (38) 74

Johnson, P. R. (133) 223

Joy, F. D. H. (190) 316

Jupp, G. W. (135) 226

Kettlewell, H. W. (123) 205

Leat, E. J. (189) 313

Lee, F. M. (141) 236

Leeston-Smith, F. A. (39) 75

Lewis, A. E. (119) 198

Lillington, G. G. (37) 71

Lock, E. J. (70) 123

Lyall, C. R. (204) 339

MacBryan, J. C. W. (208) 345

Macdonald, H. L. S. (105) 175

STEVE ELLIS

Hillsborough

A 21-YEAR PHOTOGRAPHIC HISTORY

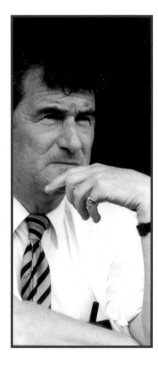

Captions by Keith Farnsworth

The **Hallamshire** Press 1997

All Photographs by Steve Ellis
Photographs © 1997 Steve Ellis and Sheffield Newspapers Ltd
Text © 1997 The Hallamshire Press

Published by The Hallamshire Press
The Hallamshire Press is an imprint of
Interleaf Productions Limited
Broom Hall
Sheffield S10 2DR, UK

Typeset and designed by Interleaf Productions Limited
Printed in Singapore

British Library Cataloguing in Publication Data:
   A catalogue record for this book is available from the British Library.

ISBN 1-874718-41-5

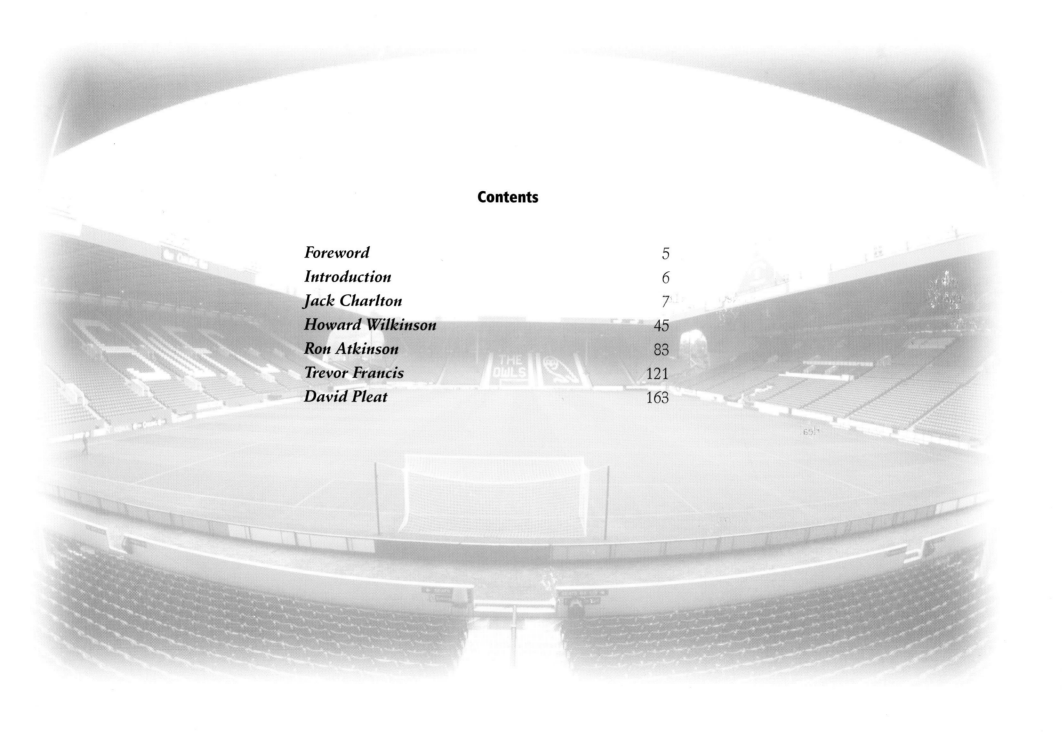

Contents

Foreword

It is often said by art experts that the greatest portraits, films and photographs are those taken by cameramen who are in love with their subjects.

Football has many millions of fans who idolise their heroes—who bring them great joy or great grief, often inside the same minute. There are so many television re-runs of the magnificent goals and intense highlights that often we get blasé about the game and its skill, sweat, anger and tears, and the passion and pain inside the ground.

A photographer that can capture that authentic emotion in a split second is a very gifted person. To be able instantly to sense the atmosphere, the mood, the moment that will recall the feel and smell of the event twenty or thirty years later is a treasured talent.

All of us at Hillsborough have known Steve Ellis as a brilliant 'snapper', as they are called in the trade. For many years we have admired him not just for his work, but as a great colleague who travels with the team far and wide carrying the heavy tools of his trade often under difficult circumstances.

He comes with us to bring to our fans those fantastic split-second events that not only thrill, but also augment our history and heritage. It is possible to look at some of his photographs over and over again and always discover something new. Which is the sign of the great professional Steve is.

Joe Ashton MP
Director, Sheffield Wednesday Football Club
Chairman, Houses of Parliament All-Party Football Committee

Introduction

For Steve Ellis, this superb collection of over 200 pictures is a celebration of his 21 years as Sheffield Wednesday's official photographer. It captures a colourful and eventful phase in the club's history which Steve has witnessed and recorded from a unique standpoint as a respected and trusted 'insider'.

Steve, 42, the son of a Stocksbridge steelworker, has been connected with Sheffield Newspapers since leaving school in 1971. He started as a junior in the photographic department, later spent many years working behind the scenes in the editorial darkroom, and, after commercial and freelance experience, eventually graduated to full-time staff photographer on The Star.

It was through football that he gained his initial professional opportunities in his spare time while still a junior in the early 1970s. The Morning Telegraph's chief photographer Frank Travers started taking him to matches, and by 1976 Steve's progress was such that he was soon invited to cover games for Wednesday's match programme. Steve quickly gained a formal appointment as the club's official photographer, and since then he has not only won coveted awards but widespread recognition among his fellow professionals as an outstanding exponent of his art.

His secret is not only in his ability to take excellent action pictures under pressure in all kinds of conditions, but his knack of being able to exercise his skills without being intrusive…a gift he shares with all the best press photographers.

'When I started taking photographs of Wednesday matches, I was just a fan with a camera, but I soon learned that it was necessary to have certain professional detachment to take the best pictures,' he said. 'Having been a Wednesdayite since I was a small boy, it's a great thrill to have been able to travel far and wide watching them play, but it's been especially fulfilling to be able to capture all the goals, all the players and all the moments that have mattered to the club in the last 21 years. Of course, I couldn't have done it without a lot of help from a lot of people. I shall always be grateful for the lessons that people like Wilf Atkinson and Frank Travers taught me, and, over the years at

Hillsborough, the directors, officials and especially the managers and players have been very helpful and co-operative.'

Steve is married to Karen, and they have three sons: Jamie (8), Ashley (7) and George (18 months).

Keith Farnsworth
October 1997

Steve Ellis

Jack Charlton
1977–83

'Big Jack' was a great character who arrived at Hillsborough one Saturday in October 1977. He soon halted a long and dramatic decline which had seen Wednesday slump from the old First Division to the bottom end of Division Three in just a few painful years.

Charlton inspired a revival that touched a peak with promotion to Division Two in 1980. In 1983 the Owls reached the FA Cup semi-final, but within a couple of months Jack elected to bow from the scene without fulfilling his dream of guiding the club back to the top grade.

Before coming to Sheffield, Charlton had been a famous Leeds centre-half—he had played in 770 games and scored 95 goals while sharing in many great Leeds triumphs, and also collected 35 England caps. He had then become an outstanding manager with Middlesbrough between May 1973 and April 1977. It's now part of football folklore that, starting in 1986, he enjoyed a great run as the most successful national team boss in the history of football in the Republic of Ireland.

Jack Charlton, pictured with his wife, Pat, as they sat together in the North Stand at Hillsborough on 8th October 1977 to watch the managerless Owls beat Chesterfield 1–0 with a Tommy Tynan goal. A few hours after the game, he emerged from boardroom talks with the Wednesday directors to be revealed as the club's new team boss.

One of the wisest decisions 'Big Jack' made when he arrived at Hillsborough was to promote former Sheffield United manager John Harris from chief scout to an initial role as his assistant. Harris had the experience and knowledge that was crucial in several key signings, and his presence enabled Charlton to take time off for some fishing!

A typical Jack Charlton pose on the training pitch. He seems to be telling the lads they've got to show some fight—but then he might be said to be looking to the heavens for inspiration! Wednesday were in such trouble when he arrived that Jack wasn't alone in feeling it might take a miracle to save them.

Jack Charlton, wearing the familiar cloth cap, with his backroom team: (left to right) John Harris, Tony Toms and Maurice Setters. Harris and fitness expert Toms were inherited from the Len Ashurst era, and in 1978 Jack brought in Setters, a former Doncaster Rovers boss, as his senior coach.

This is no ordinary housewife serving tea to the Wednesday players during a training break in the Yorkshire Dales. It is the remarkable Mrs Cissie Charlton, mother of Jack and Bobby and cousin of the legendary Tyneside star of the early post-war era, Jackie Milburn. Son Jack Charlton had bought her a farmhouse where she revelled in the company of footballers. In this picture are Jeff Johnson, coach Ken Knighton and Jimmy Mullen as well as 'Big Jack'.

A view of floodlit Hillsborough taken during Jack Charlton's second season as Wednesday's manager. The lights had been switched on to enable the ground staff to work on the pitch.

Hillsborough has rather changed since the heyday of Jack Charlton, when the Kop was still a standing area and uncovered. The old South Stand has since been the subject of dramatic improvements. Anybody who left in 1980 would barely know the place now!

Rodger Wylde, who scored 66 goals in 193 games for Wednesday, is remembered as one of the club's most flamboyant characters of the 1970s. This picture of him on his knees enjoying the adulation of the fans was taken after he completed a hat-trick in a League Cup-tie against Doncaster Rovers, a few weeks before Jack Charlton arrived at Hillsborough. In February 1980 Charlton sold him to Oldham for £80,000.

Mel Sterland was destined to become a great Wednesday favourite who played over 300 games for the club. He is seen here with Jack Charlton at the start of a career that began when he joined the club from school in June 1978 and reached its first important milestone when he signed professional forms in October 1979.

They don't come any tougher than Mick Pickering, the defender who captained Wednesday in the 1979–80 promotion campaign. The 'wounded hero' in this picture, taken at the end of a duel with Sheffield United, made some 130 appearances for the Owls after arriving from Southampton.

Volunteers helping clear the Hillsborough pitch of snow ahead of the first match with Arsenal in the FA Cup third-round 'marathon' of January 1979.

Joe Ashton—the Member of Parliament who later became a director but in 1979 was just an ordinary Owls fan—was among the leading snow-shifters battling to ensure the Arsenal game could be played. The tie ended with a 1–1 scoreline, and it took five games to settle it.

Brian Hornsby having a crack at the Arsenal goal in the fifth and final match of the FA Cup 'marathon', when the brave Owls finally bowed out of the competition with a 2–0 defeat. Arsenal went on to win the trophy, beating Manchester United at Wembley in May 1979.

Brian Hornsby scoring Wednesday's second equaliser from the penalty spot in the 2–2 draw with Arsenal in the first of the three replays staged at Filbert Street, Leicester, January 1979.

Ray Blackhall scored only one goal in 140 games for Wednesday, and it came at Bristol Rovers in October 1980. This occasion at Hillsborough, when he pounced on a shooting chance, is interesting because of the backcloth showing what the old 'open' Kop end looked like.

Terry Curran, pictured here with Rodger Wylde, was even more flamboyant than his strike partner, and he emerged a big Owls favourite following his £100,000 move from Southampton in March 1979.

Curran in a classic Steve Ellis picture of January 1980 hammering a free-kick through Plymouth Argyle's defensive wall, but failing to beat the goalkeeper. Curran scored 39 goals in 138 games for Wednesday before electing to move to Sheffield United in the summer of 1982.

Most Wednesday fans of the period would agree that Terry Curran was a 'big noise' in the Hillsborough squad. He could also hit the top notes in the recording studio!

Referee Pat Partridge leads the teams out for the Sheffield derby duel of 26th December 1979 at Hillsborough, where there was an 11 am kick-off. Wednesday, captained by Mick Pickering, won the game 4–0 and it passed into Owls' folklore as 'The Boxing Day Massacre'!

Ian Mellor being congratulated by Mark Smith, Terry Curran and Jeff Johnson after giving Wednesday a 1–0 lead against the Blades after 25 minutes.

Terry Curran and Jeff Johnson celebrate after Curran's 63rd-minute header made it 2–0 to Wednesday.

Mark Smith completes the 4–0 defeat of the Blades with a late goal from the penalty spot at the Leppings Lane end.

Andy McCulloch celebrates the 100th League goal of his career in Wednesday's 1–1 draw at Mansfield in March 1980.

McCulloch, who scored 49 goals in 149 games for the Owls, wins an aerial duel against Luton in September 1981.

Occasionally, there are tears in football. This young footballer, holding his head after being caught in the face by the ball during a boys' training session at Middlewood, gets a sympathetic look from Jack Charlton. 'I honestly thought my passing was more accurate than that', sighed the Wednesday manager!

Jack Charlton and Martin Peters, who both played in England's 1966 World Cup-winning team, met up again in Sheffield when Peters joined the Blades, first as a player and later for a brief and traumatic spell as manager. Here Peters makes a point to the Wednesday team boss.

Ian Mellor seals a crucial 2–1 victory for Wednesday in their vital promotion duel with Blackburn at Ewood Park in late April 1980. His superb diving header from Ray Blackhall's cross four minutes from the end of the match meant Wednesday were poised for a return to Division Two.

Jubilant scenes in the home dressing room at Hillsborough after Wednesday had finished the 1979–80 season with a 0–0 draw against Carlisle to confirm their promotion from Division Three.

Meanwhile, on that sunny May afternoon in 1980, there were incredible scenes of jubilation as Wednesday supporters invaded the Hillsborough pitch and hailed their promotion heroes.

You could call it the icing on the cake as twelve-goal Andy McCulloch is joined by John Harris and chairman Bert McGee to savour a model of Hillsborough commemorating Wednesday's 1980 promotion triumph.

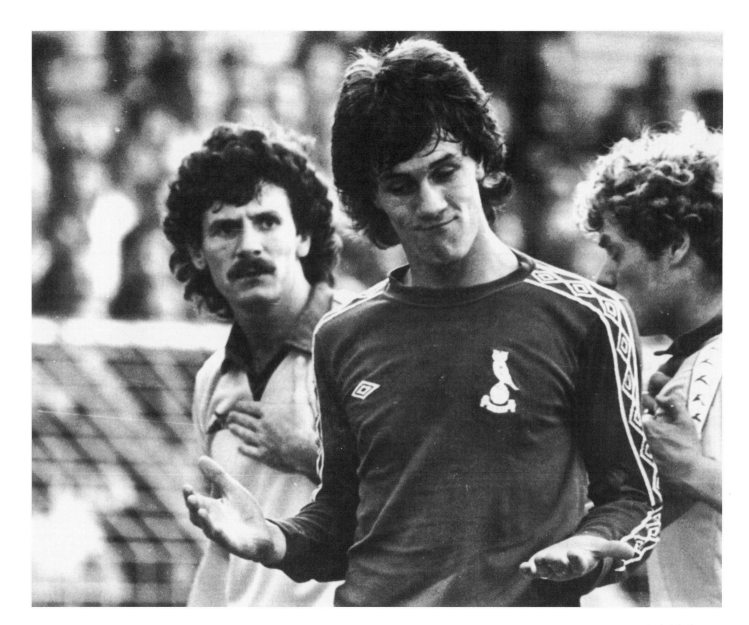

Exactly what was the significance of Oldham striker Simon Stainrod's gesture with his hands as Terry Curran looks on in this picture has probably been long forgotten. An incident involving the pair in the 27th minute of a game at Boundary Park in September 1980 prompted referee George Tyson to send off the Wednesday man— and the decision sparked astonishing crowd scenes.

A section of the crowd in the visitors' end of the Oldham ground poured onto the pitch, and the game was held up for more than half an hour as the police attempted to restore order.

Owls manager Jack Charlton, along with club chairman Bert McGee (not in picture), endeavoured to help the police halt the riot.

Charlton was in despair as he walked away from the Wednesday end of the Oldham ground.

The consequences of the trouble at Boundary Park in September 1980 included a ban on Wednesday having travelling fans at four away games, and (as in this picture) standing areas at Hillsborough were closed for four home matches. Incidentally, in February 1985, Stainrod joined Wednesday for a record £260,000 fee, but he made only fifteen appearances.

A happier event in that
1980–81 season was the arrival
of Yugoslavian Ante Mirocevic
for a record £200,000 fee. He is
seen here enjoying a 'hands-on'
celebration with Peter Shirtliff
after scoring on his Football
League debut in the 2–2 home
draw with Orient on 25th
October 1980.

Wednesday defender Charlie Williamson, who made 67 senior appearance between 1979 and 1985, calls for Tony Toms to use his 'magic sponge' to wipe away the blood after suffering a blow to his face.

A photographer collects a lot of favourite shots over the years, and this through-the-net shot of striker Gary Bannister has a special place in the Steve Ellis scrapbook.

Gary Bannister, seen here scoring in the 2–0 defeat of Leicester in March 1982, claimed 66 goals in 143 outings for the Owls between 1981 and 1984.

Jack Charlton stands on the touchline at Kenilworth Road being restrained by a Luton player as he tries to make a point. This shot serves to highlight just how emotional football can be.

But Jack Charlton always knew how to 'get away from it all'...and here he enjoys a relaxing day in the Derwent Dam at Ladybower. Meanwhile, the sign on his office door at Hillsborough reads simply: 'Gone Fishing'!

Is Mel Sterland telling Kevin Taylor to stop picking his nose, or are they simply plotting something special with a free-kick?

Central defender Mark Smith, seen here in action in a game at Blackburn, was another of the local lads who made good with Sheffield Wednesday. He played over 350 games between April 1977 and May 1987.

Ian Bailey's playing days were prematurely ended by an injury suffered in April 1983 at Bolton, where he is seen in this picture getting treatment from physio Jon Honey. Bailey, an £80,000 signing from Middlesbrough in August 1982, was limited to 45 games for Wednesday, and this injury occurred just a week before the Owls' FA Cup semi-final date with Brighton.

Ante Mirocevic raises his arms
in triumph after claiming
Wednesday's 57th-minute
equaliser in the FA Cup
semi-final with Brighton at
Highbury in April 1983.
Sadly, twenty minutes later,
the Seagulls regained the lead
and went on to dash
Wednesday's Wembley dreams
with a 2–1 victory.

Hail the conquering Owls! Wednesday fans were never slow to salute the achievements of Jack Charlton, who might not have taken Wednesday all the way back to the top grade but certainly set them well on course before vacating the Hillsborough 'hot seat' at the end of the 1982–83 season.

Howard Wilkinson
1983–88

'Wilko' was a former Sheffield grammar schoolboy international who had made 22 League appearances for the Owls as a winger. He returned to Hillsborough in the summer of 1983 after ending his top-class playing career at Brighton and serving his managerial apprenticeship at Boston United and Notts County.

In his first season as Wednesday's team boss, he ended the club's fourteen-year wait for a return to the top grade by plotting the memorable promotion triumph of 1984; and in 1986 the Owls reached the FA Cup semi-final.

Ironically, Wednesday had wanted Watford's Graham Taylor as Jack Charlton's successor, but Wilkinson—a former FA regional coach based in Sheffield and a degree graduate in physical education at Sheffield University — proved the ideal choice. He had the additional qualification of having been a 'true' Wednesdayite almost from birth!

He left Wednesday for Leeds United in October 1988 and took the Elland Road club from the bottom end of the old Second Division to the Football League Championship in 1992. Axed by Leeds in September 1996, he later became the Football Association's first Technical Director.

Howard Wilkinson with Owls chairman Bert McGee on the day the man who had led Notts County to promotion to the old First Division was told: 'Now do the same for your favourite football club!'

Wilkinson's first appointment was to bring Peter Eustace (right) back to Hillsborough as his number two. Eustace, having had two spells with the club as a player, was a surprise choice, but soon justified Wilkinson's decision.

Training sessions under 'Wilko' were invariably tough, but the players were at least able to enjoy the local countryside. Here, in the bleak winter of 1983, they forget the cold and snow as they get down to business on the hills above Bolsterstone.

Mike Lyons was a player who, quite literally, gave blood in Wednesday's cause, as illustrated by this picture taken at Southend in January 1983. 'Wilko' was delighted to inherit Lyons from the Jack Charlton era, and the big defender proved an inspiring captain in the 1983–84 promotion success.

A smiling Gary Megson looks on as Imre Varadi celebrates his equalising goal in a 3–1 win at Oldham in late September 1983.

Goalkeeper Martin Hodge grabs the ball as Mike Robinson prepares to pounce in Wednesday's Milk Cup fifth-round tie with Liverpool at Hillsborough in January 1984. The game ended 2–2. Other Owls players in the picture are Lyons, Madden and Smith.

Gary Shelton scoring the spectacular winner at Newcastle in April 1983—perhaps the most memorable of his 24 goals in 239 games for Wednesday between 1982 and 1987.

Joyful emotions expressed by Howard Wilkinson as he celebrates that famous Gary Shelton goal at Newcastle.

Peter Shirtliff, who was destined to make 292 League appearances for Wednesday in two spells, denies Newcastle's Peter Beardsley possession in that April 1984 match at St James's Park.

The goal that clinched promotion to the First Division for Wednesday after fourteen years. Mel Sterland puts his sixth penalty kick of the season into the Crystal Palace net in a famous 1–0 victory on the last Saturday in April 1984.

Howard Wilkinson **53**

Gary Shelton, Wednesday's 'Player of the Year' in the 1983–84 promotion campaign, lost everything but his underpants and needed some help from the police when jubilant Owls fans invaded the Hillsborough pitch and stripped him of his shirt and shorts after the final fixture of the season.

Celebration time for Howard Wilkinson and his players and backroom staff as the champagne flows to mark Wednesday's long-awaited promotion to Division One after fourteen years in the wilderness.

Tony Cunningham, an £85,000 buy from Barnsley, is seen here celebrating his goal on his home debut in Wednesday's memorable 4–2 defeat of Newcastle at Hillsborough in November 1983. Tony made only 28 League appearances for Wednesday before moving on to Manchester City, but his five goals proved crucial to the Owls' promotion push.

The inset pictures capture Wednesday's goals against Newcastle. From the top: Imre Varadi scores the first two; Cunningham hammers the third; and Gary Bannister notches the fourth.

Howard Wilkinson's spadework ahead of the first season back in Division One in 1984–85 had little to do with helping to re-lay the Hillsborough pitch, and everything to do with making important signings. One of them was Brian Marwood, who cost £125,000 from Hull City. Marwood proved as handy on the ball as he was with a shovel!

A picture that captures the enthusiasm, discipline and precision of Howard Wilkinson as the Wednesday manager turns starter and timekeeper in training at Middlewood.

Brian Marwood (number 7) turns in delight as Wednesday celebrate his goal against Tottenham in September 1984. It was the first of the 35 goals Marwood scored for the Owls in 161 games.

Gary Shelton scoring in Wednesday's famous 2–0 triumph at Liverpool in September 1984. The goalkeeper is Bruce Grobbelaar, and the defender looking on is a youthful Steve Nicol, who some years later was recruited for the Owls by David Pleat. Grobbelaar came to Sheffield on loan in 1997.

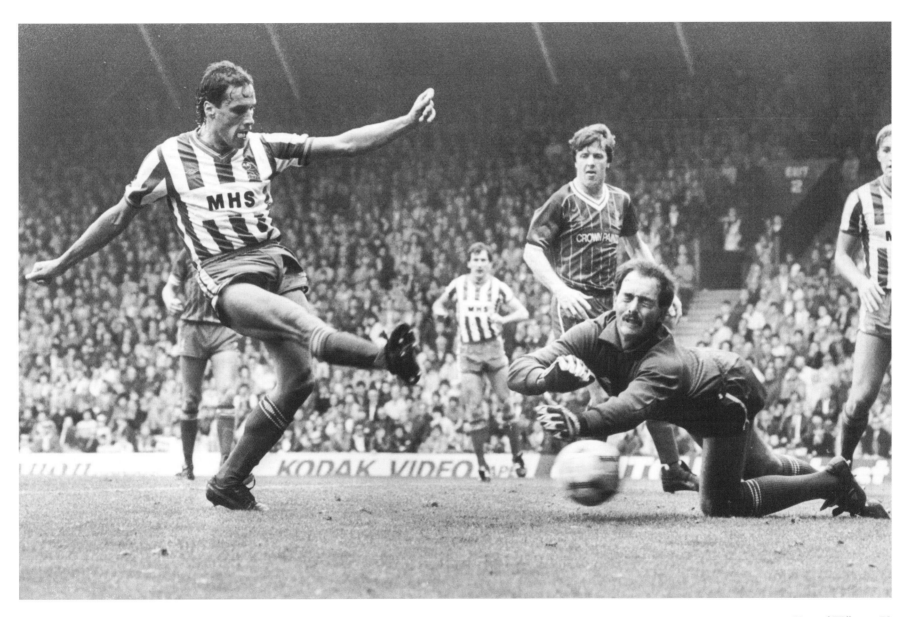

Lee Chapman was a big, brave striker who had a lean time at Arsenal and Sunderland before his career took a dramatic upswing after his £100,000 move to Wednesday ahead of the start of the 1984–85 campaign in Division One.

He arrived following the departures of Tony Cunningham and Gary Bannister and went on to score 79 goals in 187 games. He was good with his head, rapidly improved with his feet, and certainly gave it everything...scoring with fierce shots and flying headers, and always ready to go in where it hurts.

He had plenty to celebrate and his team-mates were not slow to share in the joy of his success!

Martin Hodge enjoyed a record-breaking run of 214 consecutive League and Cup appearances for Wednesday after his £50,000 move from Everton in 1983. The goalkeeper who proved to be one of Howard Wilkinson's best signings produced some golden moments...like in this picture, when he dived to his left to make a penalty save to deny Gordon Strachan when the Owls won 2–1 at Old Trafford in January 1985.

Martin Hodge made another notable penalty save at Anfield in January 1986. This time he chose to dive to his right to frustrate Liverpool's Jan Molby as the Owls earned a well-deserved 2–2 draw.

Wednesday's Brian Marwood and Chelsea's Mickey Thomas both concentrate hard as they watch Mel Sterland take the famous penalty kick that salvaged a 4–4 draw for the Owls in an unforgettable League Cup quarter-final replay at Hillsborough in January 1985.

That Chelsea cup game was incredible, for Wednesday led 3–0 at half-time, then trailed 4–3 before Sterland's dramatic equaliser in the dying seconds of normal time made the score level. Here, before the start of extra time, Howard Wilkinson, Peter Eustace, physiotherapist Alan Smith and coach Mick Hennigan seek to inspire the players for one final fling.

The frustration shows in the faces of a weary Peter Shirtliff and Lawrie Madden after the 4–4 draw means another replay with Chelsea, and a match that was to end in a 2–1 defeat at Stamford Bridge.

Howard Wilkinson **63**

Kevin Pressman, who by the autumn of 1997 boasted some 250 games for Wednesday, arrived at Hillsborough in 1984, early in the Wilkinson era. Here, in his early days, he is working under the supervision of former England and Sheffield United goalkeeper Alan Hodgkinson.

Carl Shutt, a Sheffield product who arrived at Hillsborough from non-League Spalding in 1985, made a sensational start to his Wednesday career and went on to score 16 goals in 40 League games. Here he heads what proved to be a consolation goal in a 4–1 defeat the Owls suffered at Newcastle in March 1986.

Wednesday's Chris Morris, in action at West Brom in April 1986, is pursued by a long-legged youngster called Carlton Palmer, who was later destined to join the Owls.

Wednesday lost 2–1 in extra time in the FA Cup semi-final against Everton at Villa Park in April 1986, and this headed goal by Carl Shutt, which made the score 1–1 after 53 minutes, was their happiest moment.

Shutt celebrates his goal while Everton's Rotherham-born goalkeeper Bobby Mimms looks back in anger.

Howard Wilkinson is seen here
with Everton manager Howard
Kendall at the end of the 1986
FA Cup semi-final. Everton
always seemed to get the better
of the Owls in Wilkinson's time.
Kendall, of course, later had a
spell at Sheffield United.

Alas, the FA Cup semi-final
of 1986 ended in tears for
Mel Sterland and many other
Wednesday fans, as well as the
pair offering consolation to the
Owls defender.

Wednesday's FA Cup fourth-round replay with Chester at Hillsborough in February 1987 had barely started when Owls defender Ian Knight, seen here being consoled by assistant manager Peter Eustace, suffered a compound fracture of his right leg following a wild and high challenge by Chester's Gary Bennett.

Knight was carried off and, though he did eventually make a comeback, the injury effectively shattered a highly promising career. He never enjoyed the success that had been predicted for him and, after a spell at Grimsby, was forced to hang up his boots. The irony was that, in late 1997, Bennett, whose actions caused the injury, was still playing League football.

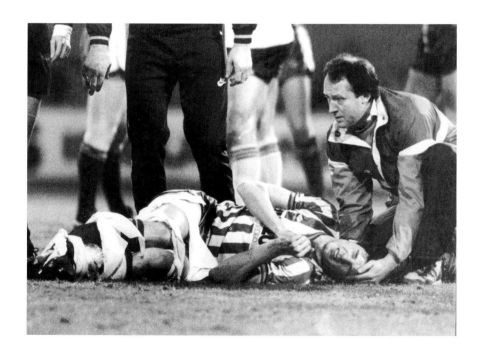

David Hirst was destined to become a great Wednesday favourite and scorer of some 130 goals in around 350 games up to the start of the 1997–98 campaign. Here he is being welcomed to Hillsborough by manager Howard Wilkinson following his signing from Barnsley in the summer of 1986.

A goal David Hirst especially enjoyed was this flying effort against his old club Barnsley at Oakwell.

It's not always fair weather! Marwood and Shelton are the Wednesday men lost in the snow at Coventry.

'Come snow or sunshine...the job never stops!' is the motto of Wednesday's award-winning groundsman David Barber as he continues to work on the Hillsborough pitch despite the snow.

72 Howard Wilkinson

Howard Wilkinson with defender Nigel Worthington. Worthington cost £100,000 from Notts County in 1984 and went on to make 417 appearances for Wednesday and become the club's most-capped player with 50 Northern Ireland caps.

Work in progress as the famous old Hillsborough Kop is finally given a roof in 1986 at a cost of £1 million.

Her Majesty the Queen, who came to Hillsborough in December 1986 to open the new-look Kop, appears rather amused by a comment from Wednesday chairman Bert McGee.

The Queen talks to Wednesday goalkeeper Martin Hodge, while manager Howard Wilkinson looks on. Hodge, who made 249 appearances for the club, had a long spell as captain and was a great ambassador for the Owls.

Wednesday seeking to sail to success as Howard Wilkinson and Peter Eustace take the players on a boat trip during FA Cup training at Scarborough in 1987. The man waving is Siggi Jonsson, an Icelandic international who made 67 appearances before moving to Arsenal.

Mark Smith finds time to reflect on his long Hillsborough career in a deserted dressing room after his testimonial game. The lad from Shirecliffe made 282 League appearances for the Owls between April 1978 and May 1987.

When Mel Sterland was capped by England against Saudi Arabia in November 1988, the Sheffield-born defender did not forget that it was Charlie Wain who set him on the road to success, and the veteran scout was rewarded with Mel's England shirt.

Sterland prods in his first goal in Wednesday's 2–1 defeat of Watford in August 1985.

Sterland needs no prompting to celebrate, with Simon Stainrod saluting the goal while Watford's John Barnes does not appear to be exactly amused!

Steve Ellis describes this as his favourite picture of Mel Sterland, a great crowd favourite and a defender who played in some 300 games for Wednesday between 1979 and 1989. Indeed, he even had one spell as a centre-forward. The fans called him 'Zico' and were sorry when he moved on to Glasgow Rangers and then Leeds United.

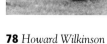

Shortly before Howard Wilkinson left Wednesday in October 1988, he brought goalkeeper Chris Turner back to Hillsborough from Manchester United. Here he and Turner reflect on a picture of Turner in his first spell at the club, during which he made 115 senior appearances before joining Sunderland in July 1979. He added another 75 League games to his Owls record and helped win the League Cup in 1991.

Howard Wilkinson **79**

Imre Varadi, pictured here in action wearing Wednesday's green and white change strip, also had two spells at Hillsborough. However, on his return in 1988, he did not repeat the form that had brought him 40 goals in 94 games in Wilkinson's first two seasons at the club.

Peter Eustace pins up his first-team selections following his formal promotion to succeed Howard Wilkinson in October 1988. Unfortunately, he remained in the job only until February 1989.

This picture of Nigel Pearson sharing a goal celebration with Mark Proctor and Imre Varadi captures one of the joyful moments from the last year of the Wilkinson era, and offers an excuse to note that one of the most rewarding decisions Peter Eustace made in his short spell as manager was to appoint Nigel Pearson as captain. Pearson, who made 224 appearances between October 1987 and 1994, took over in December 1988.

Ron Atkinson
1988–91

'Big' Ron Atkinson was a larger-than-life character, a man with a reputation as one of the Football League's most flamboyant managers. Those who knew him found him rather different from the public image—a down-to-earth but enthusiastic guy, passionate about football and widely respected as a serious student of the game who insisted good football was a top priority.

His three years at Hillsborough were certainly eventful, with a rare mixture of trauma and triumph. He will always be remembered for having given the fans plenty to savour, and for promoting a dramatic change in Wednesday's approach to investing big in the transfer market.

He had previously managed Cambridge, twice been in charge of West Brom, and had a five-year spell at Manchester United, but he joined the Owls in February 1989 after a 96-day stint at Atletico Madrid in Spain.

In his initial three months he plotted a successful fight against relegation, but his first full season in charge saw Wednesday suffer an unexpected fall from the First Division on goal-difference following a 3–0 last-day home defeat.

However, in 1990–91 the Owls not only won promotion but also lifted their first major trophy for 56 years: the Rumbelows Cup. Alas, while the cheers were still echoing around Sheffield, Atkinson shocked supporters when he elected to turn his back on the Owls and move to Aston Villa. He later managed Coventry City.

Ron Atkinson persuaded Richie Barker (second from left) to leave Luton and join him as Wednesday's coach, while Alan Smith (extreme left) and Frank Barlow (right) were key figures in his backroom team. Also in this picture is Imre Varadi.

When Wednesday went to Newcastle in late March 1989 and won 3–1, Dean Barrick scored to emerge a hero on his Football League debut. However, Barrick made only eleven League appearances before moving to Rotherham.

Wednesday's Alan Harper in a duel with Tottenham's Paul Gascoigne in the April 1989 game that saw the Owls claim a precious point to aid their battle for safety.

Nigel Pearson gives it everything with a diving header in the home draw with Wimbledon in April 1989.

Steve Whitton, a £275,000 buy from Birmingham who scored the goal that booked Wednesday's safety from relegation in the 1–0 win against Middlesbrough in May 1989.

Say one for me, Ron! The Wednesday boss seems to be praying for success as the Owls fight to stay in the top grade.

Such joy and relief! Atkinson hugs a young Wednesday fan after victory over Middlesbrough had kept the Owls in the First Division.

Ron Atkinson **89**

*Ron Atkinson shows his delight
as the final whistle blows in the
Middlesbrough game.*

Wednesday's Juniors had their own moment of triumph at the end of that 1988–89 season when they won the Northern Intermediate League Cup. Local lads Jon Newsome (second from left) and Graham Hyde (third from right), both in the front row, went on to become first-team favourites.

The 1988–89 season was blighted by the tragedy of the Hillsborough disaster, which occurred at the FA Cup semi-final between Liverpool and Nottingham Forest on 15th March 1989. Steve Ellis's picture captures the deep and spontaneous expression of public sorrow in the floral and other tributes that were laid at the Leppings Lane entrance to the Wednesday ground.

When, in November 1989, Liverpool paid their first visit to Hillsborough since the disaster, floral tributes were laid at the Leppings Lane end by Liverpool captain Alan Hanson (left) and Wednesday's Chris Turner. It was an occasion of great dignity and emotion.

The day after the Hillsborough tragedy, Prime Minister Margaret Thatcher and Football Association chairman Bert Millichip visited the ground. Wednesday secretary Graham Mackrell is in the rear.

Wednesday won only one of their first eleven matches in the First Division in 1989–90, and that victory came in a game against Aston Villa in September when Kevin Pressman saved this Nigel Callaghan penalty.

Dalian Atkinson, a £450,000 buy from Ipswich, ended his only season with Wednesday with fifteen goals, including the one that brought that eagerly awaited first League victory against Aston Villa.

Roland Nilsson, a superbly skilled Swedish international full-back, arrived from Gothenburg for a bargain £375,000 in December 1989 and proved an instant hit with the fans.

Ron Atkinson **95**

Trevor Francis shares a joke with manager Ron Atkinson at a press conference following his arrival in January 1990 on a free transfer from Queen's Park Rangers. The former England striker brought a touch of class to the Wednesday front line.

Francis, once English football's first £1-million player, was already 35 when he came to Sheffield, but he still had the ability to give Wednesdayites some memorable moments and a few special goals to savour!

David Hirst, Wednesday's
leading scorer with sixteen goals
in 1989–90, makes a point to
referee Neil Midgley.

Hirst wins a heading duel
against Manchester United in
March 1990, but this time he
failed to find the net.

Chairman Bert McGee, who often recalled being taken to Hillsborough by his father in the late 1920s, finds himself in reflective mood as he stands on the Kop in March 1990 after announcing his retirement from the board.

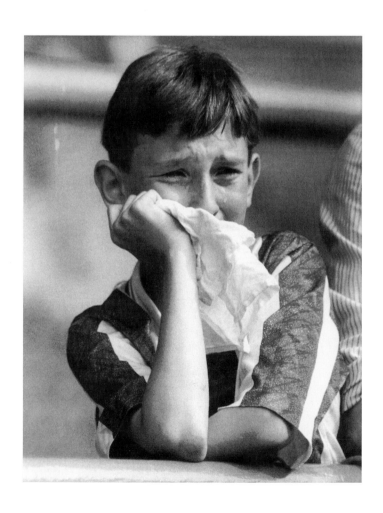

The 1989–90 campaign ended in tears for many young Wednesdayites such as this one when a home defeat against Nottingham Forest on the last day of the season doomed the Owls to relegation on goal-difference.

'Big Ron', in pensive mood after the final game of the season, simply can't believe that Wednesday are down. Everyone thought the Owls were safe after a late-season revival, but a 3–0 setback against Forest provided a painful twist to the story.

100 *Ron Atkinson*

Wednesday's quest for a prompt promotion success was launched with a 2–0 victory at Ipswich on the opening days of the 1990–91 season. These travelling Owls fans left nobody in any doubt about how confident they were that 'Big Ron' would take them back to Division One at the first attempt.

Nigel Worthington celebrates his only goal in the 1990–91 promotion run, against Barnsley in September. The other Wednesday man in the picture is striker Paul Williams, whose partnership with David Hirst was a key feature of the team's success.

In 1990–91 Bristol City played their home games at Bath, and, with cover not even provided for visiting directors, Owls chairman Dave Richards got caught in the icy December rain.

Owls captain Nigel Pearson in a typically resolute pose as he goes full length to thwart an attacking burst by Oldham's Andy Ritchie.

Viv Anderson, the former England defender who arrived from Manchester United on a free transfer in January 1991, solving a problem for Ron Atkinson when Harkes and Worthington were both unavailable to play in the first team.

Carlton Palmer in a duel with Chelsea's Andy Townsend in the Rumbelows Cup semi-final, first leg, at Stamford Bridge.

Danny Wilson, the Irish international midfielder recruited from Luton for a bargain £200,000, is seen here at full stretch when limbering up before the Cup game with Chelsea.

Danny Wilson, one of Wednesday's most popular players of the period, and physiotherapist Alan Smith share the joy of a famous victory as they leave the field after the Cup game at Stamford Bridge.

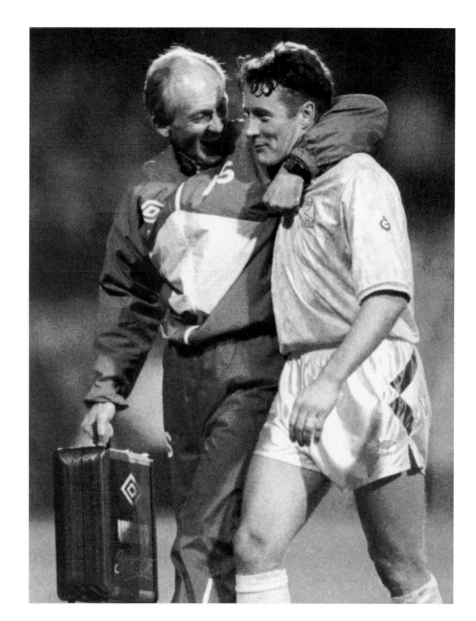

After the 1989 Hillsborough disaster, the Leppings Lane end at the ground was closed for some time. Before it was eventually brought back into use in the early 1990s, extensive improvements were made, with the upper stand upgraded and seats being installed on the lower terrace. That work was in progress when this picture was taken.

Carlton Palmer's dreams of playing in the 1991 Rumbelows Cup Final were shattered when he was sent off in a Second Division match at Portsmouth in early April. Pearson and Sheridan are the team-mates looking dismayed by the referee's red card.

Delight for John Sheridan as he salutes the fans after converting a penalty in the defeat of Blackburn in April 1991.

John Harkes gets a hug from Nigel Worthington after scoring for the Owls against Barnsley in April 1991.

Ever enthusiastic and always young at heart, 'Big Ron' was never happier than when participating in a five-a-side match with his players. 'Watch this for quality and style', he would comment as he burst into a dribble...and the lads never argued!

Alex Ferguson and Ron Atkinson are the rival managers, and Bryan Robson and Nigel Pearson the captains, as Manchester United and Sheffield Wednesday take the field at Wembley on Sunday 21st April 1991.

The Rumbelows Cup Final was 38 minutes old when Wednesday's John Sheridan latched onto a clearance and walloped the goal of a lifetime, a right-foot shot past Les Sealey which brought the only score of the game.

Owls captain Nigel Pearson holds the Rumbelows Cup aloft after climbing the famous 39 steps at Wembley. Pearson was also named 'Man of the Match'.

Cup final match-winner John Sheridan with Wednesday's first major trophy since 1935.

Yankee Doodle Dandy! John Harkes, the American kid from Kearney, New Jersey, pays tribute to his British roots by sporting bowler and brolly in this picture specially set up by Steve Ellis ahead of the Rumbelows Cup Final.

Holding the Stars and Stripes of the USA, John Harkes, who wasn't even at Hillsborough when Wednesday kicked off the 1990–91 season, was proud to end it as the first American to play in a Wembley cup final. His parents are both Scots who emigrated to New Jersey.

Jubilant Wednesday players after the Wembley triumph.

Hold onto your hats! These Wednesdayites are happy to let the Owls Cup success go right to their heads.

Full-back Phil King leads his Wednesday team-mates in song as they celebrate the Cup triumph at their hotel.

Home are the heroes. The Owls players take a triumphant ride through the Hillsborough district en route to a civic reception.

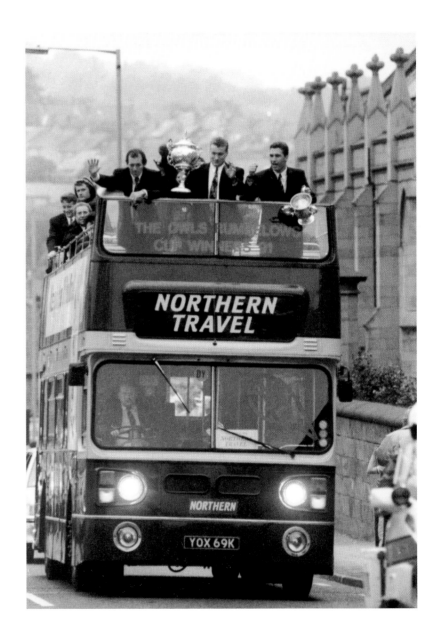

The Rumbelows Cup was the first major trophy Wednesday had won for 56 years, and it was appropriate that chairman Dave Richards should make a point of visiting Ronnie Starling, captain of the Owls side that brought the FA Cup home in 1935, to show him the trophy.

Danny Wilson celebrating after Wednesday had added a promotion success to their Wembley Cup triumph.

Some fans had to wait nearly a lifetime to see the Owls win a major trophy, but it happened to these youngsters early in their lives…and they will remember it forever!

Ron Atkinson was a hero with Wednesday supporters, and they never stopped singing his praises until, in June 1991, he walked out and took a job with Aston Villa. Only a week earlier 'Big Ron' had insisted he was staying, and now some fans felt betrayed. However, in the long run, most people looked back and remembered the Atkinson era with affection. He put a smile on our faces, and, for the most part, helped us see the sunny side of football!

Trevor Francis
1991–95

'Tricky Trev' has a place in British football folklore as the one-time boy wonder who became the game's first £1-million player when he moved from Birmingham to Nottingham Forest in 1979. Though the former England striker with 52 caps was nearing the end of his playing days when he joined Wednesday in 1990, he still had a lot to offer.

He arrived on a free transfer after a short spell as player-manager of QPR, and in 89 games for the Owls he raised his aggregate tally of goals in English domestic football to over 200. He had also scored freely in Italian, American and Scottish football.

Francis succeeded Ron Atkinson as team boss in June 1991 and his four years in charge were, to say the least, eventful, featuring many highs and lows and a string of major signings.

In his first season Wednesday finished third in the old Division One and qualified for Europe for the first time since 1964. His second term saw the Owls visit Wembley four times but lose in both major domestic cup finals, and, of course, the campaign featured the unique all-Sheffield FA Cup semi-final clash with the Blades.

Wednesday finished seventh in the Premier League in 1994 and also reached the Coca-Cola Cup semi-final but, after they ended the 1994–95 season in thirteenth place, Francis was invited to leave. He later managed Birmingham City.

It was not without irony that Wednesday's first match under Francis was at home to Ron Atkinson's Aston Villa. Though 'Big Ron' got a daunting and antagonistic reception from Owls fans when his team arrived at Hillsborough on that sunny afternoon in August 1991, he had the last laugh because Villa won 3–2.

Francis paid the first £1 million-plus fee in Wednesday's history when he signed England goalkeeper Chris Woods from Glasgow Rangers in August 1991.

Showing the way! Trevor Francis turns in triumph after scoring the winning goal in the 88th minute against Nottingham Forest in September 1991. He had come on as a late substitute, then 'retired' immediately after finding the net!

On the bench at Liverpool, Francis with his backroom boys Richie Barker (assistant manager) and Alan Smith (physiotherapist), and players Gordon Watson and Kevin Pressman. Liverpool manager Graeme Souness and coach Roy Evans are also in the picture.

Nigel Jemson, an early Francis signing who scored only nine goals in 51 games, is seen in a heading duel with Liverpool's Steve Nicol, who was destined to join Wednesday in the David Pleat area.

The intriguing thing about this picture is the colourful protective mask being worn by Southampton goalkeeper Bruce Grobbelaar, but it is just as interesting to note that Chris Bart-Williams played in more League games (124) for Trevor Francis than any other Wednesday player. Grobbelaar was destined to join the Owls on loan in 1997.

Trevor Francis **127**

Chris Waddle, seen here dribbling past Manchester United's Ryan Giggs, joined Wednesday from Marseille for £900,000 in June 1992. The former England star was an instant hit with Owls supporters. He played in over 100 games before leaving in 1996 and playing with Falkirk, Bradford City and Sunderland. He was later player-manager at Burnley.

Footballer of the Year...Chris Waddle's brilliant form in the double cup run of 1992–93, epitomised by his stunning first-minute free-kick in the FA Cup semi-final against Sheffield United at Wembley, earned him the coveted Football Writers' Association trophy.

Waddle produced many memorable moments and some unforgettable goals. Who will forget his performance against West Ham in December 1993? Yet it wasn't always glory for the Geordie with the golden boots. He had a spell when injury sidelined him for a long period, and here he is seen reflecting on the pain of Wednesday's League Cup semi-final defeat against Manchester United in 1994. That was an occasion when he was rushed back after a lay-off and, sadly, it didn't pay off.

It was in the late spring of 1993 that the major redevelopment of the famous Hillsborough South Stand started. Replacement of the roof with a new and higher one marked the first stage in a remarkable transformation of that area of Wednesday's headquarters. The pitch, too, was re-laid after new undersoil heating had been installed.

The 1992–93 season was to end in bitter personal disappointment for Owls skipper Nigel Pearson when he broke a leg during the Coca-Cola Cup run and missed the trips to Wembley. However, it started on a high note with this superb goal in the 1–1 draw at Everton in August.

132 *Trevor Francis*

Viv Anderson, pursued by Carlton Palmer, celebrates one of his goals in the 8–1 defeat of Spora Luxemburg in the UEFA Cup-tie at Hillsborough in September 1992.

The 1992–93 campaign was especially eventful for Paul Warhurst. Converted from defender to striker by Trevor Francis, he enjoyed outstanding success with 18 goals, but this picture of him with Alan Smith serves as a reminder that only the quick reactions of the Owls physio saved Paul's life when his throat was blocked after being knocked unconscious in a collision with the Spora goalkeeper in the Hillsborough game of September 1992.

134 *Trevor Francis*

After a comfortable triumph over Spora, the Owls faced a nerve-jangling ordeal in the red-hot cauldron of Kaiserslautern in the next round of the UEFA Cup. Home supporters' flares made for a colourful scene at the German ground in October 1992, but the atmosphere was overwhelmingly intimidating!

The Kaiserslautern experience started well for Wednesday when David Hirst shot them in front after only five minutes, but Hirst was later sent off in controversial circumstances when a German opponent 'dived', and the Owls felt their ultimate 3–1 defeat had more to do with cynical gamesmanship than football.

Tension on the touchline for Trevor Francis.

John Sheridan scoring with a diving header in the Coca-Cola Cup fifth-round tie at Ipswich in January 1993, when Wednesday had to settle for a 1–1 draw after the home side equalised from a dubious late penalty.

Paul Warhurst scored twice in four minutes in Wednesday's brilliant 4–2 triumph at Blackburn in the Coca-Cola Cup semi-final, first leg, in February 1993. Four years later, in August 1997, the Owls, by then managed by David Pleat, were destined to suffer a 7–2 thrashing at Ewood Park.

Wembley-bound! Wednesday players Danny Wilson, Roland Nilsson, Viv Anderson and Carlton Palmer, plus physio Alan Smith, are in joyful mood on that evening of 14th March 1993 when the Owls completed a 6–3 aggregate triumph over Blackburn to book a Coca-Cola Cup final date with Arsenal.

John Sheridan and Nigel Worthington salute Wednesday's 1–0 defeat of Derby County in the FA Cup quarter-final replay of 17th March 1993. The vital goal had been scored by Warhurst from Sheridan's pass.

More celebrations in the Wednesday dressing room after that 1993 success against Derby meant a unique FA Cup semi-final date with Sheffield United.

History being made as the teams
take the field before the unique
all-Sheffield semi-final played in
front of a 75,000 crowd on 3rd
April 1993.

Sheffield may have been divided
by the clash of Wednesday and
United in the 1993 FA Cup
semi-final, but the majority of
young fans remained good
friends and shared a spirit of
mutual goodwill despite the
intense rivalry, as this picture of
two face-painted youngsters at
Wembley confirms.

Mark Bright, a September signing from Crystal Palace, rises to meet American John Harkes's corner and head the extra-time winner that enabled Wednesday to beat Sheffield United in the 1993 FA Cup semi-final.

Wednesday's Wembley marksmen, Chris Waddle and Mark Bright, celebrate after the triumph over Sheffield United. Waddle hammered a memorable free-kick past Alan Kelly for the Owls' first goal barely 65 seconds after the kick-off, while Bright made it 2–1 seventeen minutes into extra time.

The blue-and-white-painted faces of a happy Wednesday couple ahead of the Coca-Cola Cup final with Arsenal at Wembley on 18th April 1993.

144 *Trevor Francis*

Wednesday's second appearance at Wembley in fifteen days ended in despair with a 2–1 defeat against Arsenal in the Coca-Cola Cup final. The disappointed players here are Chris Waddle (sitting) and Viv Anderson, who suffered a head injury during the game in a collision with Arsenal's Ian Wright.

The giant Wednesday flag that came to the fore in the Cup runs of 1992–93 gets an airing on the Hillsborough Kop before the Premiership derby duel with Sheffield United in April 1993.

Ahead of Wednesday's first FA Cup final appearance in 27 years, some of the boys from the 1966 Wembley team made an appearance on the Hillsborough pitch. They are (left to right): David Ford, Gerry Young, Wilf Smith, Johnny Quinn, Graham Pugh, John Fantham and Don Megson.

Wednesday's third visit to Wembley in 1993 was on 15th May when they drew 1–1 with Arsenal in the FA Cup final. Viv Anderson, the team's third captain of the season, is seen leading out the Owls as the teams take the field.

HRH the Duchess of Kent talking to Carlton Palmer before the 1993 FA Cup final.

Wembley ecstasy...David Hirst, Mark Bright and John Harkes share mutual delight after Hirst's 62nd-minute equaliser in the 1993 FA Cup final.

Wembley agony...The FA Cup final replay on 20th May 1993 ended in painful circumstances when Andy Linighan headed Arsenal's winner in the last seconds of extra time! No wonder the Wednesday lads fell to the ground in despair.

Wednesday's Chris Bart-Williams, a substitute in the replay, is consoled by Arsenal men Dixon and Smith.

Words cannot express the sorrow evident in this picture of defeated manager Trevor Francis.

Last stand at Hillsborough! This was the last time Wednesday fans stood on the famous Kop for a Saturday match, on 1st May 1993, the game that day being against Middlesbrough. Seats were installed on the Kop before the start of the 1993–94 season.

152 *Trevor Francis*

In fact, the very last time supporters stood on the Kop to watch Wednesday was for the game against Arsenal on Thursday 6th May 1993 and, that night, chairman Dave Richards, the Walkley product who always described himself as 'a man of the people and an ordinary fan at heart', chose to join the Koppites at the end of an era. Two years later, he went back onto the Kop to ask the fans what they thought of Trevor Francis, and when they said 'he'll have to go' it marked the beginning of the end for the manager!

After all the pressure and excitement of the 1992–93 campaign, Trevor Francis was happy to take a relaxed view of preparations for the new season. Alas, his final two seasons as manager proved rather less rewarding than his first two.

The Owls and the Blades met up again, this time at Bramall Lane, in August 1993 for Derek Dooley's testimonial match. Dooley, a former Wednesday centre-forward and manager who later became United's managing director, leads the teams out, helped by his grandson, also called Derek.

154 *Trevor Francis*

In 1993–94 Wednesday lost four times to Manchester United, twice in the Premiership and twice in the Coca-Cola Cup, and Frenchman Eric Cantona, seen here in a duel with David Hirst, scored twice in United's 5–0 Premiership triumph.

The irony of Cantona's success at Manchester United was that Wednesday had been the first English club to whom he offered his services after giving up French football. He arrived in Sheffield in late January 1992, and is seen here in Owls colours. His only appearance, however, was in a six-a-side indoor match against Baltimore Blast at Sheffield Arena. He didn't stay and soon joined Leeds before moving on to Old Trafford.

Des Walker, the England defender who returned from Italian football to join Wednesday in a £2.7-million deal in the summer of 1993, is seen here in a duel with Manchester United's Mark Hughes.

Wednesday's run to the Coca-Cola Cup semi-finals in 1993–94 featured a number of memorable goals, not least one flying effort from local lad Ryan Jones which sealed victory at QPR in the fourth-round duel in December 1993. Nobody has ever been so delighted at being flat out on the ground, which is how Ryan finished up after scoring! Unfortunately, the Sheffield player's promising career was later marred by injury problems.

Fancy-dress time for the Wednesday players as they exhibit an imaginative range of clothing from Sheridan's impression of John Wayne to David Hirst's idea of a Canadian Mountie! And doesn't the 'lady' with him remind one of a big centre-half called Pearce?

During the 1993–94 season, ironically just after signing a lucrative new contract, defender Roland Nilsson decided he had to follow his family back to Sweden. They had suddenly become homesick and fallen out with Sheffield, so, in May 1994, the immensely popular Nilsson, granted a free transfer on compassionate grounds, quit English football. The fans gave him a wonderful send-off after his final match, and here he is being 'chaired' by Trevor Francis and Andy Pearce. Ironically, in 1997 he returned to English football with Coventry.

A major signing ahead of the 1994–95 campaign was Rumanian international Dan Petrescu, seen scoring against West Ham. Sadly, he never performed as well at Hillsborough as he later did after moving to Chelsea.

Ian Taylor, who arrived from Port Vale for £1 million in the summer of 1994, seen in action in a Coco-Cola Cup match against Southampton. Unfortunately, he was destined to make only fourteen League appearances before being sold to Aston Villa in the deal that brought Guy Whittingham to Hillsborough in December 1994.

This unusual shot of Wednesday striker Mark Bright and Manchester United goalkeeper Peter Schmeichel, taken at Old Trafford in May 1995, won Owls official club photographer Steve Ellis a 'Picture of the Year' award from the Sports Council's Yorkshire Region. The fixture, incidentally, was Trevor Francis's penultimate match as Wednesday's team boss. Two weeks later, on FA Cup final day, he was called to Hillsborough by the club chairman and sacked.

David Pleat
1995–

David Pleat may lack the flamboyance of Ron Atkinson and the playing pedigree of Trevor Francis, but, when he arrived at Hillsborough in the summer of 1995 at the age of 50, it was with a reputation as a seasoned and respected manager who had served a long and thorough apprenticeship. He was known as an astute tactician and a master of the art of operating on limited resources.

A former winger with Nottingham Forest, Luton, Shrewsbury, Exeter and Peterborough whose playing days were dogged by injury, Pleat found his true niche when he launched his management career at Nuneaton in 1971. Later, after four years on Luton's coaching staff, he managed them from January 1978 to May 1986.

Success at Luton prompted Tottenham to recruit him, but, sadly, within barely 18 months, and despite taking Spurs to an FA Cup Final and third place in Division One, his stay at White Hart Lane ended on a sour note in circumstances unrelated to football. He later spent three years at Leicester and was four years into his second spell at Luton when a move to Wednesday offered him a second crack at the big time.

His first season at Hillsborough saw the Owls struggle and finish fifteenth in the Premiership, but the 1996–97 campaign marked a dramatic improvement as Wednesday climbed to seventh place and only narrowly missed qualifying for Europe.

However, Wednesday made a disappointing start to the 1997–98 campaign and Pleat was again under pressure.

This picture of Ian Nolan, seen celebrating his first goal for Wednesday, at Liverpool in October 1994, serves to remind us that the defender's career continued to thrive under David Pleat.

The Pleat era started with a trophy success in the form of the Steel City Cup which the Owls won thanks to a 3–1 defeat of Sheffield United at Bramall Lane in August 1995. David Hirst, Peter Atherton and Mark Bright got the goals, and the day was memorable for teenager Ritchie Humphreys, who made his senior debut as a late substitute.

Incidentally, the new manager's arrival coincided with a decision to dispense with the traditional and popular blue and white stripes.

Wednesday's Welsh international Mark Pembridge, a £900,000 signing from Derby ahead of the 1995–96 campaign, here battles for possession with Wimbledon's Vinnie Jones in August 1995.

David Hirst has had his share of misfortune with injuries over the years, but the Owls striker has never lost his sense of humour.

David Hirst won this duel with Tottenham's Sol Campbell at Hillsborough in September 1995. However, though the striker scored in this game, he was unable to prevent Wednesday losing 3–1.

Klas Ingesson, who had a disappointing time with Wednesday following his arrival from PSV Eindhoven in September 1994, is seen in a duel with Chelsea's Mark Hughes on his final senior appearance for the club before his transfer to Bari in November 1995.

Uruguayan Danny Bergara, seen here in pensive pose at the training ground, was one of David Pleat's first recruits to the Hillsborough coaching staff. They had once been together at Luton. Sadly, it was an appointment that did not work out as well as had been hoped, and Bergara left after barely a year with the Owls.

Wednesday endured a nail-biting start under David Pleat with only two wins in the first nine games, and here the new manager and his coach Danny Bergara feel the tension as they watch a match from the Hillsborough bench.

170 *David Pleat*

Belgian Marc Degryse, a £1.5-
million buy from Anderlecht,
scoring Wednesday's third goal
in the 6–2 defeat of Leeds
United in December 1995.

Marc Degryse celebrates his
double strike against Leeds in
December 1995. He finished his
only season at Hillsborough
with twelve goals, then was sold
to PSV Eindhoven for £1.8
million in the summer of 1996.

David Hirst and Leeds United defender David Wetherall in a duel in December 1995. Wetherall, who started his career with Wednesday, is a product of High Green.

Darko Kovacevic, who cost around £2.5 million from Red Star Belgrade, was hardly one of Wednesday's most successful foreign signings, and he did not remain long at Hillsborough. However, he is seen here scoring one of the two goals he managed in a 4–2 defeat of Bolton on New Year's Day 1996.

A Wednesday supporter nicknamed 'Tango' captured a lot of publicity in the 1990s when he started appearing at matches with a naked upper body, no matter how cold the weather. What some people will do to get their picture in the papers!

The other half of Wednesday's £4.5-million double signing from Yugoslavia was defender Dejan Stefanovic, seen here winning a duel with Wimbledon's Dean Holdsworth in February 1996. Stefanovic remained long after Kovacevic went back home.

A feature of the 1990s has been the astonishing number of football people who have taken to working in the media. Owls manager David Pleat, ever keen to supplement his income, often operates in commentary teams on radio and television in his spare time. However, here he is actually being interviewed for BBC Radio Five by former Wednesday player Brian Marwood, who also complements his PFA role with broadcasting duties.

Chris Waddle managed 32 League appearances in Pleat's first season at Hillsborough and raised his overall tally of games for the Owls to around 140. However, by the autumn of 1996 he was considered surplus to requirements and left the club on a free transfer. He went on to play with Falkirk, Bradford City and Sunderland before becoming player-manager at Burnley in the summer of 1997.

Ritchie Humphreys in action at Bolton in March 1996 when he started a Premiership game for Wednesday for the first time.

This wasn't exactly the nightmare it might have been for Wednesday goalkeeper Kevin Pressman. Though he faced a dozen shots at the same moment, the 'strikers' in this instance were children from Hillsborough Junior School, and they were 'going for goal' as part of a 'Football in the Community' exercise.

By March 1996 Wednesday were anxious to sign a player who had special skills plus an ability to become a 'cult' figure and capture the imagination of the fans in the way Chris Waddle had once done. So they signed winger Regi Blinker from Feyenoord, and the introduction of 'Blinker wigs' proved a big hit with the young supporters pictured here with the Dutch favourite.

Regi Blinker celebrates with Guy Whittingham after his colleague's goal in the 2–0 home defeat of Aston Villa in March 1996. Regi actually scored twice on his Wednesday debut, but managed only three goals in 45 games before leaving to join Glasgow Celtic in August 1997.

A talented trio…Dutchman Regi Blinker, Belgian Marc Degryse and Englishman Chris Waddle in training at Middlewood.

Sheffield-born defender Jon Newsome, who returned to Wednesday from Norwich for £1.5 million late in David Pleat's first season, celebrated his first goal under the new Owls manager in the 1–1 draw at West Ham in May 1996. The result enabled Wednesday to finish two points clear of the relegation zone.

After a disappointing first season in charge of the Owls, David Pleat had good cause to wear a serious expression. The 'experts' were predicting woe for the Wednesday manager. Happily, he proved them wrong and was soon to enjoy an upturn in his and Wednesday's fortunes before another difficult spell early in the 1997–98 campaign.

David Pleat **183**

Hillsborough, which staged its first international match as long ago as 1920, was the venue for three Group D games in the European Championship in June 1996. Danish supporters, in their red and white favours, were very happy to make themselves at home in Sheffield, where they enjoyed great hospitality and saw Denmark win, draw and lose in the space of ten days.

184 David Pleat

The Croatia and Denmark teams line up for the traditional playing of the national anthems before their Euro '96 match at Hillsborough on 16th June 1996. Croatia won 3–0 before a 33,671 crowd.

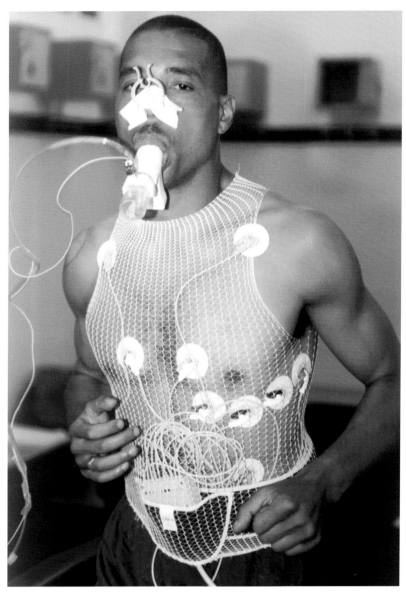

The medical and related technology in which clubs such as Wednesday have invested in recent times is truly remarkable, and the equipment attached to defender Des Walker reveals an astonishing range of data about his physical condition. Unfortunately, it can't predict or influence results on the field!

Young Wednesday striker Ritchie Humphreys kicked off the 1996–97 season with a memorable goal in the 2–1 defeat of Aston Villa at Hillsborough. It was the first of four successive wins which constituted Wednesday's best winning start at the top level since 1932!

A spectacular attempt on goal from Wednesday's £3-million signing Benito Carbone in the FA Cup fifth-round tie at Bradford City in February 1997. Carbone made his debut for the Owls in October 1996 and proved an instant favourite with supporters.

Young striker Andy Booth had an excellent first season with the Owls following his £2.6-million move from Huddersfield. Here he is seen scoring the second goal in the 2–2 draw with Leeds at Hillsborough in March 1997.

190 *David Pleat*

Italian Paulo Di Canio, who joined Wednesday in a £4.5-million deal from Glasgow Celtic in August 1997, was unsuccessful with this spectacular attempt against Leeds United on his home debut for the Owls. Note that the 1997–98 campaign saw the return of the traditional blue and white stripes!

Benito Carbone voiced a few strong words in broken English to referee Paul Durkin when the official told the Wednesday man he was being booked for retaliating after seeing his Italian compatriot Di Canio fouled by a Leeds United player in August 1997. How do you say 'You mustn't take the law into your own hands' in Italian?

Overleaf:
This panoramic shot of Hillsborough in 1997 serves to show how much the ground has developed in the 21 years since Steve Ellis started covering games as the club's official photographer.

David Pleat **191**

to be continued…